China's Struggle for

At the end of the cold war, the People's Republic of China found itself in an international crisis, facing severe problems in both domestic politics and foreign policy. Nearly two decades later, Yong Deng provides an original account of China's remarkable rise from the periphery to the center stage of the post–cold war world. Deng examines how the once beleaguered country has adapted to, and proactively realigned, the international hierarchy, great-power politics, and its regional and global environment in order to carve out an international path within the globalized world. Creatively engaging with mainstream international relations theories and drawing extensively from original Chinese material, this is a well-grounded assessment of the promises and challenges of China's struggle to manage the interlacing of its domestic and international transitions and the interactive process between its rise and evolving world politics.

YONG DENG is a professor in the Department of Political Science at the United States Naval Academy. He has published widely on Asian international relations and Chinese foreign policy.

For Aijin, Andrew, and Ashley

China's Struggle for Status

The Realignment of International Relations

YONG DENG
United States Naval Academy, Maryland

CAMBRIDGE
UNIVERSITY PRESS

CAMBRIDGE UNIVERSITY PRESS
Cambridge, New York, Melbourne, Madrid, Cape Town, Singapore, São Paulo, Delhi

Cambridge University Press
32 Avenue of the Americas, New York, NY 10013-2473, USA

www.cambridge.org
Information on this title: www.cambridge.org/9780521714150

First published 2008
Reprinted 2009

Printed in the United Kingdom at the University Press, Cambridge

A catalog record for this publication is available from the British Library.

Library of Congress Cataloging in Publication Data

Deng, Yong
China's struggle for status: the realignment of international relations / Yong Deng.
   p. ; cm.
Includes bibliographical references and index.
ISBN 978-0-521-88666-6 (hardback) – ISBN 978-0-521-71415-0 (pbk.)
1. China – Foreign relations – 1976–   2. China – International status.   I. Title.
DS779.27.D46   2008
327.51–dc22   2007044430

ISBN   978-0-521-88666-6 hardback
ISBN   978-0-521-71415-0 paperback

Contents

Figure and Tables

Figure

Tables

Preface

The end of the cold war initially thrust China to the periphery of world politics; today, it is at center stage. The country's foreign policy path has markedly differed from those of its past and other great powers in history. As such, China's rise has not simply challenged the international status quo, but also challenged the conventional wisdom on international relations. Intense scholarly inquiries, media coverage, and public and policy debates have led to an explosive growth of knowledge about the various dimensions, dyadic relationships, and issues in China's ever expanding foreign relations. Left unclear, however, are vital questions concerning precisely how distinctive and uncertain is China's international trajectory: What is the nature of its discontent and revisionism regarding the world order? What can one expect of its behavior? And finally, how should the international community evaluate and react to the China challenge? These questions are difficult, but they must be confronted. Just as China's rise poses both dangers and opportunities, so does exploring the international politics surrounding it hold difficulties and promises for innovative thinking on how states relate to each other in the current world.

This book attempts to answer these questions by combining an overarching analytical approach and a multilevel empirical inquiry. My primary goal is not theory building, although I draw out implications pointing to new ideas on international relations in general. My main goal is to properly account for the dynamics and patterns of China's foreign relations. Analytically, as the book's title makes clear, I do not view the country's foreign policy in terms of horizontally arrayed states being locked in an unmitigated struggle for power, as posited by Hans Morgenthau and Kenneth Waltz. Instead, I focus on China's uphill struggle for status through adapting to, and realigning, the power, authority, and social structures of world politics. To devise an effective conceptual framework, I engage various theories in international relations and draw on insights from other fields without being limited

to one particular approach; theories, after all, are proposed to help
us better understand the world. Neither do I see China's foreign policy as derivative from a one-off strategic choice. Instead, I lay out the
parameters that have embedded China's quest for great-power status
within the world, paying particular attention to the interlacing of its
leadership's domestic and international agendas, to the debate among
the Chinese elites over their country's foreign course, and to the interactive process between China's rise and evolving world politics. Empirically, I uncover China's struggle by investigating its policy and diplomacy on issues ranging from the world order to great-power politics,
to Asia and the developing world, and to Taiwan. The result, I hope,
is a clear specification of the motivations, uncertainties, strengths, and
weaknesses in China's foreign relations. I argue that China has sought
change to the international status quo, but that it is equally determined
to eschew the path of violent power transition; it is as determined to
pursue power to address its vulnerabilities as it is confident and skillful in managing threat perception; it has put a premium on positive
recognition, but it has not followed the path of liberal peace; and it has
overall taken advantage of the opportunities that the open, globalized
world has to offer, but it is doing so on its own terms. World politics
has undergone major changes since the end of the cold war, many of
which did not result from Beijing's initiative, but more often than not
they seemed to have aligned well with China's policy adjustments on
issues from the world order to Taiwan. Yet many questions have persisted regarding the country's domestic transition and the character of
its power, and so have the real limits, difficulties, and uncertainties in
its international environment. Unwilling to acknowledge the benefit of
the openness and order underpinned by the U.S. hegemony, the Chinese elites have complained about what they perceived to be Western
pressures and mistreatments. As their nation's power and influence
grow, however, they may find it even harder to navigate the unfamiliar, rapidly evolving world politics while they struggle to define and
manage China's new international role.

I started to work on some of the ideas in this book nearly a decade
ago. Since I undertook the project, the studies of Chinese foreign relations have thrived both inside and outside China. I gained insights into
the Chinese perspectives and debates in discussions with many Chinese colleagues as well as through their writings. My understanding
of Chinese foreign relations has been enriched and stimulated by the

vibrant community of scholars outside China. I am fortunate to have collaborated with many of them in two earlier volumes that I coedited: *In the Eyes of the Dragon* (1999) and *China Rising* (2004), as well as in other projects, and they have taught me much. Various parts of the book were presented at the American Political Science Association Annual Conference and at meetings of the International Studies Association and the American Association for Chinese Studies, as well as at two workshops funded by the Stanley Foundation, a symposium in honor of Professor Allen Whiting in Tucson, and in the Department of Government and Public Administration of the University of Hong Kong, School of International Studies of the Chinese Renmin University, School of International Service of American University, Watson Institute of Brown University, Fairbank Center of Harvard University, and St. Anthony College of Oxford University. I thank the following colleagues for inviting me to present my work at the various venues: Sherry Gray, Richard Hu, Iain Johnston, Seung-Ho Joo, Guoli Liu, Jonathan Pollack, Bob Ross, David Shambaugh, Song Xinning, Steve Tsang, Vincent Wang, Yong Wong-Lee, Zhang Xiaojin, and Quansheng Zhao. The International Studies Association and the Stanley Foundation funded two workshops that I codirected in the late 1990s that facilitated my exchange with fellow China scholars and prominent Chinese experts.

David Blainey, Lowell Dittmer, Iain Johnston, Bob Ross, Gilbert Rozman, Fei-ling Wang, and Allen Whiting read earlier versions of various chapters in the book and offered written critiques and advice. I also benefited from discussions with and suggestions by Tom Christensen, John Garver, Peter Gries, Stephanie T. Kleine-Ahlbrandt, Victor Koschmann, Barry O'Neil, Margaret Pearson, Helen Purkitt, Lucian Pye, Arthur Rachwald, Mark Selden, J. J. Suh, Robert Sutter, Michael Swaine, and William Zimmerman. The anonymous reviews for Cambridge University Press were most helpful in sharpening my thinking. The Naval Academy Faculty Research Council generously funded my field research in China as well as the research and writing of the book. I am grateful for all the assistance, but the views expressed in this book, as well as its weaknesses, are all mine.

Earlier versions of Chapters 4, 5, and 7 have been published, respectively, in Alastair Iain Johnston and Robert Ross, eds., *New Approaches to the Study of Chinese Foreign Policy*, ch. 7 (Stanford, CA: Stanford University Press; © 2006 by the Board of Trustees of the Leland Stanford Jr. University, all rights reserved); the *Journal of Strategic Studies*, vol. 20, no. 4 (Aug. 2007); and Steve Tsang, ed., *If China Attacks Taiwan: Military Strategy, Politics and Economics*, ch. 10 (London: Routledge, 2006). I thank the publishers for permission to use the material.

I dedicate the book to my wife, Aijin, and our children, Andrew and Ashley; they are the nucleus of my in-group. My wife has always supported me, despite her own busy career. My children have shown remarkable understanding of my preoccupation with the research and writing of this book in the last couple of years. Thanks to J. K. Rowling, my son thought being an author was cool, and my daughter was old enough to be fascinated with "chapter books."

1 | *Introduction*

In the immediate aftermath of the Tiananmen incident in 1989 and the subsequent end of the cold war, the People's Republic of China (PRC) found itself in presumably the worst – albeit brief – international crisis it had ever faced. The beleaguered and isolated country forged ahead, defying the enormous odds stacked against it on both domestic and international fronts. The PRC has since achieved remarkable success in diplomacy, notwithstanding the misgivings and uncertainties about its international trajectory. Barely several years into the new millennium, American news magazines began to declare the arrival of "China's century."[1] If in the early 1990s China's international environment primarily depended on the policy choices of other, outside players, today much of it is of the country's own making. There is no denial that China's rise is arguably the most important reality in contemporary world politics. Such a diplomatic track record in the past some twenty years cries out for a comprehensive dissection and fresh explanation. That is exactly the intent of this study. It does so by focusing on China's struggle for international status.

At the outset, several caveats on status are in order, because the concept is used in different ways. In sociology, treated analytically as separate from material factors, status is about social recognition that often leads to privileged treatment that may or may not lead to material gains. In international relations (IR), status is often neglected. Constructivist theories have great implications for status, but they do not clearly illuminate how status matters in IR. Ironically, when the term is used in IR, it is often by realists, who equate the status struggle with the state's jockeying for a higher position in the pecking order of power. Chinese leaders and analysts frequently refer to status as if it was the sole, noble goal of their nation's foreign policy, but they have

---

[1] Cover Story, "Special Report: China's Century," *Newsweek*, May 9, 2005; Michael Elliott, "The Chinese Century," *Time*, Jan. 22, 2007, pp. 33–42.

refrained from elaborating on what status means and how it differs from other motives.

My application of status here is based on a rejection of key assumptions in the mainstream realist paradigm in IR.[2] Realism sees international politics in terms of horizontally arranged sovereign states struggling for power and survival. But China has to wrestle with a world politics defined in significant measure by a hierarchy of power and authority. While realism sees the state as a unitary actor, whose behavior is dictated by the international structure, the PRC state is porous to global forces and much of its foreign policy is driven by the interaction between domestic and international politics. For realist theories of varied persuasions, the state's motivation is a given, whether it is to maximize power or to be secure. But Chinese foreign policy has proven to be dynamic and responsive to domestic evolution and changes on the world stage.

In determining their country's international course, leaders of the ruling Chinese Communist Party (CCP) have to ask two essential questions. First, what can they do to create an international environment conducive to their domestic agenda for sustaining the state-directed growth and gradualist reforms? Second, how can China pave a path to great-power status under a Western-dominated international hierarchy, which is buttressed by the U.S. hegemony, strong enough to render unimaginable a radically restructured, alternative world order? The realist paradigm positing the state's single-minded pursuit of relative power cannot clearly decipher how the Chinese elites have answered these questions. We thus develop the notion of status. Our concern is the process whereby the PRC has moved from the periphery to the center stage in world politics while attending to both domestic and international demands. As such, China's struggle for status has been a struggle for great-power recognition by balancing acceptance and autonomy, compliance and revisionism, power and legitimacy, and globalization and nationalism.

From our perspective, status is about the state's concerns over its material wellbeing and international treatment with the goal to engineer mutually reinforcing growth in both. Its pursuit is thus marked by a sensitivity to mitigate power politics so as to avoid violent power transition as posited by structural realists and an emphasis on upward

---

[2] The classical exposition of realist propositions is found in Kenneth N. Waltz, *Theory of International Politics* (New York: McGraw-Hill, 1979).

mobility through participation in the globalized world. Specifically three dimensions have characterized China's foreign policy after the cold war. First, the Chinese leadership is acutely aware that their country's initial, post-Tiananmen out-group status fuels fear of its growing power. And such fear, if not reversed, risks negating the international environment essential for both self-strengthening domestic reforms and international recognition. Second, while suspicious of the outside world, the Chinese leadership has remained confident that the international environment is an important part of its making. And positive foreign reactions to China's rise decidedly depend on the choices it makes, a belief that has over time been vindicated by the PRC's diplomatic success. Third, in carving out an alternative path for great-power recognition, China has pursued a strategy that combines power with reassurance and change with acceptance, a balancing act designed to secure a positive interactive process between its rise and world politics.

This has decidedly not been easy. The challenge is hardly surprising, as scholarship of the realist persuasion has long established that international politics is ill-equipped to facilitate peaceful change to the status quo when prompted by a power shift of such magnitude. Indeed, elements of traditional great-power politics persist, especially when China's rise poses the greatest threat to the U.S. global position and Japan's regional clout in Asia. Tied to the great-power competition, Taiwan becomes a central battleground where the PRC cultivates and defends regional and global recognition. At the core, important questions have remained regarding the role of China's military in its international future. However, the country's new aspirations abroad necessitate eschewing an unrestrained power politics in its international relations that would lead to an unmitigated arms race, a wholesale confrontation, or war. The central challenge is to bring about a world supportive of its leadership's agenda for engineering orderly modernization at home and a steady great-power rise abroad.

The Puzzle about Chinese Foreign Policy

Through the post–cold war era, Chinese leaders have espoused or acquiesced to various ideas that have supposedly guided the PRC's foreign policy, including most notably "lie low, bide our time," "responsible power," "peaceful rise," "peace and development," "multipolarization and globalization," "multicolored world," "peaceful development," and "harmonious world." While trying to address developments unfavorable to China, they have opted to do so as an active participant in world politics. In articulating their aspirations, they have emphasized ideas of responsibility, development, and peace. To be sure, the strategic choice of a great power like China cannot be settled by its leadership's rhetorical refrains or declaratory statements. Nor is it a function of unilateral preferences, which can themselves change. Consider, for example, the quick retraction of "peaceful rise" in 2004, after the Chinese leadership had espoused it several months earlier. Taken together, these variegated terms revealed profound anxieties about the world, but they also reflected the CCP leadership's determination to adapt to changing realities and proactively remold its international environment.

These foreign policy dynamics represent a significant departure from Chinese practices from the ancient era to the waning days of the cold war. Whereas the Middle Kingdom was the source of power, authority, and legitimacy in the premodern Sino-centric Asian order, the PRC in the post–cold war world had to ascend from a relatively disadvantaged position. During the century of domestic chaos and foreign invasions, which started with the Opium War (1839–42) and lasted until the 1940s, China was forced to be a semicolony with a nominal Chinese government that enjoyed little substance of governance or sovereignty and much less international respect. Too weak to fend for itself, according to the official Chinese interpretation, the nation was subjugated to the worst abuse and humiliations by Western imperial powers and Japan in its history.

This experience, together with the new communist China's revolutionary radicalism and the imperative of state survival under the cold war bipolarity, would essentially define Maoist diplomacy. Maoist China was a revolutionary power, as it was decidedly nonconformist and rejected formal and informal international institutions as the creation of either the superpowers or the Western capitalist camp.[3] In

---

[3] For a review of Maoist rejections of the major international economic institutions, see Harold K. Jacobson and Michel Oksenberg, *China's Participation in the IMF, the World Bank, and GATT: Toward a Global Economic Order* (Ann Arbor: University of Michigan Press, 1990). For an authoritative Chinese overview of Mao's diplomatic thoughts, see Pei Jianzhang, ed., *Mao Zedong Waijiao Shixiang Yanjiu* [Studies on Mao Zedong Thoughts on Diplomacy] (Beijing: Shijie Zhishi Chubanshe, 1993).

reality, the Maoist revolutionary impulse was reined in by the imperatives of national security that dictated conformity with "normal"
power politics practices in its foreign relations.[4] Nonetheless, the PRC
at the time preferred a radically restructured world, whose fruition
called for and justified violent means and confrontational tactics.

Under the official banner of "opening up to the outside world," post-
Mao China started to engage the world, but it did so gingerly lest the
West infringe on its independence and sovereignty. In the early 1980s,
Deng Xiaoping and other Chinese leaders were disappointed by the
U.S. support for Taiwan and the less-than-enthusiastic economic assistance from the West. The reformers reassessed the benefits–costs equation in China's strategic alignment with the United States, factoring in
the lessening Soviet threat as well. The result was an explicit "independence and autonomy" foreign policy line proclaimed in the report
by CCP General Secretary Hu Yaobang to the Twelfth Party Congress
in 1982.[5] Concerned about the popular view that exaggerated China's
dependence on the United States, Deng Xiaoping proclaimed that his
country was "not afraid of evil spirits" and "acts according to its own
views."[6] In tandem with the promulgation of the independence line,
Deng Xiaoping spearheaded a pragmatic turn in foreign policy based
on a reassessment of the world as being defined by prevailing forces of
"peace and development." Concurrently, for Deng and his chief foreign policy adviser Huan Xiang, the bipolar structure was unraveling
and giving way to a process of multipolarization whereby a great-
power nuclear war had become ultimately avoidable.[7] The relaxed

---

[4] An early work on how international anarchy tames revolutionary powers is John
 H. Herz, "Idealist Internationalism and the Security Dilemma," *World Politics*,
 vol. 2, no. 2 (1950), pp. 157–80.
[5] Lu Ning, *The Dynamics of Foreign-Policy Decisionmaking in China*, 2nd ed.
 (Boulder, CO: Westview Press, 2000), pp. 168–9.
[6] Deng Xiaoping, *Deng Xiaoping Wenxuan, vol. 2* [The Selected Works of Deng
 Xiaoping] (Beijing: Renmin Chubanshe, 1983), p. 376. See also Huan Xiang,
 Zhongheng Shijie [Overview of the World] (Beijing: World Affairs Press, 1985),
 pp. 321–4.
[7] Gao Jingdian, ed., *Deng Xiaoping Guoji Zhanlue Sixiang Yanjiu* [Studies on
 Deng Xiaoping's Thoughts on International Strategy] (Beijing: Guofang Daxue
 Chubanshe, 1992); Peng Guangqian and Yao Youzhi, eds., *Deng Xiaoping Zhan-
 lue Sixiang Lun* [On Deng Xiaoping's Thoughts on Strategy] (Beijing: Jiefangjun
 Kexue Chubanshe, 1994); Wang Taiping, ed., *Deng Xiaoping Waijiao Sixiang
 Yanjiu Lunwenji* [Anthology on Deng Xiaoping's Diplomatic Thoughts] (Beijing: Shijie Zhishi Chubanshe, 1996). On Huan Xiang's role and statements

international environment allowed the Chinese reformers to instru-
mentally manage growing economic interdependence necessitated by
their domestic agenda. At the same time, they held on to a rigid Westphalian interpretation of sovereignty as the world underwent a more
dispersed power reconfiguration, eventually leading to the end of the
cold war.[8]

From a historical perspective, the changes in Chinese foreign policy in the post–cold war era have been truly remarkable. The ancient
"center-of-the-world" mentality has given way to a premium placed
on cultivating legitimate recognition from the international society.
Maoist revolutionary diplomacy has been overridden by a deepening
relationship with the globalized world. Rigid definitions of independence and sovereignty have been reconfigured to embrace multilateral
institutions, ideas of international responsibility, and rethinking on
U.S. hegemony. Chinese leaders have talked and behaved in such a
way that it seems as if they have carved out a nonviolent, independent
international path that can lead their nation to great-power status.

These dynamics and patterns do not easily lend themselves to the
analysis of ready-made research programs in the academic IR field.
Most notably, they do not conform to realist theories, which supposedly have the most to say about great-power politics. The PRC has
already experienced a major shift in the relative distribution of power
in its favor. Given the scale and the speed of its rise, conventional wisdom would have us expect a hostile balance of power characterizing
China's international relations.[9] But in reality, China and the United
States have constantly attempted crisis management while struggling

concerning the idea of multipolarity, see Michael Pillsbury, *China Debates the
Future Security Environment* (Washington, DC: National Defense University
Press, 2000), pp. 9–13.

[8] For an excellent dissection of the Chinese views, see Wang Jisi, "International
Relations Theory and the Study of Chinese Foreign Policy: A Chinese Perspective," in Thomas W. Robinson and David Shambaugh, eds., *Chinese Foreign
Policy: Theory and Practice* (New York: Oxford University Press, 1994), pp.
481–505.

[9] Some of the reasoning highlighting the danger of power shift is laid out in Robert
Gilpin, *War and Change in World Politics* (Cambridge: Cambridge University
Press, 1981; A. F. K. Organski and Jacek Kugler, *The War Ledger* (Chicago:
University of Chicago Press, 1980); Joshua S. Goldstein, *Long Cycles: Pros-
perity and War in the Modern Age* (New Haven, CT: Yale University Press,
1988); John Mearsheimer, *The Tragedy of Great Power Politics* (New York:
W. W. Norton, 2001).

to find a strategic formula that would stabilize their relationship. It is true that the PRC is not satisfied with many aspects of the international arrangement, but the changes it has sought to secure a route for great-power ascent are not the same as the status quo–shattering changes associated with hegemonic wars. From these perspectives, both the remarkable focus and the success in the PRC's diplomacy to lessen the fear of its power represent an even greater anomaly.

As a result, while China's foreign policy is a matter of intense interest, an overview of scholarly debates, policy discussions, and media reports quickly reveals the difficulties of grappling with how it has evolved, where the country is positioned in world politics, and what international trajectory it will follow. Fortunately, studies of Chinese foreign policy conducted both inside and outside the country have experienced a renaissance. As Chinese leaders look for ideas and rely on expert advice to manage their country's increasingly complex international relations, prestigious think tanks in Beijing and Shanghai are now much better funded and are staffed with better-trained analysts than ever before. Their quality of analysis has improved by leaps and bounds. They are less restricted in disseminating their work to the public, and in fact they have greater incentives do so, not least for personal career advancement. Spurred by their country's growing influence abroad, aspiring world-class Chinese universities have competed to recruit top-notch scholars and establish respectable curricula in international studies. The process has yet to generate a real debate about such important ideas as China's foreign policy choice, as one would expect from a country on the path to "national rejuvenation." Nor has it led to a "golden age" of international studies whereby innovative, pluralistic thinking not only thrives to inspire China's foreign policy but also contribute to IR theory building in general. (Again, if China has truly arrived as a great power, one would expect such contributions from the Chinese academic community.) Despite these failings, the progress is unmistakable. It becomes even more remarkable, considering that the subject matter was traditionally the most restricted, highly controlled area of study. Their studies yield insights into the perimeters and parameters of the Chinese foreign policy debate.

Studies of China's foreign policy in the United States and Europe have also experienced a boom. The past decade saw a sizable body of English-language literature covering a wide array of issues and bilateral ties. With greater methodological and theoretical sophistication, some of the literature identifies elements in China's distinctive path of international quest. Still other works have detailed the country's key dyadic relationships. This book draws on the literature but advances it through an analytically focused, multilevel empirical analysis of the track record of China's diplomacy in the post–cold war world. As such, it specifies the change and continuity while outlining the distinctive pattern in Chinese foreign policy. We hope to address not simply the questions of what happened but also what all these developments mean in totality.

Focus on International Status

I apply the concept of status to the study of Chinese foreign policy. As stated earlier, I do not use the term in a purely sociological sense. Developed with domestic society in mind, the concept as used by sociologists and social psychologists tends to emphasize its separateness from material factors while downplaying power and noninstitutionalized means of change. I adapt the concept for this study for several reasons. First, the Chinese are intensely sensitive to their nation's "international status," treating it as if it were the overriding foreign policy objective. Second, it remedies the problem of fixation on power and interest while allowing us to explore what separates contemporary China's diplomacy from its past record as well as from the experiences of other rising powers. Third, status sensitizes us to the domestic and international politics behind the country's dynamic interaction with the outside world, thereby avoiding the pitfalls of viewing China's foreign policy in terms of a one-off strategic choice. Last but not least, status brings to focus China's discontent with and participation in the world order as well as the process whereby the country has struggled to overcome the material, political, and social barriers to its great-power aspirations.

Chinese officials and analysts alike have, since the mid-1990s, evoked "international status" (*Guoji Diwei*) as if it were the most desirable value, the one that leads to power, security, and respect. Judging by the frequency of the term's use in official Chinese discourse and scholarly analyses, the PRC may very well be the most status-conscious country in the world. Perhaps China's premodern historical greatness has inculcated a sense among the contemporary Chinese political elites that their nation is entitled to great-power status and that they are obligated to make that happen. As Michael Hunt perceptively argued, "To the extent that this long and rich imperial past defines the future for which Chinese strive, it is not in the crude sense some would have it – as a system of middle kingdom arrogance to be revived – but rather as a standard (or perhaps more accurately a national myth) of cultural achievement and international power and influence to live up to."[10] Similarly, highlighting the affirmative historical reference, Yan Xuetong, director of the Institute for International Studies at Qinghua University, recently wrote, "[T]he Chinese regard their rise as regaining China's lost international status rather than obtaining something new . . . . [They] consider the rise of China as a restoration of fairness rather than gaining advantages over others."[11] By the same token, China's century of disastrous domestic chaos and foreign humiliations after the Opium War is viewed as the worst nationalist experience in its international history.[12]

Although history matters, contemporary China's status-consciousness would not be so acute if it were not for its ongoing phenomenal ascendancy in comprehensive power. Growing wealth generates an expectation of greater respect. Faced with the established – albeit still evolving – world order, the PRC naturally feels that its great-power rise is yet to be duly recognized. Such grievances are natural so long as the rise of expectations outstrips the pace of actual status improvement.[13] Regardless of its origins, China's status sensitivity appears unparalleled. At first glance, this seems curious, especially considering the fact that the country occupies a veto-wielding permanent seat on the United Nations Security Council

---

[10] Michael H. Hunt, "Chinese Foreign Relations in Historical Perspective," in Harry Harding, ed., *Chinese Foreign Relations in the 1980s* (New Haven, CT: Yale University Press, 1984), pp. 38–9. A similar theme is developed in Lowell Dittmer and Samuel S. Kim, *China's Quest for National Identity* (Ithaca, NY: Cornell University Press, 1993).

[11] Yan Xuetong, "The Rise of China in Chinese Eyes," *Journal of Contemporary China*, vol. 10, no. 26 (2001), p. 34.

[12] See Zhang Yijun, "PRC-U.S.-Japanese Relations at the Turn of Century," Guoji Zhanwang, no. 14 (July 15, 2000), *Foreign Broadcast Information Service*: CPP20000726000070, pp. 8–11.

[13] The classic work on the origin of such social discontent is Ted R. Gurr, *Why Men Rebel* (Princeton, NJ: Princeton University Press, 1970). For a concise summary of the multidisciplinary insights along this line, see Michael A. Hogg and Dominic Abrams, *Social Identifications: A Social Psychology of Intergroup Relations and Group Process* (New York: Routledge, 1988), pp. 37–42.

and is already ranked higher than some members of the G8, the world's so-called rich man's club on many items on the economic and military index. However, as the late paramount leader Deng Xiaoping said, "We should count as a great power, but this great power is also a small power."[14] Given its population, physical scale, UN role, and now fast growing power, the PRC would always measure up as a great power in some areas. But it remains a developing country with persistent vulnerabilities at home, as the CCP government struggles to maintain sustainable growth and strengthen governance. Beyond its secured borders, the country faces critical challenges from the Taiwan issue to the uncertainties in world politics at large. As such, its foreign policy must balance the competing demands of being both a great power and a small power. Sometimes, China's small-power status has given it an edge in solidifying ties in the developing world. But more often than not, it limits its options in foreign policy choice. In a similar vein, Michael Swaine and Ashley Tellis have argued that "a hybrid 'weak-strong' state security strategy" historically underpinned a conservative Chinese foreign policy and continues to do so in the contemporary era.[15] The realignment in the world order after the cold war further renders problematic the "greatness" in Chinese power. At the same time, as China rises, its interaction with the rest of the world also intensifies, heightening awareness by the Chinese as to how their country is treated.

What is indeed striking is the extent to which the Chinese elites attribute their country's foreign policy predicament to how it is mistrusted and mistreated. For example, during the North Atlantic Treaty Organization (NATO) air campaign against Yugoslavia, an American warplane mistakenly bombed the Chinese embassy in Belgrade on May 7, 1999, causing widespread anti-American demonstrations in China and violent mob attacks on the American embassy in Beijing and diplomatic facilities in several major cities, the worst of its kind since the

---

[14] Deng Xiaoping, "Heping Fazhan Shi Dangdai Shijie De Liangda Wenti [Peace and Development Are the Two Major Issues in Contemporary World]," in *Deng Xiaoping Wenxuan, vol. 3* [Selected Works of Deng Xiaoping] (Beijing: Renmin Chubanshe, 1993), p. 105.

[15] Michael D. Swaine and Ashley Tellis, *Interpreting China's Grand Strategy: Past, Present, and Future* (Santa Monica, CA: Rand, 2000). Susan Shirk highlights the same problem limiting China's international role in her *China: Fragile Superpower* (New York: Oxford University Press, 2007).

Cultural Revolution. A hotline between the American and Chinese leaders designed to deal with such crises had been set up in 1998 based on an agreement reached during President Jiang Zemin's official visit to the United States a year earlier. But it took until May 14 for presidents Bill Clinton and Jiang to talk to each other on the telephone, a delay that fueled China's conspiracy theories, virulent nationalism, and attribution of malign intentions to the United States. Reflecting on the incident six years later, one prominent Chinese strategy analyst blamed mutual mismanagement of the crisis on the lack of expeditious communication at the highest level, resulting from profound mistrust and "severe immaturity" in the bilateral relationship.[16]

The Sino-American relationship hit yet another crisis when a Chinese fighter jet collided with an American surveillance plane near Hainan in April 2001. The Beijing-based analyst, Zhang Tuosheng, similarly attributed the badly fumbled efforts for crisis management by both parties to the unresolved, fundamental question of how the bilateral relationship was to be defined (*Dingwei*). He wrote, "Under the new, post–cold war international structure, are China and the United States friends or enemies? Or, as many have pointed out, are they neither enemies nor friends? This is a very complex and rather controversial question." Looking forward, he argued, the Sino-American relationship is characterized by "coexistence of cooperation and disagreement," with the former exceeding the latter. And "both sides are making efforts to develop a constructive cooperative partnership."[17] The "definition" issue he raised reflects the fundamental Chinese concern about the United States' ambiguities in its overall China policy, including in the economic area. The problems in the Sino-American relationship, Chinese commentators maintain, are fundamentally rooted in the prejudiced U.S. attitude toward the rising power. In the words of a Beijing-based think-tank analyst,

---

[16] Wu Baiyi, "Zhongguo Dui 'Zhaguan' Shijian De Weiji Guanli [China's Crisis Management over the Embassy Bombing Incident]," *Shijie Jingji Yu Zhengzhi*, no. 3 (2005) http://www.iwep.org.cn/guojizhengzhi/wubaiyi.pdf (accessed May 25, 2005). p. 6.

[17] Zhang Tuosheng, "Zhongmei Zhuangji Shijian jiqi Jingyan Jiaoxun [The China-U.S. Midair Collision Incident and Its Lessons]," *Shijie Jingji Yu Zhengzhi*, no. 3 (2005), p. 11. http://www.iwep.org.cn/guojizhengzhi/zhangtuosheng.pdf (accessed May 9, 2005). p. 11.

At bottom, the real "big question" in Sino-American economic and trade relations does not lie with the so-called trade deficit, Renminbi [Chinese currency] exchange rate, or textile dispute, but rather with the notions that "the speed is too fast," "the momentum too strong," "the future too unpredictable" in China's rise posited by certain quarters in the United States. They are not contented if they do not think of ways to impede and check China. Thus, in the final analysis, to truly "de-politicize" [economic disputes], it is necessary that the American policy-makers and people of all walks of life face squarely at and accept China's peaceful rise with a new mentality and strategic vision.[18]

During 2004–5, controversies flared up over the lifting of an arms embargo on China by the European Union (EU). Although the ban on arms sales was initially imposed in response to the violent end of the Tiananmen demonstrations in 1989, those opposed to its removal some fifteen years later cited China's human rights record, the military threat to Taiwan, and broader strategic implications such a move would entail for China's foreign relations. In the PRC's opinion, this punitive measure had simply been prolonged by political discrimination and strategic distrust.

The Chinese have sometimes used the term "international status" as if it were their only foreign policy goal and at other times have used status and "real power" (*Shili*) in the same breath. From what we can glean from Chinese writings, it is clear that status entails some magical qualities with which core national interests can be secured. The belief in China's steady rise has become almost an article of faith. Yet, there remains a deep concern over the fate of China's domestic and international transition. Nonetheless, Chinese leaders and analysts alike have refrained from openly discussing their concern. Presumably, the only exception is their candidness about the PRC's role in the United Nations insofar as Chinese diplomats are most comfortable in detailing concrete markers of their nation's growing influence in the context of this international organization.[19] Where scholarly treatments are attempted, status is left to be so ambiguous as to retain little analytic leverage. Given the utmost value the PRC has attached to this idea,

---

[18] Yuan Peng, "Morang Fuyun Zhewangyan [Don't Let the Floating Clouds Block Your Vision]," *Renmin Ribao*, overseas edition, June 2, 2005, p. 1.

[19] See, for example, "China's International Status Becomes Increasingly Important: Interview," *People's Daily Online*, Nov. 1, 2004. http://english. peopledaily.com.cn (accessed Nov. 15, 2004).

one would expect more careful Chinese specifications of the distinguishing and supposedly superior qualities of its ongoing status quest as opposed to other conventional modes of power politics. Chinese reticence for clarity may have to do with the very sensitivities of the notion itself; Systematic exposition of the concern would underscore the need for China to seek international recognition and as such would risk simultaneously giving too much credence to the legitimacy of the existing international social structure, emboldening Western pressures, on the one hand, and on the other, conceding China's inferiority, vulnerabilities, and need for unilateral compliance. Thus, the ubiquitous use of the term stands in contrast to its scanty analysis.

To explicate this concern and its significance in this study, we ask the following questions: What are the real sources of China's foreign policy predicament? What is the role of power in China's quest for status? And how does the status pursuit manifest itself in China's foreign policy record? Unfortunately, no ready-made IR theories can provide us with the analytical guidance. Mainstream paradigms assume that states act as individualistic, egoistic actors seeking to maximize relative power or absolute material gains.[20] Liberalism is preoccupied with identifying ways to generate cooperative outcomes that maximize the state's interests. Realism tends to view international politics as fundamentally defined by an asocial or presocial anarchy of self-help. In the few instances where "status" is considered, it is treated as simply a power struggle in the form of zero-sum "positional conflict." Status is thus said to be determined by either war-fighting capabilities or war fighting itself.[21] But this clearly does not tally with what the Chinese mean. The so-called British School in IR highlights the institutional

---

[20] For trenchant critiques along these lines, see Peter Katzenstein, ed., *The Culture of National Security* (New York: Columbia University Press, 1996); Alexander Wendt, *Social Theory of International Politics* (Cambridge: Cambridge University Press, 1998).

[21] See Randall L. Schweller, "Realism and the Present Great Power System: Growth and Positional Conflict over Scarce Resources," in Ethan K. Kapstein and Michael Mastanduno, eds., *Unipolar Politics: Realism and State Strategies after the Cold War* (New York: Columbia University Press, 1999), ch.. 2; William C. Wohlforth, "Hierarchy, Status, and War," American Political Science Association Annual Meeting, 2002; Jack S. Levy, *War in the Modern Great Power System, 1495–1975* (Lexington: University Press of Kentucky, 1983); Jesse Wilkins, "The Pursuit of Great Power Status: War as an Information Revealing Mechanism," American Political Science Association Annual Meeting, 2005.

features of the world order.[22] The popularity of constructivism in IR has brought about growing attention to social and ideational forces in international relations. However, constructivism fixates on social and cultural dynamics in interstate relations, often downplaying the uninstitutionalized nature of world politics.

Clearly, none of these schools of thought alone is adequate in accounting for the complex dimensions of China's discontent and aspirations. Realist logic would suggest looking at the country as just another state caught in a power transition, which will tragically end with war – most likely with the reigning hegemon, the United States.[23] But China's strategists have consciously vowed to avoid that pattern, and the development of the Sino-American relationship does not indicate the inevitability of that outcome. In fact, both sides have chosen an engagement path designed to steer clear from the traditional path of unmitigated great-power rivalry. The significantly lessened balancing logic in international responses toward China's rise speaks to the inadequacy of the realist framework. Liberalism suggests that change on China's part toward interest and value compatibility with the established powers, coupled with its institutional entanglement, will lead to a peaceful outcome.[24] It assumes that the Chinese elites are fully open to an "exit" strategy, abandoning its "old" domestic and international practices in order to join the established great powers.[25] However, the need to carve out their own strategic space and limitations to domestic

---

[22] The two classics in the British School are Hedley Bull, *The Anarchical Society: A Study of Order in World Politics* (New York: Columbia University Press, 1977); and Hedley Bull and Adam Watson, *The Expansion of International Society* (Oxford: Oxford University Press, 1984). For an application of the British School to China, see Yongjin Zhang, *China in International Society since 1949: Alienation and Beyond* (New York: St. Martin's, 1998).

[23] See, for example, Mearsheimer, *The Tragedy of Great Power Politics*; Dale Copeland, *The Origins of Major Power* (Ithaca, NY: Cornell University Press, 2000).

[24] One such study offering liberal solutions to the power transition problem is Ronald L. Tammen, *Power Transitions: Strategies for the 21st Century* (New York: Chatham House, 2000).

[25] For discussions of this strategy, see Henri Tajfel, *Human Groups and Social Categories: Studies in Social Psychology* (Cambridge: Cambridge University Press, 1981), pp. 246–7, 252–3, 278–9, ch. 14; Roger Brown, *Social Psychology*, 2nd ed. (New York: Free Press, 1986), pp. 556–85; Albert O. Hirschman, *Exit, Voice, and Loyalty: Responses to Decline in Firms, Organizations, and States* (Cambridge, MA: Harvard University Press, 1970).

political reforms render inconceivable a choice of a self-liberalizing "exit strategy." Also, strikingly, China has experienced the most problematic relations with those players (the United States, Japan, and Taiwan) that it has the tightest interdependence with, raising further question about the applicability of liberal propositions. The importation of constructivism into the study of Chinese foreign policy has led to some of the most innovative studies directing our attention to various new ideas, most notably, China's self-identification as a responsible power. However, the constructivist approach tends to overstate the power of ideational forces and to understate the interactive diplomacy driven by both material and nonmaterial forces.[26]

In deciphering the logic of China's status struggle in the post–cold war era, I tap into useful sources from other disciplines as well as insights from the foregoing IR theories.[27] I also carefully track China's worldview and its foreign policy manifestations. Taken together, our studies suggest that China's status quest is a function of the international power and normative arrangement, the predominant patterns of great-power politics, and China's self-definition of identity and interests in world politics. The country's foreign policy is thus best considered in terms of interaction between domestic and international politics, between China and other great powers, and between China's rise and evolution of the world order at large.

Traditionally, as Jack Levy argues, "Nearly all definitions of Great Powers focus primarily on military might," as great powers had to literally fight their ways to the top of the international pecking order.[28] The Chinese political elites are determined to develop "comprehensive national power," with an aim to improve their country's economic and technological prowess as well as software strength on domestic governance and social stability. To be sure, the Chinese have also stepped up their military modernization, most notably through an aggressive

[26] See, for example, the discussions in Jeffrey W. Legro, *Rethinking the World: Great Power Strategies and International Order* (Ithaca, NY: Cornell University Press, 2005), pp. 173–8.

[27] For the importance of not being limited by a particular theory, see Jack Snyder, "Anarchy and Culture: Insights from the Anthropology of War," *International Organization*, vol. 56, no. 1 (2002), pp. 7–45; J. J. Suh, Peter J. Katzenstein, and Allen Carlson, eds., *Rethinking Security in East Asia: Identity, Power, and Efficiency* (Stanford, CA: Stanford University Press, 2004).

[28] For a concise overview of the literature, see Levy, *War in the Modern Great Power System*, pp. 10–19. Quote on p. 11.

space program. Many of the Chinese postures warrant concerns and corresponding hard-nosed reactions. We need to consider the power politics surrounding China's rise, not least because the regional order in Asia and the mechanism of power transition in world politics at large are still weakly institutionalized. But as Jeffrey Legro writes, despite their conformist policy toward the world order,

> Chinese leaders pay close attention to power and geopolitics. Indeed, to the extent China is interested in joining international society, it should by the very principles of the system have an interest in balance of power politics. . . . Yet attention to power is hardly the sign of a revisionist country. Indeed, one might argue that the *neglect* of power realities is the hallmark of revisionist states – for example, Nazi Germany's utopian goals of world conquest, Japan's gamble at Pearl Harbor, and Brezhnev's expansionism in the face of decline.[29]

Not all competitive politics are alike. Realism cannot monopolize the "truth" about international politics just because interstate competition exists. While attentive to the competitive dynamics, we also need to consider other underlying forces, including those mitigating great-power rivalry. In contrast to the choice of military expansion by the traditional great powers, China's foreign policy in the past twenty some years has been markedly driven by the CCP's agenda to achieve a stable, economically prosperous home front. The Chinese leadership and analysts alike have been conservative in assessing their nation's capabilities, especially in terms of influencing events beyond the Asian region. They do not see forcing a radical change to either the international or regional order through all-out confrontation with the United States or Japan as in their national interest.

The Chinese policy elites seem to have understood that if their country were to achieve its great-power dream, a full-blown security dilemma surrounding its rise would have to be forestalled. They have thus shown a heightened awareness of an international fear of China's rising power and have proactively tried to assuage such concern. In attempting to bring about international outcomes more to their liking, the policy elites have tempered the revisionist impulse vis-à-vis the world order with a conformist approach. They have put a premium on cultivating respect and acceptance by the established

---

[29] Legro, *Rethinking the World*, p. 174. Italics in original.

"status group" of great powers, their Asian neighbors, and other parts of the world.[30] In a nutshell, they have looked beyond traditional, crude realist measures to deliberately manage their country's precarious international environment. The result is a Chinese foreign policy that employs wide-ranging diplomatic tools in order to ensure an overall positive interactive pattern between China's rise and international reactions to it.

Because simply borrowing existing models or applying familiar approaches does not suffice, the concept of status promises to facilitate an appropriate alternative line of inquiry into China's foreign relations. It helps broaden our analysis beyond rationalist-materialist forces, alerting us not only to the state's power and interests, but also to how the definition and attainment of power and interests are contingent upon the political, social, and cultural factors in world politics. As such, the analytical focus dovetails with the overriding question confronting the Chinese political elites: How should they shape an international environment conducive to China's domestic modernization drive and great-power rise under the U.S. hegemonic order? It underscores that at the core of China's foreign policy is the struggle to overcome its material and nonmaterial disadvantage in order to cultivate positive recognition as a great power in international society. In adapting a concept originating from the studies of domestic society, I am particularly attentive to the distinctive dynamics of the international arena. While giving due consideration to the reality of hierarchy, the factor of legitimacy, and intergroup dynamics, I also recognize the reality of power, the factor of contested authority, and the fluidities and uncertainties in international politics.

The Structure of the Book

My central concern is not to build a new IR theory in, but to disentangle the puzzle about China's foreign relations. From our perspective, the PRC's foreign policy has been an uphill struggle. After the end of the cold war, the PRC found it at a denigrated position in world politics. With no other creditable option conspicuously available, the CCP leaders have sought to engineer China's great-power reemergence within

---

[30] The term "*status group*" is from Max Weber, *Economy and Society: An Outline of Interpretive Sociology* (New York: Bedminster Press, 1968).

the world order. To that end, they have geared their diplomacy toward changing the international hierarchy to facilitate China's great-power ascent. The process has by no means been easy, and China's foreign relations have been beset by uncertainties at home and abroad. Despite this fact, they have overall succeeded remarkably. To elucidate how China has managed its international relations, the book undertakes a four-level analysis.

After the Introduction, Chapter 2 provides an overview of China's status predicament, sketches the patterns and parameters of its foreign policy response, and identifies the key variables driving its foreign policy choice. The overriding question that Chinese elites have to ask concerns how to deal with the dominant great-power grouping and the corresponding normative and institutional arrangements that define the international hierarchy. The first level of analysis thus investigates how China reacts to the international human rights regime and the generally negative character attribution associated with "China threat theories" (Chapters 3 and 4).

As regards the Western great-power center per se, I do not treat the Sino-American relationship in a separate chapter. As Peter Katzenstein argues, the United States exercises its hegemonic role (which he calls "imperium") as "both an actor and a system" of global reach.[31] Indeed, the American factor permeates the analysis throughout the book. I do, however, offer some focused discussions of the parameters of China's diplomacy toward the United States and other Western powers in the subsequent comparative analyses of its great-power diplomacy.

The PRC has formed "strategic partnerships" with Russia, the EU, and India, but it has failed to do so with Japan. Chapter 5 looks at the former through a comparative study of China's three strategic partnerships, although the greatest attention is devoted to Sino-Russian ties. To the extent that the EU is a key part of the Western alliance, this inquiry sheds important light on how China directly engages the dominant great-power grouping. Most notably, however, two of the three strategic partners, Russia and India, are non-Western, rising powers. As such, this chapter represents the second level of analysis

---

[31] Peter J. Katzenstein, *A World of Regions: Asia and Europe in the American Imperium* (Ithaca, NY: Cornell University Press, 2005), p. 245.

exploring how the PRC recasts its relationships with fellow aspiring major powers.

By virtue of its international identity and its treaty alliance with the United States, Japan is part of the "West." It has also enjoyed a de facto leadership role of some sort in Asia. Thus, China's Japan problem straddles its problems with both the United States, on the one hand, and the regional order, on the other. Chapter 6 probes beneath the nationalist emotions, economics–politics dichotomy, and balance-of-power manifestations to uncover the unifying status logic behind the paradoxical interactions between the two Asian giants.

Taken together, Chapters 5 and 6 elucidate the complex great-power politics and point to the regional dynamics in Asia surrounding China's rise. Looking beyond the major powers, Chapter 7 focuses on China's diplomacy in Asia and, to a lesser extent, in Africa. The third level of analysis is not about China's "third-world" diplomacy, as the traditional notion of third-world solidarity hardly means anything anymore. Rather it is about how the PRC adapts its relations with the relatively minor neighboring countries and African states in order to reorient the regional and global order.[32] In so doing, I focus on China's multilateral diplomacy, as it best reflects the rising power's strategic objectives while providing a political framework for bilateral ties with individual states. Thus, Chapter 7 investigates the differentiated PRC approaches to the multilateral processes in Northeast Asia, Southeast Asia, and Central Asia, respectively, focusing on its role in the Six-Party Talks, the Association for Southeast Asian Nations–centered regionalism, and the Shanghai Cooperation Organization. The chapter also offers a synopsis of China's presence in Africa by focusing on the Forum on China–Africa Cooperation.

Chinese analysts and political elites alike have considered Taiwan as a litmus test for whether or not China has arrived as a great power. Exactly how does Taiwan fit into China's rising strategy? Despite the obvious importance of this question, the literature on the cross-Straits relations is remarkably oblivious to it. The fourth level of analysis, Chapter 8, addresses this question. Lastly, I summarize the findings of the book and highlight the implications of China's status struggle for

---

[32] The seminal study on variegated modes of interaction between the big and small powers is Brantly Womack, *China and Vietnam: The Politics of Asymmetry* (New York: Cambridge University Press, 2006).

the development of Chinese nationalism, the evolving regional order in Asia, and the emerging great-power politics.

With the analytical approach and a multilevel empirical inquiry, we hope to bring to sharp relief China's struggle to simultaneously overcome material weaknesses and political, social, and cultural disadvantages in contemporary world politics. We further explore how that struggle has been manifested in its diplomacy toward the international status quo, other emerging powers, its neighboring regions and developing countries, and Taiwan. As such, we cast a new light on the human rights factor in China's foreign relations. We reconsider reputation in China's international relations. We show that the country's foreign policy cannot be shoehorned into Western IR theories and concepts, such as offensive realism, structural realism, status quo power, and revisionist power. Nor can we take at face value the dizzying array of ideas about China's harmonious rise that has been advanced by the Chinese elites. We also hope to uncover the unifying logic underwriting the PRC's diplomacy toward individual countries and specific issues. The result, I hope, is a clearer specification of the distinctiveness and uncertainties in China's international trajectory. By focusing on the dynamic interactions between the domestic and international forces that have underpinned China's diplomacy, the study offers serious reflections on the possibility of an alternative path to great-power status, as opposed to the offhand proverbial uncertainties in China's future. In the end, through this study we hope to distill some insights into the unique challenges and opportunities posed by China's extending global reach.

2 | International Status and Chinese Foreign Policy

Influenced by Max Weber's classical definition of status as "effective claim to social esteem,"[1] sociologists treat status as a separate analytic category from materialist bases of social stratification.[2] In International Relations (IR), when the term is used in realist theory, status is no different from – and is, in fact, interchangeable with – power. For realists, status, like power, is zero-sum, and the means to advance it is through materialist means most prominently associated with war and war-fighting capacities. Our use of "status" here differs from both the standard use in sociology and mainstream IR theory. For our purposes, China's struggle for status is about creating an international environment that allows the Chinese Communist Party (CCP)-state to continue self-paced reforms at home; increase power and recognition abroad to secure China's core interests; reassure other states of China's nonthreatening intent; and projects its influence in Asia and beyond. Our definition conforms to the conviction of the Chinese political elites that the path for their nation's revival starts with the domestic front, but must join an international path to cultivate acceptance abroad on their own terms. It also reflects the reality in post–cold war world politics, where an amalgam of power, security, and social recognition drives great-power politics.

Without power, there is no recognition. Yet power without recognition fuels the fear of a China threat, obviating the international opportunities necessary for economic growth. Also, in pursuing comprehensive power the People's Republic of China (PRC) has to determine how much priority is to be given to economic development as compared to

---

[1] Max Weber, *Economy and Society: An Outline of Interpretive Sociology* (New York: Bedminster Press, 1968), vol. 1, p. 305.
[2] Cecilia L. Ridgeway, "Status Construction Theory," in Peter J. Burke, ed., *Contemporary Social Psychological Theories* (Stanford, CA: Stanford University Press, 2006), p. 301.

military modernization. In pursuing international recognition, it has focused on extracting deference to its core security interests on Taiwan, legitimating its power, and reforming the Western-dominated world order. These status interests may also conflict with each other. The question regarding how China should balance these competing agendas has been the foremost concern of the Chinese leadership and analysts alike.

Three fundamental realities have conditioned China's foreign policy since the end of the cold war. The CCP elites complain about the disadvantage their country faces in the international hierarchy, wherein democratic values, capitalism, and the idea of international responsibility are *promoted*. But they also recognize the world order is structured such that a radical reconfiguration to China's international environment through confrontation appears neither feasible nor worthwhile. Established great powers led by the United States set barriers for aspiring newcomers like the PRC, but ultimately they have opted to engage, rather than contain, them. The globalized world has posed challenges to the authority of the CCP at home and abroad, but it has also presented opportunities for China's great-power ascendancy, which the political elites have seized in order to reconcile the party-state's domestic legitimacy and the nation's international recognition.

Power, Authority, and Categorization: Sources of China's Foreign Policy Predicament

With the end of the cold war, both power and authority in world politics started to coalesce around the triumphant West, thereby prompting a shift from alliance to group politics in international relations. In the face of the new power reality and uncertainties, according to insights from the social identity theory, the leading advanced democracies would naturally attempt to establish their in-group "superior distinctiveness" by promoting a set of values as the basis of social comparison and categorization.[3] In this way, the boundaries

---

[3] For a succinct discussion of the dynamics of "self-enhancement and uncertainty reduction," see Michael A. Hogg, "Social Identity Theory," in Peter J. Burke, *Contemporary Social Psychological Theories*, pp. 120–21. The classic work on small-group dynamics is Henri Tajfel, *Human Groups and Social Categories: Studies in Social Psychology* (Cambridge: Cambridge University Press, 1981), quote on p. 278.

separating "us" from the "others" (the out-group) are delimited and maintained.

For Max Weber, a dominant, privileged "status group" in a society is not just sustained by economic interest, but more importantly underpinned by in-group values and a strong "we" feeling.[4] Indeed, enduring group identity must entail what John C. Turner and his colleagues call "a shift towards the perception of self as an interchangeable exemplar of social category and away from the perception of self as a unique person."[5] The intensity of shared identification determines the group cohesion and the strength of the corresponding social arrangement. The phenomenon of differentiating people into insiders-outsiders or us-them is what social psychologists call "categorization," whose essence, argues Henri Tajfel, is to "simplify or systematize, for purposes of cognitive and behavioral adaptation, the abundance and complexity of the information received from the environment."[6] With the axiomatic assumption that "very often we are what we are because 'they' are not what we are,"[7] categorization makes it easy to differentiate between insiders and outsiders, to locate sources of enmity and amity, and to determine whom to trust or fear.

To facilitate favorable social comparisons, the dominant group promotes its most important traits through the representation of the "category prototype," whose values typify the supposedly superior qualities in the society.[8] Constructed through social interactions, in the words of Robert M. Entman and Andrew Rojecki, "Prototypes serve as ideal examples of categories."[9] The most prominent, often idealized values the in-group identifies with serve as both the standards for its membership and the basis for justifying separate treatment of the outsiders. The group dynamic effectively underpins "social closure," whereby

[4] Weber, *Economy and Society*. For an elaboration of Weberian views, see Barry Barnes, "Status Groups and Collective Action," *Sociology*, vol. 26, no. 2 (May 1992), pp. 259–70.

[5] J. C. Turner, et al., *Rediscovering the Social Group: A Self-Categorization Theory* (Oxford: Blackwell, 1987), p. 50. Quoted in Marilyn B. Brewer, "The Many Faces of Social Identity: Implications for Political Psychology," *Political Psychology*, vol. 22, no. 1 (2001), pp. 118–19.

[6] Tajfel, *Human Groups and Social Categories*, p. 145.

[7] *Ibid.*, p. 297.

[8] Leonie Huddy, "From Social to Political Identity: A Critical Examination of Social Identity Theory," *Political Psychology*, vol. 22, no. 1 (2001), pp. 133–34.

[9] Robert M. Entman and Andrew Rojecki, *The Black Image in the White Mind: Media and Race in America* (Chicago: University of Chicago Press, 2000), p. 61.

the ruling elites enjoy privileged status to the exclusion of others.[10] In other words, defining "us" is symbiotically affirming superiority, as it confers positive valuation on the self at the expense of others. This is the process that social psychologists characterize as in-group positive stereotyping and favoritism vis-à-vis out-group negative stereotyping and discrimination. The ubiquity and power of categorization in defining social relations and motivating behavior is well documented in the social psychology literature.[11] And this insight has forcefully informed studies on topics ranging from racial tensions in the United States to anti-immigrant movements in Europe.[12]

These sociological findings have made inroads in IR, riding in particular on the recent popularity of various constructivist theories. The new paradigm uncovers how ideas, identity, and interaction matter and as such lays bare a normative, authoritative basis of legitimacy in world politics.[13] Alexander Wendt has consistently called our

---

[10] Raymond Murphy, *Social Closure: The Theory of Monopolization and Exclusion* (Oxford: Clarendon Press, 1988).

[11] See Tajfel, *Human Groups and Social Categories*; Michael A. Hogg and Dominic Abrams, *Social Identifications: A Social Psychology of Intergroup Relations and Group Process* (New York: Routledge, 1988), p. 23 and passim; Vamik Volkan, *Blood Lines: From Ethnic Pride to Ethnic Terrorism* (New York: Farrar, Straus and Giroux, 1997); Will Kalkhoff and Christopher Barnum, "The Effects of Status-Organizing and Social Identity Processes on Patterns of Social Influence," *Social Psychology Quarterly*, vol. 63, no. 2 (2000), pp. 95–115; Jan E. Stets and Peter J. Burke, "Identity Theory and Social Identity Theory," *Social Psychology Quarterly*, vol. 63, no. 3 (2000), pp. 224–37; Roger Brown, *Social Psychology*, 2nd ed. (New York: Free Press, 1986), ch. 15, 16; Brewer, "The Many Faces of Social Identity," pp. 115–25; Huddy, "From Social to Political Identity," pp. 127–56.

[12] Entman and Rojecki, *The Black Image in the White Mind*; Paul M. Sniderman, Pieranngelo Peri, Rui J. P. de Figueiredo, Jr., and Thomas Piazza, *The Outsider: Prejudice and Politics in Italy* (Princeton, NJ: Princeton University Press, 2000).

[13] For a sampling of the literature, see Christian Reus-Smit, *The Moral Purpose of the State: Culture, Social Identity, and Institutional Rationality in International Relations* (Princeton, NJ: Princeton University Press, 1999); Mlada Bukovansky, *Legitimacy and Power Politics: The American and French Revolutions in International Political Culture* (Princeton, NJ: Princeton University Press, 2002); Rodney B. Hall, "Moral Authority as a Power Resource," *International Organization*, vol. 51, no. 4 (Autumn 1997), pp. 591–622; John W. Meyer, John Boli, George M. Thomas, and Francis O. Ramirez, "World Society and the Nation-State," *American Journal of Sociology*, vol. 103, no. 1 (July 1997), pp. 144–81; Peter Katzenstein, ed., *The Culture of National Security* (New York: Columbia University Press, 1996).

attention to the power of social identification in interstate relations, which may vary "from conceiving the other as anathema to the self to conceiving it as an extension of the self."[14] Other scholars have shown that where a state is located in that social-psychological continuum with other states decisively influences the interpretation of information and inference of intentions in its interstate interactions.[15]

In grappling with the meaning of the post–cold war world, many IR experts have sketched out a graded world order defined by member states' varying success of democratization, economic growth, and peaceful development at home and abroad. In crude or nuanced formulations, much of the literature tends to differentiate zones of world politics based on static standards. For example, writing in the early 1990s, James Goldgeier and Michael MacFaul posited that North America, Europe, and Japan had formed a "great-power society," characterized by stable nuclear deterrence, reliable democratic peace, and firm liberal economic beliefs; whereas, old-style power politics and violence were commonplace throughout the rest of the world. The "core" of the great-power society developed in isolation from the "periphery," they argued, and was largely inward looking and indeed sought to dissociate further from the periphery.[16]

But with power and authority intensely contested in world politics, the established powers must fight to preserve the status quo. Referring to such efforts, Ian Clark observes, "[W]ithin the still universal ideal of international society, there has increasingly been articulated the doctrinal rationale for an 'inner' grouping entitled to the fullest enjoyment

---

[14] Alexander Wendt, "Collective Identity Formation and the International State," *American Political Science Review*, vol. 88, no. 2 (June 1994), p. 368. See also Wendt, *Social Theory of International Politics* (Cambridge: Cambridge University Press, 1998).

[15] See, for example, Jonathan Mercer, *Reputation and International Politics* (Ithaca, NY: Cornell University Press, 1996); Deborah W. Larson, *Anatomy of Mistrust: U.S.-Soviet Relations During the Cold War* (Ithaca, NY: Cornell University Press, 1997); David Campbell, *Writing Security: United States Foreign Policy and the Politics of Identity* (Minneapolis: University of Minnesota Press, 1998); Mark L. Haas, *The Ideological Origins of Great Power Politics, 1789–1989* (Ithaca, NY: Cornell University Press, 2005).

[16] John M. Goldgeier and Michael McFaul, "A Tale of Two Worlds: Core and Periphery in the Post–Cold War Era," *International Organization*, vol. 46, no. 2 (Spring 1992), pp. 467–91. See also Henry R. Nau, *At Home Abroad: Identity and Power in American Foreign Policy* (Ithaca, NY: Cornell University Press, 2002).

of the rights of membership, and also to be the interpreters and execu-
tors of the wishes of international society as a whole."[17] Many of
the Western values, such as human rights and capitalism, were indeed
universalized to become what Ralf Dahrendorf dubbed "socially established values" of the new world order.[18] And the prototypical Western
image based on select values constituted the basis of categorization
that conferred different statuses on the states. The upshot was a quite
stable – albeit fiercely contested – international social hierarchy based
on a significant overlapping of power and authority.

The prototypical member of the established in-group is one that
takes seriously the collective responsibility of maintaining the international order, practices liberal democracy, and embraces free-market
principles. Based on this image, the established in-group members are
projected to be unified by common political ideals, follow "the logic
of a separate peace" in intragroup relations, and demonstrate considerable like-mindedness on fundamental issues of global governance.[19]
Attempts to stratify the world according to these principles has centered on the promotion of democratic peace, which as an IR theory
strictly means that democracies don't fight war with each other. However, the proposition has often been expansively taken to suggest that
the democratic in-group represents a superior mode of both domestic
and international organization of political life.

The core assumption about the exclusive quality of lasting peace
among democracies has been questioned by both scholarly inquiries

---

[17] Ian Clark, *Legitimacy in International Society* (Oxford: Oxford University Press, 2005), p. 159.

[18] Ralf Dahrendorf, "On the Origin of Inequality among Men," in Edward O. Laumann, Paul M. Siegel, and Robert W. Hodge, eds., *The Logic of Social Hierarchies* (Chicago: Markham Publishing, 1970), pp. 20–21.

[19] "The logic of a separate peace" was coined by Michael Doyle. For further discus-
sion, see his *Ways of War and Peace: Realism, Liberalism, and Socialism* (New York: W. W. Norton, 1997), especially ch. 8. A sampling of the literature that differentiates states along these lines includes Goldgeier and McFaul, "A Tale of Two Worlds"; Emmaneul Adler and Michael Barnett, eds., *Security Communities* (Cambridge: Cambridge University Press, 1998); Richard Rosecrance, ed., *The Great Power Coalition* (Boulder, CO: Rowman & Littlefield, 2001); Robert Jervis, "Theories of War in an Era of Leading-Power Peace," *American Political Science Review*, vol. 96, no. 1 (March 2002), pp. 1–14; G. John Ikenberry, *After Victory: Institutions, Strategic Restraint, and the Rebuilding of Order after Major Wars* (Princeton, NJ: Princeton University Press, 2001), ch. 1, 8.

and empirical evidence. Skeptics have raised doubts about the statistical correlation, normative-cultural factor, and structural-institutional variable said to cause separate peace among democratic polities.[20] Many empirical cases, too, appear to defy the democratic peace logic. Consider, for example, in China's neighborhood the ten members of the Association for Southeast Asian Nations (ASEAN), which are of mixed regime types. Without a common democratic foundation, the ASEAN has nonetheless managed to prevent military conflict amongst its members since its formation in 1967. More broadly, the sovereignty-respecting, nonlegalistic, and flexible institutions in the Pacific Asia, in which ASEAN has played a central role, have evolved and consolidated to mitigate the security dilemma in the region.[21]

However, these contrasting arguments and evidence have done little to negate the power of the democratic peace idea in practice, as categorization does not have to rest on "empirical laws"[22] – even though it is often justified as such. As regards the proposition itself, a leading political scientist explicitly calls democratic peace a set of "norms." And "repeating the norms as descriptive principles can help to make them true."[23] In a similar vein, Michael W. Doyle advocates

---

[20] Notable works skeptical of democratic peace can be found in Michael E. Brown, Sean Lynn-Jones, and Steven Miller, eds., *Debating the Democratic Peace* (Cambridge, MA: MIT Press, 1996); Joanne Gowa, *Ballots and Bullets: The Elusive Democratic Peace* (Princeton, NJ: Princeton University Press, 1999).

[21] See Andrew Mack and John Ravenhill, eds., *Pacific Cooperation: Building Economic and Security Regimes in the Asia-Pacific Region* (Boulder, CO: Westview Press, 1995); Alastair Iain Johnston, "The Myth of the ASEAN Way? Explaining the Evolution of the ASEAN Regional Forum," in Robert O. Keohane, Helga Haftendorn, and Celeste Wallander, eds., *Imperfect Unions: Security Institutions over Time and Space* (New York: Oxford University Press, 1999); Miles Kahler, "Legalization as Strategy: The Asia-Pacific Case," *International Organization*, vol. 54, no. 3 (Summer 2000), pp. 549–71; Amitav Acharya, "Will Asia's Past Be Its Future?" *International Security*, vol. 28, no. 3 (Winter 2003/4), pp. 149–64.

[22] Jack Levy famously declared, "The absence of war between democracies comes as close as anything we have to an empirical law in international relations." Levy, "Domestic Politics and War," in Robert Rotberg and Theodore K. Rabb, eds., *The Origin and Prevention of Major Wars* (Cambridge: Cambridge University Press, 1989), p. 88. Much of the criticism of democratic peace focuses on such absolutist statements.

[23] Bruce Russett, "Why Democratic Peace?" in Brown, et al., *Debating the Democratic Peace*, p. 112.

"discrimination" toward fellow liberal democratic states.[24] And Thomas Risse-Kappen contends that "the zone of the 'democratic peace' in the Northern Hemisphere did not fall from heaven, but was created through the processes of social interaction and learning," which entails categorization of "us" from "them."[25]

In addition to promoting democracy, Western powers have also promoted free-market capitalism and international responsibility as prevailing values. Just as with democracy, assigning states into different categories based on these standards inevitably entails ambiguities and debate. The well-entrenched forces and assumptions of rationality and anarchy in international relations generate powerful theoretical arguments and empirical evidence that counter the collective image projected by the liberal democracies.[26] In reality, countries do not always practice what they preach. Besides, the values are themselves contested in terms of both their definitions and their roles in organizing world politics. Uncertainties are compounded when it comes to generalize transitional states undergoing transformation in domestic and international politics. There also may be major variance in members' commitment to the shared in-group values. Japan, for example, has exhibited significant deviance from the orthodox liberal doctrines when it comes to its domestic political economy and international trade practices.[27] The United States and its major democratic allies

[24] Michael W. Doyle, "A Liberal View: Preserving and Expanding the Liberal Pacific Union," in T. V. Paul and John A. Hall, eds., *International Order and the Future of World Politics* (Cambridge: Cambridge University Press, 1999), ch. 2.

[25] Thomas Risse-Kappen, "Collective Identity in a Democratic Community," in Katzenstein, *The Culture of National Security*, pp. 366–71. Similar dynamics are at work shaping Israeli-U.S. relations. See Michael N. Barnett, "Identity and Alliances in the Middle East," in Katzenstein, *The Culture of National Security*, ch. 11. Elements of the in-group consciousness are driving U.S.-Taiwan relations, as demonstrated in John W. Garver, *Face-Off: China, the United States and Taiwan's Democratization* (Seattle: University of Washington Press, 1997).

[26] For a realist restatement, see Kenneth Waltz, "Structural Realism after the Cold War," *International Security*, vol. 25, no. 1 (Summer 2000), pp. 5–41.

[27] There is disagreement over the depth and "stickiness" of the liberal international identity of Japan. For a wide range of views, see Michael E. Brown, Sean Lynn-Jones, and Steven Miller, eds., *East Asian Security* (Cambridge, MA: MIT Press, 1996), particularly chapters by Peter Katzenstein and Nobuo Okawara, Thomas U. Berger, Richard K. Betts, and Aaron L. Friedberg.

have squabbled over many bilateral and global issues. Yet their sense of a special bond has proven to be quite enduring.

Scientifically based or not, the upshot of the generalization and promotion along the lines of democracy, free-market capitalism, and international responsibility is a restructuring of world politics that raises serious questions about the international legitimacy of "other" powers struggling to comply with these standards. From this perspective, major powers can be differentiated into status quo powers and non–status quo powers based on whether they play a preponderant role in rearranging the world order. Unlike many realists who differentiate major powers into those that seek change (revisionist powers) and those defending the status quo (status quo powers),[28] our approach focuses on whether or not the state was among the triumphant great-power group that took it upon itself to reshape the original post–cold war world order. (Clearly, the post-9/11 U.S. pursuit of radically transformative foreign policy has effectively invalidated the realist typology.)

China is a non–status quo power, insofar as it must *react* to the international hierarchy. Judged along the dimensions of polity, market transition, and international responsibility, the PRC has exhibited marked deviance from the collective image projected by leading liberal democracies. Throughout the 1990s, numerous scholarly analyses of Chinese foreign policy in the United States questioned whether the People's Republic was deserving of great-power respect because of its noncompliance with and cynicism toward human rights and other principal international norms. As regards its international behavior, much concern was raised about China's wounded nationalism, its rigid notion of sovereignty, and a foreign policy agenda driven by the CCP-state insecurity at home. Despite the significant strides China has since made in all three areas, especially in economic liberalization and foreign policy reforms, the gap separating it and the U.S.-led great-power group has persisted. Throughout the post–cold war era, leading advanced democracies have singled out China and Russia as the problematic major powers that don't fit into the mainstream great-power group bound by lasting democratic peace.[29]

---

[28] For a cogent review of the two types of great powers in the literature, see Alastair Iain Johnston, "Is China a Status Quo Power?" *International Security*, vol., 27, no. 4 (Spring 2003), pp. 8–10.

[29] For noted scholarly works that differentiate great powers this way, see Goldgeier and McFaul, "A Tale of Two Worlds"; Rosecrance, ed., *The Great Power Coalition*; Jervis, "Theories of War in an Era of Leading-Power Peace"; Ikenberry,

China's status disadvantage became more pronounced as its material power started to grow rapidly in the early 1990s. In this regard, various schools of realist theory in international relations provide an elegant, if incomplete, explanation for international concern about China rooted in its growing materialist power.[30] For example, the power transition perspective has consistently expressed fear that China's growing power and ambitions would pose the greatest threat to the international order.[31] From yet another approach, John Mearsheimer has confidently predicted an unmitigated Chinese threat to U.S. hegemony.[32] Although none of the direst predictions has proven fully founded, they do underscore the material sources of the international anxieties over China's rise. Such concern is amplified by suspicion of the domestic and international character of the CCP state. Ominously for the

After Victory; Nau, *At Home Abroad*. Specifically on China's disqualifications as a great power, see Lucian Pye, "China: Not Your Typical Superpower," *Problems of Post-Communism*, July/Aug. 1996, pp. 3–15; Samuel Kim, "China as a Great Power," *Current History*, Sept. 1997, pp. 246–51; Gilbert Rozman, "China's Quest for Great Power Identity," *Orbis*, vol. 43, no. 3 (Summer 1999), pp. 392–402.

[30] The most important works on balancing include Kenneth Waltz, *Theory of International Politics* (New York: McGraw-Hill, 1979); Stephen Walt, *The Origins of Alliance* (Ithaca, NY: Cornell University Press, 1986); and Randall L. Schweller, *Deadly Imbalances: Tripolarity and Hitler's Strategy of World Conquest* (New York: Columbia University Press, 1998). Representative works on power transition and hegemonic stability include A. F. K. Organski and Jacek Kugler, *The War Ledger* (Chicago: University of Chicago Press, 1980); Kugler and Organski, "The Power Transition: A Retrospective and Prospective Evaluation," in Manus Midlarsky, ed., *Handbook of War Studies*, (Boston: Unwin Hyman, 1989), ch. 7; Robert Gilpin, *War and Change in World Politics* (Cambridge: Cambridge University Press, 1981); Robert Keohance, *After Hegemony: Cooperation and Discord in the World Political Economy* (Princeton, NJ: Princeton University Press, 1984). For a comprehensive discussion of how China's future is conjectured from IR theories, see Avery Goldstein, "Great Expectations: Interpreting China's Arrival," *International Security*, vol. 23, no. 3 (Winter 1997/98), pp. 36–73.

[31] See Jacek Kugler and Douglas Lemke, "The Power Transition Research Program: Assessing Theoretical and Empirical Advances," in Manus Midlarsky, *Handbook of War Studies II* (Ann Arbor: University of Michigan Press, 2000), pp. 129–63; A. F. K. Organski and Marina Arbetman, "The Second American Century: The New International Order," in William Zimmerman and Harold K. Jacobson, eds., *Behavior, Culture, and Conflict in World Politics* (Ann Arbor: University of Michigan Press, 1993).

[32] John J. Mearsheimer, "The Future of the American Pacifier," *Foreign Affairs*, vol. 80, no. 4 (Sept./Oct. 2001), pp. 46–61, and his *The Tragedy of Great Power Politics* (New York: W. W. Norton, 2001).

CCP leadership, uncertainties over power transition may intensify categorization, thereby inviting ultrasensitivity to power redistribution and zero-sum logic in other countries' calculations when dealing with China.

Throughout the 1990s, the Gallup Polls of American public opinion on China showed that unfavorable views consistently outweighed favorable ones.[33] Surveys from other sources yielded similar results. Taken together, these findings clearly showed that American optimism about the prospect of, and the U.S. role in, China's transformation in the Western image in the 1980s had given way to a strong sense of resignation and disillusionment. The majority or plurality of American respondents worried that China's development and U.S.-China relations might not be on the right track. They expressed deep concern over China's human rights record, and many failed to see any positive signs of democratic change. They did not even believe that China had made much progress toward free-market capitalism. Even though the majority of the respondents did not yet see China as an enemy to be contained, their mistrust and generally negative views were strong enough to generate an overall estranged feeling toward the PRC.[34] Indeed, according to the four surveys conducted by the Chicago Council on Foreign Relations in 1995, 1999, 2002, and 2004, China's ratings by the American respondents on the "feeling thermometer" stayed between 44° and 48° (below the 50° neutral point). Among all the major powers, the American public expressed the coolest feeling toward China.[35]

[33] Gallup Organization, at http://www.gallup.com/poll/indicators/IndChina.asp (accessed June 23, 2001); Gallup Organization, at http://www.nexis .com/research/sear . . . 5=569893dd52c50ba6b1620a7d7df3714b; Princeton Survey Research Associates, at http://www.nexis.com/research/sear . . . 5=74c8fbc49eef3723740950ef9632a2be.

[34] See a comprehensive summary of the various survey data at the website of Program on International Policy Attitudes. at http://www.americansword.org/ digest/regional_issues/china/china1.cfm (accessed July 6, 2001); the Pew Research Center for the People and the Press Report at http://www.people-press.org/china01rpt.htm. For American perceptions of China in the 1980s, see Harry Harding, *A Fragile Relationship: The United States and China since 1972* (Washington, DC: Brookings Institution, 1992); James Mann, *About Face: A History of America's Curious Relations with China* (New York: Vintage Books, 2000).

[35] The reports of the surveys are posted on the website of the Chicago Council on Foreign Relations at http://www.ccfr.org/.

These findings showed that American public opinion on China was heavily influenced by several highly consistent beliefs, similar to what psychologists call a "schema." As Entman and Rojecki contend, "[P]eople are more 'theory-driven' than 'data-driven.' That is, we more often than not approach life with assumptions that lead us to confirm expectations rather than to inscribe fresh interpretations of daily experience upon a blank mental slate."[36] Similarly, Eugene Burnstein and his colleagues conclude that the schema on the out-group, once formed "through considerable culling and refining to maximize consistency," discounts nuanced, factual "case information" in order to enhance conformity to the preconceived notion.[37] American public opinion on China did not cohere into an enemy image. But these negative perceptions seem to have formed a rather consistent, if still evolving, schema through which China was treated as one of "them," removed from the trustworthy in-group.

In parallel to public opinion, key American policy makers, while in favor of an engagement policy, have nonetheless refrained from embracing the PRC as fully integrated into the international mainstream.[38] In 1993, Anthony Lake, President Clinton's National Security Adviser, publicly labeled China one of the "backlash states" in the company of Iran, Iraq, Burma (Myanmar), and North Korea.[39] Such a harsh statement wasn't atypical in the aftermath of the Tiananmen crisis. But even after the United States formalized its engagement policy, U.S. official views, subtly or bluntly stated, on the People's Republic have consistently been marked by ambiguity and uncertainty despite twists and turns in the bilateral relationship. Ten years after Lake's speech, the strategic report released by the George W. Bush administration in September 2002 states, "We welcome the emergence of a

---

[36] Entman and Rojecki, *The Black Image in the White Mind*, p. 48.

[37] Eugene Burnstein, March Abboushi, and Shinobu Kitayama, "How the Mind Preserves the Image of the Enemy: The Mnemonics of Soviet-American Relations," in Zimmerman and Jacobson, *Behavior, Culture, and Conflicts in World Politics*, pp. 197–229. Vamik D. Vokan argues that a similar force is at work driving ethnic conflict. See his *Bloodlines: From Ethnic Pride to Ethnic Terrorism* (New York: Farrar, Straus, and Giroux, 1997).

[38] For a listing of these official remarks, see Johnston, "Is China a Status Quo Power?" pp. 5–8.

[39] Michel Oksenberg, "China and the Japanese-American Alliance," in Gerald L. Curtis, ed., *The United States, Japan, and Asia: Challenges for U.S. Policy* (New York: W. W. Norton, 1994), p. 100.

strong, peaceful, and prosperous China. . . . Yet, a quarter century after beginning the process of shedding the worst features of the communist legacy, China's leaders have not yet made the next series of fundamental choices about the character of their state."[40] In testimony at the U.S. Senate Armed Services Committee in February 2005, Secretary of Defense Donald Rumsfeld characterized China as "a country that we hope and pray enters the civilized world in an orderly way without the grinding of gears and that they become a constructive force in that part of the world and a player in the global environment that's constructive."[41] On the "schematic" level, official U.S. formulations on China have invariably emphasized the uncertainties and unresolved questions regarding its domestic and international future.

European powers and Japan have differed with the United States on policy means in dealing with China, but they fundamentally share the view that the PRC poses a categorically different type of challenge from other major powers – except perhaps for Russia. Their engagement tactics may differ, and their policies toward China have enjoyed some autonomy that opens up opportunities for Beijing to fend off a Western united front. They also have exerted some influence over U.S. policy. Yet Europe and Japan ultimately have deferred to the U.S. leadership and its policy adjustments on Taiwan and human rights, and their overall strategies align with, rather than undercut, U.S. interests.[42] Open transatlantic fissures over various international issues,

[40] The Bush administration, "The National Security Strategy of the United States," released in Sept. 2002, at http://www.whitehouse.gov/nsc/nss.pdf, p. 27.

[41] Eric Schmitt, "Rumsfeld Warns of Concern about Expansion of China's Navy," *New York Times*, Feb. 18, 2005, p. A9.

[42] On Sino-European relations, see Katinka Barysch, with Charles Grant and Mark Leonard, *Embracing the Dragon: The EU's Partnership with China* (London: Center for European Reform, 2005); David Shambaugh, *European and American Approaches to China: Different Beds, Same Dreams* (Washington, DC: Sigur Center for Asian Studies, George Washington University, 2002) and the special issue of *China Quarterly*, no. 169 (March 2002), particularly Kay Moller, "Diplomatic Relations and Mutual Strategic Perceptions: China and the European Union," pp. 10–32; Eberhard Sandschneider, "China's Diplomatic Relations with the States of Europe," pp. 33–44. On Sino-Japanese relations, see Morton Abramowitz, Funabashi Yoichi, and Wang Jisi, *China-Japan-U.S.: Managing the Trilateral Relations* (Tokyo: Japan Center for International Exchange, 1998); James Przystup, "China, Japan, and the United States," in Michael J. Green and Patrick Cronin, eds., *The U.S.-Japan Alliance* (New York: Council on Foreign Relations Press,

such as Iraq and the EU attempt to lift the arms embargo on China during 2003–05, no doubt had some effect in undermining Western cohesion. While one should not overstate the unity in their China policies among advanced democracies, their largely compatible approaches have fundamentally defined China's international environment. By the same token, irreparable damage to the transatlantic alliance would have profound implications for China's foreign relations.

In response, the Chinese have complained about the unfair international arrangement, and some have suspected a systematic Western attempt to tarnish their country's image. The unfair and simplistic portrayals of China in the Western media were particularly to be blamed. They argued, as a result of what they viewed to be biased media reporting, the policy makers and the general public in the West did not adequately recognize China's struggle for modernity under its unique conditions or its progress in increasing citizens' private space and individual freedoms, improving the nation's economic well-being, introducing grassroots rural democracy, strengthening the rule of law, and acting responsibly in foreign policy.[43]

To the extent that the United States holds the key to China's international recognition, the PRC's foreign policy concerns have focused on the Sino-American relationship. Thus, China's self-assessment of its international status fluctuates largely based on the state of Sino-American relations. The period of 1997–98 witnessed the most optimistic Chinese evaluations, as the United States and China jointly declared that they would build a strategic partnership (which translated into exchanges of summit meetings), and President Bill Clinton verbally pledged not to support Taiwan independence; one China, one Taiwan; or Taiwan's membership in international organizations for which sovereignty is required.[44] Also important at the time, the

1999), ch. 2; Mike Mochizuki, "Terms of Engagement: The U.S.-Japan Alliance and the Rise of China," in Ellis S. Krauss and T. J. Pempel, eds., *Beyond Bilateralism: U.S.-Japan Relations in the New Asia-Pacific* (Ithaca, NY: Cornell University Press, 2004), pp. 87–114.

[43] Jia Qingguo, "Frustrations and Hopes: Chinese Perceptions of the Engagement Policy Debate in the U.S.," *Journal of Contemporary China*, no. 27 (2001), pp. 321–30; Wu Xinbo, "To Be an Enlightened Superpower," *Washington Quarterly*, vol. 24, no. 3 (Summer 2001), pp. 63–71; Jia Qingguo, "Disrespect and Distrust: The External Origins of Contemporary Chinese Nationalism," *Journal of Contemporary China*, vol. 14 (Feb. 2005), pp. 11–21.

[44] Commentator, "Making Efforts to Establish Sino-U.S. Constructive Strategic Partnership," *Renmin Ribao* (Internet), June 18, 1998, p. 1, Foreign

two countries closely coordinated with each other in dealing with the nuclear proliferations crisis in South Asia. The United States publicly praised China's responsible choice not to devalue its currency while chiding Japan's manipulation of the yen during the Asian financial crisis. The United States and China were both also opposed to the Japanese proposal for an Asian Monetary Fund. After a brief honeymoon, more-sober analyses followed, and the Sino–American relationship returned to its "normal" state of ambivalence, characterized by mutual suspicion and a high degree of uncertainty.

While Chinese analysts differ in their evaluations of the balance between cooperative and conflict dynamics in the Sino–American relationship, the consensus discerns a mixed, "ambiguous" pattern that could conceivably turn either more antagonistic or more cooperative.[45] While the events after September 11, 2001 infused a greater cooperative spirit in Sino–American relations, Chinese leaders and analysts alike, nonetheless, reacted to Secretary Colin Powell and other U.S. State Department officials' exuberant praise of the bilateral ties with subdued enthusiasm. They doubted that the United States had unambiguously accepted China as a legitimate great power. As the prominent America watcher Zi Zhongyun observed, "During China's transitional period, the delicate state of [Sino–American relations] won't change for a while. In addition, as long as the Taiwan issue remains unresolved, the fundamental suspicion and hedging will not dissipate simply because of the anti-terror campaign."[46] The Chinese

Broadcast Information Service (hereafter cited as FBIS): FTS19980618000362; He Chong, "Yearender: China's Diplomatic Activities This Year Attract World Attention," *Hong Kong Zhongguo Tongxun She,* Dec. 30, 1998, FBIS: FTS19990114001801; Wang Jisi, "Achievements, Effects of Clinton's China Visit," *Hong Kong Wenwei Po,* Sept. 14, 1998, p. A7, FBIS: FTS19980922000344.

[45] Zhang Yijun, "PRC-U.S.-Japanese Relations at the Turn of Century," *Shanghai Guoji Zhanwang,* no. 14 (July 15, 2000), p. 7, FBIS: CPP20000726000070; Jianwei Wang, *Limited Adversaries: Post–Cold War Sino-American Mutual Images* (New York: Oxford University Press, 2000); Philip C. Saunders, "China's American Watchers: Changing Attitudes Towards the United States," *China Quarterly,* no. 161 (March 2001), pp. 41–65.

[46] Quoted in Guo Xuetang, "Zhuazhu Zhanlue Jiyu, Bizhanlue Fengxian" [Seize Strategic Opportunities, Avoid Strategic Risks], *Huanqiu Shibao* [Global Times], Feb. 21, 2003, p. 2, at www.people.com.cn/GB/paper68/8525/800379.html. See also Chen Peiyao, "Changes in the U.S. Security Strategy and Adjustments of Its China Policy," *Zhongguo Pinglun,* no. 51 (March 1, 2002), pp. 6–9, FBIS: CPP20020307000097; Jin Canrong, "An Assessment of Two Types of New Factors in China's International Environment," *Xiandai*

complained, in particular, that China's core security interests on Taiwan were not fundamentally respected and that the fear and hostility toward Chinese power and intentions still lingered in the U.S. policy communities.

For prominent Chinese IR experts, their country's foreign policy predicament is marked by the "isolation," "exclusion," "discrimination," and distrust by the United States and its allies.[47] The corollary is that China is somewhat separated from what Wang Jisi, Dean of the School of International Studies at Peking University, dubs a "pattern of coordination and cooperation among the world's major powers, institutionalized through the G-8."[48] The transatlantic division over the war on Iraq in 2003–04 reduced the collective pressures from the established great powers on China, but mainstream Chinese analysts tended not to overstate the damage to the Western alliance. They believed that the ties among the leading democratic powers might have been somewhat reconfigured, but they were still tenacious. The division separating their country and the status quo powers remained to define its international environment.

In international relations, material power is an essential determinant of international status for any country, China included. As Samuel Crafton observed, "Even after you give a squirrel a certificate which says he is quite as big as any elephant, he is still going to be smaller, and all the squirrels will know it and all the elephants will know it."[49] The Chinese were acutely aware that its disadvantage abroad

Guoji Guanxi, no. 2 (Nov. 20, 2002), pp. 7–9, FBIS: CPP20021206000159; Xiong Guangkai, "The Global Challenge of International Terrorism," speech at the Munich International Security Policy Conference, Feb. 8, 2003, at www.securityconference.de/konferenzen/rede.php?menu_20 (accessed March 29, 2003).

[47] See Yan Xuetong, et al., *Zhongguo Jueqi – Guoji Huanjin Pinggu* [International Environment for China's Rise] (Tianjin, China: People's Press, 1998), ch. 3, quotes on pp. 170, 173–4; Yan Xuetong, *Meiguo Baquan yu Zhngguo Anquan* [American Hegemony and China's Security] (Tianjin, China: Renmin Chubanshe, 2000), pp. 24–9; *Yan Xuetong*, "Yu Fazhan De Zhongguo Xiangchu" [Getting Along with a Growing China], *Global Times*, Aug. 8, 2002, at http://www.people.com.cn/GB/paper68/6948/674845.html; Zhang Yijun, "PRC-U.S.-Japanese Relations at the Turn of Century."

[48] Wang Jisi, "China's Search for Stability with America," *Foreign Affairs*, vol. 84, no. 5 (Sept./Oct. 2005), p. 42.

[49] Quoted in William Zimmerman, *Soviet Perspectives on International Relations, 1956–1967* (Princeton, NJ: Princeton University Press, 1969),

owed much to its material weakness. In its official historical discourse, China's worst status loss during the century after the Opium War was associated with the worst economic and technological backwardness. Such remembrance heightens Chinese sensitivity to its economic backwardness. Moreover, it was after all Deng Xiaoping and other CCP reformers' painful realization of China's economic backwardness and their embrace of the developmental idea of "opening up to the outside world" in the late 1970s that prompted the pragmatic turn in post-Mao Chinese foreign policy in the first place.

The public awareness of China's relative backwardness is evident in a nationwide survey by the newspaper *China Youth Daily* in 1995 on the worldviews of its young readers. When asked about their three-dimensional appraisals of China's standing in the world, the respondents gave the highest mark to China's "political status" (largely equated with its permanent membership in the United Nations Security Council), ranked the military status in the middle, and considered economic status as significantly lagging behind. In addition, they were optimistic about the all-round advancement in the decades to come.[50]

Government-affiliated researchers attempted to develop more scientific measures to gauge China's national power in a comparative light. Leading think tanks – such as the Academy of Military Science, the Chinese Academy of Social Sciences (CASS), and the China Institute of Contemporary International Relations (CICIR) – have all conducted such studies since the 1990s. Their assessments of China's ranking in comprehensive national power vary, but they are generally conservative and cautious, particularly when comparing their nation's strengths with those of the United States.[51] Modesty in self-ranking helps

---

p. 123. Zimmerman in turn borrows this quote from William T. R. Fox, *The Super-Powers* (New York: Harcourt, Brace, 1944), p. 3.

[50] Guan Fu, "Analytical Report of the Chinese Youth Look at the World Survey," *Zhongguo Qingnian* [Chinese Youth], July 24, 1995, p. 1, FBIS: FTS19950724000041.

[51] See Chen Yue, *Zhongguo Guoji Diwei Fenxi* [Analysis of China's International Status] (Beijing: Contemporary World Press, 2002), pp. 43–65; Michael Pillsbury, *China Debates the Future Security Environment* (Washington, DC: National Defense University Press, 2001), ch. 5; Yong Deng and Fei-ling Wang, "Introduction," in Yong Deng and Fei-ling Wang, eds., *China Rising: Power and Motivation in Chinese Foreign Policy* (Boulder, CO: Rowman & Littlefield, 2005), pp. 2–3.

unify China's national purpose behind self-strengthening development, realistically set national expectation of its role abroad, and defuse foreign concerns over China's power.[52] Also, Chinese self-assessments of power have emphasized the notion of "comprehensive national power" (*Zhonghe Guoli*). The Chinese definitions of the term are vastly expansive to include national cohesion and government effectiveness or even its history and culture of international benevolence and diplomacy – even though it is primarily about China's economic, technological, and military strengths.[53] Such a notion of power probably reflects a deepseated concern that China's material power cannot continue to grow without domestic institutional reforms, a national spiritual renewal of a kind, and a supportive international environment.

China's material growth has brought to the fore the unsettled question of how the international community should deal with China's rising power. The uncertainties and misgivings in the capitals of the established great powers and the Asian region could lead to further denigration of the PRC as a dangerous outsider and could conceivably spark a U.S.-led containment. At the same time, as China accrues more wherewithal, its diplomatic stage has extended from its periphery to Asia and beyond. As its power and aspirations grow, China's international politics has become more complicated and requires even more careful management.

Status Drive and China's Foreign Policy

The literature in sociology and social psychology has suggested various strategies to overcome status disadvantage, ranging from unilateral emulation of the high-status traits to totally challenging the social arrangement.[54] Notably, leading social psychologists Henri Tajfel and Roger Brown, among others, explicitly borrowed the economist Albert Hirschman's terms "exit" and "voice" to underscore, respectively,

---

[52] According to Randall Schweller, a real power contender must have at least half of the military strength of the strongest power in the international system. See Schweller, *Deadly Imbalances: Tripolarity and Hitler's Strategy of World Conquest* (New York: Columbia University Press, 1997).

[53] See Chen Yue, *Analysis of China's International Status*, pp. 43–65; Pillsbury, *China Debates the Future Security Environment*, ch. 5.

[54] See Hogg and Abrams, *Social Identifications*, ch. 3; Tajfel, *Human Groups and Social Categories*; Brown, *Social Psychology*, pp. 558–60, 577; Kalkhoff and Barnum, "The Effects of Status-Organizing."

the routes of adopting high-status traits or seeking changes in the standard of social comparison that created the social hierarchy in the first place.[55] These insights are suggestive, but they are not wholly applicable to the international arena where, in comparison to domestic society, power politics still prevails under relatively weakly congealed authority. Thus, for our purposes, to examine China's quest for great-power status, it is imperative to give due consideration to the power politics logic still persistent in world politics. China's approach to the existing international arrangement is likely to comprise an amalgam of conformity and revisionism with persistent uncertainties.

The stability of the international social hierarchy, China's relative material weakness, and the CCP leadership's definition of national interests have made an outright confrontational strategy prohibitively costly. The need to carve out its own strategic space and limitations to domestic political reforms render inconceivable a choice of a self-liberalizing "exit" strategy to break away from the periphery. Equally impossible is a rule-based, orderly status change along the line of participation in a mature democracy, which was envisioned by way of Hirschman's "voice." The ideas of exit and voice are useful in illuminating China's foreign policy choice insofar as the former underscores the imperative of compliance and the latter brings to the fore discontent with the status quo and an intention to change. China's foreign policy pattern after the cold war has demonstrated various combinations of status strategies that have overall excluded either a wholesale pro-Western choice or a systematically confrontational choice. Its quest for great-power status has entailed laying the material basis of international recognition through power growth and power practice, on the one hand; and, on the other, enhancing international legitimacy through constructive participation in the international society. Achieving both requires restraining power politics for the sake of cultivating legitimate recognition. Such a strategic choice seeks to redraw the boundaries disadvantaging its international status, but that revisionism is balanced by the need to seek acceptance from, and interdependence with, the dominant great-power group, neighboring states in Asia, and other key players in world politics.

---

[55] Tajfel, *Human Groups and Social Categories*, pp. 246–7, 252–3, 278–9, and ch. 14; Brown, *Social Psychology*, pp. 556–85; Albert O. Hirschman, *Exit, Voice, and Loyalty: Responses to Decline in Firms, Organizations, and States* (Cambridge, MA: Harvard University Press, 1970).

In essence, China's status strategy is to engineer its great-power rise through a path alternative to traditional power transition marked by hostile balancing, escalating zero-sum competition, and the ineluctable outcome of war. Specifically, it shows a heightened sensitivity to the social and structural dynamics of the fear of a China threat. Thus, the PRC has adroitly adapted its foreign policy to changes in, and has proactively influenced, its international environment in order to maximize the opportunity of peaceful ascent. It has carefully managed its international relations to secure an overall mutually reinforcing pattern of interaction between its material power and international recognition.

In charting the country's international course, international studies in China at the outset of the new century have become more diversified in theoretical orientations in comparison to the 1990s, when nascent liberal thinking struggled to make inroads into the realist-dominated field.[56] Now Chinese IR is witnessing a remarkable coexistence of realism, liberalism, and constructivism. Led by Yan Xuetong, director of the Institute of International Studies at Qinghua University, scholars of realist persuasion have continued to focus on the inevitable "structural conflict" intensified by China's rising power. The liberal research program has experienced steady consolidation. Closely associated with Wang Yizhou, the long-time deputy director of the Institute of World Economics and Politics at the CASS, the Chinese liberal IR school has seen an impressive growth in the research agenda on interdependence, institutions, "soft power," and global governance. Most remarkably, constructivism seems to have found the most hospitable audience in China – albeit with Chinese style. Spearheaded by Qin Yaqing, vice president of China's Foreign Affairs University, the theory has gained speedy popularity, with a following particularly strong among young scholars. As a testimony to his growing influence in both the academic and policy worlds, Qin was the only formally trained IR scholar invited to speak to Chinese leaders on world affairs at a seminar chaired by President Hu Jintao and organized by the political bureau of the CCP Central Committee in February 2004.[57] Creatively and

---

[56] Yong Deng, "The Chinese Conception of National Interests in International Relations," *China Quarterly*, no. 154 (June 1988), pp. 308–29.

[57] Xinhua, Feb. 24, 2004, at http://news.xinhuanet.com/newscenter/2004-02/24/content_1329708.htm.

selectively applying constructivist insights, these scholars have asked what kind of new ideas and right choices China can adopt and promote to remake its identity in, and revamp its relations with, the world.

In the aftermath of the Tiananmen incident in June 1989, Chinese foreign policy was in a defensive, crisis management mode.[58] In face of the dire international environment, Deng Xiaoping propounded the famous twenty-eight-character instruction for handling Chinese foreign relations, which roughly means – "Calmly observe the situations; secure our footing; cope changes with confidence; conceal capacities and bide our time; skillfully keep a low profile; avoid sticking [one's] head out; be proactive" (*Lengjing Guancha, Wenzhu Zhenjiao, Chenzhuo Yingfu, Taoguang Yanghui, Shanyu Shouzhuo, Juebu Dangtou, Yousuo Zuowei*).[59] The period of 1989–92 saw a besieged CCP leadership struggling to resist Western sanctions and thwart what it called the Western conspiracy of "peaceful evolution," designed to overthrow the Chinese government. In light of the domestic and international crisis that struck fear among the Chinese leaders of a repetition of domestic chaos and foreign disasters during the century of national humiliation after the Opium War, Deng urged calm and confidence to pursue a low-profile diplomacy. This was especially necessary for a badly shaken CCP leadership, which had just survived so severe a division at the very top over how to handle the student demonstrations that nearly collapsed the regime. The immediate goal was clearly to stabilize China's domestic front and break its pariah status in world politics, although greater activism was later emphasized in mainstream Chinese interpretations. Deng's injunction was subsequently questioned during foreign policy crises and more recently when China has become significantly stronger. But Chinese officials and mainstream analysts

---

[58] Qian Qichen, *Waijiao Shiji* [Ten Episodes in Diplomacy] (Beijing: Shijie Zhishi Chubanshe, 2003), pp. 164–201.

[59] Deng Xiaoping, *Deng Xiaoping Wenxuan III* [Selected Works of Deng Xiaoping, vol. 3], (Beijing: Renmin Chubanshe, 1993). See also Gao Jingdian, ed., *Deng Xiaoping Guoji Zhanlue Sixiang Yanjiu* [Studies on Deng Xiaoping's Thoughts on International Strategy] (Beijing: Guofang Daxue Chubanshe, 1992); Peng Guangqian and Yao Youzhi, eds., *Deng Xiaoping Zhanlue Sixiang Lun* [On Deng Xiaoping's Thoughts on Strategy] (Beijing: Jiefangjun Kexue Chubanshe, 1994); Wang Taiping, ed., *Deng Xiaoping Waijiao Sixiang Yanjiu Lunwenji* [Anthology on Deng Xiaoping's Diplomatic Thoughts] (Beijing: Shijie Zhishi Chubanshe, 1996).

have insisted on heeding the spirit of Deng's advice that their country should balance activism with caution to improve its international environment through steady, successful domestic transformation and skillful, patient diplomacy rather than confrontation.

Concurrent to the easing of post-Tiananmen diplomatic isolation was a new reality check in China's international thinking. Despite wishful thinking for multipolarization briefly popular among Chinese analysts in the early half of the 1990s, the reality that decision makers in Beijing were compelled to grapple with was that none of the supposed candidate power centers, be they Europe, Japan, or Russia, showed any determination to balance against the United States. Rather, U.S. primacy appeared to be more secure than ever. The cluster of U.S.-led advanced democracies demonstrated remarkable unity in managing international affairs and considerable pull as the global center, thereby significantly limiting any centrifugal forces.[60]

While recognizing the new constraints imposed by this international arrangement, mainstream Chinese analysts have also emphasized the great opportunities that China could seize to achieve its great-power goal. Having reviewed China's impressive record of participation in international institutions, Wang Yizhou concludes that the "implied message" is that despite complaints about the world order, "China recognizes the legitimacy and efficacy of the existing international institutions and conventions."[61] Professor Shi Yinhong, now at Renmin University of China, wrote in 2000 that "the fundamental question" facing Chinese foreign policy is "how to deal with the comprehensive advantage in the world's politics, economics, and military as well as its values, norms, and rule system enjoyed by the U.S.-led community of Western advanced countries." He called for a unified Chinese strategy that placed "coordination and compliance" ahead of "hedging and struggle."[62]

---

[60] I discussed China's polarity debate in detail elsewhere. See Yong Deng, "Hegemon on the Offensive: Chinese Perspectives on U.S. Global Strategy," *Political Science Quarterly*, vol. 116, no. 3 (Fall 2001), pp. 343–65.

[61] Wang Yizhou, *Quanqiu Zhengzhi He Zhongguo Waijiao* [Global Politics and China's Foreign Policy] (Beijing: Shijie Zhishi Chubanshe, 2003), p. 46.

[62] Shi Yinhong, "Dangjin He Weilai Shijie Zhengzhi De Jiben Wenti" [The Basic Questions in World Politics of Today and Tomorrow], *Taipingyang Xuebao*, no. 2 (2000), p. 20. See also Shi Yinhong and Song Dexin, "21 Shijiqianqi Zhongguo Guoji Xintai, Waijiao Zhexue He Genben Zhanlue Sikao" [Reflections on China's International Mentality, Diplomatic Philosophy, and

Other influential Chinese analysts have openly advocated increasing Chinese "identification with" (*Rentong*) and "fusing into" (*Rongru*) the regional and global community. For Qin Yaqing, how the rising China "peacefully fuses into the international society" should be the overriding question animating China's international studies.[63] These arguments should not be taken as calls for unconditional Chinese submission to international demands. In fact, some analysts took issue with these liberal and constructivist notions for their implications that China must Westernize itself (*Ziwo Xihua*).[64] However, even those more skeptical of the world order would agree with Zhang Yunling, director of the CASS Institute of Asia-Pacific Studies, who contended that a more favorable international order "cannot be realized merely by reversing or smashing the existing order and pattern. Instead, it can be realized by improving and adjusting the current order and pattern. Therefore, China is not an enemy against the existing order and pattern, but a participant."[65] To secure China's vital developmental opportunity, he further maintained that China must "actively participate in the existing order and defend its self-interests through participation."[66]

Basic Strategy in the Early Period of the 21st Century], in Niu Jun, ed., *Zhongguo Waijiao Juan* [China's Foreign Affairs] (Beijing: New World Press, 2007), pp. 27–44.

63 Chu Shulong, "Quanmian Jianshe Xiaokang Shehui Shiqi De Zhongguo Waijiao Zhanlue" [China's Diplomatic Strategy During the Period of Comprehensively Building a Well-off Society], *Shijie Jingji Yu Zhengzhi* [World Economics and Politics] (hereafter cited as *WEP*), no. 8 (Aug. 2003), pp. 8–14; Qin Yaqing, "Guojia Shengfen, Zhanlue Wenhua He Anquan Liyi" [State Identity, Strategic Culture, and Security Interests], *WEP*, no. 1 (2003), pp. 10–15; Qin Yaqing, "Guoji Guanxi Lilun De Hexin Wenti Yu Zhongguo Xuepai De Xingcheng" [The Core Question in International Relations Theories and the Formation of the Chinese School], *Zhongguo Shehui Kexue*, no. 3 (2005), pp. 165–76, at http://www.irchina.org/pdf/qyq05b.pdf.

64 Yin Chengde, "Jiangou Hexie Shijie" [Building a Harmonious World], China Institute of International Studies, at http://www.ciis.org.cn/index-news.asp?NewsID=20070109141845255&d=4&classname=%C9%EE%B6%C8%B7%D6%CE%F6&classid=9 (accessed March 6, 2007).

65 Zhang Yunling, "Oberving China's Security Environment," *Liaowang*, April 3, 2000, no. 14, pp. 24–6, FBIS-China, April 11, 2000, p. 2.

66 Zhang Yunling, "Ruhe Renshi Zhongguo Zai Yatai Diqu Mianlin De Guoji Huanjing" [Making Sense of China's International Environment in the Asia-Pacific Region], *Dangdai Yatai* [Contemporary Asia-Pacific Studies], no. 6 (2003), p. 4.

Reflecting these positive beliefs about the world order, Chinese leaders have put a premium on ensuring that their country's "activity is accepted as right and proper by a preponderant portion of the active" members in the international society, particularly among those established great powers and neighboring states in Asia.[67] The result is a predominant pattern in Chinese foreign policy compliant to the "established 'patterns' or 'international orders' to international interactions," which Jacek Kugler and Douglas Lemke call the international "status quo."[68] While seeking legitimacy through compliance, the PRC has also demonstrated its discontent with the existing world order. In a nutshell, unrestrained Western dominance is not conducive to its status advancement; that is why the PRC has considered multipolarization as an ultimate goal. But in articulating this preference, the Chinese have stressed multipolarization as a process and a trend, a position that justifies gradual change. To defuse the anti-American tone, the PRC has refrained from advocating balancing against the United States through aggressive self-armament or military alliance with others. Instead, since the late 1990s China's multipolar vision of the world has shown greater concern over how the U.S. hegemony is managed than over the power configuration itself, with policy geared toward restraining U.S. unilateralism and reducing Western dominance in the name of promoting "democratization," "pluralization," and "harmony" of international relations.[69]

[67] This is Robert A. Dahl's definition of legitimacy. Quote from his *A Preface to Democratic Theory* (Chicago: University of Chicago Press, 1956), p. 138. See also Leslie. H. Palmier, *Social Status and Power in Java* (New York: Athlone Press, 1969), pp. 10–11.

[68] Kugler and Lemke, "The Power Transition Research Program, p. 131. For a comprehensive review of China's cooperative international behavior, see Johnston, "Is China a Status Quo Power?" pp. 5–56. See also Avery Goldstein, "The Diplomatic Face of China's Grand Strategy: A Rising Power's Emerging Choice," *China Quarterly*, no. 168 (Dec. 2001), pp. 935–64; Michael D. Swaine and Ashley J. Tellis, *Interpreting China's Grand Strategy: Past, Present, and Future* (Santa Monica, CA: Rand, 2000).

[69] Chen Yue, *Analysis of China's International Status*, ch. 4; Tang Shiping, "China's Periphery Security Environment in 2010–2015," *Zhanglu Yu Guanli*, no. 5 (Oct. 2002), pp. 34–45, FBIS: CPP20021017000169; Wang Yi, "Safeguard Peace, Promote Development, Create a New Situation for Diplomatic Work," *Shijie Zhishi*, Jan. 16, 2003, pp. 8–10, FBIS: CPP20030204000110; Hu Jintao's speech on April 21, 2006 at Yale University, New Haven, CT, at http://paper.people.com.cn/rmrb/html/2006-04/23/content_4376427.htm.

The PRC clearly prefers a more "democratic," pluralistic world where one set of values does not become the sole standard; the Western political system is not the only legitimate form of government; and no single power center dictates world affairs. Typical of the official support for international diversity since the early 1990s was the statement made by former President Jiang Zemin at the UN Millennium summit meeting on September 6, 2000: "The world is multi-colored. Just as the universe cannot have only one color, so too can't the world just have only one civilization, one social system, one developmental model, or one set of values."[70] His report to the sixteenth CCP Congress reaffirmed these views, proclaiming, "[W]e stand for protecting pluralism in the world, advocate democratization in international relations and diversity in developmental models."[71] His successor, Hu Jintao, built on these themes in his call for building a harmonious world. In his speech at the UN summit meeting commemorating the organization's sixtieth anniversary in September 2005, President Hu recast the Chinese world vision as building a "harmonious world" based on multilateralism, greater support for the developmental right of the third-world countries, respect between civilizations, and democratic interstate relations.[72] For the Chinese leaders, a world that respects member states' sovereignty and diversity in political systems, economic models, and cultural beliefs would necessarily call into question Western superiority, value dominance, and interventionism. The upshot would be a relaxation of the intergroup boundaries in great-power relations and much reduced pressures on China's unilateral compliance.

The PRC has chosen to work within the world order to promote change. Its diplomacy has focused on finding ways to simultaneously project influence and build legitimacy in order to secure great-power

---

[70] Ni Jianmin and Chen Zhishun, *Zhongguo Guoji Zhanlue* [China's International Strategy] (Beijing: Renmin Chubanshe, 2003), ch. 8, quote on p. 204.

[71] Jiang Zemin, "Quanmian Jianshe Xiaokang Shehui, Kaichuang Zhongguo Teshe Shehuizhuyi Shiye Xinjumian" [Building a Well-off Society in an All-out Effort, Creating a New Situation for the Cause of Chinese-Style Socialism], *Renmin Ribao*, overseas ed. (hereafter cited as *RMRB*), Nov. 18, 2002, p. 3.

[72] Hu Jintao, "Nuli Jianshe Chijiu Heping, Gongtong Fanrong De Hexieshijie" [Striving to Build a Harmonious World with Lasting Peace and Common Prosperity], *RMRB*, Sept. 17, 2005, p. 2. See also Wang Yizhou, "Yige Zhongda De Guoji Changyi" [A Major International Initiative], *RMRB*, Sept. 24, 2005, p. 1.

recognition through a sustained, constructive interaction in foreign relations. To that end, it has found institutional activism to be indispensable to its diplomacy. The United Nations carries supreme, irreplaceable value, thanks to China's permanent membership in the Security Council. Thus, events such as the wars on Yugoslavia (1999) and Iraq (2003), both of which bypassed the UN, deeply worried Beijing. In response, China has tried to support a central role for the international organization in world affairs. Little wonder that Chinese commentators are proud of the instrumental role their country played in convening the Millennium Summit of the permanent UN Security Council members in New York City in September 2000. China's preferred world has always featured a robust UN. The world's only universal organization not only grants the PRC certain status prerogatives, but also represents an effective instrument for Beijing to promote multilateralism and a "democratic" mode of international relations – with a small financial contribution, especially compared with the shares of the United States, Japan, and Germany.

Besides the United Nations, China has demonstrated great enthusiasms toward other international institutions, as illustrated in its participation in the World Trade Organization (WTO). For Chinese commentators, economic rationale aside, their country's accession to the WTO in December 2001 was a major status booster. Besides these high-profile organizations, China has also joined many other institutions dealing with a whole spectrum of economic, security, and political issues. Judging by the sheer number of its formal memberships, the PRC is no doubt fully integrated into the international society. The Chinese approach to WTO underscores the fact that when the Chinese elites judge the benefits of complying with institutions and norms outweigh the costs, they will do so. By the same token, if the CCP leadership determines that compliance is too costly, it will resist connecting China's domestic and international trajectories to the global norms and trends.[73]

The same can be said about China's approach to the notion of international responsibility. The idea originally came from China's

---

[73] Shuming Bao, et al., eds., *The Chinese Economy after WTO Accession* (Burlington, VT: Ashgate, 2006); Wang Hongying, "'Linking Up with the International Track': What's in a Slogan?" *China Quarterly*, no. 189 (March 2007), pp. 1–23.

self-identification starting in the mid-1990s, when the country came under widespread criticisms as a spoiler of the international order. While the notion of responsibility is always contested, depending on perspectives, it generally involves compliance with multilateral institutions and norms and contributions to problem-solving to issues commonly believed to pertain to global governance or regional order. While China takes the idea seriously, it bristles at the Western imposition of its own definition on it.

Since the mid-1990s, the PRC government has been simultaneously drawn into the international institutional and normative framework and subject to mounting international pressure to do more in dealing with regional and global problems. As such, the country's policy elites are compelled to wrestle with how best to configure national interest in the age of globalization and to adapt sovereignty to be inclusive of international responsibility.[74] To be sure, Chinese compliance has varied, depending on the issues, and in some cases it has encountered setbacks.[75] Compared to previous eras, however, the Chinese notion of sovereignty at the outset of the new century has become significantly more flexible and porous, making possible unprecedented PRC participation in international cooperation on both conventional and unconventional security issues. For example, China has dispatched military and civilian personnel to many of the trouble spots in Asia, Africa, Latin America, and even the Middle East under the auspices of the UN Peacekeeping Operations, and recently Chinese officers have increasingly assumed commanding responsibilities. First participating in 1990, according to Xiong Guangkai, by the end of 2006 China had deployed nearly 6,000 troops in sixteen such missions, more than any other permanent member of the UN Security

---

[74] Wang Jun, "Zhongguo De Zhuquan Wenti Yanjiu" [Research on Sovereignty in China], in Wang Yizhou, ed., *Zhongguo Guoji Guanxi Yanjiu (1995–2005)* [IR Studies in China (1995–2005)] (Beijing: Beijing University Press, 2006), pp. 341–69; Wang Yizhou, *Tanxun Quanqiu Zhuyi Guoji Guanxi* [Exploring International Relations from a Globalist Perspective] (Beijing: Beijing University Press, 2005), pp. 329–57; Wang Yizhou, *Guojia Liyijuan* [National Interests] (Beijing: New World Press, 2007).

[75] For reviews of the Chinese record in the 1990s, see Elizabeth Economy and Michel Oksenberg, eds., *China Joins the World: Progress and Prospects* (New York: Council on Foreign Relations Press, 1999); David M. Lampton, ed., *The Making of Chinese Foreign and Security Policy in the Era of Reform* (Stanford, CA: Stanford University Press, 2001).

Council.[76] In the following year Beijing sent another contingent to Darfur, Sudan, whose mission was focused on local peace, service, and infrastructure construction.

After the government under President Hu Jintao and Premier Wen Jiabao was sworn in, China adjusted its approach toward the G8, which it had long viewed as the world's "rich men's club" composed exclusively of Western powers. Having turned down earlier invitations by three hosting nations in 1996, 1998, and 2000, President Hu decided to attend the G8-sponsored meetings held in France in 2003. He subsequently accepted similar invitations when the United Kingdom, Russia, and Germany hosted the meetings in 2005, 2006, and 2007. Concurrent with engagement with G8, the PRC also has begun formal consultation with G7 on economic and financial matters. Commenting on their country's engagement with G8, Chinese analysts emphasized the benefits to engage this "great-power forum," not the least of which was the increase of China's acceptance as a willing and influential player in world affairs. At the same time, they continued to express reservations about the "discriminatory" nature of this great-power gathering.[77] For them, until and unless the forum

[76] Bates Gill and James Reilly, "Sovereignty, Intervention and Peacekeeping: The View from Beijing," *Survival*, vol. 42, no. 3 (Autumn 2000), pp. 41–59; Allen Carlson, "More Than Just Say No: China's Evolving Approach to Sovereignty and Intervention since Tiananmen," in Alastair Iain Johnston and Robert S. Ross, eds., *New Directions in the Study of China's Foreign Policy* (Stanford, CA: Stanford University Press, 2006), pp. 217–41. The Xiong quote is from "Adapting to Change," *Beijing Review*, Feb. 1, 2007, p. 17.

[77] Wang Fang, "Zhongguo Nanbei Fenghui Xian Fenliang" [China Shows Its Weight at the South-North Summit], *Global Times*, June 4, 2003, at www.snweb.com.cn/gb/gnd/2003/0604/a0604001.htm; "Hu's Trip Represents China's Global Diplomatic Perspective," *People's Daily*, English ed. (Internet), July 6, 2003, at http://english.peopledaily.com.cn/200306/06/eng20030606_117795.shtml; Zheng Yu, "Zhongguo Keyi Jiaru Baguo Jituan" [China Is Ready to Join the Group-8], *Global Times*, May 30, 2003, at www.snweb.com.cn/gb/gnd/2003/0530/o0530001.htm; Antoaneta Bezlova, "China Enters the G8 Big League," *Asia Times*, May 23, 2003, at www.atimes.com/atimes/China/EE23Ad01.html; Shen Jiru, "Zhongguo Bu Keyi Zhuiqiu Jiaru Baguo Jituan" [China Won't Single-Mindedly Seek G8 Membership], at www.iwep.org.cn/fangtan/baguojituan.htm (accessed Aug. 15, 2003); Sun Jinzhong, "Baguo Fenghui Youyinian" [Another Year of G8 Summit], http://www.ciis.org.cn/item/2005-07-01/51046.html (accessed July 15, 2005); Shen Jiru, "Baguojituan Ying Gengxin Guoji Hezuo Guannian" [G8 Should Renew Concept of International Cooperation], *RMRB*, July 18, 2006, p. 1.

becomes less Western-dominated, China's membership would be all but out of the question; and even if it makes it into the club, it might still face isolation, much as Russia has.

While adopting a pragmatic approach to G8, the PRC focused on managing bilateral ties with Russia, the EU, India, and Japan as well as the United States. It has consolidated a comprehensive strategic partnership with Russia since the mid-1990s and has built more limited strategic partnerships with the EU and India in the early years of the new century. While a common strategic vision has been elusive for its relationships with the United States and Japan, through conscientious efforts on both sides, the United States and China have managed to regularize formal and informal mechanisms of consultation and communication. Despite continued mutual strategic hedging, the two countries have accumulated experience in crisis management and dispute settlement that they can build and draw on in steering their broad relationship. The Sino-Japanese relationship recently encountered major setbacks, but at the same time the two Asian giants have a compelling interest not to allow their rivalry to destroy interdependence between them, destabilize the Asian region, or derail their global aspirations.

China is highly sensitive to how neighboring Asian states react to its power. Its remarkable attentiveness to regional diplomacy is in part attributable to China's deepening interdependence with its neighbors. But the simultaneous separateness of regional dynamics and their close connection to the great-power politics generates a potent logic for China to integrate its regional diplomacy into a broad strategic objective.[78] To cement ties with neighboring countries, excepting most notably its continued dispute with India, China has settled historical disagreements along its long land borders from the east section with Russia to the south with Vietnam. The PRC good-neighbor policy in Asia has increasingly entailed greater attempts than ever before to project a responsible image, adopt confidence-building measures, strengthen economic ties, and advocate regional institution building.

---

[78] On the development of regionalism under U.S. hegemony, see Barry Buzan and Ole Weaver, *Regions and Powers: The Structure of International Security* (Cambridge: Cambridge University Press, 2003); Peter Katzenstein, *A World of Regions: Asia and Europe in the American Imperium* (Ithaca, NY: Cornell University Press, 2005).

A similar spirit has led to recent Chinese efforts to create an economic and security community with Southeast Asian nations.[79] In promoting "cooperative security," the PRC is in effect offering the antithesis of, a counterweight to, traditional military alliances and other forms of "cold war mentality."[80] Most of the Asian countries are willing to reciprocate Beijing's positive engagement, so long as doing so serves their national interests, helps with growth and stability in the region, and increases their diplomatic options.

PRC activism in multilateral diplomacy in Asia in the early years of the new century represents an even more remarkable departure from the traditional hostility to it in the Maoist era and skeptical involvement through much of the 1980s and 1990s. The country hosted the first post-9/11 summit of the Asia-Pacific Economic Cooperation forum (APEC) in Shanghai, whose success was widely regarded by the Chinese as marking their country's growing international influence.[81] China has also been an active participant of the multiple cooperative efforts explicitly led by the ASEAN. In Northeast Asia, it played a high-profile role after 2003 in hosting and coordinating a multi-party diplomatic mechanism designed to rid the Korean peninsula of nuclear weapons. Chinese commentators are particularly proud of their nation's leadership role in the creation and continued growth of the Shanghai Cooperation Organization (SCO), "the first international organization named after a Chinese city."[82] The organization evolved

---

[79] See Wang Jisi, "China's Changing Role in Asia," Atlantic Council of the United States, Jan. 2004, at www.acus.org/Publications/occasionalpapers/Asia/WangJisi-Jan-04.pdf; Fu Ying, "China and Asia in a New Era," *China: An International Journal,* vol. 1, no. 2 (Sept. 2003), pp. 304–12; "ASEAN, China Forge Strategic Partnership," at http://english.peopledaily.com.cn/200310/09; "China, ASEAN Sign Nonaggression Pact," *Hong Kong AFP,* Oct. 8, 2003, FBIS: CPP20031008000023.

[80] For reviews of China's regional shift in foreign policy during the reform era, see Michael Yahuda, *The International Politics of Asia-Pacific, 1945–1995* (New York: Routledge, 1996), ch. 6; Mark Selden, "China, Japan, and the Regional Political Economy of East Asia, 1945–1995," in Peter Katzenstein and Takashi Shiraishi, eds., *Network Power: Japan and Asia* (Ithaca, NY: Cornell University Press, 1997), ch. 9; Bin Yu, "China and Its Asian Neighbors," in Yong Deng and Fei-ling Wang, eds., *In the Eyes of the Dragon: China Views the World* (Boulder, CO: Rowman & Littlefield, 1999), ch. 9.

[81] Geng Jianrong and Li Rong, "Jiefang Ribao Reporters Interview Minister Tang Jiaxuan on the Eve of the APEC Meeting," *Shanghai Jiefang Ribao* (Internet), Oct. 17, 2001, FBIS: CPP 20011018000294.

[82] Wu Yingchun, "China's International Status Has Markedly Risen," *Renmin Ribao* (Internet), Sept. 30, 2002, FBIS: CPP 20021004000066.

from the "Shanghai Five," the annual meeting for leaders of China, Russia, Kazakhstan, Kyrgyzstan, and Tajikistan, which was started in 1996 to enhance border security and confidence building among the member states. The meeting's addition of Uzbekistan, the formation of SCO in Shanghai in June 2001, and the establishment of a permanent secretariat based in Beijing and an antiterrorism coordination center in Tashkent, Uzbekistan in 2004 marked a steady institutionalization and formalization of the cooperative mechanism. For Beijing, the SCO consolidates Sino-Russian cooperation and represents a model of China's new diplomacy based on comprehensive, open, and voluntary cooperation that is intended to enhance security for all states, but threaten none.[83]

Along with its growing influence in Asia, China's diplomacy has also branched out in other parts of the developing world. Finding their country on the unfamiliar international stage, Chinese policy elites and analysts have debated over their country's self-identity in world politics. To fulfill its international responsibilities, argued respected IR specialist Pang Zhongying, China needed a "normal mentality" in engaging the world with a forward-looking definition of national interest. In a rare occurrence in the Chinese IR community, he even questioned the wisdom of China's use of its veto power in 1999 to block the UN-sponsored peaceful operation in Macedonia, in retaliation of that country's diplomatic recognition of Taiwan.[84] Veteran America watcher Zi Zhongyun wrote in early 1999, "No longer can China always use the excuse of 'five thousand years of civilization plus one hundred years of humiliations.' As they enter into the twenty-first century, the Chinese can, and urgently need to, create new spiritual sources for inspiration."[85] Jin Dexi, China's top expert on the Sino–Japanese relationship, asked in a 2002 article, "Our accession to

---

[83] "Summit Meeting Launches Shanghai Cooperation Organization," *People's Daily*, at http://english.peopledaily.com.cn/200106/15/eng20010615-72740.html; Xie Rong, "Shanghai Hezuo Zuzhi – Quyu Hezuo De Dianfan" [The Shanghai Cooperation Organization – Model for Regional Cooperation], Xinhua, May 28, 2003, at http://past.people.com.cn/GB/shizheng/252/10778/10780/20030528/1002621.html.

[84] Pang Zhongying, "China's International Status and Foreign Strategy after the Cold War," *Renmin Wang*, May 5, 2002, FBIS: CPP20020506000022.

[85] Zi Zhongyun, "Zhongmei Jianjiao Shizhounian Yu Ershi Zhounian: Bian Yu Bubian [Tenth Anniversary and Twentieth Anniversary of Sino-American Diplomatic Normalization: Change and Continuity], *Meiguo Yanjiu*, no. 1 (1999), p. 12.

WTO demonstrated that we have made up our mind to fuse into the international system economically. Then how should we treat the same system in the future in the political and security arenas?" Arguing that China's self-image should not be mired in the victim mentality based on selective memories of Western humiliations in modern history, he called for a new outlook with "a modernization of national consciousness."[86] Without such a change, warns Wu Jianmin, veteran diplomat and president of the Foreign Affairs University, China would be ill equipped to properly handle the complex international reactions to China's rise.[87]

Other prominent IR experts echoed ambassador Wu's warning against narrow-minded, emotional nationalism, while at the same time they forcefully argued for the embrace of inspiring ideas and moral values to guide China's rise.[88] Evidently dissatisfied with Chinese efforts to integrate itself into the international mainstream, Wang Jisi, former director of the CASS Institute of American Studies, bemoaned the lack of "a systematic approach to [constructively and proactively] dealing with the existing world order seen by the Chinese as 'United States-led.'"[89] Most remarkably, one senior scholar from the CCP Central Party School attributed China's disadvantaged international status to its undemocratic polity.[90] Another scholar at Peking University similarly contends that flaws in the Chinese political system "damage China's international image, negatively impact China's international influence, and limit the growth of China's comprehensive national power." Hence, a Chinese-style democracy is needed so that China

[86] Jin Dexi, "Zhongguo Xuyao Daguo Xintai" [China Needs Great-Power Mentality], *Global Times*, Sept. 12, 2002, at http://www.people.com.cn/GB/paper68/7239/698878.html.

[87] "Wu Jianmin Urges Chinese Nationals to Abandon 'Weak Nation Mentality,'" *Hong Kong Ta Kung Pao* (Internet), March 8, 2006, Open Source Center (formerly known as FBIS, hereafter cited as OSC): CPP20060308508003; Wu Jianmin, "A Long Way to Go Before China Abandons Weak Nation Mentality," *Zhongguo Qingnian Bao* (Internet), March 21, 2006, OSC: CPP20060321510008.

[88] "Xuezhe Tan Daguo Zeren Yu Xintai" [Scholars on Great-Power Responsibility and Mentality], at http://news.xinhuanet.com/fortune/2005-08/17/content_3366770.htm.

[89] Wang Jisi, "China's Changing Role in Asia," p. 5.

[90] Liu Jianfei, "Zhongguo Minzhu Zhengzhi Jianshe Yu Zhongmei Guanxi" [The Construction of Democratic Politics in China and Sino-U.S. Relations], *Zhanlue Yu Guanli*, no. 2 (2003), pp. 76–82.

would not be handicapped in international competition.[91] These views reflect a conviction explicitly or implicitly shared by many thoughtful Chinese analysts that their country's orderly democratic reforms would strengthen its domestic front *and* international standing. Framed this way, democratic change at home becomes a national strategic interest in fulfilling China's great-power aspiration.

The flourishing of contending views propounded by influential scholars and governmental advisers in and of itself represents a change of great significance, especially in light of the fact that Chinese foreign policy had historically been the most strictly controlled subject. Not all of these new ideas have translated into practice, to be sure. But some have, as manifested in the many foreign policy adjustments China has made in the past fifteen years. Taken together, they represent an unmistakable sign that the PRC has been under mounting pressure to wrestle with the choices it must make to fulfill its international aspirations.

China's discontent with its international status has been a source of both inspiration and frustration. Its leaders have been careful not to set their nation's expectations dangerously high. As noted earlier, through the 1990s and early years of the new century assessments by Chinese officials and policy analysts of their country's comprehensive national power were generally conservative. Most of them would agree with the characterization of China as a "regional power with limited global significance."[92] The new century has seen a de-emphasis of China's mere regional power status and the Hu-Wen leadership has been bolder than their reformist predecessors in propouding supposedly Chinese global visions of harmony. But such rhetoric shift has not contained concrete alternative policy prescriptions, nor has it led to a fundamental shift in China's foreign policy direction. As China's global clout grows, the CCP leadership must continue to balance confidence and expectation because unrealistic foreign ambitions could be deeply destabilizing at home and abroad. This has proven to be no easy task. Frustration

---

[91] Ye Zicheng, *Zhongguo Dazhanlue* [The Grand Strategy of China] (Beijing: Zhongguo Shehuishexue Chubanshe, 2003), pp. 116–26, quote on p. 117.

[92] Chen Yue, *Analysis of China's International Status*, ch. 5, 6; Mao Xiaojun, "Transforming Concepts and Proactively Responding to Factors," *Xiandai Guoji Guanxi*, no. 11 (Nov. 20, 2002), pp. 22–4, FBIS: CPP20021209000250.

over perceived status immobility and denial has fueled virulent nationalism and a power politics impulse.[93] Limitations in domestic political
change have continued to generate a political drawback in its international relations. The PRC strategy of peacefully contested change
that seeks to strike a balance between power and legitimacy has been
tested by its own power politics impulse and foreign concerns over the
implications of its phenomenal rise in material power.

Overall, Chinese leaders have shown an unprecedented sensitivity
to sources of categorization that could worsen China's international
environment, but their compliance with global norms and institutions
has been conditioned by equally potent concern to undertake domestic
and foreign policy reforms on their own terms. They have been keen
on cultivating legitimate recognition without appearing to be weak in
power. They have strived for peaceful development, but they have also
worried that their vulnerabilities might be exploited. They seek to join
the world and take advantage of the opportunities the globalized world
has to offer. At the same time, they have also sought to change the
Western-dominated world and expand China's control over Taiwan
and influence over its international environment in general.

Making the Choice: Opportunity and Constraints

As a status seeker, how China sees its future in relation to the existing world order determines its foreign policy choice. That judgment
is in turn derivative from how the international system is arranged,
the predominant patterns of international relations directly pertaining
to how it is treated, and the CCP leadership's definition of national
interest. Specifically, China's foreign policy has to do with how its
political elites view the U.S. hegemonic order, the most efficacious way
to achieve China's rise, and the nexus between their domestic and
international agenda. Now we turn to these key parameters shaping
China's international course.

---

[93] Alastair Iain Johnston, "China's Militarized Interstate Dispute Behavior, 1949–
1992," *China Quarterly*, no. 153 (March 1998), pp. 1–30; Joseph Fewsmith
and Stanley Rosen, "The Domestic Context of Chinese Foreign Policy: Does
'Public Opinion' Matter?" in Lampton, *The Making of Chinese Foreign and
Security Policy*, ch. 6; Peter H. Gries, "Tears of Rage: Chinese Nationalism and the Belgrade Embassy Bombing," *China Journal*, no. 45 (July 2001),
pp. 25–43.

International Hierarchy: Reality and Perceptions

In the world arena as in domestic society, status politics is decisively determined by power distribution and legitimacy of the social arrangement. It becomes most orderly when the dominant group possesses supreme material capacities to defend the status quo *and* when the prevailing view among key members "cannot imagine things otherwise arranged."[94] The post–cold war power and authority structure in world politics has similarly driven China's foreign policy, dissuading it from forcing systemic change. The cooperative PRC posture has largely reflected recognition of the lasting U.S. hegemony and the CCP elite's judgment that a radically restructured, alternative order is simply unrealistic, at least in the next quarter of a century or so.

Chinese perceptions of U.S. power after the cold war underwent several noticeable mutations. From 1989 to 1992, the United States emerged as the winner of the cold war and the world's sole superpower. For its part, the Chinese government was preoccupied during this period with acute domestic insecurity in the aftermath of the Tiananmen incident, which was aggravated by a perceived U.S. scheme to destabilize the CCP regime. Internationally, Beijing had to cope with a U.S.-led diplomatic isolation. Around 1993, Chinese analysts reassessed the international situation and argued that the unipolar U.S. power had to contend with emerging powers, such as Europe, Japan, Russia, China, and other states. The trend was multipolarization, but they soon discovered that this assessment reflected more wishful thinking than reality.

By the latter half of the 1990s, it had become clear that the U.S. preponderance had become even more secure, as the only superpower gained greater material advantage over other states and second-tier powers were decidedly unwilling to balance against it. Accordingly, the consensual Chinese view began to hold that "the superpower is more super, and the many great powers are less great."[95] Coming

---

[94] Brown, *Social Psychology*, p. 562; Tajfel, *Human Groups and Social Categories*, p. 246; Hogg and Abrams, *Social Identifications*, pp. 26–9 and *passim*; Michael A. Hogg, *The Social Psychology of Group Cohesiveness* (New York: New York University Press, 1992); Hogg and Abrams, *Social Identifications*; Kalkhoff and Barnum, "The Effects of Status-Organizing"; Jan E. Stets and Peter J. Burke, "Identity Theory and Social Identity Theory."

[95] Wang Jisi, "Building A Constructive Relationship," in Abramowitz, et al., *China-Japan-U.S.*, p. 22.

to recognize the preponderance and longevity of the U.S. power was by no means easy, as such a change of mind represented not only a departure from the long-standing official line but also a shift toward an emphasis on finding a way to accommodate the fundamental reality in world politics. Instead of insisting on the myth that the rest of the world would rise up to end Western dominance, Chinese leaders and analysts could now more realistically assess the opportunities and restraints for their country's foreign policy choices.

Starting in the mid-1990s, the view that the United States was on the decline had given way to a new consensus that multipolarization would be a "long and tortuous historical process."[96] None of the Chinese analysts was confident enough to specify a precise date of the onset of a genuinely multipolar world. Instead, they focused on the ongoing struggle between unipolarity and multipolarity, emphasizing that the process was about policy choices rather than dictated by the balance-of-power logic. Questioning the wisdom of traditional polarity thinking in the first place, Beijing University Professor Ye Zicheng recently argued that multipolarity might not be in China's best interest, nor is the American unipolarity necessarily incompatible with China's rise.[97] Indeed the Hu-Wen leadership has toned down the call for multipolarity, instead opting to alternatively advocate multilateralism and democratization.

Prior to the events on September 11, 2001, Chinese analysts had conceded the fact that materialist power had accrued to the United States. They also took note of the strengthening of U.S. leadership, not only among like-minded advanced democracies but also through control of "the moral and legal high ground" in the world.[98] They argued

---

[96] Yu Sui, "Shijie Duojihua Wenti" [The Problem of Multipolarization of the World], *WEP*, no. 3 (2004), pp. 15–20; Li Zhong, "On the Great Debate over Unipolarity and Multipolarity," *Liaowang*, no. 21 (2000), pp. 14–15, reprinted in China Renda Social Sciences Information Center (hereafter cited as CRSSIC), *China's Diplomacy*, no. 9 (2000), pp. 2–3; Yang Jiemian, "The World Situation at the Turn of the Century and U.S. Global Strategy," *Guoji Wenti Yanjiu* [International Studies], Nov. 13, 2000, pp. 23–30, OSC: CPP20001215000150.

[97] Ye Zicheng, "Chaoyue Duojihua Siwei, Cujin Daguo Hezuo" [Transcending Multipolarity Thinking, Promoting Great-Power Cooperation], in Qin Yaqing, ed., Guoji Zhixun Juan [The World Order] (Beijing: New World Press, 2007), pp. 62–86.

[98] Su Ge, "The New World Order and International Security," *Guoji Wenti Yanjiu*, Nov. 13, 2000, pp. 7–12, OSC: CPP20001215000148. See also Wang Jisi, "China's Search for Stability with America."

that Western-dominated international institutions, values, and standards have allowed the United States to categorize other countries into different groups based on these ideational factors. The policy consequences of the graded world order were dramatically demonstrated in the neo-interventionism promoted by the United States and its NATO allies, justifying disrespect of sovereignty toward those countries that threatened the West.[99] Unrivalled American hegemony provided the country with unparalleled freedom to consolidate its international primacy.

From the Chinese perspective, the U.S. policy toward the People's Republic has overall been characterized by ambiguities with both elements of acceptance and suspicion, engagement and containment. Some Chinese analysts attributed U.S. mistrust and hostility to a reigning hegemon's fear of a rising power, an explanation whose logic is not dissimilar from that of structural realism. Others resort to less materialist analysis, blaming the U.S. containment impulse to Washington's ideological, religious, and racial bias. In response, Zheng Bijian, a top adviser to the CCP leadership, called for the United States to abandon "drawing line[s] [between friends and enemies] according to ideology and [a] social system based on the cold war mentality," "values based on 'the cultural superiority theory,'" and "the traditional notion that the rising power must challenge the existing hegemony."[100]

Chinese political elites have been deeply concerned about U.S. power and policies, particularly when the United States dispatched aircraft carrier groups to the vicinity of the Taiwan Strait during the missile crisis, led NATO to wage war against Yugolavia, and launched a preventive war against Iraq. These events increased China's commitment to self-strengthening economic and military modernization. At the same time, even amidst these crises, no mainstream Chinese analyst advocated a tit-for-tat, all-out confrontational response; instead, they

---

[99] See, for example, Shen Qurong, "On the Struggle over Building the New International Order," *Xiandai Guoji Guanxi* [Contemporary International Relations], Jan./Feb. 2000, pp. 8–12, reprinted in CRSSIC, *International Politics*, no. 5 (2000), pp. 8–11; Hu Wenlong, "The Kosovo War – Strategic Issues Research," *Guofang* [National Defense], Feb. 15, 2001, pp. 4–8, OSC: CPP20010319000184.

[100] Zheng Bijian, "Zhongmei Guanxi De Sige Zhanlue Jiyu" [Four Strategic Opportunities in Sino-American Relationship], *RMRB*, July 12, 2005, p. 5.

called for coordinated, far-reaching diplomatic responses.[101] While determined to defend its core territorial, political, and developmental interests, the PRC has refrained from unduly antagonizing the status quo powers lest such provocation fuel the fear of a China threat and invite a tightening grip of the international order by the advanced democracies to contain China. As other political scientists have argued elsewhere, the enduring nature of the U.S. hegemony has effectively lessened the balancing logic in international relations.[102] For a second-tier power like China, a confrontational policy appeared futile and counterproductive due to its own relative material weakness, lack of reliable allies, and fear of being further isolated.

Moreover, as liberal IR theorists such as G. John Ikenberry have argued, the U.S.-led international order is uniquely equipped to assuage systemic discontent, thanks to the open and pluralist character of the American polity itself and the liberal ideas and institutions conducive to upward mobility that have characterized the U.S. hegemony.[103] Mainstream Chinese analysts echoed this judgment, albeit with significantly less certitude about American openness to a peaceful power transition. For example, Yang Jiemian, vice president of the Shanghai Institute of International Studies, argued that compared with the world orders after the two world wars, the post–cold war world is "more just and fair," making it possible for reformist change.[104] Those liberal propositions, however persuasively made, do not automatically translate into reassurance in practice. And there are plenty of skeptics toward the U.S. policy agenda on China. The Chinese, whose views are heavily influenced by the state of the Sino-American relationship, have more reasons than their realist colleagues

---

[101] For an excellent exposition of Chinese debate triggered by the NATO war, see David M. Finkelstein, *China Reconsiders Its National Security: 'The Great Peace and Development Debate' of 1999* (Alexandria, VA: CNA, 2000).

[102] G. John Ikenberry, ed., *America Unrivaled: The Future of Balance of Power* (Ithaca, NY: Cornell University Press, 2002).

[103] Ikenberry, *After Victory*, pp. 20, 266–70 and passim. See also Daniel Deudney and G. John Ikenberry, "Realism, Structural Liberalism, and the Western Order," in Ethan B. Kapstein and Michael Mastanduno, eds., *Unipolar Politics: Realism and State Strategies after the Cold War* (New York: Columbia University Press, 1999), ch. 4.

[104] Yang Jiemian, *Da Hezuo: Bianhuazhong De Shijie He Zhongguo Guoji Zhan-lue* [Grand Cooperation: The Changing World and China's Global Strategy] (Tianjin, China: Renmin Chubanshe, 2005), pp. 73–4.

in the United States to doubt the U.S. commitment to self-restraint, multilateralism, and openness to accept emerging powers like China.[105] While U.S. unilateralism over Iraq and its ambitious blueprint to transform the world after 9/11 did not directly affect China, as did the earlier NATO war on Yugoslavia or the 1995–96 Taiwan crisis, these events did raise doubts and angst among the Chinese elites over the prospect of a institutionalized power transition involving China's rise.

The United States has not fully embraced the PRC as a strategic partner, but it has shown enough deference to its core national interests both at home and abroad to reassure the Chinese of a cooperative possibility in their bilateral relationship. In this light, the U.S. Deputy Secretary of State Robert Zoellick's speech on September 21, 2005 underscoring the "need to encourage China to become a responsible stakeholder in the international system" was both timely and important.[106] While the notion of "stakeholder" has yet to be clearly defined, the speech did help provide some direction to the U.S.-China strategic dialogue started in 2004. More broadly, Zoellick's speech in effect responded to the idea of the "peaceful rise" propounded by Zheng Bijian and others with a reaffirmation of the U.S. desire for a positive engagement with China. Several years into the new century, mainstream Chinese analysts are no longer saying that U.S. preeminence would last for twenty or thirty or fifty years, as some of them used to write prior to 9/11. Instead, they have argued that the world is still U.S.- and Western-dominated, but it is now more dynamic, with more dispersed power than at any time during the post–cold war era. They are also more positive about the direction of the Sino-American relationship, although they complain that the notion of "stakeholder" is U.S.-centered and demanding. The Chinese maintain that the United States continues its hedging strategy vis-à-vis China, but they are now

---

[105] Alastair Iain Johnston and Daniela Stockmann, "Chinese Attitudes Toward the United States and Americans," in Peter J. Katzenstein and Robert O. Keohane, eds., *Anti-Americanism in World Politics* (Ithaca, NY: Cornell University Press, 2007), ch. 6. For realist skepticism toward propositions of a liberal U.S. agenda, see Randall L. Schweller, "The Problem of International Order Revisited: A Review Essay," *International Security*, vol. 26, no. 1 (Summer 2001), pp. 161–86; Waltz, "Structural Realism after the Cold War."

[106] Robert B. Zoellick, "Whither China: From Membership to Responsibility?" at http://www.ncuscr.org/articlesandspeeches/Zoellick.htm.

more confident about their influence in shaping the Sino-American relationship.[107]

The Opportunity of Status Rise: Frustrations and Confidence

China's foreign policy is in large part a response to its own valuation of the opportunity for status mobility in the world order. Optimism over the success of its peacefully contested rise strengthens support for the strategy of orderly change through a balanced pursuit of power and legitimacy. Conversely, perception of a U.S.-led containment has fueled emotional nationalism and confrontational backlashes in Chinese foreign policy.[108] Events such as the NATO bombing of the Chinese embassy in May 1999 and the collision of the U.S. surveillance plane with a Chinese jet fighter in April 2001 led to despair over true Western intentions. They brought to the fore the deeply embedded Chinese sense of rejection and victimization by Western powers, even leading to suggestions that there was a racial dimension to the American discrimination against the country.[109] Such frustrations lessened incentives for "good behavior" on China's part.

These incidents notwithstanding, the enduring strength of the international arrangement, coupled with confidence with their own diplomatic acumen, has dissuaded Chinese leaders from opting for a confrontational course. Since the mid-1990s, the PRC has directed its diplomatic efforts toward promoting an alternative world vision, wherein sovereignty remains the prerogative of individual states; no political system is superior; the diverse cultures, beliefs, values, and modes of international relations are equally valid; and ultimately

---

[107] Jin Canrong, ed. *Daguo Zhanluejuan* [Strategies of the Great Powers] (Beijing: New World Press, 2007); Qin Yaqing, *The World Order*; Yuan Peng, "Sino-U.S. Relations: New Changes and New Challenges," *Xiandai Guoji Guanxi*, May 20, 2006, pp. 29–37, in OSC: CPP20060606329001.

[108] See Fewsmith and Rosen, "Public Opinion and Foreign Policy"; Suisheng Zhao, *A Nation-State by Construction: Dynamics of Modern Chinese Nationalism* (Stanford, CA: Stanford University Press, 2004).

[109] Wang Xiaode, "Zhongzhu Youyuegan Touying Meiguo Waijiao" [Racial Superiority Projected in U.S. Diplomacy], *Shijie Zhishi* [World Affairs], no. 8 (2000), pp. 38–9, reprinted in CRSSIC, *International Politics*, June 2000, pp. 137–8; Wang Jisi, "Zhongmei Keyi Bimian Xinlengzhan" [China and the United States Can Avoid Another Cold War], *Global Times*, June 22, 2001, at http://www.snweb.com/gb/gnd/2001/0622/g062200.htm.

external resistance to its rise is minimized. While pursuing these changes, the PRC has also sought to accumulate "social capital" in the international community, by which I mean acceptance of China as a responsible member and a relatively stable commitment by other countries to maintain friendly ties with it.[110] The PRC has pursued multilayered, omnidirectional partnership diplomacy, designed to forge long-term, cooperative relations with countries in Europe, Asia, Africa, Latin America, and elsewhere.[111] It has worked to forge a new pattern of great-power politics and solidify its newfound influence in Asia and Africa.

Consolidating ties with Asian neighbors is essential for the CCP government's domestic agenda on social stability and economic growth, regional agenda on gaining an upper hand in its rivalry with Japan and preventing anti-China coalitions along its periphery, and global agenda on securing the gateway to great-power status. Despite setbacks and difficulties, the concerted PRC effort to win over its neighbors has paid off and boosted its regional leadership position in its first rounds. This success is, more than anything else, due to China's diplomatic skills in taking advantage of its considerable compatibility with neighboring governments in terms of the need for development, stability, and peace at home and in the region.

The need to achieve a commonly desired and only jointly attainable "superordinate goal" reduces intergroup hostility and allows for the pursuit of absolute gain through cooperation.[112] Avoiding a cold war type of unbridled division may be considered such a goal, one that can

---

[110] The term "social capital" has been widely used in the studies of American and comparative politics since the release of Robert Putnam's book *Bowling Alone: The Collapse and Revival of American Community* (New York: Simon and Schuster, 2000). My definition of the term clearly differs from his and others'.

[111] See Su Hao, "Zhongguo Waijiao De 'Huoban Guanxi' Kuangjia" [The 'Partnership' Framework in China's Diplomacy], *World Affairs*, no. 5 (May 2000), pp. 11–12, reprinted in CRSSIC, *China's Diplomacy*, June 2000, pp. 8–9; Li Zhongjie, "Xinshiji Zhongguo Quanqiu Zhanlue Gouxiang" [Thoughts on China's Global Strategy in the New Century], *Zhonggong Zhongyang Dangxiao Xuebao* [Journal of the Chinese Communist Party School], no. 1 (2000), pp. 23–40, reprinted in CRSSIC, *International Politics*, May 2000, pp. 92–102.

[112] Kalkhoff and Barnum, "The Effects of Status-Organizing," p. 101. See also Brown, *Social Psychology*, ch. 17; Burnstein, et al., "How the Mind Preserves the Image of the Enemy."

limit rivalry among major powers in the post–cold war world. Prominent Chinese analysts have indeed advanced the view that the global challenges, the web of bilateral ties, and the logic of nuclear peace pose significant limits on Sino-American rivalry.[113] Managing economic interdependence represents yet another common goal. Throughout the 1990s, globalization sometimes came under attack from perspectives of the dependency theory and the state-centric, ultranationalist views in China, as commentators subscribing to these beliefs blamed globalization for their country's economic weakness and strategic inferiority vis-à-vis the West.[114] But mainstream Chinese views have embraced globalization as a distinguishing feature in contemporary world politics. While the process presents a host of unprecedented challenges to China at the international, subnational, and transnational levels, it offers great opportunities for China to deepen domestic reforms, cultivate cooperative foreign relations, and increase international recognition.[115]

Globalization has indeed been a major source of "new thinking" in Chinese foreign policy. Again, political scientist John Ikenberry contends that the free-market system under the U.S. hegemony provides a level playing field of a sort where positive-sum gains can be cooperatively achieved.[116] With similar reasoning, Chinese analysts, too, place much hope for a cooperative Sino-American relationship on the two countries' compatible economic interests. They argue that economic interdependence and the growing formal and informal ties have

---

[113] See Qingguo Jia, "New Priorities, New Opportunities: Sino-American Relations since 9–11," *Asia Perspectives*, Spring 2002, pp. 9–12; Wang Jisi, "China and the United States Can Avoid Another Cold War"; Yan Xuetong, "Post–Cold War Continuity – Major Post–Cold War International Political Contradiction," *Strategy and Management*, June 1, 2000, pp. 58–66, in FBIS-China, June 23, 2000; Song Yiming, "The Opportunities and Challenges Our Country Faces in the World Before 2010," *Guoji Wenti Yanjiu*, March 2000, pp. 1–6, reprinted in CRSSIC, *China's Diplomacy*, Aug. 2000, pp. 12–16.

[114] The extreme antiglobalization views were propounded in He Xin, *Zhonghua Fuxin Yu Shjie Weilai* [China's National Rejuvenation and the World's Future], vol. 1, 2. (Chengdu: Sichuan People's Press, 1996); Fang Ning, et al., *Quanqiuhua Yinying Xia De Zhongguo Zhilu* [China's Road under the Shadow of Globalization] (Beijing: Chinese Social Science Press, 1999).

[115] Pang Zhongying, ed., *Quanqiuhua, Fanquanqiuhua Yu Zhongguo* [Globalization, Antiglobalization, and China] (Shanghai: Renmin Press, 2002); Wang Yizhou, *Global Politics and China's Foreign Policy*.

[116] See Ikenberry, *After Victory*, pp. 267–8.

had a "democratizing" effect on international relations restraining
U.S. power, lessening the fear of a China threat and creating opportunities for win-win competition in great-power politics.[117] Growing
Chinese demand for market access and energy has raised international
concerns about the spillover effect leading to zero-sum power politics
in its foreign relations. Issues concerning China's trade practices and
demand for natural resources directly bear upon its developmental
right, and as such they need to be managed carefully. Fortunately, a
largely market-oriented competition and cooperation in energy technologies, even if imperfectly undertaken, are eminently possible. Out
of its own national interest, the PRC has vowed not to repeat earlier
industrializers' approach to modernization through unbridled foreign
expansionism.[118]

Myriad transnational threats and a shared desire to avert another
cycle of great-power war in the nuclear era also mitigate competitive power politics. Even before the 9/11 terrorist attacks, American
public opinion considered such problems as weapons proliferation,
terrorism, drug trafficking, environmental degradation, and the AIDS
epidemic a much larger threat than the rising power of China.[119] In
the aftermath of 9/11, U.S.-Chinese cooperation in combating terrorism lessened mutual animosity fueled by NATO's accidental bombing
of the Chinese embassy in Belgrade and the EP-3 surveillance plane

---

[117] For a typical Chinese view, see Gu Ping, "Heze Liangli, Poze Liangshang:
Dangqian Zhongmei Guanxi Pinglun" [Cooperation Means Mutual Benefits; Antagonism Means Mutual Harms: Commentary on the Current Sino-
American Relationship], *RMRB*, May 31, 2001, p. 4. For a detailed treatment
of the topic, see Yong Deng and Thomas G. Moore, "China Views Globalization: Towards a New Great Power Politics," *Washington Quarterly*, vol. 27,
no. 3 (Summer 2004), pp. 117–36.

[118] Information Office of the PRC State Council, "Zhongguo De Heping Fazhan
Daolu" [China's Road to Peaceful Development], *RMRB*, Dec. 23, 2005, pp.
2–3; Zheng Bijian, "Guoji Jingyan Yu Zhongguo Teshe" [International Experiences and Chinese Characteristics], *RMRB*, July 18, 2005, p. 1; Zheng Bijian,
"China's 'Peaceful Rise' to Great-Power Status," *Foreign Affairs*, vol. 84, no.
5 (Sept./Oct. 2005), pp. 18–24.

[119] See the findings of the public opinion poll conducted in May 2001 by the
Pew Research Center and Council for Foreign Relations at http://www.people-
press.org/china01rpt.htm. For a detailed account of the common global issues
and security challenges facing the United States and China, see David M.
Lampton, *Same Bed, Different Dreams: Managing U.S.-China Relations, 1989–
2000* (Berkeley: University of California Press, 2001).

incident in April 2001.[120] Apart from offering assistance in combating the immediate terrorist threats, the PRC also took care not to appear too obstructionist against the expanded U.S. foreign policy agenda for its global antiterror campaign. Most tellingly, during the debate over Iraq preceding the war in 2003, Beijing quietly reassured Washington that it would not block a UN Security Council resolution authorizing the use of force.[121] The second Iraq war heightened Chinese concern over unilateral U.S. attempts to remold the world according to its own power politics logic and political values, while at the same time the manner in which the war unfolded has also prompted doubts about the sustainability of U.S. unilateralist practices. In the initial phase of the war, the Chinese were unnerved about the implications of the U.S. unilateralism, but soon started to doubt whether that policy could last in light of how the war was folding and the widespread international opposition to it. Chinese policy advisers and scholars alike maintained that the war damaged U.S. legitimacy and Western unity in international affairs.[122] Today they view the US with less emotional nationalism, more confidence, and more sense of equality. As the United States seemed tied down by its own choice and its power is increasingly contested, the Chinese have toned down the revisionist rhetoric of multi-polarity, while at the same time, they have stepped up efforts to deliberately realign regional and global environment to their liking.

The PRC might be considered the greatest beneficiary of globalization, having taken advantage of the opportunities of economic

---

[120] The immediate effect of 9/11 is explored in Jonathan D. Pollack, ed., *Strategic Surprise: U.S.-China Relations in the Early Twenty-First Century* (Newport, RI: Naval War College Press, 2003); Andrew Scobell, "Terrorism and Chinese Foreign Policy," in Deng and Wang, *China Rising*, pp. 305–23; John Garver, "Sino-American Relations in 2001: The Difficult Accommodation of Two Great Powers," *International Journal*, Spring 2002, pp. 283–310.

[121] Susan V. Lawrence, "How China Relations Improved: An Insider's View," *Far Eastern Economic Review*, Oct. 28, 2004, p. 16.

[122] Qin Yaqing, *The World Order*, part 2; Qian Qichen, "Xinshiji De Guanjiguanxi" [International Relations in the New Century], *Xuexi Shibao* [Study Times], no. 257, Oct. 2004, reprinted at http://www.irchina.org/news/view.asp?id=641 (accessed Nov. 5, 2004); Zhang Ruizhuang, "Meiguo Baquan De Zhengdangxing Weiji" [The Legitimacy Crisis of the U.S. Hegemony], *Guoji Wenti Luntan* [International Review], no. 35 (Summer 2004), at http://www.siis.org.cn/gjwtlt/2004/IT2/zhangluizhuang.htm.

globalization presumably better than any other country. In terms of strategic and political interests, although the international arrangements have disadvantaged China in important ways, the United States and other advanced democracies have overall pursued an engagement policy toward Beijing, with a declared readiness to welcome it to join the great-power club. Ultimately, from the Chinese perspective, the world order has been Western-dominated, but it has not been rigidly arranged to block China's rise. Great-power politics may be heavily centered on the United States, but it is in a state of flux, characterized by a struggle between centripetal and centrifugal forces. The balance-of-power logic is at work creating perils in China's foreign relations, but its international environment is not dictated by an immutable structural force; a lot depends on China's own policy choices. Their world may not be tranquil (*Bu Taiping*), as the Chinese like to say, but ultimately it *can* be managed.[123]

The Party's National Interest: Legitimacy at Home and Recognition Abroad

China's international trajectory is in large part set by its domestic track. For the Chinese historian Zhang Baijia, his nation's diplomacy since the Opium War has really been the projection of its domestic fate. The way to enhance contemporary China's international status is first and foremost through self-strengthening reforms to build a strong, vibrant, and confident nation that tap into the global mainstream.[124] His view represents a useful antidote to a prevalent notion in his country that China is always a reactive victim in world affairs. It's true that PRC foreign policy has been more developmentally oriented and domestically embedded than ever before, but it is not simply a derivative of domestic politics. To fully comprehend its dynamics, we need to be attentive to how the CCP domestic agenda interacts with international politics. What anchors Chinese integration in the world system is its domestic economic reform and opening up, which the leadership has embraced

---

[123] Qin Yaqing, *The World Order*; Jin Canrong, *Strategies of the Great Powers*; Niu Jun, ed., *Zhongguo Waijiao Juan* [China's Foreign Affairs] (Beijing: New World Press, 2007); Yan Xuetong, ed., *Guoji Anquanjuan* [International Security] (Beijing: New World Press, 2007).

[124] Zhang Baijia, "Gaibian Ziji, Yingxiang Shijie" [Transforming Self, Influencing the World], in Niu Jun, *China's Foreign Affairs*, pp. 3–26.

since the late 1970s. As China's reforms and economic growth have proceeded in tandem with its deepening integration into the world, its domestic and international politics is conditioned by the country's unprecedented depth of global participation. Chinese reformers at levels from the center to the factory have capitalized on economic globalization and substantive integration into the world mainstream to lock in and deepen key policy reforms, market transitions, and institution building. In this way, the dominant interests in Chinese society are closely tied to the world market, to major international institutions, to the advanced economies, and to neighboring regions in Asia and other parts of the developing world.[125]

Navigating the interlacement between domestic and international politics is no easy task. The CCP leadership clearly realizes that both its effective governance at home and participation abroad require domestic reforms to overcome China's weaknesses in the political, social, economic, technological, and military arenas. While the economic blueprint is in place, the political roadmap has yet to be clearly charted. But as they search for the road to a "strong" state capable of presiding over China's reemergence as a great power, Chinese leaders and strategy analysts have to grapple with how to sustain broad societal dynamism buttressed by effective state institutions, inspiring values, and national cohesion.

Making China prosperous, strong, and respected in the world is now the most important source of the CCP's domestic legitimacy. In this way, the CCP mandate to rule and the Chinese quest for great-power recognition abroad overlap. However, domestic politics fixated on the state security has sometimes held back the nation's upward mobility in the world. The post–cold war international hierarchy generally favors democracies and disadvantages nondemocracies, thereby turning China's value and polity gap with the U.S.-led great-power group into a major handicap to its foreign relations. Compliance with the dominant political value in the world is hardly the CCP government's overriding goal. China has thus chosen to remedy the problem through

---

[125] David Zweig, *Internationalizing China: Domestic Interests and Global Linkages* (Ithaca, NY: Cornell University Press, 2002); Shuming Bao, et al., *The Chinese Economy after WTO Accession*; Thomas G. Moore, "Chinese Foreign Policy in the Age of Globalization," in Deng and Wang, *China Rising*, ch. 5; Wang Yizhou, *National Interests*.

self-paced political reforms and foreign policy initiatives designed to minimize the negative international fallout of its lagging democratization. And complaints about Western prejudice has been a key source of China's discontent and revisionism vis-à-vis the world order. The persistent concern over maintaining domestic stability and territorial integrity also limits change in China's views on sovereignty and the issue of Taiwan.[126] The CCP domestic legitimacy relies on sustenance of a Chinese national identity still tied to the "chosen trauma" of humiliation by imperialist powers in modern history.[127] Foreign hostilities, pressures, or criticisms against China in turn engender popular Chinese frustrations with Western powers. Filtered and adroitly exploited by the official propaganda apparatus, these frustrations turn into nationalism that legitimizes the CCP-state, but can also challenge the government's "change- through-participation" foreign policy.

After the cold war, the reconfigured notion of international recognition in world politics has brought to the fore the domestic-foreign nexus; the two spheres simply can no longer be compartmentalized. Never before has the Chinese government felt more pressured to respond to the competing demands from the international society and diversified interests in the rapidly changing Chinese society. Parallel pursuits in domestic reforms and international participation have underlaid China's rise. By the same token, limits and uncertainties in its international trajectory are often rooted in the myriad problems in the country's domestic transition.

Since the Tiananmen incident in 1989 and the subsequent end of the cold war, despite its discontent with the U.S. hegemony and Western

---

[126] For broad discussions of the linkage between inadequate state building and rigid interpretation of sovereignty in the developing world, see Robert Jackson and Carl Rosberg, "Why Africa's Weak States Persist: The Empirical and the Juridical in Statehood," *World Politics*, vol. 35 (1982), pp. 1–24; Robert Jackson, *Quasi-States: Sovereignty, International Relations, and the Third World* (Cambridge: Cambridge University Press, 1990); Mohammed Ayoob, *The Third World Security Predicament: State Making, Regional Conflict, and the International System* (Boulder, CO: Lynne Rienner, 1995), ch. 1, 2.

[127] For a discussion of "chosen trauma" in ethnic identity construction, see Volkan, *Blood Lines*, pp. 48–9; the special issue on "Trauma and Identity," *Mind and Human Interaction*, vol. 11, no. 1 (2000). On how the "victim mentality" motivated Mao's foreign policy, see Jian Chen, *Mao's China and the Cold War* (Chapel Hill: University of North Carolina Press, 2001).

domination, the Chinese leadership has judged that its best course abroad is to carefully navigate through world politics. Thus, China's foreign policy has been geared toward adapting itself to the power, authority, and social structure in world politics while enhancing its power, leverage, and influence. To track the patterns and dynamics of interaction between China's rise and evolving world politics, we now examine exactly how the country has reacted to the pressures and expectations from the international community, approached its great-power diplomacy, enhanced its influence in Asia and Africa, and adjusted its Taiwan policy.

3 | *Negotiating the Human Rights Standard*

Fixated on the target state's behavioral outcomes in human rights, political scientists studying the normative effect generally consider the People's Republic of China (PRC) as a failed case. Within the China studies community, the consensus recognizes Chinese responsiveness, albeit in varying degrees. China scholars tend to treat human rights as just one of the many issue areas in the PRC's foreign relations. And the focus is on the diplomatic tussle, the give-and-take over specific rights concerns. This approach parallels the U.S. policy debate in the 1990s over whether it should condition market access on human rights in dealing with China. As the linkage episode passed away, scholarly interest in the human rights issue waned at the outset of the new century.

These approaches underestimate the power of human rights. From our perspective, international human rights are not just another norm to be dismissed or bargained away. They are a constitutive principle of contemporary international society. In no small measure, they demarcate political boundaries and set standards for proper great-power behavior. In this sense, China's human rights problem has represented the political origin of its status conundrum after the cold war. This chapter explores this political effect and examines the PRC human rights diplomacy in the broad context of its struggle to overcome the political barriers against its great-power aspiration.

The violent end of the student demonstrations in Tiananmen Square in June 1989 immediately led to international condemnation and isolation against the Chinese Communist Party (CCP)–run government. While the worst part of the diplomatic crisis ended quickly, the political effects of its rights-abusing image were anything but ephemeral. Subsequently, the triumphant democracies promoted human rights as a foundational principle of the post–cold war world order. With a gap between the CCP polity and the rights-respecting great-power community, the PRC has since been confronted with a persistent political advantage and diplomatic liability. To lessen censure abroad, China has been both responsive and resistant to international pressures, but the slow pace of political liberalization at home has limited compliance. The country has sought to simultaneously oppose the use of human rights to justify discriminatory treatments of illiberal states and redefine the international standard itself.

Human Rights and the World Order

Mobilized by the moral outrage against the Holocaust and other atrocities during the Second World War, the United Nations promulgated the Universal Declaration on Human Rights (UDHR) in 1948. The UN interest in human rights was also spurred by an appreciation of the linkage between human rights and international security, as is evident in Article 55 of the UN Charter proclaiming the inherent contribution of human rights progress to international peace.[1] Despite its auspicious birth, the emerging cold war soon eviscerated the universal ideals of inalienable human rights. For much of the ensuing decades, with few exceptions (most notably the global outcry against South Africa's racial segregation), human rights were subsumed and submerged under the strategic rivalry in a bipolar cold war struggle. The United States did not seriously pursue a human rights policy until the détente of the 1970s, when it strategically deployed human rights in a moral campaign against communism.[2]

While stifling human rights, the polarized cold war also proved and reinforced the power of the principled idea. The UN UDHR was given a more practical, legally specific manifestation in 1976 when the International Covenant on Civil and Political Rights (ICCPR) and the International Covenant on Economic, Social, and Cultural Rights (ICESC) officially came into effect after a decade of ratification. The two documents, together with the UDHR, came to become known as the International Bill of Rights, which has inspired regional human

---

[1] Thomas G. Weiss, David P. Forsythe, and Roger A. Coate, *The United Nations and Changing World Politics*, 2nd ed. (Boulder, CO: Westview Press, 1997), p. 132.

[2] Katherine Sikkink, "The Power of Principled Ideas: Human Rights Policies in the United States and Western Europe," in Judith Goldstein and Robert Keohane, eds., *Ideas and Foreign Policy: Beliefs, Institutions, and Political Change* (Ithaca, NY: Cornell University Press, 1993), pp. 139–70.

rights conventions (with Asia being the most notable exception) and international treaties on specific issues ranging from women's issues to genocide.[3] Over time, the idea of human rights gained so much appeal and recognition in both the West and the East that it helped tip decisively the balance of power leading to the collapse of communism in Europe.

After the cold war, human rights have been embraced to such an extent as to exemplify an international norm, commonly understood to be "collective understandings of the proper behavior of actors" in the international society.[4] Human rights are often held as an international standard required of all sovereign states.[5] In parallel to its unprecedented salience, an impressive body of IR literature has been produced to explore where, when, why, and how the norm succeeds or fails to enforce behavioral claims on target sovereign states. The academic studies of the normative effect in general tend to focus exclusively on a particular issue area. Martha Finnemore calls this approach "issue-specific," one heavily influenced by regime theory.[6] As regards human rights, treating the issue as just another norm, scholars are quick to declare its failure when states in question refuse to budge under international pressure. Indeed, Margaret Keck and Kathryn Sikkink pointedly refer to the PRC as an example of the norm's ineffectiveness. Aside from a lack of unifying purpose among human rights activists in China, they blame unavailability of Western material leverage, as the People's Republic was not receiving "large military and economic assistance."[7]

---

[3] For a list of the UN human rights treaties, see Weiss, et al., *The United Nations and Changing World Politics* pp. 140–4. Jack Donnelly provides a comprehensive review of the international, regional, and single-issue human rights regimes in his *Universal Human Rights in Theory and Practice* (Princeton, NJ: Princeton University Press, 1989), ch. 11.

[4] Jeffrey W. Legro, "Which Norms Matter? Revisiting the 'Failure' of Internationalism," *International Organization*, vol. 51, no. 1 (Winter 1997), p. 33.

[5] Kathryn Sikkink, "Human Rights, Principled Issue-networks, and Sovereignty in Latin America," *International Organization*, vol. 47, no. 3 (Summer 1993), pp. 411–41; Saskia Sassen, *Losing Control: Sovereignty in an Age of Globalization* (New York: Columbia University Press, 1996).

[6] Martha Finnemore, *National Interests in International Society* (Ithaca, NY: Cornell University Press, 1996), p. 16.

[7] Margaret E. Keck and Kathryn Sikkink, *Activists Beyond Borders: Advocacy Networks in International Politics* (Ithaca, NY: Cornell University Press, 1998), pp. 116–18, 208.

Hence, the CCP regime, they argue, could completely disregard foreign criticisms with impunity. Their view on China's total defiance is disputable, as will be demonstrated in the following pages. Granted, they are right on the CCP's recalcitrance, but they overlook the normative effect as it manifests itself in shaping the broad political basis of China's international relations.

Historically, certain norms and principles fundamentally determined the international treatment of nation-states.[8] Human rights in the post–cold war world have acquired some of the characteristics of such ideas, thanks to the spread of democracy, the promotion of global transnational networks and grassroots social movements, the moral authority of the norm per se, and the backing of the preponderant power of democratic countries. No matter how imperfectly promoted, human rights have become a source of the states' international legitimacy in ways analogous to how some of the original, Eurocentric ideas evolved into the underpinning values of the globalized Westphalian interstate system.[9] The United States and the European Community even explicitly set human rights as a criterion for sovereignty recognition for the newly independent states in Eastern Europe and the former Soviet Union.[10]

In the eyes of leading democratic powers, the superiority of rights-respecting states is further justified by the widespread belief in democratic peace, attributing reliable peace to mutual identification based on democracy and human rights.[11] Closely tied to the democratic peace notion is the corresponding values-based process of social

---

[8] The classics on how Western values and practices were applied to other "uncivilized" areas in the European-centered international system are Hedley Bull and Adam Watson, eds., *The Expansion of International Society* (Oxford: Clarendon Press, 1984); Gerrit W. Gong, *The Standard of "Civilization" in International Society* (Oxford: Clarendon Press, 1984).

[9] Ian Clark, *Legitimacy in International Society* (Oxford: Oxford University Press, 2005), ch. 9; Jack Donnelly, "Human Rights: A New Standard of Civilization?" *International Affairs*, vol. 74, no. 1 (1998), pp. 1–23; Stephen D. Krasner, "Sovereignty, Regimes, and Human Rights," in Volker Rittenberger with the assistance of Peter Mayer, eds., *Regime Theory and International Relations* (Oxford: Clarendon Press, 1995), pp. 139–67.

[10] Sassen, *Losing Control*, p. 57.

[11] For overviews of democratic peace, see Miriam Fendius Elman, ed., *Paths to Peace: Is Democracy the Answer?* (Cambridge, MA: MIT Press, 1997); Michael E. Brown, Sean Lynn-Jones, and Steven Miller, eds., *Debating the Democratic Peace* (Cambridge, MA: MIT Press 1996); Joanne Gowa, *Ballots and Bullets: The Elusive Democratic Peace* (Princeton, NJ: Princeton University Press, 1999).

construction of group differentiation and stratification in international relations. Human rights distinguish the community of liberal states from other regime types. Unlike other international principles, as Thomas Risse and Kathryn Sikkink point out, "Human rights norms . . . both prescribe rules for appropriate behavior, and help define identities of liberal states."[12] Similarly, Jack Donnelly observes, "'Inside' and 'outside,' in international no less than national societies, are defined not simply by geography or even by a history of interaction, but by cultural values that make insiders different from, and in many ways superior to, outsiders."[13] In Barry Buzan's idealized portrayal, the post–cold war international hierarchy coincided with the "concentric circles of commitment" to human rights and other transnational values promoted by the West.[14]

In a different line of enquiry, Mark L. Haas shows that the ideological gap heavily contributes to strategic enmity in great-power politics. In his theoretical scheme, ideologically opposed states tend to view each other as threatening to regime security at home and political influence abroad. They also tend to draw group boundaries based on ideological cleavages. Attributing violent predisposition to the outgroup "other," ideologically different states become strategically mistrustful, with both assuming worst-case scenario in their interaction.[15] In the post–cold war era, clearly great-power politics has been driven by other factors as well. It is also clear that the human rights issue has had a remarkably persistent, if diverse, effect on China's relations with the United States and other advanced democracies.

Insofar as human rights have become a key organizing principle of the emerging and evolving post–cold war world order, a narrow treatment fails to fully consider its political impact. In many ways, the PRC represents a perfect case to test our proposition. Since the Tiananmen incident, China's human rights record has received arguably the closest international scrutiny of any nation. While the pressures have

---

[12] Thomas Risse and Kathryn Sikkink, "The Socialization of Human Rights Norms," in Thomas Risse, Stepehen C. Robb, and Kathryn Sikkink, eds., *The Power of Human Rights: International Norms and Domestic Change* (New York: Cambridge University Press, 1999), p. 8.

[13] Donnelly, "Human Rights," p. 2.

[14] Barry Buzan, "From International System to International Society: Structural Realism and Regime Theory Meet the English School," *International Organization*, vol. 47 (1993), pp. 349–52.

[15] Mark L. Haas, *The Ideological Origins of Great Power Politics, 1789–1989* (Ithaca, NY: Cornell University Press, 2005).

undergone an ebb and flow and material interests often trump moral concerns in other countries' concrete dealings with the PRC, the CCP government has not been able to shake off the moral demand to live up to the human rights standard, regardless of how contested that standard is. The negative political effect of its illiberal polity has remained manifest in the country's international standing and has become even more pronounced, as China steps up its diplomatic campaign to be recognized as a great power.

From Crisis to Diplomatic Liability

For much of the cold war era, China was largely insulated from international scrutiny on human rights. The outside world basically ignored the worst humanitarian debacles in the PRC history during the Great Leap Forward and the Cultural Revolution. Starting in the mid-1970s, the U.S. human rights policy did not target the PRC, thanks to continued Chinese isolation and its newfound strategic importance in easing the U.S. withdrawal from Vietnam and containing the Soviet threat in general. Concerted international focus on China's human rights was also absent during much of the 1980s, when the PRC was regarded as the beacon of socialist reforms and opening to the West. For his role as the paramount leader of a reformist China, Deng Xiaoping was twice honored as "The Person of the Year" by *Time* magazine, in 1978 and 1985. Only after the mid-1980s did human rights emerge as an issue in America's relations with China.[16] The attention was then on China's draconian one-child-per-family policy, mistreatment of Tibet, and suppression of the best-known political activists. Important as these issues were, they were not viewed as reflective of the fundamental flaw of the regime, and both the Ronald Reagan and George Bush administrations took care not to allow them to fundamentally blight America's rapprochement with China.[17]

---

[16] Robert S. Ross, *Negotiating Cooperation: The United States and China, 1969–1989* (Stanford, CA: Stanford University Press, 1995), pp. 243, 260. For coverage of the U.S. interest in China's human rights in the mid-1980s, see Harry Harding, *A Fragile Relationship: The United States and China since 1972* (Washington, DC: Brookings Institution, 1992), passim, esp. pp. 198–206.

[17] Harding, *A Fragile Relationship*, pp. 202–6.

But things changed dramatically after what happened in Tiananmen Square during the spring and summer of 1989. Massive student demonstrations lasted for several months in Beijing and elsewhere in China, but they were finally met with a violent crackdown by the People's Liberation Army, leaving hundreds, if not more, dead in early June. In the ensuing waves of political repressions, thousands were thrown into prison. International reactions were dramatic and united in ways never seen before. Overnight, formerly reformist Chinese leaders became the "butchers of Beijing." Isolated even in the developing world, the CCP regime had imposed on it swift sanctions by the advanced democracies. Human rights would thereafter powerfully drive U.S. domestic politics in policy making toward China.[18]

While much of the material retribution was short-lived, international scrutiny on China's human rights has proved tenacious. Western countries and Japan must now consider human rights in their dealings with China, albeit in a less than consistent fashion. President Clinton decided on May 28, 1993 to explicitly condition China's most-favored nation (MFN) trading status on the country's concrete human rights improvements. The futility of this linkage policy soon became obvious, and it was officially ended on May 26, 1994.[19] But the U.S. Congress continued to threaten to revoke China's MFN until September 2000. Even after formally granting China's permanent trade status, the United States kept the human rights issue alive either through continuous bilateral and multilateral pressure, the U.S. State Department's annual report, and various forms of congressional intervention or simply by emphasizing political values in its foreign policy.

With the end of the cold war, the energized governmental agenda on human rights in the West was complemented by the greatly mobilized international governmental organizations (IGOs) and nongovernmental organizations (NGOs) in taking to task China's human rights

---

[18] Robert S. Ross, "National Security, Human Rights, and Domestic Politics: The Bush Administration and China," in Kenneth Oye, Robert Lieber, and Donald Rothchild, eds., *Eagle in the New World: American Grand Strategy in the Post–Cold War Era* (New York: HarperCollins, 1992).

[19] For a detailed investigation of the linkage policy and its reversal, see David M. Lampton, "America's China Policy in the Age of the Finance Minister: Clinton Ends Linkage," *China Quarterly*, no. 139 (Sept. 1994), pp. 597–621. For an updated account, see David M. Lampton, *Same Bed, Different Dreams: Managing U.S.-China Relations, 1989–2000* (Berkeley: University of California Press, 2001), pp. 111–55.

record. Most remarkably, the UN Sub-commission on Prevention of Discrimination and Protection of Minorities passed a resolution condemning the Chinese government's systematic disregard of its citizens' rights in August 1989, an unprecedented act against a permanent member of the UN Security Council.[20] Two years later, the same UN institution again formally criticized Beijing's Tibetan policy. After that, however, the Sub-commission proved unable to sustain such pressure. The multilateral battle would then be waged mainly in the UN Commission on Human Rights (UNCHR) in Geneva, Switzerland.[21]

Between 1990 and 2004 (except for 1991, 1998, 2002, 2003, and 2005), democratic members of the UNCHR would press every year for a resolution censuring China's human rights record. No such attempt fully succeeded, and in nearly all cases resolutions sponsored by the United States and European states failed even to get through the vote on a "no action" motion tabled by China and its friends, such as Pakistan.[22] The only time such a resolution passed the procedural vote was in 1995, but the unexpected withdrawal of support by Russia for the substantive resolution left it one vote short. That was the closest – and, as it turned out, the last – real chance in fifteen years for the UNCHR to endorse a resolution censuring China's human rights practices. But the yearly exercises provided a stage where governments, transnational networks, NGOs (such as Asia Watch, Human Rights in China, and Amnesty International), individual activists (such as Harry Wu, Wei Jingsheng, Wang Dan, and the Dalai Lama) could bring to global attention a wide array of China's human rights problems. And the embattled CCP regime had to respond to these criticisms in one way or another.

---

[20] Ann Kent, "China and the International Human Rights Regime: A Case Study of Multilateral Monitoring, 1990–1994," *Human Rights Quarterly*, vol. 17 (1995), p. 4.

[21] For a comprehensive account, see Ann Kent, *China, the United Nations, and Human Rights: The Limits of Compliance* (Philadelphia: University of Pennsylvania Press, 1999), ch. 2.

[22] The complete vote tallies are reported by the Xinua News Agency, at http://news.xinhuanet.com/ziliao/2004-04/16/content_1423892.htm (accessed June 8, 2006). Chen Shiqiu, then a key member of China's diplomatic contingent in Geneva, recollects the first Chinese use of the "no action" tactic in Li Lingwei and Tao Tian, "Nanwang 16 Nianqian Nage Chuntian" [The Unforgettable Spring 16 Years Ago], *Renmin Ribao*, overseas edition (hereafter cited as *RMRB*), March 17, 2006, p. 6.

The Tiananmen incident marked the beginning of human right as a full-blown factor transforming the terms of China's engagement with the rest of the world. In the immediate aftermath of the event, the PRC became a pariah in the world community. And its human rights stigma raised fundamental questions about the character of the Chinese state as an international actor.[23] Soon, China was able to soften the pressure, but its negative political image continued to invite prejudiced treatment that significantly disadvantages its national interests.

Calling international human rights "the mandate of the twenty-first century," President Clinton publicly cast China "on the wrong side of history" during the official summit exchanges in 1997 and 1998.[24] Other American officials expressed their criticisms less bluntly than did Clinton, but the issue of China's illiberal polity has pervaded overall U.S. views on China. While conditioning trade on human rights has become a thing of the past, the United States has both explicitly and implicitly linked human rights with its overall treatment of China. Europe, Japan, and the United States may disagree on how best to facilitate that country's political liberalization, but they share more than they differ on the concern about China's human rights situation. And that concern figures in their policies toward it one way or another, although its actual impact depends heavily on the domestic politics in, and calculations of interests by, the countries involved.[25]

---

[23] James D. Seymour, "Human Rights in Chinese Foreign Relations," in Samuel S. Kim, ed., *China and the World: Chinese Foreign Relations in the Post–Cold War Era*, 3rd ed. (Boulder, CO: Westview Press, 1994), ch. 10; Andrew J. Nathan and Robert S. Ross, *The Great Wall and the Empty Fortress: China's Search for Security* (New York: W. W. Norton, 1997), ch. 10.

[24] See *New York Times*, Oct. 30, 1997, p. A14, and June 28, 1998, p. A1.

[25] On Sino-European relations, see David Shambaugh, *European and American Approaches to China: Different Beds, Same Dreams* (Washington, DC: Sigur Center for Asian Studies, George Washington University, 2002) and the special issue devoted to the subject in *China Quarterly*, no. 169 (March 2002), particularly Kay Moller, "Diplomatic Relations and Mutual Strategic Perceptions: China and the European Union," pp. 10–32; Eberhard Sandschneider, "China's Diplomatic Relations with the States of Europe," pp. 33–44. For a sample of studies on human rights in Japanese policy toward China, see Hoshino Eiichi, "Human Rights and Development Aid: Japan after the ODA Charter," in Peter Van Ness, *Debating Human Rights: Critical Essays from the United States and Asia* (New York: Routledge, 1999), pp. 199–230; Yasunobu Sato, "New Directions in Japanese Foreign Policy: Promoting Human Rights and Democracy in Asia," in Edward Friedman, ed., *The Politics of Democratization: Generalizing East Asian Experiences*

The rejuvenated human rights norm in world politics represented an unprecedented source of disadvantage the PRC had to wrestle with in its international relations.[26] The fear of political isolation might explain the paradox of dire security assessment by Chinese strategy analysts during much of the 1990s, when their country's physical security had never been better since the Opium War.[27] No longer dismissing Western rights concern as a burst of self-righteous Western outrage or anachronistic cold war mentality, prominent Chinese analysts have recognized the strategic liability that China's nondemocratic polity poses. The reality of value divergence between the two countries, they argue, inevitably hamstrings Sino-American relations, as it allows the United States to denigrate their country internationally. As a result, China does not enjoy the special bond of political values that underpin relations between the United States and other mainstream great powers.[28]

China's human rights stigma has no doubt contributed to international mistrust toward its intention. Due in small part to this problem, the United States and its democratic allies have withheld

(Boulder, CO: Westview Press, 1994), pp. 102–21; Yozo Yokota and Chiyuki Aoi, "Japan's Foreign Policy Towards Human Rights: Uncertain Changes," in David P. Forsythe, ed., *Human Rights and Comparative Foreign Policy* (Tokyo: United Nations University Press, 2000), pp. 115–45.

[26] For the literature highlighting the normative problem in Chinese foreign relations, see Samuel S. Kim, "China as a Great Power," *Current History*, Sept. 1997, pp. 246–51; Alastair Iain Johnston, "International Structures and Foreign Policy," in Samuel S. Kim, ed., *China and the World: Chinese Foreign Policy Faces the New Millennium*, 4th ed. (Boulder, CO: Westview Press, 1998), pp. 55–87; Rosemary Foot, "Chinese Power and the Idea of a Responsible State," *China Journal*, no. 45 (Jan. 2001), pp. 1–19.

[27] For enumeration of these potential dangers, see Xi Laiwang, *Ershiyi Shiji Zhonguo Zhanlue Da Chehua: Guojia Anquan Zhanlue* [Grand Strategic Plans for the 21st Century: China's Security Strategy] (Beijing: Hongqi Chubanshe, 1996); Yan Xuetong, *Zhongguo Guojia Liyi Fengxi* [Analysis of China's National Interests] (Tianjin, China: Tianjin Renmin Chubanshe, 1996).

[28] Wang Jisi, ed., *Wenming Yu Guoji Zhengzhi* [Civilizations and International Politics] (Shanghai: Shanghai Renmin Chubanshe, 1995), pp. 23, 189–90; Liu Jianfei, "Zhongguo Minzhu Zhengzhi Jianshe Yu Zhongmei Guanxi" [The Construction of Democratic Politics in China and Sino-U.S. Relations], *Zhanlue Yu Guanli*, no. 2 (2003), pp. 76–82; Yan Xuetong, *Meiguo Baquan Yu Zhongguo Anquan* [American Hegemony and Chinese Security] (Tianjin, China: Tianjin Renmin Chubanshe, 2000), pp. 3–31; Niu Jun, "Wushinian: Zhongguo Yu Shijie" [Fifty Years: China and the World], *Global Times*, at wysiwyg://7/http://www.snweb.com/gb/gnd/2000/1229/g1229001.htm (accessed Dec. 29, 2000).

status recognition of China and have been unwilling to respect its core security interests. The illiberal PRC polity has fueled the fear of Chinese power, particularly since the early 1990s. As Chapter 4 will detail, human rights were variously invoked in the China threat theories from afar in the West as well as in neighboring Asian countries. As the logic went, a regime egregiously violating the rights of its citizens should not be trusted to respect the rights and interests of other countries. The logic also allowed advocates for containing China to compare the PRC to Nazi Germany, fascist Italy and Japan, and the Soviet Union.[29] In parallel to this alarmist view in the West, the fear of China becoming the new "evil empire" that would warrant containment by the West and its regional allies in Asia was eminently palpable in Chinese writings from the time of Tiananmen through the mid-1990s.

While the worst strategic consequences did not materialize, the human rights problem has been firmly embedded in the public image of China in the United States and other advanced democracies. Democratic leaders must always balance other concerns and realpolitik often seems to trump morality. Yet no elected officials can afford to appear dismissive of this problem and sometimes they do sacrifice material gains over principle in their policy advocacy regarding the PRC.[30] Democratic governments and officials are, therefore, quite reticent about rewarding China on issues that may confer significant international prestige and acceptance. With this consideration, the U.S. Congress voted to publicly oppose China's bid for hosting the 2000 Olympic Games.[31] Human rights were also a key factor that long delayed formal summit exchanges between China and the United States in the 1990s. Even when they finally took place in 1997 and 1998, President Clinton made a point of publicly criticizing China's woeful state of political liberalization. Besides the rhetorical bluntness, the Clinton administration also took concrete steps to raise the human rights profile. Most notably, the White House appointed a special

---

[29] For a summary of containment arguments, see Yong Deng and Fei-ling Wang, "Introduction," in Yong Deng and Fei-ling Wang, eds., *In the Eyes of the Dragon: China Views the World* (Boulder, CO: Rowman & Littlefield, 1999), pp. 2–5.

[30] Ming Wan, *Human Rights in Chinese Foreign Relations: Defining and Defending National Interests* (Philadelphia: University of Pennsylvania Press, 2001).

[31] Ann Kent, "States Monitoring States: The United States, Australia, and China's Human Rights, 1990–2001," *Human Rights Quarterly*, vol. 23 (2001), p. 597.

coordinator on Tibetan Affairs within the State Department while President Jiang Zemin was visiting in the United States in October 1997. Exactly ten years later, in October 2007, the U.S. Congress awarded the Dalai Lama the Congressional Gold Medal and President George W. Bush held a high-profile meeting with the exiled spiritual leader of Tibet, casting limelight on Beijing's mistreatment of ethnic minority and religious rights at a time when the PRC seemed to have gained so much international influence.

After the Tiananmen incident, even though economic sanctions by the West were short-lived, concern about empowering the authoritarian CCP regime did have some effect in hindering China's foreign economic relations. The United States and other Western powers continued arms embargoes and related dual-use technology transfers control. Human rights problems also complicated Beijing's efforts to handle the issues of Hong Kong, Tibet, and Taiwan. The United States and other leading democracies were much less deferential to Beijing's interests as they contemplated at various times offering arms sales and security commitment to Taiwan, as well as moral support to the causes of the Dalai Lama and democrats in Hong Kong.[32]

Democratization in Taiwan exacerbated the division across the Strait, which is heavily defined and justified on the grounds of human rights. Capitalizing on Western favoritism toward democracies, pro-independence political entrepreneurs in Taiwan would always contrast the island's democracy with mainland China's one-party authoritarianism to provide a new rationale for the former's sovereignty claim.[33] A consistent thrust of Taiwan's diplomacy has been to simultaneously denigrate China and promote its own international status by underscoring the political value gap across the Strait. The logic behind this identity diplomacy is analogous to that of Israel's successful effort

---

[32] Michel Oksenberg, "Taiwan, Tibet, and Hong Kong in Sino-American Relations," in Ezra Vogel, ed., *Living with China: U.S.-China Relations in the Twenty-First Century* (New York: W. W. Norton, 1997); Nancy Bernkopf Tucker, *Taiwan, Hong Kong and the United States, 1945–1992* (New York: Twayne, 1994).

[33] Robert A. Madsen, "The Struggle for Sovereignty Between China and Taiwan," in Stephen D. Krasner, ed., *Problematic Sovereignty: Contested Rules and Political Possibilities* (New York: Columbia University Press, 2001), pp. 141–93; Shi Chih-Yu, "Human Rights as Identities: Difference and Discrimination in Taiwan's China Policy," in Van Ness, *Debating Human Rights*, pp. 144–63.

to solidify American support through cultivating the shared democratic identity in contrast to the neighboring authoritarian Arab states,[34] even though the outcomes of the two efforts have been quite different.

The industrialized democracies have shown a remarkable reluctance to contemplate the possibility of admitting China to the Group-8 club, lest its membership would grant the nondemocratic polity a key positive "status cue."[35] At the invitations of the hosting countries – France, Great Britain, Russia, and Germany – President Hu Jintao attended the G8 meetings in 2003, 2005, 2006, and 2007, indicating unprecedented Chinese involvement with this great-power club. China's growing economic clout clearly calls for a reconsideration of the G8's relationship with this rising power. But its political system has caused unease in this relationship by both parties. The group was prepared to intimately involve China, whose role has become increasingly important in dealing with the management of global issues, such as international financial stability, trade regime, and third world development. But nearly a decade into the new century, the great-power club was still not ready to welcome China's formal membership. The PRC, in turn, expressed no eagerness to join, so long as the group remains Western-dominated.

In many historical cases, a state's political denigration by the international community carried tremendous costs beyond its borders.[36] The contemporary world, the country targeted, and the issue involved make the Chinese case different. But the country is by no means immune to

[34] See Ministry of Foreign Affairs of the Republic of China (Taiwan), "Our Position on China's Rise," Dec. 27, 2005, in Foreign Broadcast Information Service (hereafter cited as FBIS): CPP20051227312007; Michael N. Barnett, "Identity and Alliances in the Middle East," in Peter Katzenstein, ed., *The Culture of National Security: Norm and Identity in World Politics* (New York: Columbia University Press, 1996), pp. 432–47.

[35] Robert S. Ross, "Engagement in U.S. China Policy," in Alastair Iain Johnston and Robert Ross, eds., *Engaging China: The Management of an Emerging Power* (New York: Routledge, 1999), p. 190. For a review of the literature on status cues in social psychology, see Joseph Berger, et al., "Status Cues, Expectations, and Behavior," *Social Psychology of Groups: A Reader* (Greenwich, CT: JAI Press, 1993).

[36] A general discussion along this line can be found in Deon Geldenhuys, *Isolated States: A Comparative Analysis* (Cambridge: Cambridge University Press, 1990). For a good example, see James Barber and John Barratt, *South Africa's Foreign Policy: The Search for Status and Security, 1945–1988* (Cambridge: Cambridge University Press, 1990).

similar impacts on its foreign relations. In fact, mainstream Chinese analysts have equated Western ideological bias as a main source of international disrespect of their country's core national interests and legitimate global aspirations. To the extent that established great powers judge China's international character based on its polity, human rights could set in motion a negative interactive pattern in the aspiring power's foreign relations. Indeed, the issue once threatened to escalate enmity and ignite an all-round cold war between the United States and China in the 1990s.[37] For some analysts, both inside and outside China, the value gap represents the most potent, intractable source of mistrust and hostility in America's China policy.[38]

To be sure, exigent concerns and material interests often trump political values in the day-to-day policy making of Washington and other Western capitals. Nonetheless, in the post–cold war and post-9/11 world, policy makers and public opinion leaders in the West have rather consistently promoted democratic values and human rights as bases for their countries' foreign policies. The upshot is a social identification that intensifies affinity with democracies and suspicion toward nondemocracies. Such unease with the PRC based on human rights, coupled with the strategic challenge posed by its rapidly growing power, has generated profound misgivings in international reactions to China's rise.

China Responds: Compliance and Resistance

In terms of socioeconomic rights and individual freedoms, post-Tiananmen China has made great strides, especially in comparison to its past. The People's Republic has seen unprecedented prosperity, albeit with great costs and uncertainties over its sustainability. The

---

[37] For an excellent discussion of human rights and strategic debate in the United States, see Peter Van Ness, "Addressing the Human Rights Issue in Sino-American Relations," *Journal of International Affairs*, vol. 49, no. 2 (Winter 1996), pp. 309–31.

[38] Zhu Feng offers a thoughtful analysis along these lines from a Chinese perspective in his "Human Rights Problems and Current Sino-American Relations," Van Ness, *Debating Human Rights*, pp. 232–54. For his broad analysis, see Zhu Feng, *Renquan Yu Guojiguanxi* [Human Rights and International Relations] (Beijing: Peking University Press, 2000). For an authoritative view of the U.S. perspective, see Aaron L. Friedberg, "The Future of U.S.-China Relations: Is Conflict Inevitable?" *International Security*, vol. 30, no. 2 (Fall 2005), pp. 7–45.

economic welfare of the populace as a whole has seen tremendous improvement, although income disparity has reached a spectacularly high level. Despite (or sometimes because of) its concern over domestic stability, the Chinese leadership has attempted institution building and reforms designed to cope with the new challenges and the exacerbated social discontent, on the one hand, and to maintain the vitality in the fast-changing domestic society and globalization, on the other.

The economic and social dynamism in China has unleashed myriad challenges to the CCP government. But the nation's good economic fortune has also temporarily lessened societal demand on civil and political rights.[39] There, the reach of transnational networks and NGOs on human rights is still very limited. For the sake of securing the CCP's leadership and domestic stability, the Chinese government has often found itself at odds with the international human rights regime. However, potent claims for respect of human rights from multilateral institutions such as the UNCHR, leading democracies, and NGOs did erode China's psychological and institutional barriers to receptivity to the international norm.[40] While pacing political change largely on its own terms, the Chinese government has made efforts to improve its rights-respecting record, most of which grew out of the necessity for domestic reforms. To rationalize measures essential for China's economic transition, such as the protection of private property, which had been in wide practice, the National People's Congress, the Chinese legislature, passed a comprehensive set of constitutional amendments in 2004 to that effect. This by no means settled the ownership issue, as illustrated by the ongoing, widespread disputes over the land rights of Chinese peasants. But it clearly helped set the direction for future reforms to have written into the constitution an explicit pledge to "respect and protect human rights," after similar expressions had previously appeared in other official documents.[41] Open embrace of

---

[39] See Ming Wan, "Chinese Views on Human Rights and Democracy," in Deng and Wang, *In the Eyes of the Dragon*, pp. 97–117; Minxin Pei, "Is China Democratizing," *Foreign Affairs*, vol. 77, no. 1 (1998), pp. 68–82.

[40] Two detailed studies are Ann Kent, *China, the United Nations, and Human Rights: The Limits of Compliance* (Philadelphia: University of Pennsylvania Press, 1999); Rosemary Foot, *Rights Beyond Borders: The Global Community and the Struggle over Human Rights in China* (New York: Oxford University Press, 2000).

[41] The Chinese constitution with the latest amendments is printed in *RMRB*, March 16, 2004. For Chinese interpretations of the significance, see Xu Xiang, "Uphold 'People-Centered' Concept, Respect and Protect Human Rights: Interview with

the idea even made its way in "the Chinese-Russian Joint Statement on the World Order of the Twenty-First Century," signed by Presidents Hu Jintao and Vladimir Putin on July 1, 2005. Article six of the statement explicitly recognizes the "universal" nature of human rights, albeit with qualifications that emphasize respect for "national conditions," "sovereignty," and "dialogue" in rights promotion.[42]

The Chinese government also felt pressured enough to defend its position in front of the world audience by issuing a stream of white papers on this subject after 1991. As regards formal commitment, the PRC has signed more than twenty international treaties on human rights.[43] Most notably, China signed the International Covenant on Economic, Social, and Cultural Rights (ICESCR) in 1997 and ratified it in 2001. Two years later, the PRC submitted to the UN Economic and Social Council its first action report pursuant to the treaty. Beijing also signed the International Covenant on Civil and Political Rights (ICCPR) in 1998, although a decade later it had not ratified the treaty. The difficulties stem from the reality that China's domestic practices fell far short of the demanding stipulations in the treaty. By the same token, eventual ratification, even with likely reservations, will significantly improve the legal recourse in China's human rights protection.[44]

Famous Constitutional Scholar and Chinese People's University Professor Xu Chongde," *Renquan*, no. 2 (April 1, 2004), pp. 29–30, in Open Source Center (hereafter cited as OSC): CPP20040608000233; Dong Yunhu, "Completely and Accurately Understand, Grasp, and Implement the Constitutional Principle of the State Respecting and Safeguarding Human Rights," *Renmin Ribao* (Internet), May 11, 2004, p. 10, in OSC: CPP20040511000049.

[42] "Zhonge Guanyu Ershiyi Siji Guoji Zhixu de Lianhe Shengmin" [Sino-Russian Joint Statement on the World Order of the 21st Century], *RMRB*, July 2, 2005, p. 4.

[43] "China Makes Achievements Through International Human Rights Exchange, Cooperation," at http://english.com.cn/200403/30/print20040330_138915.html (accessed Jan. 5, 2005).

[44] Li Ling, "Zhongguo Pizhun 'Gongmin Quanli He Zhengzhi Quanli Guojigongyue' Xuyao Jiejue De Jige Wenti" [Several Problems to Be Resolved in China's Ratification of the 'International Covenant on Civil and Political Rights,'" in Zhou Qi, ed., *Renquan Yu Waijiao* [Human Rights and Diplomacy] (Beijing: Shishi Chubanshe, 2002), pp. 276–97; Mo Jihong, "Liange Guoji Renquan Gongyue Xia Diyueguo De Yiwu Yu Zhongguo" [The Obligations of the Country Signatory to the Two Human Rights Conventions and China], at http://iwep.org.cn/chinese/workingpape/zgygjzz/17.pdf (accessed Dec. 2004).

Table 3.1. *Major International Human Rights Treaties China Had Signed by 2007*

Treaties	Date of Signature	Date of Ratification
Convention against Torture and Other Cruel, Inhuman or Degrading Treatment or Punishment	1986	1988
Convention Relating to the Status of Refugees	NA	1982
Convention on the Prevention and Punishment of the Crime of Genocide	NA	1983
International Convention on the Elimination of All Forms of Racial Discrimination	NA	1982
International Convention on the Suppression and Punishment of the Crime of Apartheid	NA	1983
Protocol Relating to the Status of Refugees	NA	1982
Convention on the Rights of the Child	NA	1991
International Labor Organization Equal Remuneration Convention	NA	1990
Convention on the Elimination of All Forms of Discrimination against Women	1980	1980
International Covenant on Economic, Social, and Cultural Rights	1997	2001
International Covenant on Civil and Political Rights	1998	Not yet ratified
Geneva Conventions (All Four)	NA	1956
Geneva Conventions, Protocol I: Protocol Additional to the Geneva Conventions of 12 August 1949, and Relating to the Protection of Victims of International Armed Conflicts	1983	1983
Geneva Conventions, Protocol II: Protocol Additional to the Geneva Conventions of 12 August 1949, and Relating to the Protection of Victims of Non-International Armed Conflicts	1983	1983
UN Convention on the Rights of Persons with Disabilities	2007	Not yet ratified

Sources: Mo Jihong, "Liangge Guoji Renquan Gongyue Xia Diyueguo De Yiwu Yu Zhongguo" [The Obligations of the Country Signatory to the Two Human Rights Conventions and China], pp. 5–6, at http://iwep.org.cn/chinese/workingpaper/ zgygjzz/17.pdf (accessed Dec. 4, 2004); International Committee of the Red Cross, at http://www.icrc.org/Web/eng/siteeng0.nsf/htmlall/party_gc/$File/Conventions%20 de%20GenSve%20et%20Protocoles%20additionnels%20ENG;logo.pdf (accessed Jan. 5, 2005); Xinhua, March 31, 2007, at http://news.xinhuanet.com/ english/2007-03/31/content_5918968.htm.

Along with increasing treaty accession, China's international out-look has become receptive to the idea of human rights as well. The first human rights white paper published by the State Council Information Office in 1991 officially accepted the idea as compatible with Chinese socialism, in contrast to previous eras when human rights were thor-oughly rejected as a corrupt "bourgeois slogan."[45] Two years later, the first nominally nongovernmental organization, the China Society for Human Rights Studies, was created to engage the emerging mul-tilevel global advocacy network on human rights. Since its inception, the organization has represented Chinese positions through its pub-lications and media exposure, participation in international forums, and sponsorship of conferences and dialogues with other NGOs and individual scholars. It has facilitated a semiofficial Chinese track of human rights diplomacy. According to Ann Kent, "[B]y 1993, China had abandoned the non-intervention argument as its principal defense, and had indicated a measure of acquiescence with the human rights norms in the International Bill of Rights and the [1993] Vienna Decla-ration."[46] Through much of the 1990s, the Chinese government made available generous grants to support research and lent its blessing on numerous national and international conferences on human rights. The country also witnessed a publication boom on human rights, having issued a stunning number of books on the subject, although most of them were geared to countering Western criticisms and interferences.[47]

The ideational evolution is evident in the discourse on interna-tional relations in general in China. Wang Yizhou, the long-time deputy director of the Institute of World Economics and Politics at the Chinese Academy of Social Sciences, has been the most outspo-ken liberal-oriented scholar in this regard. Since the mid-1990s, he has consistently argued for the inclusion of human rights in the Chi-nese notion of sovereignty. For him, the need for such new think-ing stems from an obligation essential for contemporary great-power recognition as well as an imperative of national security in the age

---

[45] Dong Yunhu, "Completely and Accurately Understand, Grasp, and Implement the Constitutional Principle," quotes on p. 2.

[46] Kent, "China and the International Human Rights Regime," p. 40.

[47] *Human Rights Dialogue*, vol. 6 (Sept. 1996), p. 4; The Information Office of the State Council, "Zhongguo Renquan Shiye De Jinbu" [Progress in China's Human Rights Cause], *RMRB*, Dec. 28, 1995, p. 5.

of neo-interventionism.[48] Wang's arguments implicitly underscore the undeniable negative impact of human rights on both China's security interests and its international reputation. His views reflect those of forward-looking Chinese scholars who have come to appreciate that their nation's status advancement abroad cannot be divorced from political reforms at home, nor can human rights be brushed aside as merely outdated "cold war mentality." Instead, their country must find a way to reconcile sovereignty with human rights and to seriously address the political origin of China's foreign policy predicament. Such rethinking on human rights, when articulated on nationalist grounds, becomes hard to refute by their conservative Chinese colleagues in or out of academe.

While partially embracing the rights norm, China has also resisted theories and practices that the CCP leadership deems unacceptable. Concerns for social stability under the CCP rule and nationalism have been the main causes behind setbacks to political liberalization at home and rejection of human rights pressure abroad.[49] The dual concerns were most dramatically expressed in China's State Council response to the U.S. State Department Human Rights Report in 1995. In the Chinese rebuttal, Beijing attributed U.S. criticisms to hostility to the CCP regime and the ulterior American motive to "demonize, destabilize, and contain China." [50] The government's views resonated in Chinese society, insofar as Western criticisms on human rights were equated

---

[48] Representative of his views are Wang Yizhou, "Establishing a New Sovereignty Concept at the Turn of the Century," *Liaowang*, no. 29, July 17, 2000, pp. 8–11, in FBIS: CPP20000725000088; Wang Yizhou, SARS Yu Feichuantong Anquan [SARS and Nontraditional Security], at http://www.iwep.org.cn/zhengzhi/SARSyufeichuantonganquan_wan (accessed Sept. 10, 2003); Wang Yizhou, *Quanqiu Zhengzhi He Zhongguo Waijiao* [Global Politics and Chinese Diplomacy] (Beijing: Shijie Zhishi Chubanshe, 2003).

[49] Suisheng Zhao, "Chinese Intellectuals' Quest for National Greatness and Nationalistic Writing in the 1990s, *China Quarterly*, no. 152 (Dec. 1997), pp. 725–45; Feng Chen, "Order and Stability in Social Transition: Neoconservative Political Thought in Post-1989 China," *China Quarterly*, no. 151 (Sept. 1997), pp. 593–613; Joseph Fewsmith, "Neoconservatism and the End of the Dengist Era," *Asian Survey*, vol. 35, no. 7 (July 1995), pp. 635–51.

[50] The Information Office of the State Council, "Weihu Renquan Haishi Ganshe Neizheng?" [Promoting Human Rights or Interfering with Domestic Affairs?], *RMRB*, March 29, 1996, pp. 1, 3.

with a design to hold back China's rightful quest for great-power status.

The Chinese government is particularly irate at the public statements by Western governments castigating its human rights abuse, as, in the words of Jack Vincent, the issue "touches nerves concerned with the quality of one's domestic government."[51] It refuses to accept either the tactic or the substance of such accusations. Chinese leaders would concede that their human rights record is far from desirable, but they reject suggestions that China's inadequate rights protection is a reflection of its inferior polity. Thus, the Chinese government has since 1999 issued its own annual report on the U.S. human rights record to counter the State Department's annual human rights report documenting abuses and shaming the abusers. Initially under a pseudonym, the Chinese counter report was soon released as the work of the Information Office of the PRC State Council.[52]

Rejections of U.S. human rights policy as driven by deliberate bias and anti-China motives intensified, when the government felt acutely threatened by destabilizing domestic forces and international isolation.[53] Sacrosanct notions of sovereignty impervious to human rights pressure were invariably hardened during nationalist crises over Taiwan and in relationship with the West in broad terms, such as NATO's mistaken bombing of the Chinese embassy in Belgrade in May 1999. However, mainstream Chinese views have always suspected Western intent in using humanitarianism to justify power politics. While more open than ever before to reinterpretation of sovereignty, they have emphasized sovereignty as the precondition for human rights.[54] Such

---

[51] R. J. Vincent, *Human Rights and International Relations* (Cambridge: Cambridge University Press, 1986), p. 138.

[52] Xiong Zhengyan, "Zhuanfang Yang Zhengquan" [Special Interview with Yang Zhengquan], at http://news.xinhuanet.com/world/2007-03/19/content_5865848.htm (accessed March 19, 2007).

[53] Harry Harding, "Breaking the Impasse over Human Rights," in Vogel, *Living with China*. A succinct review of Chinese commentators' responses to the U.S. human rights policy can be found in Yang Yusheng, *Zhongguoren De Meiguoguan: Yige Lishi de Kaocha* [Chinese Views on America: A Historical Perspective] (Shanghai: Fudan Daxue Chubanshe, 1996), p. 280.

[54] A balanced, cogent review of Chinese rethinking is Wang Jun, "Zhongguo De Zhuquan Wenti Yanjiu" [Research on Sovereignty in China], in Wang Yizhou, ed., *Zhongguo Guoji Guanxi Yanjiu (1995–2005)* [IR Studies in China (1995–2005)] (Beijing: Beijing University Press, 2006), pp. 350–4. See also Zhou Qi,

reactions can be explained as much by realist concerns as by the CCP regime's insecurity and the traumatic century-long nationalist experience as a semicolony at the hands of self-righteous imperial powers after the Opium War of 1839–42.[55]

China's resistance strategy has focused on contesting the human rights norm, downplaying political differences in bilateral foreign relations, dividing the democratic alliance, blocking public censure by UN bodies, and minimizing multilateral pressures. By the late 1990s, it had achieved important successes on these fronts. Most notably, the PRC was able to move the main platform of its human rights diplomacy from the multilateral UN commission, whose negative opinions particularly concerned Beijing, to various bilateral "dialogues" prone to power plays and cynical manipulation.[56] Beijing's vehemence in standing its ground and energetic diplomacy have defused unified international pressure and dissuaded Western governments from making explicit linkage between human rights and specific policy issues.

Regaining Lost Ground Through Revisionism

The mixed record of China's human rights compliance has handicapped its foreign relations. To compensate for or remedy this political liability, the PRC has pursued a broad revisionist strategy. The revisionism is two-fold: to change the standard of great-power recognition and to reshape the human rights discourse itself.

Human Rights and Diplomacy, part 4; Liu Wenzhong, et al., "'Renquan Gaoyu Zhuquan' Shi Jiekou" ["Human Rights Superseding Sovereignty" Is an Excuse], *RMRB*, March 17, 2006, p. 6.

[55] Onuma Yasuaki, "Toward an Intercivilizational Approach to Human Rights," in Joanne R. Bauer and Daniel A. Bell, eds., *The East Asian Challenge for Human Rights* (New York: Cambridge University Press, 1999), pp. 104–6.

[56] "Behind Closed Doors: Bilateral Dialogues on Human Rights," *China Rights Forum*, no. 2 (2003), pp. 22–9; Kent, *China, the United Nations, and Human Rights*; Foot, *Rights Beyond Borders*; Kent, "States Monitoring States," pp. 583–624; Wan, *Human Rights in Chinese Foreign Relations*. On Beijing's ultrasensitivity to multilateral shaming, see Merle Goldman, "The Importance of Human Rights in U.S. Policy Toward China," in Thomas A. Metzger and Ramon H. Myers, eds., *Greater China and U.S. Foreign Policy: The Choice Between Confrontation and Mutual Respect* (Stanford, CA: Hoover Institution Press, 1996), pp. 76–83.

China's notion of its proper role in the world after the cold war was initially focused on crisis management designed not to aggravate its isolation. To rejoin the global mainstream, the PRC soon began to showcase its cooperative diplomacy while making concessions, or what Jack Donnelly calls "side payments to third parties," in its international behavior.[57] Indeed, Beijing abstained, instead of exercising its veto, in the UN vote on the use of force against Iraq after its invasion of Kuwait in August 1989.[58] Similar motivation to replenish lost legitimacy was also well documented in China's compliance behaviors on weapons proliferations and arms control, including acceding to the Non-Proliferation Treaty (NPT) in March 1992 and the Comprehensive Test Ban Treaty (CTBT) in 1996.[59] More broadly, Andrew Nathan has linked the Chinese government's moral deficit in human rights to conciliatory foreign policy in economic and security areas.[60] Other scholars, too, have shown that China's domestic fragility and need as a nondemocracy to curry international legitimacy actually contributed to its risk-averse, cooperative orientations abroad.[61]

These behaviors, often associated with good citizenship in the international society, did in no small measure mend Beijing's tattered image. Such motivation later evolved into a concerted, proactive effort to project a responsible image. Although the notion of responsibility is

---

[57] Donnelly, *International Human Rights*, p. 126. Rodney B. Hall similarly emphasizes the diplomatic value of political values in his "Moral Authority as a Power Resource," *International Organization*, vol. 51, no. 4 (Autumn 1997), pp. 591–622.

[58] See Harding, *A Fragile Relationship*, pp. 270–5.

[59] Joseph Nye, Jr., "China's Re-emergence and the Future of the Asia-Pacific," *Survival*, vol. 39, no. 4 (Winter 1997/98), p. 73; Banning Garrett and Bonnie Glaser, "Chinese Perspectives on Nuclear Arms Control," *International Security*, vol. 20, no. 3 (Winter 1995/96), pp. 43–78.

[60] Andrew Nathan, "China: Getting Human Rights Right," *Washington Quarterly*, vol. 22, no. 2 (Spring 1997), pp. 135–51; Andrew Nathan, "China and the International Human Rights Regime," in Elizabeth Economy and Michel Oksenberg, eds., *China Joins the World: Progress and Prospects* (New York: Council on Foreign Relations Press, 1999), pp. 136–60.

[61] Jianwei Wang, "Coping with China as a Rising Power," in James Shinn, ed., *Weaving the Net: Conditional Engagement with China* (New York: Council on Foreign Relations Press, 1996), pp. 133–74; Fei-ling Wang, "Beijing's Incentive Structure: The Pursuit of Preservation, Prosperity, and Power," in Yong Deng and Fei-ling Wang, eds., *China Rising: Power and Motivation in Chinese Foreign Policy* (Boulder, CO: Rowman & Littlefield, 2005), pp. 19–49.

highly contested, it certainly is meant to shift the focus of international legitimacy away from domestic polity to emphasize instead on the state's external behavioral patterns. As such, positive recognition comes from the state being generally participatory in international institutions as well as being constructive and cooperative in foreign policy choices.[62]

In tandem with aligning itself with the idea of responsibility, the PRC has undertaken a global diplomatic campaign to promote a world vision that values pluralism, sovereignty, and its own brand of "peace-and-development" diplomacy. The idea is to minimize human rights as a yardstick for international standing.[63] For Beijing, international focus on the transnational value not only threatens sovereignty, but also justifies discrimination against nondemocratic states. As an influential Chinese analyst writes, "[T]he goals of the post–Cold War international struggles are not only limited to a rivalry for a position of strength, but are expressed even more so in rivalry over the moral and legal high ground."[64] Thus, an important part of China's struggle to regain its lost political ground is to undermine Western promotion of the authoritative claims of universal human rights.

Thus, the PRC has by no means shied away from contesting what it believes to be Western domination of the human rights discourse and self-serving deployment of the standard itself. It has tried to steer attention toward its own areas of comparative advantage in social and economic rights, while at the same time it has promoted relativism on human rights and in international relations in general. After the Tiananmen incident, realizing the futility of rebuttal to Western criticisms based on rigid sovereignty and Marxist class analysis, the

---

[62] For dissections of the Chinese idea of responsibility, see Wang Yizhou, *Global Politics and Chinese Diplomacy*, pp. 307–24; Johnston, "International Structures and Chinese Foreign Policy;" Zhang Yongjin and Greg Austin, eds., *Power and Responsibility in Chinese Foreign Policy* (Canberra, Australia: Asia Pacific Press, 2001); Hongying Wang, "National Image Building and Chinese Foreign Policy," in Deng and Wang, *China Rising*, pp. 73–102.

[63] For the logic of promoting an alternative great-power standard, see Debroah W. Larson and Alexei Shevchenko, "Shortcut to Greatness: The New Thinking and the Revolution in Soviet Foreign Policy," *International Organization*, vol. 57, no. 1 (Winter 2003), pp. 77–109.

[64] Su Ge, "The New World Order and International Security," Guoji Wentiyanjiu, Nov. 13, 2000, pp. 7–12, in FBIS: CPP20001215000148, quote on p. 6.

Chinese government had by the early 1990s propounded what it calls a "comprehensive" notion of human rights that considers political-civil rights, socioeconomic rights, individual and collective rights, and national developmental rights as "mutually interdependent and indivisible."[65]

China's relativist arguments emphasize a country's cultural, societal, and economic conditions in determining its human rights practices. Some of these views can be found in relevant international agreements, and they have been invoked in the North-South dispute over human rights. As such, China's positions have received sympathetic hearing in the third world. Most notably, in the 1990s the PRC found allies in many of its neighboring countries, such as Singapore, Malaysia, and Indonesia, whose elites were intent on propounding a set of "Asian values" supposedly distinctive from the Western standard.[66] With support from developing countries, Beijing was able to escape censure by rights-related IGOs, particularly the UNCHR.[67] At the beginning of the new century, the PRC has emphasized mutual respect of civilizations and international dialogue as the right way to promote human rights. Such positions have had much traction in the third-world states unnerved by the value-based Western foreign policy. Their votes were instrumental

---

[65] Wang Xinfang, ed., *Zhongguo Yu Lianheguo* [China and the United Nations] (Beijing: Shijie Zhishi Chubanshe, 1995), ch. 15. On developmental rights, see Pitman B. Porter, "The Chinese Legal System (?): Continuing Tensions over Norms and Enforcement," in Joseph Y. S. Cheng, ed., *China Review 1998* (Hong Kong: Chinese University Press, 1998), pp. 25–59; Michael J. Sullivan, "Developmentalism and China's Human Rights Policy," Van Ness, *Debating Human Rights*, pp. 120–43.

[66] See Denny Roy, "Singapore, China, and the 'Soft' Authoritarian Challenge," *Asian Survey*, vol. 34 (March 1994), pp. 231–42; Geoffrey Robinson, "Human Rights in Southeast Asia: Rhetoric and Reality," in David Wurfel and Bruce Burton, eds., *Southeast Asia in the New World Order* (New York: St. Martin's Press, 1996); Sidney Jones, "The Impact of Asian Economic Growth on Human Rights," in James Shinn, ed., *Fires Across the Water: Transnational Problems in Asia* (New York: Council on Foreign Relations Press, 1998); Foot, *Rights Beyond Borders*, pp. 153–57; Van Ness, *Debating Human Rights*. The best multidisciplinary treatment of the "Asian values" debate is Bauer and Bell, *The East Asian Challenge for Human Rights*. For a comprehensive study of the Asian views on human rights from a Chinese perspective, see Luo Yanhua, *Dongfangren Kanrenquan: Dongya Guojia Renquaguan Toushi* [East Asians View Human Rights: Dissecting East Asian Nations' Human Rights Views] (Beijing: Xinhua Press, 1998).

[67] Kent, *China, the United Nations, and Human Rights*.

in securing China a seat at the newly created UN Human Rights Council (UNHRC) in 2006 in lieu of the Geneva-based commission (UNCHR).

In the debate leading up to the creation of the UNHRC, China was highly skeptical of the reform ideas that would favor democracies in membership selection and provide a sustained monitoring of the human rights practices across the world. In its policy statement on the UN reforms released in June 2005, the PRC explicitly called for greater attention to social and economic rights and variegated national conditions. Complaining that Western "'Witch-hunters' twisted the function of the old commission from promoting human rights world-wide to naming and shaming governments not to their liking,"[68] the Chinese government maintained in the document that "the key for UN reforms is to reverse the reality of politicizing the human rights issue." Preferring to treat human rights as a matter of "technical coop-eration" between sovereign states, Beijing reiterated its opposition to any scheme that "categorizes countries into 'democracies' and 'non-democracies.'"[69] With these these considerations, on top of its eco-nomic and energy interests, China, together with Russia and South Africa, vetoed a U.S. and British resolution in the UN Security Coun-cil in January 2007 criticizing Myanmar's (Burma's) human rights abuse.[70] When the military junta violently put down the widespread protests led by the monks in the fall of the same year, Beijing went along with a UN Security Council statement critizing the act, but made it abundantly clear its opposition to any sanction that might jeapodize the survival of the Yangon (Rangoon) regime.

In some ways, the events after the terrorist attacks in the United States on September 11, 2001 have reduced the impact of human rights on China's foreign relations in general. For one preeminent Chinese analyst, just as Sadam Hussein's invasion of Kuwait in 1989 helped

---

[68] Xiong Lei, "Turning Attention to True Human Rights Abusers," *China Daily* (Internet), June 20, 2006, in OSC: CPP20060620078001, p. 1.

[69] "Zhongguo Zhengfu Fabu Guanyu Lianheguo Gaige Wenti De Lichang Wenjian" [The Chinese Government Issues Position Documents on UN Reforms], Xinhua, June 8, 2005, at http://news.xinhuanet.com/newscenter/2005-06/08/content_3056790.htm (accessed July 13, 2005).

[70] "Miandian Ganxie Zhongguo Foujue Yingmei Caoan" [Myanmar Grateful for China's Veto on British-U.S. Draft Resolution], *Wuhan Morning News*, Jan. 19, 2007, at http://www.cnhan.com/GB/content/2007-01/19/content_736004.htm.

end China's diplomatic isolation following Tiananmen, so, too, were the 9/11 terrorist attacks critical in restoring the Sino-American relationship, which had spun downward in the preceding months.[71] The pressing needs to combat terrorism and the proliferation of weapons of mass destruction (WMD) have sometimes overshadowed the strategic and political difference between the two countries.

   This does not mean that human rights are removed from American policy toward China. Rather, the emphasis by President George W. Bush's administration on the spread of democracy and liberal values in the U.S. foreign policy underscored the long-term political problem that human rights pose for Sino-American relations.[72] Indeed, official U.S. statements from the National Security Strategy released in September 2002 to the U.S. State Department human rights report to speeches by President Bush and other key U.S. foreign policy makers continued to highlight the value gap separating China and the United States. Tellingly, after a two-year hiatus, Washington decided to sponsor a resolution on China at the 2004 UNCHR meeting. Awarding the Congresssional Gold Medal to the Dalai Lama, in tandem with his high-level treatment by the White House three years later, triggered a mini-crisis in the Sino-American relationship in fall 2007, but had similar effect in raising broader questions about the character of the Chinese polity. China's diplomatic and economic ties to rights-abusive regimes across the world have also raised concern about the political implications of its great-power rise.[73]

   While the Bush administration labeled in 2002 the Chinese Uighur Muslim group, East Turkestan Islamic Movement (ETIM), as a terrorist organization, top American officials also warned Beijing against

---

[71] Jin Canrong, "An Assessment of Two Types of New Factors in China's International Environment," *Xiandai Guoji Guanxi*, no. 2, Nov. 20, 2002, pp. 7–9, in FBIS: CPP20021206000159.

[72] For scholarly treatments of the post-9/11 U.S. strategy, see Robert Jervis, "Understanding the Bush Doctrine," *Political Science Quarterly*, vol. 118, no. 3 (Fall 2003), pp. 365–88; Philip Zelikow, "The Transformation of National Security," *National Interest* (Spring 2003), pp. 17–28; John Lewis Gaddis, "A Grand Strategy of Transformation," *Foreign Policy*, Nov./Dec. 2002, pp. 50–57. For a discussion of the relevance of the Bush strategy to China concerning human rights, see Rosemary Foot, "Bush, China and Human Rights," *Survival*, vol. 45, no. 2 (Summer 2003), pp. 167–86.

[73] Gary J. Bass, "China's Unsavory Friends," *Washington Post*, April 23, 2006, p. B5.

interpreting this as a green light for a ethnic and religious crackdown in Xinjiang. When fifteen or so Uighur detainees at Guantanamo Bay were ready for release in 2005, the United States declined to hand them over to the Chinese government out of a human rights concern.[74] Five were eventually sent to Albania in May 2006, which incensed China.[75]

The post-9/11 events have no doubt created a more relaxed international environment and new platforms for China's great-power diplomacy. The urgency of fighting terror and curbing WMD proliferation allowed Beijing to earn international recognition on both fronts. While concerned about the way the war was waged, China supported various aspects of the U.S. global antiterror campaign, including the war on the Taliban in Afghanistan and other nonmilitary areas of transnational cooperation. On the WMD front, Beijing's role in brokering and hosting the first trilateral talks and then the Six-Party Talks on the North Korean nuclear crisis earned China important international recognition. The PRC also skillfully used its influence at the UN to similar effect. The U.S. preoccupation with fighting a broad war on terror also allowed Beijing to showcase its win-win, cooperative diplomacy, which effectively brought its growing economic power to bear in boosting its great-power status.[76]

Occurrences of rights disrespect in the U.S. war on terror hampered its global leadership in criticizing China on human rights. Official Chinese media seized the Abu Ghraib prison scandal in 2004 to reinforce the point that human rights were impossible without state sovereignty and national security. The "Chinese Report on U.S. Human Rights Record in 2006," released in March 2007, devoted a whole section to

---

[74] David S. Cloud and Ian Johnson, "Friend or Foe," *Wall Street Journal*, Aug. 3, 2004, p. 1; Adam Wolfe, "China's Uighurs Trapped at Guantanamo," *Asian Times*, Aug. 4, 2004, at http://www.atimes.com/atimes/China/FK04Ad02.html (accessed Jan. 18, 2005); Robin Wright, "Chinese Detainees Are Men Without a Country," *Washington Post*, Aug. 24, 2005, pp. A1, A4.

[75] "China Demands Repatriation of the Five Terror Suspects," *People's Daily*, at http://english.people.com.cn/200605/10/eng20060510_264381.html (accessed June 6, 2006).

[76] Robert L. Suettinger, "The Rise and Descent of 'Peaceful Rise,'" *China Leadership Monitor*, Fall 2004, at http://www.chinaleadershipmonitor.org/20044/rs.html (accessed Dec. 12, 2004); T. Taylor and Evan Medeiros, "China's New Diplomacy," *Foreign Affairs*, vol. 82, no. 6 (Nov./Dec. 2003), pp. 22–35; Yong Deng and Thomas G. Moore, "China Views Globalization: Towards a New Great Power Politics," *Washington Quarterly*, vol. 27, no. 3 (Summer 2004), pp. 117–36.

detailing how the United States mistreated foreign nationals and committed atrocities in Afghanistan and Iraq. [77] The fissures between the United States and its major European allies about the Iraq war aggravated divisions among leading democracies, thereby reducing Western unity on human rights vis-à-vis China. Such transatlantic disunity was most dramatically demonstrated in the invigorated EU efforts to lift the arms embargo on China imposed after the Tiananmen crackdown, in open defiance of the U.S. opposition during 2004–5. Strenuous U.S. pressures eventually succeeded in maintaining the arms ban. Beijing's failure to remove the EU measure, which it complained was discriminatory, underscores the persistent political handicap that human rights poses to China's diplomacy.

Chinese leaders have stressed that a key feature separating their country's international path from great-power politics of the past is their lack of interest in exporting China's developmental model. However, human rights are intricately linked to China's international relations in a fundamental way since the end of the cold war. To be sure, the role of human rights has evolved along with the changing dynamics in world politics. Yet, to the extent that it constitutes a normative pillar of the world order, it exerts a pervasive impact on how states are treated in the international society. Human rights cannot be simply trumped by power or bargained away. As China's influence and interests expand abroad, the issue of its ties with autocratic regimes from neighboring Myanmar to far-away Sudan has come under international scrutiny. With China's growing global reach, its purportedly politically neutral foreign policy has become increasingly problematic.

---

[77] Information Office of the State Council, "2006 Nian Meiguo De Renquan Jilu" [The U.S. Human Rights Record in 2006], *RMRB*, March 9, 2007, pp. 5–6

4 | *Reacting to "China Threat Theories"*

The so-called "China threat theories," are essentially foreign attributions to China as having a harmful, destabilizing, and even pernicious international disposition. If human rights raise questions about China's polity and its possible foreign policy ramifications, the notion of a "China threat" has more direct bearing on how the rising power is treated abroad. As such, the battle over China threat theories has taken center stage, where the action-reaction concerning the international politics surrounding the People's Republic China (PRC) has played out.

To decipher this interactive process, I draw on the concept of the "security dilemma," but I make and demonstrate two propositions dissimilar to the standard realist expositions. First, states rely on each other's reputed character to infer intentions and to determine treatment accordingly. In the post–cold war world of U.S. hegemony and great-power peace, a state's threat reputation leads to social derogation and out-group status, which in turn intensifies the security dilemma logic in the international reaction to its power. As an emerging power, the status-conscious PRC has been doubly sensitive to the dynamics of this reputation. Second, given the clear stakes involved, the defamed state will be motivated to take corresponding steps, and may succeed, to secure power and acceptance. The way China has managed its foreign relations has shown that the security dilemma in contemporary world politic is potent but not ineluctable.

Threat Reputation and the Security Dilemma: A Reconsideration

Mainstream realism and deterrence theory argue that establishing a reputation for power and a resolve to carry out security commitments is paramount in the state's security policy. Typical of this view is Hans Morgenthau's approach to "prestige." For him, the state's "policy of prestige" is about its "reputation for power," whose purpose "is to impress other nations with the power one's own nation actually possesses, or with the power it believes, or wants the other nations to believe, it possesses." The cardinal sin for policy makers is to "be satisfied with a reputation for power which is inferior to the actual power possessed," as such a "negative policy of prestige" invites foreign predation.[1]

Similarly, deterrence theory equates reputation with the credibility of a state's resolve to protect its core interests.[2] For Thomas Schelling, the state's "reputation for action . . . consisting of other countries' beliefs (their leaders' beliefs, that is) about how the country can be expected to behave . . . is one of the few things worth fighting over."[3] Underscoring the security benefits of a tough image, neither Morgenthau nor Schelling had much to say about why contemporary China should be so terribly upset by foreign fear purported in the China threat theory. In fact, Schelling contended that "impetuosity, irrationality, and automaticity" [sic] boost deterrence.[4] In this vein, the negative costs of a bad repute do not concern those scholars preoccupied with the imperatives of power struggle and deterrence credibility under international anarchy.

Insofar as it can be used to illuminate the negative security consequences of a state's dangerous reputation, the notion of security dilemma may offer a basis for understanding Chinese sensitivities and aversions to the China threat theories. According to its proponents, the security dilemma is pervasive under international relations, as states, uncertain of each other's intentions, are engaged in worst-case security

---

[1] Hans Morgenthau, *Politics among Nations: The Struggle for Power,* 4th ed. (New York: Knopf, 1967), ch. 6, quotes on pp. 70, 76, 80. Robert Gilpin makes similar points in his *War and Change in World Politics* (New York: Cambridge University Press, 1981), pp. 31–3.

[2] See Paul Huth, "Reputations and Deterrence: A Theoretical and Empirical Assessment," *Security Studies,* vol. 7, no. 1 (Autumn 1997), pp. 75–8. For critical reviews of the deterrence literature, see Huth, "Reputations and Deterrence," *ibid,* pp. 72–99; Jonathan Mercer, *Reputation in International Relations* (Ithaca, NY: Cornell University Press, 1996), ch. 1; Dale Copeland, "Do Reputations Matter?" *Security Studies,* vol. 7, no. 1 (Autumn 1997), pp. 33–71.

[3] Thomas C. Schelling, *Arms and Influence* (New Haven, CT: Yale University Press, 1966), p. 124. For a similar definition of image, see Robert Jervis, *The Logic of Images in International Relations* (Princeton, NJ: Princeton University Press, 1970), p. 5.

[4] Schelling, *Arms and Influence,* p. 40.

planning. They tend to view power and security as zero-sum and in relative terms. Hence, a state's supposedly security-enhancing capabilities and behaviors become threatening to other states triggering responses in kind. Such a vicious action-reaction spiral leads to competitive arms build-up and an unmitigated power struggle.[5]

The literature on the security dilemma attributes the perpetual source of state insecurity to the anarchic nature of international relations. Under anarchy, it contends, states should not be overly worried about how their security-motivated measures are interpreted; inaction is not an option. Even if they did, there would not be much they could do to change others' reactions. For Kenneth Waltz, "[S]tates have to live with their security dilemma, which is produced not by their wills but by their situations. A dilemma cannot be solved; it can more or less readily be dealt with." And a robust mutual nuclear deterrence is what the most states (i.e., great powers for Waltz) can do.[6] Indeed, during the cold war the Soviet initiative of peaceful coexistence, begun in the mid-1950s, was essentially an attempt to use nuclear deterrence as the "answer" to its security dilemma with the West.[7]

With similar belief about the structural sources of the security dilemma, Robert Jervis laments, "The central theme of international relations is not evil but tragedy."[8] For him, the security dilemma is fundamentally driven by "the inability [of states] to recognize that one's own actions could be seen as menacing and the concomitant

---

[5] Robert Jervis, *Perception and Misperception in International Politics* (Princeton, NJ: Princeton University Press, 1976); Jervis, "Cooperation under the Security Dilemma," *World Politics* vol. 30, no. 2 (Jan. 1978), pp. 167–214; Charles L. Glaser, "The Security Dilemma Revisited," *World Politics*, vol. 50, no. 1 (1997), pp. 171–201. For applications of the security dilemma to East Asia, see Thomas J. Christensen, "China, the U.S.-Japan Alliance, and the Security Dilemma in East Asia," *International Security*, vol. 23, no. 4 (Spring 1999), pp. 49–80; Jennifer M. Lind and Thomas J. Christensen, "Correspondence: Spirals, Security, and Stability in East Asia," *International Security*, vol. 24, no. 4 (Spring 2000), pp. 190–200.

[6] Kenneth Waltz, *Theory of International Politics* (New York: McGraw-Hill, 1979), p. 187.

[7] Graham D. Vernon, "Controlled Conflict: Soviet Perceptions of Peaceful Coexistence," in Graham Vernon, ed., *Soviet Perceptions of War and Peace* (Washington, DC: National Defense University Press, 1981), ch. 7; Adam B. Ulam, *Expansion and Coexistence: The History of Soviet Foreign Policy, 1917–1967* (New York: Praeger, 1968), pp. 509–610.

[8] Jervis, *Perception and Misperception*, p. 66.

belief that the other's hostility can only be explained by its aggressive-ness."[9] In other words, the security dilemma persists because anarchy blocks states' "learning" about the real mechanics of, and therefore adaptation to, their undesirable security condition. And even if the danger of escalating hostility is obvious, the structural imperative of anarchy is such that, in the words of John Mearsheimer, "little can be done to ameliorate the security dilemma as long as states operate in anarchy." For him, "This situation [of security dilemma–driven great-power struggle], which no one consciously designed or intended, is generally tragic."[10]

Most security analysts hold more complex views than Mearsheimer on the state's behavior and policy choice. Jervis, for example, proposes that the security dilemma can be alleviated when status quo–oriented states are confident in the defensive nature of each other's security mea-sures and in their own ability to neutralize potential military threats. Charles Glaser introduces two additional variables, "greed" and "unit-level knowledge of the state's motives," arguing that the states' moti-vational structures and confidence in each other's intentions also deter-mine the acuteness of the security dilemma.[11] These analytical variables highlight some of complexities that the key security dynamic in interna-tional relations entails. But at the practical level, defense and offense are notoriously difficult to differentiate. In the environment of mis-trust and uncertainty and when states do not agree on what constitute each other's legitimate security interests, the offense-defense separa-tion hardly matters. Similarly, confidence building between states is hardly about discovering each other's "true" intentions.

Ultimately, much of the threat perception and mutual confidence is a matter of judgment. If, according to Jonathan Mercer, "[a] reputa-tion is a judgment of someone's character (or disposition) that is then used to predict or explain future behavior,"[12] then one can reasonably postulate that state A draws inferences of state B's intentions based on its reputation and would react accordingly. Mercer's definition closely coincides with the standard definition of image by Allen Whiting in Chinese foreign policy studies as the "preconceived stereotype . . .

---

[9] *Ibid.*, p. 75.
[10] John Mearsheimer, *The Tragedy of Great Power Politics* (New York: W. W. Norton, 2001), pp. 36, 3.
[11] Glaser, "Security Dilemma Revisited."
[12] Mercer, *Reputation in International Relations*, p. 6.

derived from a selective interpretation of history, experience, and self-image." Studies on China's relations with the United States and Japan clearly demonstrate that reputation or preconceived image decisively shapes policy making in all three capitals.[13]

Thus, a state's reputation determines how other states judge its international character and gauge its intentions.[14] A threat reputation will spark hostile reactions and aggravate the security dilemma. According to Stephen Walt, "[S]tates that are *viewed* as aggressive are likely to provoke others to balance against them."[15] Then what are the sources of threat perception? Material factors clearly matter, as specified by Walt. Under the condition of international uncertainties, states will have to base their judgment of intention on their prior experience and mutual *a priori* assumptions about their future. It is also subject to the ongoing interaction between the states involved.

The democratic peace literature actually points to social identification as the source of threat perception. Democracies are not necessarily more peaceful than other regime types. It's the shared identity precluding the resort to force that sets their relations on a virtuous interactive path. Without shared identity, there is no democratic peace.[16] Jonathan Mercer has shown that even status attributions into either an in-group or an out-group determine how the same information is interpreted differently. States tend to attribute the behavior of adversarial, out-group states to dispositional traits, which tend to harden the boundaries

---

[13] Allen S. Whiting, *China Eyes Japan* (Berkeley: University of California Press, 1989), quote on p. 18; David Shambaugh, *Beautiful Imperialist: China Perceives America, 1972–1990* (Princeton, NJ: Princeton University Press, 1991); Jianwei Wang, *Limited Adversaries: Post–Cold War Sino-American Mutual Images* (Hong Kong: Oxford University Press, 2000).

[14] Peter J. Katzenstein, "Introduction: Alternative Perspectives on National Security," in Peter J. Katzenstein, ed., *The Culture of National Security: Norms and Identity in World Politics* (New York: Columbia University Press, 1996), pp. 14–17.

[15] Stephen Walt, *The Origins of Alliances* (Ithaca, NY: Cornell University Press, 1986), quote on p. 25, italics added.

[16] See Joanne Gowa, *Ballots and Bullets: The Elusive Democratic Peace* (Princeton, NJ: Princeton University Press, 1999); Jack Snyder, "Anarchy and Culture: Insights from the Anthropology of War," *International Organization*, vol. 56, no. 1 (Winter 2002), pp. 36–8; Thomas Risse-Kappen, *Cooperation Among Democracies: The European Influence on U.S. Foreign Policy* (Princeton, NJ: Princeton University Press, 1995), pp. 32, 223; Michael E. Brown, Sean Lynn-Jones, and Steven Miller, eds., *Debating the Democratic Peace* (Cambridge, MA: MIT Press, 1996).

that separate "friends" and "enemies" in the first place.[17] The status effect is wholly consistent with the social psychology insights on group dynamics: Attribution of a negative identity to the "other" affirms and magnifies the superior distinctiveness of the in-group identity. Intergroup prejudice explains the persistence of international conflict at both the interstate- and intertransnational-group levels.[18]

Despite the robust effect of social identification on threat image, any attempt to establish the direction of the causal arrow would hardly be conclusive. As Dale Copeland observes, group differentiation in international relations starts with some judgment of the state character, including threat assessment.[19] Emanuel Adler and Michael Barnett show that the highly integrated peaceful community of democratic states nurtures a collective group identity.[20] In his U.S.–centered concentric model of world politics, Henry Nau simply bases his differentiation of the state identity and status on the factor of militarized threat: Democratic peace leads to shared democratic identity, while a security threat posed by "others" determines their outlier statuses.[21] Thus, it seems more fruitful to consider threat perception as embedded in, and symbiotically interactive with, strategic and social interactions.[22]

[17] Mercer, *Reputation in International Relations*.

[18] For analyses focusing on transnational group politics, see John M. Owen IV, "Transnational Liberalism and U.S. Primacy," *International Security*, vol. 26, no. 3 (Winter 2002), pp. 117–52; Bruce Cronin, *Community under Anarchy: Transnational Identity and the Evolution of Cooperation* (New York: Columbia University Press, 1999); Christopher Hemmer and Peter Katzenstein, "Why Is There No NATO in Asia? Collective Identity, Regionalism, and the Origins of Multilateralism," *International Organization*, vol. 56, no, 3 (Summer 2002), pp. 575–607. For state level analyses, see Jonathan Mercer, "Anarchy and Identity," *International Organization*, vol. 49, no. 2 (Spring 1995), pp. 229–52; Alastair Iain Johnston, *Cultural Realism: Strategic Culture and Grand Strategy in Chinese History* (Princeton, NJ: Princeton University Press, 1995). Mercer seeks to explain why the state as an in-group pursues relative gains, whereas Johnston draws on the social psychology insights to illuminate the role of symbolic strategic culture of Ming China.

[19] Copeland, "Do Reputations Matter?" pp. 55–61.

[20] Adler and Barnett, *Security Communities*, pp. 47–8 and passim.

[21] Henry R. Nau, *At Home Abroad: Identity and Power in American Foreign Policy* (Ithaca, NY: Cornell University Press, 2002).

[22] See Robert Latham, *The Liberal Moment: Modernity, Security, and the Making of Postwar International Order* (New York: Columbia University Press, 1997), ch. 3 and passim.

After the cold war, as militarized conflict among advanced democratic powers is no longer contemplated or even imagined, a great power "security community" has come into existence. In this age of great-power peace, a threat reputation would be particularly damaging to an aspiring great power's social standing and hence to its security interests. As the dominant great-power grouping is distinguished by its members' shared commitment to peace among themselves and international responsibilities at large,[23] a China reputed to harbor violent ambitions would justify it being treated categorically differently. Such a status loss in turn would reinforce a threat image and motivate hostile, discriminatory responses.

The status factor may also explain the validity asymmetry in states' mutual attribution of reputation. To the extent that power coincides with the prevailing normative and institutional framework in world politics, the threat attribution will have a different effect on the dominant in-group than on the out-group. The former will be less sensitive to others' threat attributions, because it tends not to stick, nor does it matter that much. In this way, threat is not a matter of mutual perception. Due to the gap in both power *and* legitimacy, the dominant group enjoys greater credibility than the subordinate group in mutual imputation of negative images. Hence, China threat theories have been quite persistent, while China's counterthreat theories on the United States, Japan, and India hardly "sell," except for its own populace.

What is clear is that a state's threat reputation exacts a loss of international legitimacy and hardens its hostile "other" status, which in turn could *a priori* give rise to what Alexander Wendt calls "no-holds-barred power politics" directed against it.[24] Because the China threat theories variously underscore how China's rise harms others' interests and threatens the international status quo, they contribute more potently than its human rights violations alone to China's ambiguous, less than advantageous international standing. True, various notions of

---

[23] Robert Jervis, "Theories of War in an Era of Leading-Power Peace," *American Political Science Review*, vol. 96, no. 1 (March 2002), pp. 1–14; Emanuel Adler and Michael Barnett, eds., *Security Communities* (Cambridge: Cambridge University Press, 1998); Richard Rosecrance, ed., *The Great Power Coalition* (Boulder, CO: Rowman & Littlefield, 2001).

[24] Alexander Wendt, *Social Theory of International Politics* (Cambridge: Cambridge University Press, 1999), p. 262. See also Latham, *The Liberal Moment*; Cronin, *Community under Anarchy*.

China threat have yet to coalesce into an enemy image in the minds of the public and various elites in the United States, Japan, or elsewhere. But if not countered, it could translate into an insurmountable security dilemma exacting irretrievable loss in its quest for great-power status. These considerations explain Beijing's ultrasensitivity and aversion to the China threat theory.

"The Chorus of China Threat"

Chinese interpretations of "China threat theories" lump together variegated negative views, propounded by nonstate, as well as state, actors in the West and Japan. Three Chinese versions have been advanced as to the genesis and precise timing of "China threat theories." A *Beijing Review* article published in 1997 attributes their origin to an August 1990 article by a professor at Japan's National Defense Academy.[25] Another account comes from Xu Xin, then president of the China Institute for International Strategic Studies and former deputy chief of staff of the People's Liberation Army (PLA). According to Xu – at a symposium hosted by the conservative Heritage Foundation in Washington, DC on August 25, 1992 – a U.S. Assistant Secretary of Defense blamed China for sparking an arms race in the Asia-Pacific region. The notion of China threat was magnified in the following month by the former U.S. ambassador to China, James Lilley, in Hong Kong, where he openly criticized China's military expansion.[26]

The official version, commonly accepted by Chinese analysts, traces the beginning of the China threat theories to the end of 1992.[27] A confluence of factors was said to explain their emergence. Deng Xiaoping's "Southern Tour" resuscitated China's market reform, leading to the economic rise of a unified China that lent credence to the fear of China's strength in lieu of the commonplace prognosis of imminent "China collapse" in the aftermath of the cataclysmic events in 1989–91. In February of that year, China's legislature, the National

---

[25] Wang Zhongren, "'China Threat' Theory Groundless," *Beijing Review*, no. 40 (July 14–20, 1997), pp. 7–8, in Foreign Broadcast Information Service (hereafter cited as FBIS): FTS19970716000009.

[26] Fang Zhi, "Who Threatens Who after All," *Liaowang*, [n.d.], in FBIS: FTS199603210000061.

[27] Guan Cha Jia [Observer], "China's Development Is Beneficial to World Peace and Progress-Refuting the 'China Threat' Theory," *Renmin Ribao*, overseas edition, Dec. 22, 1995, pp. 1, 3, in FBIS: FTS1995122000064.

People's Congress, passed a law that reaffirmed in particular China's territorial claims over the South China Sea Islands, which were fiercely disputed by several Southeast Asian countries. Meanwhile, the United States was contemplating the sale of F-16 fighter jets to Taiwan. The Japanese Diet was on the verge of passing a bill that would allow its Self-Defense Forces to participate in the United Nations peacekeeping operations. Both the United States and Japan used China's military threat to achieve their ulterior motives.

China threat theories have since unfolded along both security and economic lines. On the security front, they focused on China's threat of force against Taiwan, irresponsible arms sales, claims to contested territories, military buildups, and a lack of transparency. Also, in more general terms, a dangerous Chinese expansionism is said to have manifested itself in power, intentions, and behavior. The aggregate material power accruing from its phenomenal growth, coupled with an illiberal regime and nationalism, would lead to greater military prowess and aggressive foreign behavior.

On the economic front, its spectacular growth alone means that the PRC would out-compete other countries in areas where it enjoys comparative advantage, particularly labor-intensive manufacturing industries, and absorb much of the foreign direct investment that would otherwise be destined elsewhere. China's economic gains would be attained at the expense of its economic partners. Its mercantilist trade policy would undermine the international liberal economic regimes. At the outset of the new century, China's surging demand for natural resources has added fuel to international concerns about global competition over these finite goods. Its growing economic presence in Asia, Africa, and Latin America has also raised questions about the political, economic, and security implications of China's ever-expanding global reach.

As Table 4.1 shows, in Chinese interpretations, while security and economic threats are consistent themes, the China threat theories have taken on various other forms with a multitude of progenitors. The United States, Taiwan, and Japan have represented the most consistent sources of various notions of a China threat. The propagators in those places have fabricated a China threat in order to advocate a hostile containment policy toward China; to justify interferences in China's domestic affairs, including Taiwan; to maintain their hegemonic security structure in the Asia-Pacific region; and to enhance their own military expenditures and overall defense capabilities.

Table 4.1. *"China Threat Theories" in Chinese Interpretations (1990–2007)*

Variant	Date of Origin (approx.)	Source	Description
General notion of China's revisionist threat	1992–	United States, Japan, Taiwan	Based on its power politics, regime type, nationalism, China is regarded as a threat to the regional and international status quo as well as the three parties. The rise of these views officially marked the beginning of the most pernicious and persistent China threat theory. The three parties have since led the international smear campaign against China. Originally South Korea was also a progenitor, but it has since seen these views die away there.
Japan's China threat theory	1990? –	Japan	Japan has been a main propagator of the China threat theory to keep China down, stoke its own nationalism, and divert international attention from its motivations of remilitarization and lack of remorse for its wartime past.
India's China threat theory	1998–2003	India	India cited a China threat to justify its nuclear tests and non–status quo political and military ambitions.
Cultural sources of China threat	1993–95	Samuel Huntington, United States	Harvard political scientist Huntington's "clash of civilizations" thesis singles out Confucianist China as a threat to the West.
China's food crisis and energy shortage	1995, 2004–	Lester Brown, United States, et al.	Brown, director of Worldwatch Institute, contended that China couldn't feed its vast population and that China's food shortage was bound to trigger a global food crisis. Others argued that China's growing energy demands would motivate Beijing's aggressive policy, particularly toward the South China Sea. Later, the concerns about China's insatiable demands for natural resources were revived after 2004.

Greater China superpower	1994–97	Japan, Southeast Asia	The growing economic integration of coastal China, Hong Kong, Taiwan, and overseas Chinese communities was creating a domineering Chinese entity in Asia.
Aggressive Chinese nationalism	1995–	United States, Japan, et al.	Chinese nationalism has led to political conservatism at home and aggressive policy abroad. Rising nationalism has translated into Beijing's military threat to Taiwan, rivalry with Japan, and anti-American sentiments.
China doesn't matter	1999	Gerald Segal, United States–United Kingdom	Segal argued that China does not deserve great-power status and that other great powers need not accommodate its interests.
China's economic threat	2001–	The West and developing world	After China's WTO accession, some Asian countries blamed their own economic woes on China's competition. Economic interdependence with China has since lessened their concern. But with its growing trade, investment, and energy need, fear of Chinese growth at the expense of other economies in Africa and Latin America as well as the West has grown.
Rising Chinese power, rising Chinese threat	2001	John Mearsheimer, United States	Mearsheimer, a University of Chicago professor, singled out China as the next great power, whose rise is bound to trigger a dangerously destabilizing power transition.
China collapse theory	2001–02	Individuals in the West	This represented a new twist to China threat theory, predicting imminent collapse of the Chinese economy and political system.

Chinese official analysts are particularly concerned about the origins of the China threat theory from the United States. Reflecting hostilities and bias, they argue, various strands of American-based China threat theory smear China's image, denigrate the Chinese political system, overstate China's strengths, and assign irresponsible, destabilizing motives to Chinese external behaviors.

The Chinese views hold that Japan represents another very enthusiastic peddler of the most pernicious brand of China threat theory. As discussed earlier, one Chinese account attributes the origin of the theories to Japan in 1990. Another Chinese author even suggests that the idea of China threat was first floated in Japan as early as 1984. Japan's anti-China theme has varied widely, but it encompasses nuclear, economic, military, and/or ethnically based "greater China" threats. Chinese rebuttal directed against Japan began to take on added vigor in the mid-1990s. Since then, Japan's China threat theory has evolved from being one of the main irritants in Sino-Japanese relations to become the overriding Chinese concern vis-à-vis Japan.

India was once a leading originator of the China threat theory. India first became a main progenitor around the time when it detonated nuclear weapons, in May 1998. Prime Minister Vajpayee wrote a letter on May 11 to U.S. President Clinton citing China's nuclear arsenal and the 1962 Sino-Indian war to justify New Delhi's acquisition of nuclear weapons. The most prominent actor in India's anti-China drama was Defense Minister George Fernandes, who openly discussed the China threat before and after the nuclear tests.[28] Three years later, Fernandes made similar remarks that ignited yet another round of Chinese counterattacks that underscored India's use of the China threat as a "shield" to justify its aggressive arms purchases, expanded missile programs, and great-power ambition.[29] The Indian brand of China threat has lingered, but remarkably it has withered since 2003.

[28] Yan Xuetong, "Why Has India Created a 'China Threat Theory'?" *Guangming Ribao* (Internet), May 19, 1998, p. 3, in FBIS: FTS19980520000644; China Radio International in Mandarin to Northeast Asia, South Pacific, Hong Kong, Macao, and Southeast Asia, 0900 GMT, May 21, 1998, in FBIS: FTS19980521001220.

[29] Wang Hui, "India's 'China Threat' Unfair," *China Daily* (Internet), March 14, 2001, in FBIS: CPP20010314000063; Zhao Zhangyun, "Irresponsible Argument," *Renmin Ribao* (Internet), June 7, 2001, p. 3, in FBIS: CPP20010607000038; Wang Jiaqing, "International Watch: A 'Shield' That Doesn't Hold Water and Can't Stand Refuting," *Jiefangjun Bao* (Internet), June 14, 2001, p. 5, in FBIS: CPP20010614000020.

While the United States and Japan are the state actors most responsible for spreading the fear of China, pro-independence advocates in Taiwan were equally enthusiastic in magnifying a China threat to advance their causes. Most dramatically, President Chen Shui-bian attempted to equate Beijing's military threat with terrorism in the aftermath of the September 11 events.[30] Other substate actors and individuals in the West have also been singled out as abetting the fear of China from various perspectives. Notably, John Mearsheimer's restatement of a hardcore power politics theory in 2001 reinforces the view about the inevitable military threat a growing Chinese power poses to the status quo powers, particularly the United States.[31]

Chinese commentators also take note of the views that link Chinese history and contemporary nationalism to a China threat. In particular, the Harvard University political scientist Samuel Huntington's "clash of civilization" thesis directed attention to the Confucianist culture as a source of China's military threat.[32] Similarly, legitimate Chinese patriotism and the country's natural antipathy to Western interference were misrepresented by certain individuals as irrational, aggressive nationalism that could translate into anti-Americanism, hegemonic ambitions in Asia, and saber rattling toward Taiwan. The growing economic ties between China and overseas Chinese communities were even claimed to be evidence of the emergent, malign "greater China" superpower.[33]

For the Chinese, there is yet another strand of the China threat notion that focuses on the country's weaknesses at home and abroad.

---

[30] Liu Hong, "Taiwan Strait Observation: Who Is Engaged in Military Terrorism?" *Beijing Renmin Wang*, WWW-text, Sept. 18, 2002, in FBIS: CPP20020918000028; Kong Shengliang, "Chen Shui-bian's Political Show of 'UN Participation' Has Become a Laughing Stock of the International Community," *Renmin Ribao*, overseas edition (Internet), Sept. 16, 2002, p. 5, in FBIS: CPP20020916000072.

[31] Ren Yujun, "Always Looking for a Fight at Crucial Times, Creating an Enemy Threat," *Huanqiu Shibao* (Internet), Sept. 4, 2001, p. 1, in FBIS: CPP20010907000052.

[32] Liang Lihua, "A Political Myth of Multiple Incarnations: The China Threat Theory," *Dangdai Sichao*, no. 2 (April 20, 1998), pp. 57–63, in FBIS: FTS19980602001171. See also Wang Jisi, ed., *Wenmin Yu Guoji Zhengzhi* [*Civilizations and International Politics*] (Shanghai: People's Press, 1995).

[33] "James Lilley's Sorrow," *Renmin Ribao*, Feb. 1, 1997, in FBIS: FTS19970201000694; Yang Xuejun and Li Hanmei, "Key Factors Affecting Coming Japanese Diplomatic Strategies and Actions," *Zhanlue Yu Guanli*, no. 1 (Feb. 1998), pp. 17–23, in FBIS: FTS19980502000166.

For example, the director of the Washington, DC–based Worldwatch Institute, Lester Brown, in his 1995 book *Who Will Feed China?*, contended that China's vast population threatened to strain the world's food supply. A related but more enduring theme than Brown's food threat has been a concern that China's insatiable demand for natural resources, energy, and living space may generate pressures for an aggressive foreign policy. Gerald Segal's 1999 article in *Foreign Affairs* titled "Does China Matter?" contended that China's political, economic, and military capabilities were minuscule on a world scale. Beijing should be treated accordingly and the Western powers should not accommodate Beijing's interests based on an exaggerated estimation of China's international status.[34] Similarly, the "China collapse theory" as most notably propounded by Gordon G. Chang in 2001–2 that seriously questioned China's economic health and institutional viability was interpreted as reflective of the same hostility and prejudice against China as the China threat theories inciting fear of China's strengths.[35]

China under Threat

From the Chinese perspective, China threat theories are simply concocted by hostile forces seeking to threaten China. As such, China's interpretations reflect self-assessments of the external threats it faces. As the preceding section shows, Chinese interpretations have lumped together wide-ranging negative attributions from abroad that exaggerate China's alleged expansionist impulse, destabilizing potential at home and abroad, and anachronistic worldview. Taken together, they reveal an acute Chinese sense of insecurity about its international environment.

Clearly topping China's security concerns is its relationship with the United States. The United States plays a key role for the Chinese Communist Party (CCP) leadership's domestic and international agenda on economic modernization, maintaining domestic stability, and securing

---

[34] Gu Ping, "What Is the Motive for Belittling China?" *Renmin Ribao*, Sept. 16, 1999, p. 6, in FBIS: FTS 19991023001000.

[35] Gordon G. Chang, *The Coming Collapse of China* (New York: Random House, 2001). On Chinese reactions, see Liu Xiaobiao, "From 'Threat Theory' to "Collapse Theory,'" *Renmin Ribao* (Internet), June 11, 2002, p. 3, in FBIS: CPP20020611000045.

opportunities for upward mobility in world politics. By virtue of its global leadership position, the United States decisively influences the receptivity toward China's rise by the established great-power grouping and the international society at large. Reflecting the utmost importance the Chinese elites have attached to managing Sino-American relationship, Zi Zhongyun, the former director of the Institute of American Studies at the Chinese Academy of Social Sciences, wrote in 1999 that the U.S. hegemony "has included two aspects – 'letting those who are with it thrive and prosper,' and 'letting those who are against it come to their doom'" (*Shunzhi Zechang Nizhi Zewang*).[36] Other Chinese commentators may contend that she overstated U.S. power and Chinese constraints. But they all share her belief that America's threat rhetoric and perception vis-à-vis China has profound negative consequences for the Sino-American relationship and their nation's overall international environment. Thus, as uncertainties and suspicion have persisted in the bilateral relationship, Chinese leaders and mainstream analysts have been deeply concerned about the U.S.-based China threat theories. And avoiding sustained confrontation with the United States has been the official policy, supported by mainstream Chinese analysts.[37]

The PRC views India as an emerging power, dissatisfied with its current international status, and it is concerned that India might seek to achieve its great-power ambition at the expense of China's interests. What has worried Chinese strategists most were when India openly played up a China threat to achieve its political and military goals while seeking to bandwagon with the U.S. power.[38] It's little wonder that the Chinese response to India's nuclear tests in May 1998 showed greater concern over India's China threat theory than the weapons

---

[36] Zi Zhongyun, "For the Maximum Interests of the Nation, for the Long-Term Welfare of the People," *Taipingyang Xuebao*, no. 21 (Dec. 14, 1999), pp. 10–15, in FBIS: CPP20000725000044, p. 6.

[37] John Garver calls this Chinese view "the law of avoidance." See Garver, "Sino-American Relations in 2001: The Difficult Accommodation of Two Great Powers," *International Journal*, vol. 57 (Spring 2002), p. 309. See also Yong Deng, "Hegemon on the Offensive: Chinese Perspectives of the U.S. Global Strategy," *Political Science Quarterly*, vol. 116, no. 3 (Fall 2001), pp. 343–65.

[38] Michael Pillsbury, *China Debates the Future Security Environment* (Washington, DC: National Defense University Press, 2000), ch. 3. On India, see John Garver, *The China-India-U.S. Triangle: Strategic Relations in the Post–Cold War Era* (Seattle: National Bureau of Asian Research, 2002).

proliferation itself. Specifically, Indian Prime Minister Vajpayee's letter to President Clinton on May 11 defending its nuclear tests galvanized Beijing for a fierce reaction. Made public in American media,
the letter cited extensively the Sino-Indian border conflict in 1962 and
China's nuclear threat to justify India's nuclear program. One leading
Chinese India-watcher wrote, "Although the Chinese side expressed
understanding of India's need to carry out nuclear tests for its security needs, it could not understand why" India would use a China
threat to achieve its nuclear ambitions.[39] In addition to fiery rhetorical
rebuttal, Beijing launched diplomatic counterattacks that called the
world's attention to India's violation of the global nonproliferation
regime.[40]

Nevertheless, mutual animosities diminished significantly after April
2003, when Indian Defense Minister Fernandes, the "number one peddler" of the Indian "China threat theories," paid a high-profile visit
to Beijing at the height of the Severe Acute Respiratory Syndrome
(SARS) crisis. The improvement in their bilateral relationship further
picked up after Prime Minister Vajpayee's week-long visit to China
two months later. Mutual trust has since increased as the two Asian
giants have quickly elevated their "cooperative partnership" to a more
forward-looking "strategic partnership" designed to avoid internecine
rivalry as both strive for great-power status.[41]

---

[39] Quoted in John W. Garver, "The Restoration of Sino-Indian Comity Following
India's Nuclear Tests," *China Quarterly*, no. 168 (Dec. 2001), p. 869.

[40] *Ibid.*, pp. 865–89; Susan Shirk, "One-Sided Rivalry: China's Perceptions and
Policies Toward India," in Francine R. Frankel and Harry Harding, eds., *The
India-China Relationship: What the United States Needs to Know* (New York:
Columbia University Press, 2004), pp. 75–100; Yan Xuetong, "Why Has India
Created a 'China Threat' Theory"; [No author], Beijing China Radio Interna-
tional in Mandarin to Northeast Asia, South Pacific, Hong Kong, Macao, and
Southeast Asia, May 21, 1998, in FBIS: FTS19980521001220. For the broad
context of Chinese reactions, see Ming Zhang, *China's Changing Nuclear Pos-
ture: Reactions to the South Asian Nuclear Tests* (Washington, DC: Carnegie
Endowment for International Peace, 1999).

[41] "Chinese Premier, Indian PM Hold Talks," *People's Daily* (Internet), at
http://english.peopledaily.com.cn (accessed June 23, 2003); Fang Zhou, "China,
India Forming Strategic Ties," *China Daily*, at http://www.chinadaily.com.cn/
english/doc/2005-02/18/content_417242.htm (accessed March 24, 2005);
"Longxiang Gongwu" [The Dragon and the Elephant Dancing Together], at
http://news.sina.com.cn/c/2005-04-15/03536389989.shtml (accessed April 19,
2005).

While India's China threat theories turned out to be manageable, the Japanese version has proved to be much more deep-rooted and baneful for the Chinese. As the PRC makes gains in great-power ascent, Tokyo has become highly skeptical of its neighbor's self-proclaimed peaceful intent. Particularly since the late 1990s, Japan has shown an unprecedented firmness in dealing with China, as it has stood up to Beijing on historical and other contemporary bilateral issues, stepped up competition with the PRC over regional influence, and increased its material power through enhanced alliance with the United States and its own military armament. In a nutshell, Chinese commentators have interpreted the popularity of China threat theories in Japan as reflective of Tokyo's ulterior motive to deny China's rightful rise.

Apart from concerns about the policy directions of the United States, Japan, and India, the PRC was also worried about the China threat echoes from its neighbors in Southeast and Central Asia,[42] as these states might join other hostile powers to balance against China. In the early years of the twenty-first century, the PRC has also bristled at accusations that with its growing presence in Africa and Latin America the country is plundering natural resources, displacing local industries, and destabilizing local governments on those continents. The fear of the global marketability of the notion of a China threat underscored the precarious nature of Beijing's relations with these countries and of its overall international environment.

China's interpretations do not limit the China threat theory to the views associated with the state actors. Rather, they are much more expansive. Indeed, the chorus of anti-China voices ranges from views overstating Chinese strengths to views underscoring Chinese weaknesses. Express concerns about the rise of aggressive Chinese nationalism and the power of the greater China are denounced, and so is Huntington's view that China represents the challenge of the Confucianist civilization to the West. As the fears of China's neighbors of its increased economic competitiveness are refuted, so are various individuals' and nongovernmental groups' views highlighting the flaws and

---

[42] Allen S. Whiting, "ASEAN Eyes China: The Security Dimension," *Asian Survey*, vol. 37, no. 4 (April 1997), pp. 299–322; Xu Tao, "The Strategic Security Strategy of the Central Asian Countries and China's Western Security Environment," *Zhanlue Yu Guanli*, August 1, 1999, pp. 32–8, in FBIS: FTS19991027000867.

frailties of the Chinese political system. For Beijing, these unpalatable views may not directly lead to advocacy of a specific policy inimical to Chinese interests. They nonetheless tarnish China's image, leading to the country's political and psychological estrangement with its neighbors, other parts of the developing world, and the established great powers.

Chinese Response: Rhetoric and Policy

The PRC issued its first official rebuttal in 1995, although, according to its official view, however, the theories started a few years earlier. The lag reflected the policy elites' uncertainties about both the security implications and China's proper response. However, it did not take long before the Beijing leadership "learned" about the weighty costs of a negative image. And China's security in the seemingly enduring American unipolar world must entail a vigorous response to foreign imputation of a violent predisposition to it. The 1995-96 Taiwan crisis and Beijing's disputes with Manila over the Mischief Island in the South China Sea in the spring of 1995 added credibility to the notion of a China threat. Beijing immediately responded by sending several high-ranking military and civilian leaders on foreign trips with the exclusive purpose of rebutting China threat theories. Official media and academic writings chimed in to reinforce the government's position.

The PRC has countered the China threat theories by equating them with the cold war mentality, ill will, and bias against China. In the meantime, it has strived to reassure the international community of China's peaceful, cooperative intent. Insofar as the various notions of a China threat reveal Chinese vulnerabilities in world politics, the PRC has also taken measures to enhance its material and diplomatic leverage in shaping its international environment.

In shrill rhetorical rebuttals, the PRC has rejected the notion of its economic threat by maintaining that China is still a developing country and its growing competitiveness results from compliance with market principles. In other words, blame the game, not the players.[43] On the security front, Chinese writers dismiss foreign conjectures of a China

---

[43] Dong Fureng, "On 'Theory of China Threat,'" Hong Kong Ta Kung Pao (Internet), February 2, 2002, in FBIS: CPP20020202000017.

threat as a reflection of a cold war mentality, a trick analogous to "a thief crying 'Stop thief'" (*Zeihan Zhuozei*) played by those countries to hide their own power politics ambitions while obstructing China's legitimate aspirations.

Such an attack mode also characterizes Chinese response to views originating from nonstate actors and individuals in the West that do not lend themselves to direct policy prescriptions but are damaging to its overall reputation in international society. Chinese rebuttals show little interest in any pretense of dispassionate reasoning. As such, Huntington's civilizational-clash thesis, Brown's warning on China's food shortage, and the concerns about aggressive Chinese nationalism were attacked as simply reflective of Western "ignorance" and "bias." Other views objectionable to Beijing were equated with "malicious belittling and slandering statements" propounded by Western ill-wishers.[44] Chinese authors from the conservative political camp even attributed these malign views to racism traceable to the imperialist "Yellow Peril" theory.[45]

In more reasoned responses, the Chinese have focused on debunking the exaggeration of its material capabilities, misinterpretations of its intentions, and misunderstanding of its policy behavior. Despite the rapid growth of its national power, the arguments go, China still ranks low among the major powers in comprehensive strength with an even much lower per capita income. In terms of military power, apart from the significant unilateral troops reduction, China fell far behind the United States in military expenditures and spent less than such great powers as Japan, Great Britain, and France.[46] Most recently, as its defense budget surged yearly, the PRC has maintained that its armament is purely defensive-driven in a highly complex and uncertain global and regional security environment. Chinese writers have also debunked extrapolations of China's aggressive intentions by highlighting its peaceful historical record associated with the benevolent Confucianist culture as well as its contemporary embrace of win-win

---

[44] Wang Zhongren, "'China Threat' Theory Groundless;" Gu Ping, "What is the Motive for Belittling China," p. 2.

[45] Peng Huaidong, "From the 'Yellow Peril' to the 'China threat," *Zhenli De Zhuiqiu*, April 11, 1997, in FBIS: FTS19970602001429.

[46] Tian Xin, "China Threat Theory Collapses of Itself, as Military Spending of Both U.S. and Japan Has Far Exceeded That of China," *Hong Kong Wen Wei Po*, March 6, 2002, p. A6, in FBIS: CPP20020306000090.

economic cooperation and cooperative security. For them, China's foreign policy behaviors evidence peaceful intentions, responsibility, and restraint, even on such issues as Taiwan, the South China Sea, nuclear tests, and arms sales.[47]

In tandem with reassurance in words, the PRC has undertaken corresponding policy responses designed to cultivate recognition and acceptance from international institutions, China's neighboring countries, and other great powers. Admittedly, the behavioral impact of the China threat theory is much harder to pin down. But analytical reasoning and empirical evidence clearly establish how China's fear of foreign attribution of a threat reputation has shaped its foreign orientations.[48]

As was discussed earlier, a threat reputation attached to China, if not countered, could lead to a loss of its international legitimacy, thereby mobilizing a U.S.-led containment coalition against it. For the security-conscious Chinese policy elites, it should quickly become clear that to effectively refute the China threat theory, behavioral adjustments must also be made. These positive changes were duly recognized in the English-language literature as deriving from a new Chinese commitment to building a cooperative, responsible image in international society.[49]

---

[47] Guan Cha Jia, "China's Development is Beneficial to world Peace and Progress;" Fang Zhi, "Who Threatens Whom after All?"; Wang Zhongren, "'China Threat' Theory Groundless;" [No title] *Jiefangjun Bao*, Jan. 21, 2002, p. 5, in FBIS: CPP20020121000008.

[48] For compelling evidence, see Avery Goldstein, *Rising to the Challenge: China's Grand Strategy and International Security* (Stanford, CA: Stanford University Press, 2005).

[49] Alastair Iain Johnston, "International Structures and Chinese Foreign Policy," in Samuel S. Kim, ed., *China and the World: Chinese Foreign Policy Faces the New Millennium* (Boulder, CO: Westview Press, 1998); Alastair Iain Johnston and Paul Evans, "China's Engagement in International Security Institutions," in Alastair Iain Johnston and Robert Ross, eds., *Engaging China: Management of an Emerging Power* (London: Routledge, 1999), pp. 235–72; Michael D. Swaine and Alastair Iain Johnston, "China and Arms Control Institutions," in Elizabeth Economy and Michel Oksenberg, eds., *China Joins the World: Progress and Prospects* (New York: Council on Foreign Relations Press, 1999), ch. 3; Rosemary Foot, "Chinese Power and the Idea of a Responsible Power," *China Journal*, no. 45 (Jan. 2001), pp. 1–19; Hongying Wang, "Multilateralism in Chinese Foreign Policy: The Limits of Socialization," *Asian Survey*, vol. 41, no. 3 (May/June 2000), pp. 475–91.

To assuage foreign concerns, the PRC has been eager to show that China's rise represents an opportunity rather than a threat to its partner and to the world at large. Its approach to WTO was a case in point. According to Chinese views, concern about a China threat was a major reason for the tortuous process of China's accession negotiations, particularly with the United States.[50] China's chief negotiator on China's WTO membership, Long Yongtu, repeatedly stated both before and after China's accession that whether the rise of China was viewed as an opportunity or a threat would determine China's international environment. In fact, it was Chinese Premier Zhu Rongji who first popularized the "China opportunity" idea during his visit to the United States in the spring of 1999.[51] Similarly, other official accounts also considered dispelling notions of a China threat as a major benefit of China's WTO membership.[52] A rationale for seeking China's opening and compliance with the rule-based trade organization was that it would replace China threat theory with China opportunity theory and help create China's responsible image.[53]

Similar concern to demonstrate positive contributions of China's rise to international security and prosperity has also driven China's broad strategic choices. Indeed, since the mid-1990s the PRC has made vigorous efforts to deepen China's international interdependence,

---

[50] Yue Yang, "China's Opportunity Theory," *Zhongguo Jingji Shibao* (Internet), April 12, 1999, in FBIS: FTS19990422000265.

[51] "The Rise of China – A Threat or an Opportunity?" *People's Daily* (Internet), at http://english.peopledaily.com.cn/200212/22/eng20021222_108925.shtml (accessed March 26, 2005).

[52] See Gong Wen, "Let History Record the 15 Years – Memorandum on the Negotiations for China's WTO Entry," *Renmin Ribao* (Internet), Nov. 11, p. 2, in FBIS: CPP20011112000058; He Chong, "Major Significance of China Becoming a WTO Member," in *Hong Kong Zhongguo Tongxun She*, Nov. 11, 2001, in FBIS: CPP20011111000086.

[53] Guan YuanZhi, "China Is Not Stopping Its Efforts to Rejoin the GATT and Face Up to the Asian Financial Crisis in 1998," *Zhongguo Gaige Bao*, March 2, 2998, p. 3, in FBIS: FTS19980416000855; Long Yongtu, "Join the World Trade Organization, Fuse into the International Community Mainstream," *Guoji Maoyi Wenti*, Sept. 1999, pp. 1–10, 30, in FBIS: FTS19990929000581; "Long Yongtu: Avoiding Disadvantages While Pursuing Advantages of Globalization," *Jinan Dazhong Ribao* (Internet), Oct. 10, 2001, in FBIS: CPP20011010000223; Sun Xiaosheng and Yu Jingzhong, "Long Yongtu Says China's Accession to the WTO Creates an Image of a Responsible Power," in Beijing Xinhua Hong Kong Service, May 23, 2002, in FBIS: CPP200020524000074.

underscore its win-win diplomacy, cultivate multilevel and omnidirectional partnerships, and embrace various forms of multilateralism.[54] It has been well documented that image concerns have contributed to China's progress in compliance with the international arms control and disarmament regimes.[55] Similarly, a desire to win recognition as a responsible power was behind Beijing's constructive behavior in the 1997–98 Asian Financial Crisis, particularly in resisting the pressure to devaluate its national currency and in contributing to the rescue packages given to the hardest-hit neighboring economies.[56]

Overall, seeking legitimate power has fundamentally defined the motivational structure of the PRC's foreign policy. The CCP leaders have shown considerable awareness of how foreign judgment of the character of the Chinese state matters. For example, Li Ruihuan, former chairperson of the Chinese People's Political Consultative Conference, contended that it's mistaken to view China's growing power as a threat, because "whether a person will harm other people will not depend on the size of his build or strength, but on his moral character and conduct."[57] In conjunction with the rethinking of China's international role, its foreign policy practice witnessed a systematic set of notable adjustments. Both the timing and substance of these shifts suggest a clear linkage of its strategic choices to a concern over the rising fear of a China threat.

This, of course, does not suggest that China's response is simply to "play nice." For the CCP leaders, the China threat notions reflect the uncertainties and vulnerabilities in their country's foreign relations.

---

[54] Goldstein, *Rising to the Challenge*. See also Yong Deng and Fei-ling Wang, eds., *China Rising: Power and Motivation in Chinese Foreign Policy* (Boulder, CO: Rowman & Littlefield, 2005).

[55] Swaine and Johnston, "China and Arms Control Institutions;" Bates Gill, "Two Steps Forward, One Step Back: The Dynamics of Chinese Nonproliferation and Arms Control," in David M. Lampton, ed., *The Making of Chinese Foreign and Security Policy in the Era of Reform, 1978–2000* (Stanford, CA: Stanford University Press, 2001), ch. 9.

[56] Thomas Moore and Dixia Yang, "Empowered and Restrained: Chinese Foreign Policy in the Age of Economic Interdependence," in Lampton, *The Making of Chinese Foreign and Security Policy*, ch. 7; Hongying Wang, "National Image Building and Chinese Foreign Policy," in Deng and Wang, *China Rising*, pp. 73–102.

[57] Yang Guojun and Wang Dajun, "Li Ruihuan Comments on 'China Threat Theory,'" Xinhua Domestic Service in Chinese, Dec. 13, 1999, in FBIS: FTS19991213001045.

They have thus taken steps, including more traditional power politics practices, to hedge against perceived threats and gain initiatives in controlling their country's fate in world politics. Thus, perhaps the most important task facing the PRC in its foreign policy is to balance reassurance with the need to address its vulnerabilities.

The difficulties of this task are demonstrably clear in the rise and fall of the slogan "peaceful rise." Designed to provide a credible vision of a cooperative future in China's foreign relations, leading Chinese strategic thinkers broached the alternative idea of a peaceful rise in late 2003.[58] The concept was soon explicitly endorsed by top Chinese leaders and intensely studied by China's international relations scholars. However, the debate had died down by the summer of 2004, as the ongoing Taiwan crisis and power politics concerns vis-à-vis Japan and the United States quickly raised doubts about the wisdom of elevating "peaceful rise" to strategic prominence. The top Chinese leaders' reticence had to do with a two-fold concern that confident declaration of China's rise would be counterproductive in their campaign to defuse the fear of a China threat; yet, the unconditional announcement of peaceful intent would undermine deterrence, particularly vis-à-vis the United States, Taiwan, and Japan.

Escaping the Security Dilemma: Alternative Explanations and Assessment

Contemporary China's sensitivity and response to the China threat theories do not fully accord with traditional realist theories on deterrence, power politics, or the security dilemma. Nor does it fully align with the Maoist approach to foreign relations, whose preoccupation with demonstrating the new People's Republic's resolve led to quite frequent use of force.[59] To the extent that the way the PRC reacts to

---

[58] Song Niansheng, "Heping Jueqi, Zhongguo Fazhan Zhilu," [Peaceful Rise, China's Road to Development"), *Huanqiu Shibao* [Global Times], April 23, 2004, p. 3, at http://www.people.com.cn/GB/paper68/11864/1069451.html (accessed April 29, 2004).

[59] Allen S. Whiting, *China Crosses the Yalu: The Decision to Enter the Korean War* (New York: Macmillan, 1960); Allen S. Whiting, *The Chinese Calculus of Deterrence: India and Indochina* (Ann Arbor: University of Michigan Press, 1975); Allen S. Whiting, "China's Use of Force, 1950–1996, and Taiwan," *International Security*, vol. 26, no. 2 (Fall 2001), pp. 103–31. See also Melvin

the China threat theories has a direct bearing on the country's "general reputation," in the sense of the mainstream deterrence literature,[60] it suggests a configured reputation highly concerned to create a positive interactive pattern with the key players abroad in contemporary Chinese foreign policy.

One may speculate that China's ultrasensitivity to its less than honorable image may have to do with the country's self-conception as a paragon of virtues and benevolence in the premodern Sino-centric East Asian order.[61] Indeed, Chinese commentators often point to Confucian China's benign history and culture to support the notion of their country's benevolent contemporary foreign policy. But beyond these assertions, no compelling evidence in either Chinese writings or Western scholarship exists to demonstrate that how the country's ancient history and culture would set its contemporary interaction with foreign players on a distinctive path.

Another explanation for the Chinese reactions may be found in the supposed domestic audience effect. As well documented in the literature, both Maoist and post-Maoist Chinese leaderships have manipulated foreign threat for popular mobilization to meet its domestic agenda and for shoring up regime legitimacy.[62] From this perspective, the contemporary CCP regime has every reason to blame China's security predicament on hostile foreigners, because doing so helps divert popular attention away from serious problems in the painful domestic transition. According to this line of reasoning, to the extent that the China threat theories reflect myriad external hostilities, a persistent refutation of the theory perpetuates a sense of national insecurity,

---

Gurtov and Byong-Moon Hwang, *China under Threat: The Politics of Strategy and Diplomacy* (Baltimore, MD: Johns Hopkins University Press, 1980).

[60] On general reputation, see Jonathan Mercer, "Reputation and Rational Deterrence Theory," *Security Studies,* vol. 7, no. 1 (Autumn 1997), pp. 100–13; *ibid.,* *Reputation in International Relations,* pp. 36–42.

[61] Swaine and Johnston, "China and Arms Control Institutions," p. 134; Samuel Kim and Lowell Dittmer, "Whither China's Quest for National Identity," in Dittmer and Kim, eds., *China's Quest for National Identity* (Ithaca, NY: Cornell University Press, 1993), p. 281.

[62] Thomas J. Christensen, *Useful Adversaries: Grand Strategy, Domestic Mobilization, and Sino-American Conflict, 1947–1958* (Princeton, NJ: Princeton University Press, 1996); Alastair Iain Johnston, "Realism(s) and Chinese Security Policy," in Ethan Kapstein and Michael Mastanduno, eds., *Unipolar Politics: Realism and State Strategies after the Cold War* (New York: Columbia University Press, 1999), ch. 8.

which the Beijing regime finds useful to focus national purpose on maintaining social stability and economic growth. There is some evidence that such a calculation might have figured in Beijing reactions to China threat theories. Most tellingly, in his rebuttal in late 1999, Li Ruihuan drew on the bitter experience of a weak China's victimization by imperialist powers in modern history and quoted an old Chinese saying, "On hearing the calls of crickets, can you not plant crops?" to urge his domestic audience to "work wholeheartedly with undivided devotion" to build a strong China. In a similar vein, Luo Yuan of the Chinese Academy of Military Science compared the China threat theories to a "whetstone" that can "temper our national will" for great-power status.[63]

Indeed, there is no distinction in China threat theories over whether the barrage of "character assassinations" was directed against the communist party-state or the Chinese nation. In Chinese responses, all the hostile foreign voices are lumped together under the rubric of "China threat theories," suggesting Western conspiracy to deny the Chinese nation its rightful interests and respect in the international arena in ways harking back to the century of humiliations after the Opium War. The Chinese government has proven adept at orchestrating the use of Western hostilities for the purpose of patriotic education to compensate for its sagging, ideologically based legitimacy.[64] Purported evidence of ill will from certain Western countries no doubt helps effect popular support for the Chinese government. As such, the nationalist purpose clearly influenced the Chinese discourse on China threat theories. Propaganda targeted at the domestic audience dictated rhetorical tactics to heighten the dangers to the Chinese nation in a perilous world. But strident nationalist rhetoric designed for domestic consumption is a far cry from China's foreign policy practices. Unlike Maoist China, where nationalism was mobilized to support aggressive foreign policies, contemporary China has to rein in anti-Western

---

[63] Yang Guojun and Wang Dajun, "Li Ruihuan Comments on 'China Threat Theory,'" p. 2; Luo Yuan, "Zhongguo Xuyao Lilian Liuzhong Daguoxintai" [China Needs to Cultivate Six Types of Great Power Mentality], Oct. 21, 2005, at http://news.xinhuanct.com/world/2005-10/21/content_3662080.htm (accessed Nov. 2, 2005).

[64] Suisheng Zhao, *A Nation-State by Construction: Dynamics of Modern Chinese Nationalism* (Stanford, CA: Stanford University Press, 2004), pp. 231–4 and passim.

emotions and assuage the fear of a China threat in its conduct of international relations.

The regime-legitimating hypothesis on antiforeign nationalism ultimately offers an incomplete explanation. The status concern promises to offer a deeper, fuller account of China's sensitivity and foreign policy reactions. True, with its ideological claim to monopoly of power in doubt, the CCP relies heavily on nationalism for domestic legitimacy. But negative affirmation of its rule by playing up hostile foreign forces trying to keep China down can hardly satisfy the Chinese populace in the reform era. Nor does it serve the Chinese government's goal to capitalize on globalization for its domestic and international agenda. Internationally, the PRC must secure an international environment largely receptive to the idea that China's rise represents an opportunity for orderly change, economic prosperity, and better governance in the increasingly globalized would. This has compelled the CCP leadership to reconcile its domestic legitimacy at home with China's search for international recognition. Thus, a full and plausible explanation must also consider China's concern about international legitimacy and its fear of a dire security environment to which a threat reputation may lead.

In the age of great-power peace, a violent, revisionist reputation would further contribute to China's out-group status. Such status loss escalates the spiral of mutual hostilities and thus the security dilemma. As we've discussed previously, we know from the social categorization literature that the out-group is always the target of negative stereotyping.[65] It follows that China's out-group status would likely lead to a continued selective use of information that reinforces a stereotypical threat image. Moreover, in-group members view power as positive-sum with each other and thus are much less sensitive to a power shift within the group. In contrast, in dealing with the out-group members, they would interpret power by a zero-sum logic and be ultrasensitive to power redistribution in favor of any "other" member. In this vein, the China threat theory could intensify the fear of growing Chinese

---

[65] For evidence from social psychology and applications of group bias to international relations, see Eugene Burnstein, Mark Abboushi, and Shinobu Kitayama, "How the Mind Preserves the Image of the Enemy," in William Zimmerman and Harold K. Jacobson, eds., *Behavior, Culture, and Conflict in World Politics* (Ann Arbor: University of Michigan Press, 1993), pp. 197–229; Mercer, *Reputation in International Relations*, particularly ch. 2.

power, thereby maximizing hostile reactions to it, emboldening Taiwan independence, and sparking anti-China armament and alliance making with the United States by its Asian neighbors. The result could be a nightmarish scenario whereby a hostile United States leads an international coalition to contain China.

Chinese strategy analysts aware of the concept of security dilemma argue that the *sine qua non* of China's foreign policy is to lessen the danger of structurally induced hostilities toward its rise. Others less versed in Western IR literature have similarly cautioned against Chinese diplomacy succumbing to the power politics logic. One prominent scholar at Beijing University explicitly urges his compatriots to curb their self-righteous sense of entitlement to greater wealth and respect while being more self-conscious in appreciating how others might view China's rise with trepidation and fear.[66] He is not alone among influential Chinese scholars in publicly calling for dispassionate understanding of how other countries might find Chinese nationalism inflammatory, its approach to Asia domineering, and its growing influence disconcerting.

The Chinese policy elites clearly understand that a reputed, violently revisionist character in the Chinese state would widen the gap separating it and the U.S.-led great-power grouping. Such status denigration would intensify the security dilemma in the international politics surrounding its rise, a dynamic it must forestall in order to take advantage of the opportunity the world has to offer for its economic modernization and great-power recognition. The way the Chinese have shown empathy, learning, and adaptation in response to the China threat theories defies the realist propositions. The country's incomparable status denigration in the aftermath of Tiananmen heightened the sensitivity to its reputation abroad, but it also raised the stakes in managing its foreign policy interactions in world politics. For the highly security-conscious Chinese political elites, the danger of an unmitigated security

---

[66] Shi Yinhong and Song Dexin, "21 Shijiqianqi Zhongguo Guoji Xintai, Waijiao Zhexue He Genben Zhanlue Sikao" [Reflections on China's International Mentality, Diplomatic Philosophy, and Basic Strategy in the Early Period of the 21st Century), in Niu Jun, ed., *Zhongguo Waijiao Juan* [China's Foreign Affairs] (Beijing: New World Press, 2007), pp. 27–44; Niu Jun, "Zhongguo Jueqi: Mengxiang Yu Xianshi Zhijian" [China's Rise: Between Aspirations and Realities), in Niu Jun, *China's Foreign Affairs, ibid.*, pp. 101–3.

dilemma becomes so real and the costs of such an international environment become so unambiguously high that it did not take long before they "learned" about, and took action to forestall, such a dangerous prospect.

Studies in social psychology suggest that an effective way to build trust is through cooperative pursuit of commonly desired and only jointly attainable "superordinate goals."[67] In the age of globalization, there is a plethora of transnational issues and nonconventional threats that demand cooperative responses in the international community. Indeed, after the 9/11 events, China's analysts greatly hoped that the new realities of globalization would transform great-power politics so that it would become conducive to China's rise.[68] The war on global terrorism had an immediate effect in deflating the China threat theory. A story related by Long Yongtu is rather telling in this regard. According to Long, on the morning of September 11, 2001, he was in tough negotiations in Europe with American trade representatives over "the last details of China's WTO accession." The American delegation abruptly left its afternoon meeting upon hearing the news about the terrorist attacks (European time). Long and his Chinese colleagues feared that China's entire WTO deal might be in jeopardy. To their surprise, the American delegation returned the next day and all "the details hotly discussed at the last meeting" were quickly smoothed over. Long quoted the American representatives as saying, "At this critical moment, a rally of civilized countries is more needed."[69]

Chinese commentators took particular notice of the fact that President George W. Bush attended the unofficial summit meeting at the

---

[67] William Kalkhoff and Christopher Barnum, "The Effects of Status-Organizing and Social Identity Processes on Patterns of Social Influence," *Social Psychology Quarterly,* vol. 63, no. 2 (2000), p. 101. See also Roger Brown, *Social Psychology,* 2nd ed. (New York: Free Press, 1986), ch. 17; Burnstein, et al., "How the Mind Preserves the Image of the Enemy."

[68] See Yong Deng and Thomas G. Moore, "China Views Globalization: Towards a New Great Power Politics?" *Washington Quarterly,* vol. 27, no. 3 (Summer 2004), pp. 117–26.

[69] Chiu Li-ben, Wang Chien-min, and Chi Shuo-ming, [No title], *Hong Kong Yazhou Zhoukan,* no. 41 (Oct. 8, 2001), pp. 26–9, in FBIS: CPP20011010000088, pp. 1–2; Duan Silin, "How Long Will Friendship Between China, United States Last This Time?" *Hong Kong Kuan Chiao Ching,* no. 350 (Nov. 16, 2001), pp. 6–9, in FBIS: CPP20011116000061, pp. 4–5.

Asia-Pacific Economic Cooperation (APEC) forum in Shanghai in October 2001. More importantly, while in Shanghai he referred to President Jiang Zemin as "the leader of a great nation." Chinese analysts invariably saw in the war on terrorism an opportunity to direct the U.S. threat attention on China toward unconventional, transnational threats.[70] While encouraged by signs of the U.S. rethinking its strategic priorities, Chinese analysts are nonetheless skeptical and uncertain as to whether Washington has undertaken a complete reassessment of security threats to embrace China as a strategic partner rather than a potential rival. They continue to consider the U.S. threat perception vis-à-vis China as the root cause of the problems in Sino-American relations. They note that after only a brief respite the China threat theory has reemerged surrounding China's military power, its unfair economic practices, its policy toward Taiwan, the EU's attempt to lift the arms embargo on China, and growing Chinese clout in Asia and beyond.[71]

Overall, concerted Chinese rhetorical and diplomatic responses have, however, achieved important successes in allaying foreign hostilities. China threat theory has diminished in places, including, notably, Europe, Southeast Asia, India, South Korea, and Russia. But Chinese efforts have also encountered failures in Japan, Taiwan, and the United States. Alexander Wendt contends that effective strategies of reassurance for a country surrounded by suspicion and fear must

---

[70] Chen Peiyao, "Changes in the U.S. Security Strategy and Adjustments of Its China Policy," *Zhongguo Pinglun*, no. 51 (March 1, 2002), pp. 6–9, in FBIS: CPP20020307000097; [No author], "How to Look at U.S. Strategic Models," *Renmin Ribao* (Internet), Jan. 11, 2002, p. 7, in FBIS: CPP20020111000046; Duan Silin, "How Long Will Friendship Between China, United States Last This Time?"; Zhang Tuosheng, "What Will China Do about U.S. Preemptive Action," *Shijie Zhishi*, no. 16 (Aug. 16, 2002), pp. 24–5, in FBIS: CPP20020906000167.

[71] See, for example, Yuan Peng, "11 September's Incident and Sino-U.S. Relations," *Xiandai Guoji Guanxi*, Nov. 20, 2001, pp. 19–23, 63, in FBIS: CPP20011204000180; Liu Aicheng, "When Will the Cold War Mentality Find Its Resting Place?" *Renmin Ribao* (Internet), June 8, 2004, p. 3, in FBIS: CPP20040608000036; Huang Qing, "Anyone Who Poses Threat Shall Bear Responsibility," *People's Daily* (Internet), at http://english.people.com.cn/200503/02/eng20050302_175287.html (accessed March 25, 2005); Yuan Peng, "Sino-U.S. Relations: New Changes and New Challenges," *Xiandai Guoji Guanxi*, May 20, 2006, pp. 29–37, in Open Source Center: CPP20060606329001.

entail a wholesale embrace of genuine multilateralism, adoption of democracy (because democracies are seen as inherently more trustworthy than other polities), and "self-binding" or even "self-sacrificing" policy choices.[72] This is a tall order in international relations. If he is right, with its spectacular growth in material power, the challenge is particularly great for China in its anti-China-threat campaign.

For its broader status interests, the PRC has put a premium on removing the image of a dangerous outsider. However, it is also sensitive to a plethora of threats as revealed in the China threat theories. The CCP government will not tolerate international criticisms directed at its regime type. It harbors deep suspicion that the threat attribution represents a Western scheme to defame China, deny its great-power aspirations, and delegitimize its national interests. Official Chinese commentary has identified three ways in which the China threat theories are intended to adversely affect China's international environment:

> One, creating political opinion to apply pressures upon China and to meddle in China's domestic affairs. . . . Two, distorting China's image and driving a wedge between China and its neighboring countries to limit China's development. Three, playing the trick of "a thief crying 'Stop thief!'" to divert public attention and to direct the spearhead at China to maintain their own hegemonic position.[73]

The real intention of Western powers, warned Yang Yi, director of strategic studies at the National Defense University, was to "push China to the 'defendant seat'" so they can box China in. For him, China needs a stronger military for deterrence purposes, but also to defend his country's expanding interests abroad in safeguarding its citizens, trade, and energy access while contributing more to global governance.[74] The PRC's growing economy, coupled with its extending global presence, has provided new rationale for military modernization. Meanwhile,

---

[72] Wendt, *Social Theory in International Politics*, pp. 360–63.
[73] Guan Cha Jia, "China's Development Is Beneficial to World Peace and Progress," p. 5. See also Fang Zhi, "Who Threatens Whom after All?" p. 4.
[74] Yang Yi, "Zhongguo Jundui Conglai Shi Zhengyi Zhishi Heping Zhishi" [The Chinese Military Is Always a Force for Justice, a Force for Peace], *Renmin Ribao*, overseas edition, Jan. 8, 2007, p. 1; Yang Yi, "Caution, Engagement," *China Security*, vol. 3, no. 4 (Autumn 2007), pp. 28–38.

the PLA has also jostled to assert its own voice and interests in domestic decision-making, further fueling international debates over China's real intentions. With these forces at work, the Chinese leadership will continue to face the profound challenge of managing foreign fear of a China threat, as the country's claim to great-power status is increasingly backed up with capabilities.

5 | Strategic Partnerships with Russia, the European Union, and India

A notable achievement in China's diplomacy is its strategic partnerships with Russia (from 1996), the European Union (EU) (2003), and India (2005). From Beijing's perspective, "strategic partnership" connotes mutual acceptance of the partner states' importance to each other and to the world at large. The characterization thus signals a partner's political willingness to recognize China's legitimate rise, to manage areas of disagreement in order to steadily improve the overall bilateral relationship, and if possible to enhance coordination in promoting their common preferences in the international arena. However, just as each partnership has its own qualifier, in reality each of China's dyadic relationships has its own difficulties and limits as well as a distinctive set of dynamics.

There exists an impressive literature on the unusual relationship between Russia and China, focusing in particular on the history of the former's interaction with the latter.[1] Many observers have underscored the problems and fragilities of their ties, and some have thus predicted an imminent disentanglement of their strategic partnership.[2] Others have reduced the partnership to essentially an arms deal, beyond which

---

[1] Elizabeth Wishnick, *Mending Fences: The Evolution of Moscow's China Policy from Brezhnev to Yeltsin* (Seattle: University of Washington Press, 2001); Alexander Lukin, *The Bear Watches the Dragon: Russia's Perceptions of China and the Evolution of Russian-Chinese Relations since the 18th Century* (Armonk, NY: M. E. Sharpe, 2003); Jeanne L. Wilson, *Strategic Partners: Russian-Chinese Relations in the Post-Soviet Era* (Armonk, NY: M. E. Sharpe, 2004). The studies tend to focus on the bilateral interaction from Russian perspectives.

[2] Jennifer Anderson, *The Limits of Sino-Russian Strategic Partnership*, International Institute for Strategic Studies, Adelphi Paper 315 (Oxford: Oxford University Press, 1997); Andrew C. Kuchins, "The Limits of the Sino-Russian Strategic Partnership," in Andrew C. Kuchins, ed., *Russia after the Fall* (Washington, DC: Carnegie Endowment for International Peace, 2002), pp. 205–20; Bobo Lo, "The Long Sunset of Strategic Partnership," *International Affairs*, vol. 80, no. 2 (2004), pp. 295–309.

there is little substance.[3] Still, some analysts have viewed the new ties with alarm.[4] Similarly, confusions abound over the meanings of China's strategic partnerships with the EU and India.

This chapter takes a fresh look at Sino-Russian ties and compares them with the other two more recent dyads to gain insights into China's approach to great-power politics in general. The Sino-Russian strategic partnership is given extended treatment for its special importance and relatively long duration. I start with an overview of Sino-Russian relationship after the cold war, focusing on how the leadership on each side has resolved to steadfastly move the relationship forward by settling bilateral problems, updating bilateral ties, and coordinating their stances in the international arena. I then specify the logic behind Sino-Russian strategic interaction by uncovering their similar status disadvantage and aspirations. The third section provides a brief history of China's strategic partnerships with India and the EU. The last part comparatively evaluates the significance and limits of the three sets of strategic partnerships.

The Making of the Sino-Russian Strategic Partnership

The Soviet leader Mikhail Gorbachev, having just completed a historical visit to Beijing, where the student demonstrators hailed him as a hero, refrained from joining the Western condemnation of the Tiananmen killings in early June 1989. His country quickly disintegrated. The two former communist giants and arch ideological-strategic rivals found themselves on diametrically opposite domestic and diplomatic tracks. Post-communist Russia adopted a "shock therapy" of pro-Western liberalization at home and abroad. The idea was to decisively break away from the Soviet past and simultaneously embrace capitalism, democracy, and the "West." Also important, winning

---

[3] See, for example, Dmitri Trenin, "The China Factor: Challenge and Chance for Russia," in Sherman W. Garnett, ed., *Rapprochement or Rivalry: Russia-China Relations in a Changing Asia* (Washington, DC: Carnegie Endowment for International Peace, 2000), pp. 39–70; Robert H. Donaldson and John A. Donaldson, "The Arms Trade in Russian-Chinese Relations: Identity, Domestic Politics, and Geopolitical Positioning," *International Studies Quarterly*, vol. 47, no. 4 (Dec. 2003), pp. 709–32.

[4] Stephen J. Blank, "Russia Looks at China," in Stephen J. Blank and Alvin Z. Rubinstein, eds., *Imperial Decline: Russia's Changing Role in Asia* (Durham, NC: Duke University Press, 1997), pp. 65–98.

unconditional Western support was critical for President Boris Yeltsin in order to lock in Russia's radical domestic transition and boost his own domestic legitimacy.[5]

As these momentous events unfolded, the post-Tiananmen Chinese Communist Party leadership was alarmed and deeply fearful that a fully Westernized Russia would further isolate China. But drawing a lesson from their premature public support to the aborted coup by the communist hardliners in Moscow in August 1991, the CCP leadership judged that a better strategy was to wait until the dust settled and be prepared to deal with whoever emerged as the winning coalition in Russia's domestic power struggle.[6] Fortunately for Beijing, setbacks in both Russia's domestic transition and diplomacy soon prompted a rethinking on its earlier approach of radical, unilateralist liberalization.

As regards its relations with the People's Republic of China, initially the new Russian foreign policy team under President Yeltsin and Foreign Minister Andrei Kozyrev occasionally would raise the human rights issue, but ultimately it did not adopt a politically based, hostile policy. Instead, Moscow first chose to neglect China in its diplomatic reorientation, while at the same time leaving the door open for normalization of bilateral relations, a process formally started with Gorbachev's summit meeting with Deng Xiaoping in May 1989.[7] A key indicator of continued Sino-Russian rapprochement was the ratification of the May 1991 treaty on the eastern section of the Chinese-Russian border by both legislatures in February 1992.[8]

Spurred by its stalled relationship with Japan over the disputed four southernmost Kurile Islands (known as the Northern Territories in Japan) in the autumn of 1992, Russia started to pursue in earnest a China-oriented Asian policy. Diplomatically isolated, the PRC government had every reason to reciprocate with equal, if not greater, enthusiasm. The subsequent four years (1992–96) witnessed a drastic

[5] James M. Goldgeier, "Prospects for U.S.-Russian Cooperation," in Kuchins, *Russia after the Fall*, pp. 281–2.

[6] Li Jingjie, "From Good Neighbors to Strategic Partners," in Garnett, *Rapprochement or Rivalry?*, pp. 72–9.

[7] Cui Xiantao, *Mianxiang Ershiyi Shiji De Zhonge Zhanlue Xiezuo Heban Guanxi* [Sino-Russian Strategic and Cooperative Partnership Facing the 21st Century] (Beijing: Zhonggong Zhongyang Dangxiao Chubanshe, 2003), pp. 4–5.

[8] Qin Qichen, *Waijiao Shiji* [Ten Stories of a Diplomat] (Beijing: Shijie Zhishi Chubanshe, 2003), pp. 228–9.

improvement of Sino-Russian relationship, with rhetorical leaps from a "friendly" relationship to a "constructive partnership" to a "strategic partnership."[9] Both of the partnership ideas were first proposed by Yeltsin, in 1994 and 1996, but immediately they were embraced by his Chinese counterpart, President Jiang Zemin.[10] Growing ties led to a friendship treaty (effective for twenty years and renewable), signed by Jiang and President Vladimir Putin in July 2001. With the formal affirmation of their cooperative commitments, the strategic partnership has since proceeded more steadily than before.

These accelerated developments are remarkable, especially in light of the many domestic obstacles on both sides, stemming notably from the border demarcation, Chinese immigrants in Russia, and mutual security suspicion. The border and immigration issues were intertwined with Moscow's difficulties in keeping under control unruly regionalism in the Russian Far East. Russia's inchoate federalism gave local governments unprecedented power, without clearly delimitating the respective purviews of the center and the locales. As a result, through much of the 1990s, maverick regional leaders in the Russian Far East, such as Governor Yevgeny Nazdratenko of Primorskii Krai and Governor Viktor Ishaev of Khabarovskii Krai, used these issues as a bargaining chip vis-à-vis the center. For the sake of their own political careers and their notions of regional and national interests, they often defied Moscow's China policy.[11]

---

[9] Noting the quick three-step improvement in Sino-Russian relations has become the standard Chinese characterization. For a representative view, see Liu Guchang, "Sino-Russian Good-Neighborly, Friendly, and Cooperative Relations in the 21st Century," *Qiushi* (Internet), no. 23 (Dec. 1, 2002), in Foreign Broadcast Information Service (hereafter cited as FBIS): CPP20021205000044.

[10] Qian, *Ten Stories*, p. 240.

[11] The role of the Russian Far East in influencing Sino-Russian relations is well covered in the literature. See Michael McFaul, "The Far Eastern Challenge to Russian Federalism," Garnett, *Rapprochement or Rivalry?*, ch. 11; Wishnick, *Mending Fences*, ch. 9; Rajan Menon and Charles E. Ziegler, "The Balance of Power and U.S. Foreign Policy Interests in the Russian Far East," in Judith Thornton and Charles E. Ziegler, eds., *Russia's Far East: A Region at Risk* (Seattle: National Bureau of Asian Research/University of Washington Press, 2002), pp. 35–56; Elizabeth Wishnick, "Regional Dynamics in Russia's Asia Policy," *ibid.*, pp. 293–317; Bruce A. Elleman, "Russian Foreign Policy in the Chinese Context," in Blank and Rubinstein, *Imperial Decline*, pp. 99–126; Blank, "Russia Looks at China," pp. 72–3.

The direct cause of the Chinese immigrant problem was the visa-waiving program introduced in early 1992 that opened the floodgates for the Chinese rushing into Russia for trade, jobs, investment, and even smuggling. The Russian public reacted swiftly to the sudden surge of Chinese people on their soil with alarm, even hysteria. Exaggerated reporting of the dangers posed by the Chinese immigrants ran rampant in Russian media. The most extreme claims put the number of Chinese illegal immigrants as high as two million in the Far East area and five million across Russia.[12] Accompanying the wild numerical estimations was a rather rampant historically rooted, racially based fear of a well-planned invasion orchestrated by the Chinese government. According to Mikhail Alexseev, "Viktor Larin, director of the Vladivostok Institute of History, counted more than 150 articles in the local and national press in 1993–95 that raised the specter of the 'yellow peril,' or massive Chinese migration into the Russian Far East as part of China's territorial expansion."[13] Larin's widely cited finding was also noted by Chinese scholars.[14] In light of the public outcries, the Russian government issued a decree reinstating a visa requirement on Chinese visitors on December 6, 1993, which immediately came into effect.[15] The decisive action, coupled with aggressive interventions by local authorities on the Russian side and joint Sino-Russian efforts at border patrol, largely brought the issue under control, even though Russian concerns have persisted.

Objective scholars in both Russia and the West find it all but impossible to ascertain the precise numbers of the Chinese immigrants in Russia in general and its Asian sectors in particular. But they unanimously reject the grossly overstated Chinese expansion. According to Alexander Lukin, "A realistic estimate based on the data of authorities and local police in 1992–1993, suggests that, during the peak

---

[12] Mikhail Alexseev, "Chinese Migration in the Russian Far East: Security Threat and Incentives for Cooperation in Primorskii Krai," in Thornton and Ziegler, *Russia's Far East*, p. 319.

[13] *Ibid.*; Wishnick, *Mending Fences*, p. 154.

[14] See, for example, Cui, *Sino-Russian Strategic and Cooperative Partnership*, pp. 492–3.

[15] Li Chuanxun, "Eluosi Yuandong Duihua Guanxi De Huigu Yu Zhanwang" [Russian Far East's Relations with China: Retrospect and Prospect], *Qiushi Xukan* (Harbin), Feb. 2000, pp. 34–7, reprinted in Renmin University of China, *Chinese Diplomacy*, June 2002, pp. 24–6; Cui, *Sino-Russian Strategic and Cooperative Partnership*, p. 493.

of the border openness, the numbers of Chinese in the RFE [Russian Far East] did not exceed 50,000 to 60,000; and after 1994 it significantly decreased.... These numbers are nowhere near the 10 to 12 percent of the [Chinese] population of the RFE in 1910, nor 4 percent in the late 1920s."[16] Another well-informed study concludes, "More sober local estimates [across Russia] were in the 100,000–200,000 range, not all of them (perhaps not even the majority) permanent."[17] Western media tend to cite higher numbers, as illustrated in a *Washington Post* article on July 29, 2003 putting Chinese immigrants in the RFE at over 200,000.[18]

Emotional Russian reactions to the immigration issue were in part derived from the internal migration to the western sections of the country responsible for the decrease of the population in Russia's Far East to some seven or eight million.[19] The new demographic reality, coupled with economic woes plaguing the vast region, fueled the worst nationalist fear of being overrun by a massive Chinese influx. So, unlike the China threat theories elsewhere, which have arisen in response to problems in mutual interactions, the fear of China in Russia has its origins more in the economic weakness of the Far East and the difficulties in Moscow's relationship with its regions than in the Russian-Chinese relationship per se.[20] Recently, progress in bilateral coordination has significantly, if not fully, alleviated excessive Russian concerns about a Chinese takeover.

Border disputes had long been a major source of animosity between the two nations. Thus, legally delimiting the countries' boundaries were the centerpiece of a mutual attempt to achieve rapprochement. Following the treaty on the 4,300-kilometers-long borders along northeast China (known as the East Section), Russia and China concluded another treaty in 1994 to guide the demarcation of the mere 55-kilometers-long border along China's Xinjiang Autonomous Region

---

[16] Lukin, *The Bear Watches the Dragon*, pp. 167–8.

[17] Galina Vitkovskaya, Zhanna Zayonchkovskaya, and Kathleen Newland, "Chinese Migration into Russia," in Garnett, *Rapprochement or Rivalry?*, ch. 12, quote on p. 350.

[18] Peter Baker, "A Tense Divide in Russia's Far East," *Washington Post*, July 29, 2003, p. A9.

[19] See also Alexseev, "Chinese Migration in the Russian Far East," pp. 319–47; Wishnick, *Mending Fences*.

[20] See Lukin, *The Bear Watches the Dragon*, ch. 3.

(known as the West Section). However, because border demarcations directly impinged on the interests of the locales involved, the actual implementation of the treaties met with strenuous regional resistance. Determination on the part of both leaderships and Chinese flexibility made possible the full implementation of both treaties, in 1997 and 1998.

Left unsettled, however, were the three Russian-controlled islands – including Bolshoi Urruriiski (*Heixiazi* in Chinese, or "Black Bear") and Bolshoi in the border rivers – accounting for about 380 square kilometers or less than 3 percent of the East Section. Both sides pledged flexibility in joint use of the disputed areas in the interim and patience in finding an early amicable solution.[21] On President Putin's visit to Beijing in October 2004, China and Russia finally reached a deal resolving the last disputes. Both sides were initially tight-lipped about the specifics of the agreement, but leaked Russian sources suggested that there was a mutually agreed upon compromise. It turned out that they decided to evenly split the more important Black Bear Island. The supplementary treaty was later ratified by both countries' legislatures and actual demarcation was then quietly undertaken and completed.[22]

Clearly, growing political trust explained the success of the latest round of border negotiations where previous efforts had failed.[23] This

---

[21] Cui, *Sino-Russian Strategic and Cooperative Partnership*, pp. 17–18; Ni Xiaoquan, "China's Threat Perceptions and Policies Toward the Russian Far East," in Thornton and Ziegler, *Russia's Far East*, pp. 375–95; Georgi F. Kunadze "Border Problems Between Russia and Its Neighbors," in Gilbert Rozman, Mikhail Nosov, and Koji Watanabe, eds., *Russia and East Asia* (Armonk, NY: M. E. Sharpe, 1999), pp. 135–41.

[22] "Heixiazidao Huigui Zhongguo Quzhelu: Sishi Yunian Silun Tanpan" [The Tortuous Road of the Black Bear Island's Return to China: Four Rounds of Negotiations in over Forty Years], *Nanfang Zhoumo* [Southern China Weekend], May 26, 2005, at http://news.sina.com.cn/c/2005–05–26/17456758256.shtml (accessed June 11, 2005); Li Fenglin, "Guanyu Zhongsu/e Bianjie Tanpan Jiqi Qianjing" [On Sino-Soviet/Russian Border Negotiations and Their Prospects], at the China Institute of International Studies website, http://www.ciis.org.cn/item/2005–05–31/50988.html (accessed July 1, 2005); "Bufen Heixiazidao Jijiang Huigui" [Parts of the Black Bear Island Are to Return], *Renming Ribao*, overseas edition (hereafter cited as *RMRB*), April 9, 2007, p. 2.

[23] Kunadze "Border Problems Between Russia and Its Neighbors," pp. 135–6; Ni, "China's Threat Perception and Policies Toward the Russian Far East,"

cooperative spirit made it possible for Russia to relinquish parts of the disputed territories under its control. The completion of border demarcation and better management of border-crossing issues have helped to assuage Russia's fear of China's irredentist claims. In its anti-Soviet propaganda campaigns during the 1960s–80s, a historical "fact" held dearly in China was that the Qing dynasty lost to Tsarist Russia over 1.5 million square kilometers of land. Remarkably, in celebrating the historical settlement of the border issue, talk of such "lost territories" all but disappeared in mainstream Chinese commentary. Considering the history of border conflicts between the two countries and international history in general, the way in which China and Russia settled their territorial disputes bespoke a new set of dynamics behind their bilateral relationship.

Since the early 1990s, Russian arms sales and technology transfers to China have constantly served as a cornerstone and cement for their bilateral ties. With a Western arms embargo on China, Moscow became Beijing's only key supplier of modern weapons and military technologies. Major arms deals were successfully negotiated during the waning days of the Soviet Union, soon after Gorbachev's Beijing visit in May 1989. Arms trade and military-related technology transfers picked up and were maintained at a high level under the successor Russian Federation. According to one expert writing at the outset of the twenty-first century, "[M]ost estimates put this [the arms trade] at around U.S.$1–1.5 billion per annum." While this estimation conforms to mainstream Western analyses, unofficial Russian sources put the number significantly higher.[24] The precise items and volume transferred are all but impossible to determine thanks to the secrecy on both sides.[25]

The economic ties between the two nations were clearly out of sync with their political relationship throughout the 1990s. Bilateral trade volume hovered below $10 billion during the decade, falling short of

p. 383; Li Fenglin, "On Sino-Soviet/Russian Border Negotiations and Their Prospects."

[24] Lo, "The Long Sunset of Strategic Partnership," p. 297. See David Lague and Susan V. Lawrence, "In Guns We Trust," *Far Eastern Economic Review*, Dec. 12, 2002, pp. 32–5; Wilson, *Strategic Partners*, p. 102.

[25] For an overview of Russian arms sales to China, see Wilson, *Strategic Partners*, pp. 93–113.

the U.S.$20 billion by 2000, a goal set by presidents Yelstin and Jiang in 1996. Mismanagement in border trade, the lack of institutionalization, and confusions in customs control, together with deep-rooted structural problems on both sides, were to blame for the sluggish trade, defying political fiat from both political leaderships.[26] However, trade picked up as the new century began, thanks in part to surging Chinese demand for Russian oil and natural gas. Mutual complementarities and improving political trust suggest great potentials in deepening economic cooperation in the energy area and beyond, whilst the same time, both countries will continue to rely heavily on ties with advanced Western economies to engineer sustained growth.

In less than two decades, spearheaded by frequent and highly institutionalized leadership meetings, China's relationship with post-Soviet Russia evolved from brief ideological enmity and mutual diplomatic neglect to strategic partnership. The progress is remarkable considering the radical domestic changes in the two countries as well as the historical animosities and power shift between them. Also important, the publics on both sides were ill prepared for these diplomatic breakthroughs. This was particularly a problem in Russia, where policy debates were fiercer and foreign policy decision making was significantly more decentralized. With a bewildering array of liberal, realist, communist, ultranationalist, and even blatantly racist perspectives, Russia had probably the most variegated views on China in the great China debate across the world.[27] Moreover, in pushing their China policy, Russian leaders had to battle a domestic structural pathology of fragmentation, which one Chinese scholar aptly dubbed, "hot at the top, cool at the bottom, and clogged in the middle" (*Shangre, Xialiang, Zhongsai*).[28] In this connection, President Putin's centralization of power, while a setback to democracy, no doubt gave Moscow a much freer hand to pursue its foreign policy. The latest agreement on the small disputed islands in the East Section

---

[26] International Monetary Fund, *Direction of Trade Statistics Yearbook*, various years. For a Chinese listing of the problems, see "Why Sino-Russian Trade Not up to U.S.$20 Billion," at http://english.people.com.cn/200404/09/eng20040409_139952.shtml (accessed July 11, 2004).

[27] For an overview, see Lukin, *The Bear Watches the Dragon.*

[28] Yan Xuetong, et al., *Zhongguo De Jueqi—Guoji Huanjing Pinggu* [China's Rise: An Evaluation of the International Environment] (Tianjin: Renmin Chubanshe, 1998), pp. 270–1.

was simply inconceivable in the 1990s due to staunch local nationalism in the Russian border areas.

As a result of ten years of strategic partnership, the Chinese and Russian militaries conducted in August 2005 a series of joint military exercises, code-named "Peace Mission 2005," in Vladivostok and the Shangdong Peninsula area. With nearly 10,000 troops and advanced weaponries involved, the *Beijing Review* declared, "they are the largest-scale military exercises the PLA [People's Liberation Army] has ever launched with foreign armed forces."[29] Reportedly, the PRC tried to use the exercises to maximize deterrence on Taiwan, whereas Russia's focus was on Central Asia. As a result, they did not agree on the location of the war games until the end of 2004. Regardless of the veracity of these reports, the countries were able to smooth over differences, and in the end the drills did somewhat serve their interests on both fronts. Two years later, in August 2007, the second "peace mission" military exercise was conducted in Russia, under explicit auspices of the Shanghai Cooperation Organization (SCO).

Russia and China indeed have strengthened their comprehensive ties through the SCO, which had its start as the Shanghai Five leadership meetings in 1996, designed to facilitate confidence building about border security among China, Russia, Kazakhstan, Kyrgyzstan, and Tajikistan. In 2001, under Chinese and Russian leadership, the Shanghai Five added a sixth member, Uzbekistan to officially become the SCO, and a few years later it granted several countries observer status. The SCO has since evolved into an international organization that has played a nontrivial role in transforming the strategic landscape of the Central Asian region.

On the heels of the Tiananmen incident in 1989 and the subsequent collapse of the Soviet Union, few observers would have foreseen a Sino-Russian strategic partnership in several years. At the beginning of the new millennium, Chinese officials and analysts declared that Sino-Russian relations had never been better, a sentiment echoed by their Russian counterparts. Strikingly, in the short span of their new relationship, the two countries have settled (if not solved altogether) outstanding bilateral issues that historically have derailed amity; developed frequent, regularized meetings at the highest levels; and pledged

[29] Ni Yanshuo, "Aiming for Security," *Beijing Review*, Sept. 1, 2005, p. 13.

and sometimes worked jointly to promote a less Western-dominated world order.

China and Russia: Fellow Travelers out of the Periphery

The collapse of the Soviet empire forfeited the diplomatic gains expected by the two communist giants from the historical summit meeting between Mikhail Gorbachev and Deng Xiaoping in May 1989. The cataclysmic change not only exposed the PRC as the only major ideological foe of the West, but also gave birth to a post-communist Russia that could potentially join the West to gang up against China. After all, inspired by an intellectual paradigm known as "Atlanticism," the new Russian political elite sought a wholesale Westernization of domestic and foreign policy.[30] Foreign Minister Andrei Kozyrev and his liberal cohorts in the government had little interest in being associated with Beijing. However, domestic woes and international frustration soon dampened the Russian hope to rebuild a new country in the Western image.

In terms of foreign relations, the disputes over the four southernmost Kurile Islands (Northern Territories) with Japan in 1992 underscored the substantive barriers in Russia's reorientation. But it was the subsequent expansion of the North Atlantic Treaty Organization that created a real sense of crisis in the Russian foreign policy establishment. Seeing NATO as a relic of the cold war, Moscow had proposed an alternative security institution inclusive of all European states, but to no avail. Subsequently, various NATO arrangements with Russia failed to fundamentally assuage Moscow's concerns over the organization's growing reach. Russia's political elite fundamentally viewed NATO expansion as evidence of Western distrust and a symbol of its failed struggle to join the West. As such, the psychological denigration, humiliation, and betrayal inflicted on them cannot be overstated. The 1999 NATO war against Yugoslavia over Kosovo only confirmed the worst Russian fear of the security organization's malicious implications for its international stature and core interests.[31]

---

[30] Alexander A. Sergunin, "Discussions of International Relations in Post-Communism Russia," *Communist and Post-Communist Studies*, vol. 27, no. 1 (March 2004), pp. 20–1.

[31] For the trauma inflicted on Russia by the NATO expansion, see Margot Light, John Lowenhardt, and Stephen White, "Russia and the Dual Expansion of

Russia's flawed political and economic transition, the Chechnya war, and weapons proliferation disputes further alienated its relationship with the West. Moscow, in turn, saw a consistent pattern of Western disrespect of its national pride and relentless attempts to encroach on its sphere of influence. Putin's support for the U.S.-led war on terror after 9/11 failed to qualitatively improve Western treatment of Russia. Instead, during 2003–05 Moscow found its influence eaten away with the downfalls of traditional pro-Russian leaders in largely peaceful, popular democratic movements known as "color revolutions" in Georgia, Ukraine, and Kyrgyzstan. Moscow invariably saw these nearby changes as inspired and abetted by the West.

By the mid-1990s, the Russian elite had concluded that its erstwhile unilateral pro-Western approach had proven counterproductive to both its security interests and its international status.[32] The liberal Atlanticist foreign policy had failed to secure a place for Russia at the great-power table. As two Russian analysts wrote, "The West is yet to accept Russia as it is, and Russian society has yet to develop its identification with the West."[33] The result was a profound disillusionment with the West. An alternative idea known as Eurasianism, which seeks to balance Russia's European and Asian identities, was revived and gained ground in Russian foreign policy thinking. In

---

Europe," in Gabriel Gorodetsky, ed., *Russia Between East and West: Russian Foreign Policy on the Threshold of the Twenty-First Century* (London: Frank Cass, 2003), pp. 61–74; William D. Jackson, "Encircled Again: Russia's Military Assesses Threats in the Post-Soviet World," *Political Science Quarterly*, vol. 117, no. 3 (Fall 2002), pp, 373–400; Sergei Medvedev, "Power, Space, and Russian Foreign Policy," in Ted Hopf, ed., *Understandings of Russian Foreign Policy* (University Park: Pennsylvania State University Press, 1999), p. 46; Vladimir Branovsky, "Russian Views on NATO and the EU," in Anatol Lieven and Dmitri Trenin, eds., *Ambivalent Neighbors: The EU, NATO, and the Price of Membership* (Washington, DC: Carnegie Endowment for International Peace, 2003), pp. 269–94; Dmitri Trenin, *The End of Eurasia: Russia on the Border Between Geopolitics and Globalization* (Washington, DC: Carnegie Endowment for International Peace, 2002), pp. 270–97.

32 See Michael McFaul, "A Precarious Peace: Domestic Politics in the Making of Russian Foreign Policy," *International Security*, vol. 22, no. 3 (Winter 1997/98), pp. 5–35; Dimitri Simes, *After the Collapse: Russia Seeks Its Place as a Great Power* (New York: Simon & Schuster, 1999); Bobo Lo, *Russian Foreign Policy in the Post-Soviet Era: Reality, Illusion and Mythmaking* (New York: Palgrave Macmillan, 2002).

33 A. P. Tsygankov and P. A. Tsygankov, "New Directions in Russian International Studies: Pluralization, Westernization, and Isolationism," *Communist and Post-Communist Studies*, vol. 37, no. 1 (March 2004), p. 4.

comparison to Atlanticism, Eurasianism shows a greater awareness of Russia's distinctive values and special interests, especially in securing its strategic space in the former Soviet republics; is characterized by a heightened fear of marginalization and threat in an uncertain world; and advocates a more diversified foreign policy beyond a fixation on the West.[34] The new idea coalesced with other schools of thought and ideological persuasions to prompt a paradigm shift in Russian foreign policy.[35]

Russia thus began to aggressively pursue a diversified foreign policy with particular attention to the Islamic and Pacific Asia, believing that such multidirectional diplomacy would advance, rather than impede, its relationship with the West. As Deputy Foreign Minister Alesandr Panov stated in late 1994, "[T]he stronger [Russia's] positions are in the East, the more confidently and decisively we can act in the West."[36] For Yeltsin and his supporters, the PRC was the centerpiece of Russia's diplomatic diversification toward the East. He stated in 1995, "We can rest on the Chinese shoulder in our relations with the West. In that case the West will treat Russia more respectfully."[37] For him, reforming the tight, discriminatory international structure required concerted effort with China.[38]

---

[34] For a concise discussion of Atlanticism and Eurasianism, see Sergunin, "Discussions of International Relations in Post-Communism Russia," pp. 20–23. A well-researched Chinese account is Bi Hongye, "Ouya Zhuyi Diyuan Zhengzhiguan Yu Eluoshi Waijiao Zouxiang" [Eurasianist Geo-Political Thinking and Russia's Diplomatic Trend," in Feng Zhaolei and Xiang Lanxin, eds., *Zhuanxing Zhong De Eluoshi Duiwai Zhanlue* [Russia's Foreign Strategy in Transition] (Shanghai: Renmin Chucanshe, 2005), pp. 44–69. For the implications of this debate for Russia's policy choices in Asia, see Oles M. Smolansky, "Russia and the Asia-Pacific Region: Policies and Polemics," in Blank and Rubinstein, *Imperial Decline*, pp. 7–39.

[35] For discussions of liberal and realist views, see Pavel A. Tsygankov and Andrei P. Tysygankov, "Dilemmas and Promises of Russian Liberalism," *Communist and Post-Communist Studies*, vol. 37, no. 1 (March 2004), pp. 53–70; Shakleyina and Bogaturov, "The Russian Realist School of International Relations."

[36] Quoted in Smolansky, "Russia and the Asia-Pacific Region," p. 22; Tatyana A. Shakleyina and Aleksei D. Bogaturov, "The Russian Realist School of International Relations," *Communist and Post-Communist Studies*, vol. 27, no. 1 (March 2004), pp. 37–51.

[37] Quoted in Lukin, *The Bear Watches the Dragon*, p. 305.

[38] See, for example, Aleksandr Grigoryevick Yakovlev, "Russia and China in the Structuring of a New World Order," *Moscow Problemy Dalnego Vostoka*, no. 6 (Nov.—Dec. 1998), pp. 23–9, in FBIS: FTS19990316000015; Lukin, "Russia's

While few, if any, Chinese observers had anticipated such a quick Russian turnabout, they unanimously described Russia's move away from the West as fully expected. Rooted either in civilizational division or strategic rivalry, they argue, the West has always kept Russia at arm's length and at bay. The United States and Europe took advantage of Russia's weakness, disrespected core Russian national interests, and treated Russia with a great deal of ambivalence and suspicion.[39] This remained unchanged under President Putin. The common themes in Chinese studies of Russian foreign relations boil down to three points. First, Russia is weakened, humiliated, and disenchanted with the West. Second, the driving force behind Russia's foreign policy is the restoration of its great-power status. And third, Russia's great-power potential should not be underestimated.[40]

China and Russia thus saw themselves as natural allies, insofar as they both purportedly exhibit traits that would justify being treated as outliers to the U.S.-led Western great-power group.[41] They, in turn,

Image of China and the Russian-Chinese Relations"; Lo, *Russian Foreign Policy in the Post-Soviet Era*, pp. 57–9.

[39] Pan Deli and Xu Zhixin, eds., *Eluosi Shinian* [Ten Years of Russia: Politics, Economics, and Foreign Policy], vol. 2 (Beijing: Shijie Zhishi Chubanshe, 2003); Li Jingjie, "Shilun Zhonge Zhanlue Xiezuo Huoban Guanxi" [On Sino-Russian Strategic Partnership of Coordination], *Dongou Zhongya Yanjiu*, no. 2 (1997), at http://www.cass.net.cn/chinese/s24_oys/chinese/Magazine/Yanjiu/9702/001.htm (accessed July 12, 2005). Yang Jiemian, "Chongzhanlue Huoban Dao Yidiyiyou De Meie Guanxi" [U.S.-Russian Relations: From Strategic Partnership to Mixture of Enmity and Friendship], *Guoji Guancha*, no. 1 (2000), in Renmin University of China, *International Politics*, no. 5 (2000), pp. 80–84; Feng Yujun, "Xifang Weihe Paichi Eluosi" [Why Does the West Exclude Russia?], *Huaqiu Shibao*, Aug. 29, 2002, p. 4; Michael Pillsbury, *China Debates the Future Security Environment* (Washington, DC: National Defense University Press, 2000), pp. 173–5.

[40] Jiang Yi, et al., *Chongzhen Daguo Xiongfeng: Pujing De Waijiao Zhanlue* [Reinvigorating Great-power Ambitions: Putin's Diplomatic Strategy] (Beijing: Shijie Zhishi Chubanshe, 2004); Feng Shaolei and Xiang Lanxin, eds., *Pujing Waijiao* [Putin's Diplomacy] (Shanghai: Shanghai Renmin Chubanshe, 2004); Feng Zhaolei and Xiang Lanxin, *Russia's Foreign Strategy in Transition*; Xu Zhixin, "Pujing Shiqi Eluosi Duiwai Zhanlue Jiexi" [Diagnosis of Russian Foreign Strategy During the Putin Era], *Eluoshi, Zhongya, Dongou Yanjiu* [Russian, Central Asian, and East European Studies], no. 3 (June 2004), pp. 50–7; Pillsbury, *China Debates the Future Security Environment*, ch. 4.

[41] Robert Jervis, "Theories of War in an Era of Leading-Power Peace," *American Political Science Review*, vol. 96, no. 1 (March 2002), pp. 1–14; Richard Rosecrance, ed., *The Great Power Coalition* (Boulder, CO: Rowman & Littlefield, 2001); John Garver, "Sino-Russian Relations," in Samuel S. Kim, ed.,

resent such a treatment and have expressed their revisionist preferences in the mantra of promoting "multipolarity." The use of the realist term would seem to suggest a traditional alliance-making, balance-of-power logic against the West. But the substance behind the rhetoric refrain reveals a much more nuanced approach and a more dynamic trilateral interaction involving the United States and Europe. The PRC has long preferred multipolarity, but its assessment of both the likelihood and content of such a world have evolved over time. Chinese discourse always envisions China and Russia as independent poles. Beyond that, however, other than offering a broad contour of that preferred world, the idea of multipolarity never translated into a practical game plan for bringing it about. It almost never conveyed a concrete policy prescription for Chinese activism through alliance making or audacious diplomatic shifts.

By the late 1990s, Chinese analysts started to accept the enduring strength of U.S. hegemony and to characterize multipolarization as a drawn-out process.[42] Similarly, their Russian counterparts have expressed a strong preference for multipolarity. But caution is urged: Do not get caught up in wishful thinking, but recognize the lasting nature of the U.S.-led Western power dominance. And Russian national interest is best served by improving ties with the West and by strengthening its own domestic front.[43] For both countries, the notion of multipolarization serves to justify their calls for change to features of the world order that they perceive to be unfair and discriminatory.

Thus, despite the polarity language, the Sino-Russian strategic partnership does not fully accord with the realist prescription of an alliance geared toward balancing against Western power. It cannot be explained by such zero-sum logic, nor is it marked by such confrontation toward the international status quo. For example, the 2001 bilateral treaty signed did not stipulate any commitment to a direct

---

China and the World: Chinese Foreign Policy Faces the New Millennium (Boulder, CO: Westview Press, 1998), pp. 114–32.

[42] Yong Deng, "Hegemon on the Offensive: Chinese Perspectives of the U.S. Global Strategy," *Political Science Quarterly*, vol. 116, no. 3 (Fall 2001), pp. 343–65.

[43] Shakleyina and Bogaturov, "The Russian Realist School of International Relations"; Simes, *After the Collapse*, pp. 206–7; Lo, *Russian Foreign Policy in the Post-Soviet Era*, pp. 24–6.

military role in assisting each other. It twice stressed that it is "not directed against any third country."[44] The PRC and Russia both have disavowed any characterization of their partnership as an anti-Western alliance, while acclaiming it as representative of a new paradigm in international relations.

To say that the Sino-Russian partnership overall does not conform to the traditional power politics model does not negate the impulse on both sides to form a robust alliance to counter U.S. power. The Russians were more explicit in flirting with such an idea. Most notably, in late 1998 Prime Minister Yevgeniy Primakov openly suggested including India to create a non-Western tripartite coalition. With Russian seriousness in doubt, neither India nor China cared to issue any official reactions to his proposition. Perhaps the most serious interest in a separate global grouping surfaced in the aftermath of the NATO air war against Yugoslavia and the mistaken bombing of the Chinese embassy in Belgrade in May 1999. For a brief period, China and Russia did step up military ties, but the drive for an exclusive alliance proved to be feeble and short-lived.[45] Subsequently, Chinese official commentaries took pains to reiterate the Sino-Russian partnership's nonhostility toward any third party.[46]

For both Chinese and Russian leaderships, fulfilling their countries' international aspirations requires not only good ties with each other but also with the West. Such win-win interaction is both desirable and feasible,[47] whereas the alternative strategy of building a

---

[44] See the Chinese text of the treaty, *RMRB*, July 17, 2001.

[45] Alexander Lukin, "Russia's Image of China and the Russian-Chinese Relations," at http://www.brookings.org/dybdocroot/fp/cnaps/papers/lukinwp-01.pdf, p. 5; Rong Ying, "A Strategic Triangle," *Beijing Review*, Aug. 5, 2005, p. 10; Bin Yu, "Historical Ironies, Dividing Ideologies and Accidental 'Alliance': Russian-Chinese Relations into the 21st Century," in Carolyn W. Pumphrey, ed., *The Rise of China in Asia: Security Implications* (Carlisle, PA: Strategic Studies Institute, 2002), pp. 144–6; Wishnick, *Mending Fences*, p. 157; Jackson, "Encircled Again," pp. 373–400.

[46] Editorial, "New Milestone in Sino-Russian Relations," *RMRB*, July 16, 2003, p. 1; Zhou Zhunnan, "Shining Example for a New Mode of International Relations," *RMRB*, July 16, 2002, p. 3; Gu Ping, "A Model of New-Style State Relations," *Renmin Ribao* (Internet), Dec. 4, 2002, p. 3, in FBIS: CPP20021204000039.

[47] On Russia, see Jack Snyder, "Russia: Responses to Relative Decline," in T. V. Paul and John A. Hall, eds., *International Order and the Future of World Politics* (Cambridge: Cambridge University Press, 1999), pp. 146–54; MacFaul,

confrontational alliance appears to be neither desirable nor feasible.[48] Consequently, the countries' ties are seen as indispensable for both sides in supporting their domestic agendas and securing their strategic spaces. Thus, the Sino-Russian strategic partnership is marked by a lack of hostile exclusiveness and a binding mutual commitment directed against the West or the United States.

Both Chinese and Russian quests for the great-power status are hampered by their material weaknesses and domestic problems. The most tangible status benefits of their strategic ties are the security dividends between themselves and the substantial mutual support for their respective domestic agenda geared toward enhancing comprehensive national power. Their new entente effectively removed a security threat that historically had dominated strategic planning in both capitals. The steady Russian supply of high-tech weapons significantly boosted China's arsenal, essential for deterrence or military scenarios across the Taiwan Strait. Economic cooperation, particularly in the energy sector, has registered impressive growth several years into the new century. China's participation in the economy of the Russian Far East has helped revitalize the region and dampened the centrifugal forces that have deeply worried Moscow.

A path-dependent effect is also at work, fortifying a domestic-international nexus that underpins their respective approaches to the strategic partnership. For Chinese reformers, their domestic reforms (*Gaige*) were to be undertaken in tandem with openness (*Kaifang*) to the outside world. *Perestroika* ("restructuring," especially of the Russian economy) in the Soviet Union in the 1980s and the subsequent Westernization effort by Russia marked a rejection of the earlier Soviet goal to build a totalitarian, anti-Western bloc. The upshot is that in both countries an anti-Western strategic choice would represent too radical a reversal and would meet stiff resistance from the dominant social interests so deeply tied to the globalized world. The

---

"A Precarious Peace." On China, see Alastair Iain Johnston, "Is China a Status Quo Power?" *International Security*, vol. 27, no. 4 (Spring 2003), pp. 5–56.

[48] Bin Yu, "Historical Ironies, Dividing Ideologies and Accidental 'Alliance,'" pp. 111–59; Gilbert Rozman, "China's Quest for Great Power Identity," *Orbis*, vol. 43, no. 3 (Summer 1999), pp. 395–9; Alexei D. Voskressenski, "Russia's Evolving Grand Strategy Toward China," in Garnett, *Rapprochement or Rivalry?*, pp. 133–4.

economic fortunes of both countries are tied to the global system and to Europe, Japan, and North America in particular. The PRC is already at the center of economic globalization, while Russia is striving to better position itself in it. Sino-Russian trade represented only a fraction of Sino-American trade, suggesting an asymmetry of China's economic reliance decisively favoring the United States and other Western markets.

In terms of the bilateral relationship, the mutual trust and shared interests were simply not strong enough to sustain an anti-Western alliance. Overlaying diverse Russian perceptions on the PRC were a sense of unease about its rise. Contrasting economic fortunes of the two countries cast a long shadow over their strategic ties. As Dmitri Trenin of the Carnegie Moscow Center writes, "[I]n the highly improbable case of [an anti-American] alliance actually emerging, Russia is likely to play a subordinate role. The supreme but bitter irony could be that having refused to be a junior partner of the United States, Moscow would end up as Beijing's 'little brother' and 'ammunition bearer.'"[49] For Trenin, it would be strategic folly for Russia to pursue such a one-sided, anti-Western policy. Instead, he believed, Russia should keep a watchful eye on China. On the Chinese side, a formal alliance did not figure in Beijing's calculations in the first place.[50] Sino-Soviet experiences in the 1950s left too many bitter memories. Besides, for the Chinese elite, while Russia might resent the West, it ultimately would not turn its back on it.[51]

In terms of their international agendas, both China and Russia are simultaneously driven by a prosystem bias and a revisionist agenda vis-à-vis the world order. Thus, both take pains to reassure the outside world that their strategic ties are emphatically not aimed at any third party. Yet they need each other's support to enhance their diplomatic leverage in a world where the West clearly has an upper hand. In the words of one Chinese analyst, Sino-Russian strategic ties

---

[49] Dmitrti Trenin, "From Pragmatism to Strategic Choice: Is Russia's Security Policy Finally Becoming Realistic?" in Kuchins, *Russia after the Fall*, p. 192.
[50] See Anderson, *The Limits*.
[51] See, for example, Jiang Yi, "Eluosi De Guoji Diwei Yu Waijiao Zhengce Xuanze" [Russia's International Status and Diplomatic Choice], *Dongou Zhongya Yanjiu*, no. 3 (2002), at http://www.cass.net.cn/chinese/s24_oys/chinese/Magazine/Yanjiu/0203/020301.htm (accessed July 7, 2005).

are a "response" and "warning" to Western pressure and U.S. hege-monism.[52] As another Chinese analyst writes, "The restraint of [the] Sino-Russian strategic partnership on the United States should also be the kind of mutual restraint of pluralistic politics under a constitutional structure, instead of the life-and-death or zero-sum relations limited only to safeguarding one's own interests and independence."[53] Pro-claimed lofty ideals aside, at bottom what drives Sino-Russian strate-gic partnership is a common pursuit for change to the international arrangement such that they face significantly reduced collective pres-sure from a united West setting standards and dictating rules.[54] By the same token, neither country accepts a world tightly controlled by the United States and its democratic allies. Thus, they prefer a multipo-lar, pluralistic, democratic world order that would confer upon them greater strategic space and political legitimacy. And both sides believe, to that end, that they need to capitalize on each other's strengths and support.

To be sure, the scholarly and policy community in Russia tends to display more diverse views, more open and heated debate, and more robust liberal voices than in China. But at the strategic level, the political elites on both sides seem to realize that their countries have many convergent interests, insofar as they face similar foreign policy predicaments rooted in the U.S. power preponderance and Western dominance. The "Joint Statement on the World Order for the Twenty-first Century," signed at the conclusion of President Hu Jintao's visit to Moscow on July 1, 2005, systematically articulated their shared international discontent and preferences. Most revealingly, it pro-claimed, "[T]he international community should thoroughly rid itself of confrontational and alliance-making mentalities, should not seek monopoly and domination in international affairs, and should not categorize member states into leadership and subordinate types."[55] And as the statement made it clear, the solution was a more pluralized and multipolarized world.

---

[52] Cui, *Sino-Russian Strategic and Cooperative Partnership*, pp. 78–81.

[53] Zhuang Liwei, "Hu Jintao's Crucial Future," *Nanfeng Chuang*, June 1, 2003, pp. 12–14, in FBIS: CPP20030611000023, quote on p. 4.

[54] See also Rozman, "Sino-Russian Relations."

[55] For the Chinese version of the full text, see "Zhonge Guanyu Ershiyi Siji Guoji Zhixu de Lianhe Shengming" [Sino-Russian Joint Statement on the World Order of the 21st Century], *RMRB*, July 2, 2005, p. 4.

They issued a joint statement advocating "multipolarity" in world politics in 1997; and in 2005, they propounded a vision of a "new world order." To soften their calls for change, Chinese and Russian leaders have recently equated multipolarization to democratization in world politics. On his first foreign visit to Moscow as the newly inaugurated Chinese president in late May 2003, Hu Jintao spoke of the need to "democratize international relations."[56] Similarly, senior Russian leaders and diplomats have stressed what they and their Chinese counterparts really want is the democratic principles of sovereignty, mutual respect of national interests, and nonmilitary solutions to international conflicts. For both Russia and China, multipolarity is an antidote to what they perceive to be U.S. unilateralism and Western discrimination against them. Insisting on multipolarity serves to deny legitimacy to the U.S.-led international hierarchy or the arbitrary standards employed by the West to justify separate treatments of different categories of states.[57]

Their shared status interests have manifested themselves in concrete areas of cooperation. At the annual meetings of the United Nations Human Rights Commission (UNHRC), Russia had since the mid-1990s provided support to China in its efforts to ward off any formal resolution criticizing its human rights record. After casting its decisive vote – which saved China from what would have been the first official UNHRC censure in 1995 – Russia's vote pattern on China in this UN body shifted from implicit, reluctant support to an explicit and unequivocal siding with Beijing. Russia joined hands with China to block U.S. attempts to reform the UNHRC in 2005. The two countries were also staunch defenders of sovereignty against the so-called Western power politics practices and humanitarian interventionism, especially after the NATO war against Yugoslavia.[58]

In many instances, China and Russia pooled their diplomatic resources to try to curb U.S. unilateralism. A notable example was

---

[56] *RMRB*, May 29, 2003, pp. 1, 4.

[57] L. N. Klepatskii, "The New Russia and the New World Order," in Gorodetsky, *Russia Between East and West*, pp. 3–11; Lukin, *The Bear Watches the Dragon*, p. 306.

[58] Sergei V. Chugrov, "Russian Foreign Policy and Human Rights: Conflicted Culture and Uncertain Policy," in David P. Forsythe, ed., *Human Rights and Comparative Foreign Policy* (Tokyo: United Nations University Press, 2000), pp. 156–61; Dittmer, "The Sino-Russian Strategic Partnership," p. 410.

their cooperation in opposing the U.S. decision to build a national missile defense system. Both countries warned of the destabilization of strategic balance such a U.S. move might engender. Presidents Jiang and Putin issued in July 2000 a joint declaration defending the 1972 Anti-Ballistic Missile (ABM) treaty.[59] Their efforts failed. And when the United States abandoned the treaty in December 2001, their separate public reactions were mild, and no joint statement was subsequently crafted. But parallel interests in opposing U.S. development of missile defense systems with its allies in Eastern Europe and the Western Pacific later drew common, if not coordinated, opposition from Russia and China. They similarly worked in tandem to register their disapproval of the U.S.-Iraqi war and to limit the U.S. options in the North Korean and Iranian nuclear crises.

China and Russia have provided mutual support in international institutions and each other's bid for institutional membership. Both see their permanent membership in the UN Security Council as a key marker of their international status. Both see the UN as the embodiment of multilateralism and therefore prefer a central UN role in world affairs. As demonstrated through the diplomacy over the war on Iraq in 2003, Russia and China have pursued parallel, if not coordinated, diplomacy in restraining the United States through the UN mechanism.

Similarly, the SCO, which is led by China and Russia, has been hailed by both sides as setting a model of "new cooperative security" antithetical to traditional power politics. Contrary to the prediction that the post-9/11 events had rendered it irrelevant, the SCO has forged ahead. In 2004–5, the organization witnessed further institutionalization and expansion, admitting Mongolia, Pakistan, Iran, and India as observers. To be sure, the SCO is still confronted by limited resources and weak authority, as well as unsettled issues concerning its organizational mode, agenda, identity, and, most importantly, its relationship with the United States.[60] But with limited emphasis on formal rules and centralized structure, the organization has served important needs of its member states on the cheap. Remarkably, the SCO summit held

[59] The Chinese text can be found in *RMRB*, July 19, 2000, p. 1.
[60] For a rare candid Chinese analysis, see Zhao Huasheng, "Shanghai Hezuo Zuzhi: Pinggu Yu Fazhan Wenti" [The Shanghai Cooperation Organization: Assessment and the Problem of Development], *Xiandai Guoji Guanxi*, no. 5 (2005), at http://www.irchina.org/news/view.asp?id=946 (accessed July 25, 2005).

in Astana, Kazakhstan in July 2005 called for setting a "deadline" for the end of the U.S. and other coalition members' military presence in SCO member states, including U.S. air bases in Kyrgyzstan and Uzbekistan used in support of the war on the Taliban.[61] Unhappy with the U.S. human rights pressures and encouraged by SCO support, Uzbekistan officially announced termination of the lease agreement less than a month after the SCO declaration.

The SCO has served as a platform for Sino-Russian leadership in shaping regional affairs. In fact, a principal purpose of their "Peace Mission 2005" military exercises was to demonstrate their determination and capacities to defend other SCO states' interests in combating terrorism and other potential threats through military means. The emphasis on "stabilizing" the region suggests greater interest by the SCO in proactive intervention in both domestic and regional developments.[62] But just as one should not overstate Sino-Russian cooperation in challenging the world order, so should one not exaggerate the SCO's role as an anti-Western alliance. For their own reasons, smaller members, notably Kazakhstan, do not want to see the organization evolving in that direction either. Seemingly aware of its limited military role, the organization's mission has over the past several years realigned to focus on economic development and cooperation.

As for membership bids for certain international institutions, both countries have extended mutual support to reduce their exclusion. Chinese support proved instrumental in Russia's joining the Asia-Pacific Economic Cooperation (APEC) forum in 1998. Sino-Russian partnership probably helped overcome Tokyo's recalcitrance in resisting Russian entry into the Group-7 club in 1997.[63] To be sure, G8 membership does not end Russian isolation. As Dmitri Trenin observes, "Membership in the G-8, when it came at last in 1998 at Birmingham,

---

[61] "Shanghai Hezuo Zuzhi Chengyuanguo Yuanshou Xuanyan" [The Leaders' Declaration of the Shanghai Cooperation Organization Member States], *RMRB*, July 6, 2005, p. 5.

[62] Artur Blinov, "Moscow and Beijing Do Not Scare Pentagon; But Exercises on Shandong Peninsula Bring Closer Formation of Military Component in SCO," *Moscow Nezavisimaya Gazeta*, Aug. 25, 2005, pp. 1, 5, in FBIS: CEP20050825019001; Li Yong, "SCO: Conglinian Miaixiang Shijian" [SCO: Leaping from Idea to Practice], *Jiefangjun Bao*, Nov. 4, 2005, at http://jczs.sina.com.cn/2005–11–04/1325328739.html (accessed Nov. 8, 2005).

[63] Wishnick, *Mending Fences*, pp. 142–3.

was regarded as a mere sop."[64] But it marked a key step in Russia's status quest. As regards China's membership in this great-power club, for the time being neither did China officially express a desire to join as a permanent member nor was the group ready to formally invite China's application. Should Beijing decide to make an earnest bid for the G8 meeting, it's more likely than not that Russia will offer its support, for Chinese participation could reduce Russian isolation.

In Article 17 of the 2001 Sino-Russian friendship treaty, China and Russia pledge:

> The contracting parties shall conduct cooperation in world financial institutions, economic organizations and forums, and in line with the rules and regulations of the above-mentioned institutions, organizations and forums, make efforts to promote the participation of a contracting party in the above-mentioned institutions of which the other contracting party is already a member (or member state).[65]

In this spirit, China publicly supported Russia's membership in the World Trade Organization (WTO), even though resolving the myriad difficulties in their trade relationship proved to be a rather difficult process. By the time of Premier Wen Jiabao's visit to Russia in September 2004, bilateral negotiations over the terms of Russian accession had been near completion, thus dispelling suspicion in Russia about China's sincerity. The negotiations were concluded a month later, during Putin's visit to Beijing, when the two countries also officially recognized each other as a "market economy." The Chinese emphasized the special bond of strategic partnership as a key impetus behind these negotiations. And the Russian side admitted relative ease and swiftness of the final WTO deal with China in comparison with its dealings with the European Union and the United States.[66]

Measured against relevant theoretical propositions, neither their mutual commitment nor their hostility toward the United States

---

[64] Trenin, *The End of Eurasia*, p. 274.

[65] From the English translation of the treaty published at the website of the Chinese Ministry of Foreign Affairs at http://www.fmprc.gov.cn/eng/wjb/zzjg/dozys/gjlb/3220/3221/t16730.htm (accessed Aug. 18, 2004).

[66] Natalya Meliova, "Putin Delights Chinese Comrades with Russian Reforms, and Chinese Comrades Delight Putin with Alla Pugachava's Songs 'About Love and Sincere Impulse of the Soul,'" *Moscow Nezavisimaya Gazeta*, Oct. 15, 2004, p. 3, in FBIS: CEP20041015000178.

amounts to an anti-Western alliance as posited by the realist paradigm.[67] True, its formation has to do with the broad systemic forces embedded in the post–cold war international arrangement.[68] The world they find themselves in is not just about power distribution under anarchy, but rather it is defined by a hierarchy of power *and* authority. The distinctive domestic-international nexus underpinning the two emerging powers' foreign policy in the age of globalization has also conditioned their approaches to strategic ties. Both aspire to secure a seat at the great-power table, but they plan to do so on their own terms. As fellow travelers out of the periphery, they share parallel interests in resisting Western dominance and restraining U.S. power.

Strategic Partnerships with India and the EU

As early as the 1980s, the PRC began to see its cooperation with India as a possible counterweight to the increasingly institutionalized economic dominance in Asia by the United States and Japan. Following Indian Prime Minister Rajiv Gandhi's visit to Beijing in late 1988, Sino-Indian tensions eased considerably. On President Jiang Zemin's visit to India in 1996, both sides pledged to build a "constructive, cooperative partnership." But the relationship was soon stalled due to disputes over India's nuclear testing in May 1998. India had long sought to develop its own nuclear weapons, while China had long supported the Pakistani weapons program and kept up international pressures to limit India's nuclear ambition. During the crisis, the United States enlisted Beijing's support in dealing with the fallouts of the nonproliferations debacle,

---

[67] Neil MacFarlane, "Realism and Russian Strategy after the Collapse of the U.S.SR," in Ethan B. Kapstein and Michael Mastanduno, eds., *Unipolar Politics: Realism and State Strategies after the Cold War* (New York: Columbia University Press, 1999), pp. 218–60; William C. Wohlforth, "Russia's Soft Balancing Act," in Richard J. Ellings and Aaron L. Friedberg with Michael Wills, eds., *Strategic Asia 2003–04: Fragility and Crisis* (Seattle: National Bureau of Asian Research, 2003), pp. 165–79.

[68] Sherman Garnett, "Challenges of the Sino-Russian Strategic Partnership," *Washington Quarterly*, vol. 24, no. 4 (Autumn 2001), pp. 41–54; Gilbert Rozman, "Sino-Russian Relations: Mutual Assessments and Predictions," in Garnett, *Rapprochement or Rivalry?*, pp. 147–74; Lowell Dittmer, "The Sino-Russian Strategic Partnership," *Journal of Contemporary China*, no. 28 (2001), pp. 399–413; Garver, "Sino-Russian Relations."

treating China, from the Indian perspective, as a responsible great power and a trustworthy partner in the proliferation crisis precipitated by a rogue state, India.[69] India meanwhile openly cited the "China threat" to justify its nuclear program.

Both the U.S.-led isolation of India and the U.S.-China strategic partnership during 1997–98 proved short-lived. The U.S. engagement with India soon after the crisis motivated the PRC to mend its ties with India lest it be disadvantaged in the emerging new triangular relations.[70] Effectively granting India de facto nuclear power recognition, a leading analyst at the Chinese Academy of Social Sciences wrote in 2000, "China considers nuclear non-proliferation as a global issue. It does not view India's nuclear program as a threat to China, nor does it regard India's nuclear testing as an obstacle in bilateral relationship."[71]

While improvements had already been under way in Sino-Indian relationship prior to September 11, 2001, events after the terrorist attacks added impetus for cooperation. The exchange of visits by Chinese Premier Zhu Rongji in January 2002 and Indian Defense Minister George Fernandes in April 2003 demonstrated the new dynamics. Occurring in the aftermath of the terrorist attacks on the Indian parliament in December 2001, Zhu's trip underscored China's support for India's struggle against terrorism, which by definition signaled sympathy toward India's plight in the India-Pakistan conflict. The Chinese delegation also sought to spur economic and technological cooperation with its southern neighbor. A month after being sworn in by the National People's Congress, the new Chinese leadership under Hu Jintao and Wen Jiabao hosted Indian Minister of Defense George Fernandes in April 2003, amidst cancellations of high-level visits at the height of the Severe Acute Respiratory Syndrome (SARS) scare, an event made even more remarkable given the Fernandes's previous record as the leading figure in drumming up a China threat. While

---

[69] Baldev Raj Nayar and T. V. Paul, *India in the World Order*, ch. 6; John W. Garver, *Protracted Contest: Sino-Indian Rivalry in the Twentieth Century* (Seattle: University of Washington Press, 2001), ch. 12.

[70] John W. Garver, *The China-India-U.S. Triangle: Strategic Relations in the Post-Cold War Ear* (Seattle: National Bureau of Asian Research, 2002).

[71] Sun Shihai, "Zhouxiang Ershiyi Shiji de Zhongying Guanxi" [Sino-Indian Relationship Moving Toward the 21st Century], at http://www.cass.net.cn/chinese/s28_yts/wordch-en/ch-lzssh7.htm (accessed Oct. 21, 2005).

the visit itself indicated its moral support for China's fight against the SARS epidemic, India also was among the first countries to extend material assistance, albeit symbolically. The amount of 400,000 rupees (approximately U.S.$8,400) was paltry, but official Chinese media gratefully acknowledged this gift from the "Indian government and military."[72]

In 2003, India formally accepted China's sovereignty over Tibet, and the PRC implicitly recognized de facto Indian control over Sikkim. The two sides subsequently started negotiations to reopen the historically important Nathu La, a pass between Sikkim and Yadong County of Tibet for border trade. A final agreement was reached in June 2006 to reestablish the trade link, cut off when the Sino-Indian border war erupted in 1962. Highly tentative and limited due mostly to India's wariness, the first reopening failed to facilitate meaningful trade. However, the opening itself reaffirmed Beijing's recognition of Indian authority over Sikkim, promised a thriving border trade, and symbolized a new chapter in Sino-Indian relationship.[73]

The two sides reached an agreement in April 2005 on the political principles for facilitating settlement of the conflicting border claims involving 125,000 square kilometers. Recognizing the reality of decades of concerted efforts to consolidate control by China over the West Section (some 33,000 km) and by India over the East Section (approximately 90,000 km), the joint political framework appeared to emphasize that the line of actual control be the basis for boundary demarcation, a spirit similar to the one behind the successful conclusion of Sino-Russian negotiations.[74] But even sections of the line of actual control were contested. The dispute over Arunachal Pradesh

---

[72] Xinhua, "International Community Offers Assistance to China's Anti-SARS Campaign," *RMRB*, May 15, 2003, p. 5.

[73] "Zhongying Chongqi Zhongduan Duonian Bianmao Gudao" [China and India Reopen Ancient Border Route after Many Years of Closure," *RMRB*, June 22, 2006, p. 1; Xinhua, "China, India to Reopen Border Trade at Tibetan Mountain Pass," at http://news3.xinhuanet.com/english/2006–06/19/content_4713143.htm (accessed June 24, 2006).

[74] For a sampling of Chinese and Indian media reports, see Guo Nei, "Friendly Move Stressed in Sino-Indian Border Rift," *China Daily* (Internet), April 14, 2005, FBIS: CPP20050414000020; Manoj Joshi, "The Bigger Picture – Found in Translation," *New Delhi Hindustan Times* (Internet), April 14, 2005, FBIS: SAP20050414000066.

of the East Section has proven particularly intractable. Military skirmishes occurred over the dispute between the border troops in the 1980s, to which India's parliament responded with legislation making the region a formal Indian state. The PRC never accepted India's claim, whereas India's party politics and popular emotions were so deeply involved as to preclude any easy solution to the issue.

Bilateral amity culminated in China's about-face on India's bid for permanent membership in the UN Security Council. Having dropped its opposition, the PRC expressed a preference for India, albeit implicitly, over other Group-Four members (namely, Japan, Germany, and Brazil) during 2004–5. With no realistic solution to the problem of the Security Council's expansion in sight, Beijing's support was relatively cost-free. On the economic front, starting from a very low base, China-India trade jumped to $13.6 billion in 2004, $18.7 billion in 2005, and has since maintained robust growth.[75] While India, being a democracy, has seen more diverse, skeptical views on the relationship than has China, policy makers on both sides have nonetheless emphasized the compatibilities of their great-power pursuits. After 9/11, China made noticeable changes to its long-standing, one-sided support for Pakistan in South Asia. In contrast to their past tendency to downgrade India's strategic weight, mainstream Chinese writings now emphasize that India is a rising great power, much like China. This PRC respect, in turn, has reduced India's historical distrust of China, as evidenced by the ebb of China threat theories there. The new spirit animated the two Asian countries to pledge in April 2005 to forge a "Strategic and Cooperative Partnership for Peace and Prosperity."

Despite growing cooperative momentum, Sino-Indian amity is hampered by a lack of mutual affinity and thin experience of strategic understanding, as well as concrete irritants in the bilateral relationship.[76] Besides their bilateral difficulties, India's distrust of China's South Asia policy is profound. Thus, some Indian analysts attributed

---

[75] Xinhua, "Wen's Trip to Boost Sino-Indian links," at http://news3.xinhuanet.com/english/2005–04/08/content_2802289.htm (accessed June 24, 2006); Xinhua, "China, India to Reopen Border Trade at Tibetan Mountain Pass."

[76] For a succinct discussion of the perceptual gap between India and China, see Stephen P. Cohen, *India: Emerging Power* (Washington, DC: Brookings Institution Press, 2001), pp. 256–9. For an extensive study of bilateral conflicts, see Francine R. Frankel and Harry Harding, eds., *The India-China Relationship: What the United States Needs to Know* (New York: Columbia University Press, 2004).

the PRC neutrality in the India-Pakistan military showdown at Kagil in 1999 to heightened Chinese vulnerability stemming from the NATO war against Yugoslavia.[77] Compounding this distrust is the U.S. factor in the trilateral interactions.[78] After 9/11, the PRC was particularly worried about the prospect of India joining the United States to form an anti-China coalition. When the United States struck a nuclear deal with New Delhi in March 2006, effectively conferring upon India much desired international recognition on the nuclear issue and beyond, Beijing's unease was unmistakable, albeit somewhat muted.

While mutually vigilant, rather than denigrating each other's international standing, China and India have publicly embraced a concurrent great-power rise through their framework of strategic partnership. After all, as John Garver points out, they share a sense of "inferiority to the power of the Western alliance."[79] Like the PRC, India has long harbored a deep sense of denial of its rightful place in the world by the U.S.-led great-power coalition. As Baldev Raj Nayar and T. V. Paul argue, "[T]he major powers of the international system, especially the U.S., have been somewhat instrumental in the isolation of India.... [And] the U.S. thrust for hegemony, in one shape or another, and the Indian thrust for autonomy set the two countries on a long-term course of political conflict."[80] As Chinese analysts have maintained, a similar need to focus on domestic development and positive-sum status gains has lessened the balance-of-power logic in Sino-Indian relations.[81] Indeed, active U.S. engagement in South Asia and China

[77] Tang Shiping, *Shuozhao Zhongguo de Lixiang Anquan Huanjin* [Constructing China's Ideal Security Environment] (Beijing: Zhongguo Shehuikexue Chubanshe, 2003), p. 153. For a synopsis of India's concerns vis-à-vis China, see Sumit Ganguly, "Assessing India's Response to the Rise of China: Fears and Misgivings," in Carolyn W. Pumphrey, ed., *The Rise of China in Asia: Security Implications* (Carlisle, PA: Strategic Studies Institute, 2002), pp. 95–104.

[78] For Chinese analyses, see Zhao Gancheng, "Yingdu duihua Zhengce Bianxi" [A Diagnosis of India's China Policy], *Dangdai Yatai*, Contemporary Asia-Pacific Studies, no. 11 (2003), pp. 44–54; Sun Shihai, "Sino-Indian Relationship Moving Toward the 21 Century."

[79] Garver, *Protracted Contest*, p. 353.

[80] Baldev Raj Nayar and T. V. Paul, *India in the World Order: Searching for Major-Power Status* (Cambridge: Cambridge University Press, 2003), pp. 10, 222.

[81] For a balanced assessment, see Zhao Gancheng, "Zhongyin Guanxi: Gongtong Jueqi Yu Heping Gongchu" [Sino-Indian Relations: Rising Together and Coexisting Peacefully), *Guoji Wenti Luntan* [International Review], no. 35 (Summer 2004), at http://www.siis.org.cn/gjwtlt/2004/IT2/zhaogancheng.htm (accessed Sept. 12, 2005).

after 9/11 boosted India's international confidence, while having the effect of reassuring the two aspiring powers of the possibility of compatible status ascent.[82] In the first years of the twenty-first century, both leaderships appeared to realize that their countries' internecine struggle, if not restrained, would only impede their upward mobility in the world order. Bilateral ties can be complementary, rather than contradictory, to their international aspirations. Yet compared with Sino-Russian ties, the inchoate Sino-Indian strategic partnership is marked by greater caution on both sides, less political fanfare, and greater emphasis on functional technological and economic cooperation. China and India have most recently held joint military drills, but compared with the two Peace Mission exercises, they were on a significantly lesser scale and had more symbolism than substance.

While Russia and India are adjacent to China with historically troublesome border disputes, Europe as a whole is geographically distant from East Asia. During the cold war, Maoist China's preoccupation with security under bipolarity effectively assigned Europe to what Michael Yahuda aptly terms a "secondary role."[83] In contrast, economic globalization and the realignment in world politics after the cold war have elevated Europe to a matter of prime importance for China's foreign policy. Starting in the mid-1990s, the EU has proved highly adroit in proactively adjusting its policy toward the rising China. The Chinese side is more than happy to reciprocate, given the EU's newfound power and influence. As a result, in the first years of the new century, Sino-EU relationship has witnessed perhaps the most dramatic growth among great-power dyads. Economic ties have reached a new height. Cultural and social exchanges have expanded exponentially, due in no small part to the unprecedented European openness to Chinese tourists and the proliferation of research institutions devoted to mutual understanding on both sides. Political relationships have also improved, not least because of joint

---

[82] For how U.S. policy impacted Sino-Indian relations after September 11, see Garver, *The China-India-U.S. Triangle.*

[83] See his succinct review of China-Europe relationship during the cold war in Michael B. Yahuda, "China and Europe: The Significance of a Secondary Relationship," in Thomas W. Robinson and David Shambaugh, eds., *Chinese Foreign Policy: Theory and Practice* (New York: Oxford University Press, 1995), pp. 265–82.

leadership derived from the EU-PRC annual summit meeting since 1998.[84]

The two sides affirmed a commitment to building an "All-around Strategic Partnership" in October 2003. The new bilateral relationship immediately raised questions about the *raison d'être* of the EU arms embargo imposed as a punishment of the PRC for the Tiananmen crackdown in 1989, a demeaning treatment leaving China in the company of Sudan, Mynamar, and Zimbabwe. The CCP leaders in turn called the arms ban an act of political discrimination contrary to the Sino-EU strategic partnership and the tremendous progress in China. They made an explicit request for its end in China's "Document on Policy toward the EU" issued in October 2003.[85] With French President Jacques Chirac taking the lead, calls for lifting the embargo soon gained considerable support through the continent. In early May 2004, the joint Sino-EU *communiqué* specifically acknowledged China's interest in seeing the ban lifted "as quickly as possible... so as to further strengthen mutual political trust and cooperation."[86] But the seemingly unstoppable move was stalled by the summer of 2005, thanks to determined U.S. and Japanese opposition, China's enactment of the antisecession law against Taiwan the previous spring, and the growing argument in Europe that the PRC had not made enough progress on human rights to warrant the political recognition.

The arms embargo episode revealed both the strengths and weaknesses in the Sino-EU strategic partnership. On the economic front, the strategic partnership enjoys much stronger ties than China's dyadic relations with either Russia or India. Bilateral trade volume exceeded both leaderships' earlier expectations, reaching over $U.S.177 billion in 2004, higher than China's trade with any other economy and only second to the United States in the EU's foreign trade. The EU

---

[84] For the best Chinese account, see Gao Hua, "Zhongou Guanxi Sansinian: Guoqu, Xianzai Yu Weilai" [Third Years of Sino-European Relationship: Past, Present, and Future], at http://www.iwep.org.cn/pdf/2006/zhongouguanxi30nian_gaohua.pdf (accessed Jan. 24, 2006). The best work from the European perspective is Katinka Barysch, with Charles Grant and Mark Leonard, *Embracing the Dragon: The EU's Partnership with China* (London: Center for European Reform, 2005).

[85] The Chinese text of the document is published at http://www.fmprc.gov.cn/chn/wjb/zzjg/xos/dqzzywt/t27700.htm (accessed Jan. 9, 2005).

[86] "China-European Union Joint Press Communiqué (May 6, 2004)," Xinhua Domestic Service, May 6, 2004, in FBIS: CPP20040506000202.

is also the leading source of advanced technologies to China, in the forms of direct investment, equipment supplies, and high-tech trans-fers.[87] The most important project concerned PRC participation in Galileo, the EU civilian global navigation satellite system. The two sides signed a political agreement in October 2003 securing China's participation. A year later, they finalized a concrete agreement stip-ulating full-scale PRC involvement in the financing, development, and management of the ambitious EU program. With €200 million investment, this would constitute China's largest endeavor in foreign high-tech cooperation.[88] However, deepening economic ties notwith-standing, the EU has refused to grant China formal designation as a "market economy," and mutual complaints about unfair trade have continued.

The embargo debate reflected transatlantic divergence on global issues and how to deal with China, on the one hand; and on the other, it has presented a test of EU autonomy under U.S. hegemony. The Sino-EU strategic partnership has rested on a positive European atti-tude toward China's rise, their shared economic interests, and parallel international preferences. Yet persistent European concerns over the PRC polity, economic transition, and international role have provided a strong rationale for cross-Atlantic policy coordination on managing China's rise. Moreover, the EU quest for a unified, independent voice in the international arena is hampered by its continuing struggle to rec-oncile its supranational entity with the sovereignty of the twenty-seven member states, especially when interests of the big three (Great Britain, France, and Germany) diverge.[89] Ultimately, the origins and intensity

---

[87] Gao Hua, "Thirty Years of Sino-European Relationship," pp. 5–6.

[88] Yu Zheng, "Jialilue Daohang Weixing Shengkong" [The Galileo Navigational Sattellite Lifts Off], *RMRB*, Dec. 29, 2005, p. 2; "Yearender: Sino-European Ties Push Strategic High-Tech Cooperation," at http://english.people.com.cn/200512/13/eng20051213_227700.html (accessed July 12, 2006).

[89] For assessments from various perspectives, see Liu Jiansheng, "Tanjiu Oumei Zai Jieche Duihua Junshou Shang De Maodun" [Exploring the EU-U.S. Contradictions on Lifting the Arms Sales Ban on China], at http://www.ciis.org.cn/item/2005–04–07/50917.html (accessed July 9, 2005); Huo Zhengde, "Lun Zhongou Zhanlue Guanxi" [On Sino-EU Strategic Partnership], in Jin Canrong, ed., *Daguo Zhanluejuan* [Strategies of the Great Powers] (Beijing: New World Press, 2007), pp. 334–44; Gao Hua, "Thirty Years of Sino-European Relationship"; "Ouzhong Zjian Wenti Zhengjie Hezai" [Where Is the Crux of the Problem Between EU and China?], *RMRB*, July 2, 2005, p. 5; Barysch, with Grant and Leonard, *Embracing the Dragon*; David Shambaugh, "The New

of the EU's discontent with the world order qualitatively differ from those of China. The transatlantic ties proved too important for the EU as a whole to be unduly jeopardized by an intra-alliance confrontation over the Chinese embargo issue.

Alternative Path to Change

The three partners of China show a similar emphasis on positive engagement with the PRC. They also seek change in the international status quo. But the depths of their identifications differ, as do their revisionist agendas. Among them, the Sino-Russian pair has had the longest history and shares the closest set of status interests. Starting in the early 1990s, their foreign policy grievances and agendas began to converge. Their need for each other has stood the test of time. Fundamentally, the Sino-Russian strategic partnership rests on the domestic, bilateral, and international logic of each other's foreign policy. Such combined logic has precluded alliance making aimed at confronting the reigning hegemonic power, the United States, or the existing international arrangement in total.

The present interactions between China, Russia, and the West fundamentally differ from their trilateral past during the Soviet days. During the cold war era, the PRC and the Soviet Union could imagine fulfilling their international aspirations by identifying with the socialist group or the third world.[90] But in the post–cold war era, the world order is characterized by both largely unrivaled Western dominance and an overall cooperative pattern in great-power relations. Moreover, the domestic agendas of both reformist China and post-communist Russia have favored integration into and identification with the global mainstream. The emphasis on autonomy in their partnership has allowed the two former rivals to build trust, adjust mutual expectations, and freely pursue their own foreign policy agendas. While hailed as a new model in great-power relations by both sides, this approach also has

Strategic Triangle: U.S. and European Reactions to China's Rise," *Washington Quarterly*, vol. 28, no. 3 (Summer 2005), pp. 7–25.

[90] Lowell Dittmer, *Sino-Soviet Normalization and Its International Implications, 1945–1990* (Seattle: University of Washington Press, 1992); Lowell Dittmer and Samuel S. Kim, eds., *China's Quest for National Identity* (Ithaca: Cornell University Press, 1993).

allowed for self-interested calculations impeding bilateral cooperation and international coordination.[91]

Preoccupation with a daunting domestic agenda by both leaderships has limited their international activism. Chinese analysts have maintained that their country has kept a more low-profile foreign policy than has Russia. And they have argued that the two countries should learn from each other's strengths.[92] The implication is that a Russia more effectively governed at home and a China more active abroad would be in stronger positions to collaboratively enforce their international priorities. Failures to bring economic ties to match political rhetoric have raised doubts about the depth of their friendship. In particular, the leaderships' pledge to develop major cooperative projects as the locomotive for economic relationships has not come to fruition. Most notably, ten years after the massive Angarsk-Daqing pipeline deal designed to ship Siberian oil to northeast China was first proposed in 1994, Moscow unilaterally shelved it, despite strenuous lobbying by top Chinese leadership. Rather than being tied exclusively to the Chinese market, Russia chose to build a trans-Siberian pipeline that could be branched to China but also reach the Pacific coast. In the end, the new scheme disappointed the Chinese but also dissatisfied the Japanese, who had tried to secure a priority access to Russian oil.

The reasons for Russia's change of mind on the pipeline project were complex, including environmental concerns, Japanese intervention, Russian interagency conflicts, and Moscow's calculations on economic and security interests. The abortive effort not only meant a lost chance to build a flagship Sino-Russian economic project, but also dampened Chinese enthusiasm for bilateral friendship. Even on the arms deal issue, complaints could be heard in China about the high price and the greater Russian willingness to sell better weapons systems to India than to the PRC. Meanwhile, the Chinese were in no better position to complain excessively about Russia's pragmatism. Russian

---

[91] Zhao Huasheng, "Zhonge Guanxi: Diwei, Moshi, Qushi" [Sino-Russian Relationship: Status, Mode, and Trends], *Shijie Jingji Yu Zhengzhi*, no. 5 (2004), pp. 38–43.

[92] Xu Zhixin, "Diagnosis of Russian Foreign Strategy During the Putin Era," p. 52; Feng and Xiang, *Putin's Diplomacy*, p. 501.

companies did not fare well in their bids to win some of the major infrastructure projects in China.

In terms of their foreign policies, their divergent interests on a host of issues have limited unison in crafting common international responses. The Chinese were palpably disappointed when Russia forfeited leading international opposition to the U.S. withdrawal from the ABM treaty, leaving China vulnerable to a potentially robust American national defense system. Russian acquiescence to the U.S. decision on such a strategically important issue led one frustrated Chinese military analyst to wonder "Where is the 'bottom line' of Russian concession? To what extent would the Western world embrace and accommodate Russia?"[93] The ABM issue underscores the asymmetry of interests between Russia and China on an array of issues that have appeared to unite them, including the NATO expansion, Taiwan, human rights, and the U.S. alliances in East Asia. In an unusually candid review of the Sino-Russian relationship published in 1998, two prominent Chinese experts at the Chinese Academy of Social Sciences pointed out that Russia abstained rather than oppose the anti-China motion at the 1997 UNHRC meeting thanks to Moscow's reliance on the international organ to protect ethnic Russians vulnerable in many of the former Soviet republics. Meanwhile, China's opposition to the NATO expansion was hampered by its interest in winning the diplomatic battle against Taiwan in Eastern Europe.[94]

Ultimately, Sino-Russian interaction to jointly promote a revisionist agenda vis-à-vis the existing world order has been determined by the supreme value both countries attach to their relationship with the West. Fear of jeopardizing their ties with the West has effectively lessened incentives for alliance building. As they pursued an open relationship, the Sino-Russian strategic partnership was inevitably limited by inadequate coordination on important international issues of mutual

---

[93] Su Kaihua, "Emei Zhanlue Tiaozheng Jiqi Yingxiang" [Russian and U.S. Strategic Adjustments and Their Impact], *Dangdai Yatai*, no. 4 (April 15, 2003), p. 40. See also Lo, "The Long Sunset of Strategic Partnership," p. 299; Donaldson and Donaldson, "The Arms Trade in Russian-Chinese Relations," pp. 728–30.

[94] Jiang Yi and Zheng Yu, *Siji Zhijiao De Zhonge Guanxi* [Sino-Russian Relationship at the Turn of the Century], (Beijing: Institute for Eastern Europe and Central Asia Studies, Chinese Academy of Social Sciences, 1998), at http://www.cass.net.cn/chinese/s24_oys/chinese/Production/projects29/mulu.html ch. 4 (accessed June 29, 2005).

concern. As a leading Chinese analyst wrote in June 2005, the problem of "incongruities and incompatibilities" has prevented China and Russia from jointly influencing developments, such as the U.S. military presence in former Soviet republics in Central Asia and the "color revolutions" in SCO member states.[95] The Japan factor also underscores the nonexclusive nature of Sino-Russian relationship. Undoubtedly, both Russia and China have found their strategic partnership to be useful in their respective dealings with Japan. President Jiang Zemin's tough stand on the issue of Japanese war guilt on his visit in November 1998 presumably had something to do with the fact that the visit came on the heels of his successful trip to Moscow. Yet as the aforementioned oil pipeline saga illustrates, their partnership does not lock them in an exclusive alliance that precludes their diplomatic options with Japan.

To the extent that managing relationships with Western countries remains the top priority for both countries, China and Russia could likely find themselves in competition for status recognition. Indeed, this was made amply clear in the post-9/11 triangular interactions. President Putin took a series of decisive steps to support the U.S.-led global campaign against terrorism, including offering military assistance to the United States in its war on the Taliban regime in Afganistan and acquiescing to the U.S. troop deployments in its former Central Asian republics. Although the United States did not reciprocate with equitable favors to Russia, Moscow was granted full G8 membership and a market economy designation.[96] To the chagrin of the Chinese, Putin was too eager to please the United States and made a host of concessions that were potentially detrimental to China's interests. However, the events after 9/11 only temporarily questioned the strategic rationale behind Sino-Russian ties. Before long, the two countries began to share unease about the expanded U.S. global agenda. They complained

[95] Wang Xianju, "Meiguo Yinsu Kaoyan Zhonge Guanxi" [The U.S. Factor Tests Sino-Russian Relations], *Global Times*, June 6, 2005, p. 15, at http://www.people.com.cn/GB/paper68/14920/1323720.html (accessed June 12, 2005).

[96] For an excellent overview of Russia's American policy, see Alex Pravada, "Putin's Foreign Policy after 11 September: Radical or Revolutionary?" in Gorodetsky, *Russia Between East and West*, pp. 39–57. On cooperative Russian reactions to U.S. initiatives in central Asia, see Kathleen A. Collins and William C. Wohlforth, "Central Asia: Defying 'Great Game' Expectations," in Ellings and Friedberg with Wills, eds., *Strategic Asia*, pp. 291–317.

that the United States had practiced "double standards," refusing to lend full support to the Russian and Chinese fight against their own terrorist threats.[97]

In the subsequent opposition to the U.S. war on Iraq, as a Chinese scholar admitted, "their strategic coordination did not play a prominent role, although China and Russia maintained strategic consultation and cooperation. Russia's main cooperative partners were Germany and France. China supported Russia, France, and Germany, but refrained from being too deeply or directly involved."[98] The great-power realignment because of the Iraqi war also underscored that division within the Western coalition represented a major vulnerability of the current world order. Neither Russia nor China would have openly opposed the United States on the Iraqi war in 2003, if France and Germany had not led the opposition.[99] But subsequently the two countries have become more assertive in articulating their parallel positions and offering mutual support, as they did in 2007 on issues, such as opposition to UN sanctions on the Myanmar military junta for the latter's domestic repressions, NATO deployment of missile defense in Poland and Czech, and Chinese missile testing on an aged weather satellite.

Like Russia, India also shares China's sense of exclusion in the world order as well as its preference for a multipolar world. But New Delhi historically also blamed the PRC for denigrating its role in the world. The Sino-Indian strategic partnership has been beset by their problematic historical legacies and unresolved bilateral issues. Beginning in the last year of the Clinton administration, the United States has reversed its past policy of keeping India down to recognize instead India's status as a regional power and emerging global player.[100] But India has preserved its independence because it is unwilling to join any anti-China,

---

[97] See the Joint Statement signed by Presidents Hu Jintao and Vladimir Putin, May 14, 2004, *RMRB*, Oct. 15, 2004, pp. 1, 3; "Sino-Russian Joint Statement on the World Order of the 21st Century."

[98] Su Kaihua, "Russian and U.S. Strategic Adjustments and Their Impact, pp. 39–43; Zhao Huasheng, "Sino-Russian Relationship," p. 43.

[99] Xing Guangcheng, "Considerations Arising from Changes in Sino-Russia-U.S. Relations," *Xiandai Guoji Guanxi*, no. 4 (April 2003), pp. 16–18, FBIS: CPP20030514000198.

[100] Lloyd I. Rudolph, "Making U.S. Foreign Policy for South Asia: Off-Shore Balancing in Historical Perspective," American Political Science Association Annual Conference, 2006.

much less anti-Western, alliance. The Sino-Indian strategic partnership is rooted in a shared belief that stronger ties fundamentally serve their respective domestic self-strengthening agendas and international aspirations. However, they also jostle with each other to favorably position themselves in their relationship with the West. As dramatically demonstrated by the diplomatic wrangling over India's nuclear testing in 1998, the Sino-Indian relationship deteriorated into mutual acrimony when both countries tried to curry favor with the United States at the expense of the other. India enjoys political proximity with the West by virtue of being the largest democracy. The United States, Japan, and European powers have most recently shifted attention to India for geopolitical as well as economic reasons. The U.S. promotion of democracy and anti-terror campaign has further strengthened India's diplomatic position. Thus in the past several years, India has broken free from the confines of the sub-continent. Along with a robust effort to boost its material capacities, the country now sets eyesight on the bigger stage of Asia and the world having notably intensified its bid for the UN Security Council permanent seat, engaged SCO as an observer, and joined the East Asian Summit. To the extent that the geopolitical fissures among great powers are defined by ideological division, India has gained diplomatic weight, as democracies try to win over India to their side.[101] As if to respond to the talk about a new fault line in great-power politics, the China-India joint statement signed on Prime Minister Singh's visit to China in January 2008 eschewed any mention of "multipolarity," whilst at the same time, it declared, "The two sides favour [sic] an open and inclusive international system and believe that drawing lines on the ground of ideologies and values, or on geographical criteria, is not conducive to peaceful and harmonious coexistence."[102]

Fundamentally, the PRC, Russia, and India all see their international futures as lying within the globalized world. This effectively prevents any exclusive alliance building between or among them. It's little wonder that neither China nor India took seriously Russian Prime Minister Yevgeniy Primakov's proposal to form a tripartite alliance, reportedly

---

[101] Azar Gat, "The Return of Authoritarian Great Powers," *Foreign Affairs 86*, no. 4 (2007), pp. 59–69

[102] English version of the text at http://news.xinhuanet.com/english/2008–01/14/content_7422097.htm (accessed Jan. 14, 2008).

made in late 1998. The three countries have shown some interest in trilateral coordination, but the idea of an anti-Western bloc has proved to be too far-fetched. Tellingly, at the G8 summit held in St. Petersburg in July 2006, President Putin of Russia, President Hu of China, and Prime Minister Singh of India held a separate meeting on the sideline, but they focused on energy cooperation, while steering clear of any collective reference to multipolarization. Through open strategic partnerships, the emerging powers can have more diversified friends; have greatly strengthened leverage in dealing with the United States, Europe, and Japan; and assist each other's pursuit of international aspirations.[103]

Given the centrality of transatlantic alliances in defining the world order, the Sino-EU strategic partnership directly contests the boundaries separating established great powers and newcomers. The disagreements between the United States and the EU (particularly its leading powers, France and Germany) has a lot to do with the latter's impulse for a "free-ride" on U.S. leadership in dealing with an aspiring power like China. As Barry Barnes reasons, such a ubiquitous problem constantly threatens the unity of the dominant social group.[104] But overall the transnational alliance has remained strong, despite the arms ban episode. In fact, the United States and the EU subsequently saw a notable improvement in reaffirmation – if not in policy coordination, in their parallel stands on the PRC on a whole set of economic, security, and human rights issues. The loss of power first by German Chancellor Gerhard Shroder and then French President Jacques Chirac, dampened the momentum behind Sino-EU strategic partnership and movement toward ending the arms ban on China. Although the EU remained publicly committed to removing the embargo, but no concrete road map to that end had been proposed by the end of 2007.

Insofar as the EU represents a key member of the Western group, its strategic partnership with China takes on particular significance, but it has also encountered a unique set of barriers. The Sino-Indian

---

[103] On Sino-Indian relationship, see Ashley J. Tellis, "China and India in Asia," in Frankel and Harding, *The India-China Relationship*, pp. 134–77; John H. Gill, "India: Regional Concerns, Global Ambitions," in Ellings and Friedberg with Wills, eds., *Strategic Asia*, pp. 181–207; Garver, *The China-India-U.S. Triangle: Strategic Relations in the Post-Cold War Era*.

[104] Barry Barnes, "Status Groups and Collective Action," *Sociology*, vol. 26, no. 2 (May 1992), pp. 259–70.

partnership has generated little impetus for their joint push for multi-polarization in world politics. In all of the three cases, the cooperative momentum is real, and yet so are the obstacles and uncertainties in the evolution of their strategic partnerships. China's strategic partnerships with Russia, the EU, and India reflect its efforts to remold great-power politics such that the international environment is, in the main, friendly to its rise. Despite competition and tensions in these dyads, there is a compelling logic on both sides to maintain a mutually positive interactive pattern in their relationships. There seems to be an acute awareness by China and its partners that hostile balancing, exclusive alliance making, and violent revisionism ultimately do not pay in the contemporary globalized world. Yet, these partnerships are not binding, nor are their relationships individually and collectively with the West preordained.

6 | *Interdependent Rivalry with Japan*

In contrast to the cooperative momentum in China's strategic partnerships with Russia, India, and the EU, Sino-Japanese relations at the outset of the twenty-first century seemed to have evolved in the opposite direction, dipping to a new low under the administration of Prime Minister Junichiro Koizumi. Amidst the competitive dynamics, it's easy to forget that in the aftermath of Tiananmen, Japan became the closest major power for the beleaguered People's Republic of China. A little over ten years later, all the red-button issues – strategic rivalry, territorial conflict, historical animosities, mutually hostile popular nationalism, and Taiwan – flared up at the same time. Yet the already remarkably strong interdependence in terms of economic and social ties has continued to grow. Even during the gloomiest episode of the relationship since 1972, both leaderships were careful to keep the promise of reconciliation alive.

The literature is strong in describing the seemingly paradoxical developments in the Sino-Japanese relationship. Various narratives follow three conventional lines of inquiry, treating the relationship as driven by separate paths of economics and politics, balance of power, and nationalism. But to analytically account for the relationship in its totality, we need to consider the unifying logic behind its seemingly contradictory pattern. To that end, while focusing on the Chinese perspectives, I consider how their respective notions of great-power status affect mutual approaches to the relationship. The competitive impulse is strong because of Japan's dual identity as both a transitional and an established power most vulnerable to the repercussions of China's rise. Yet their economic complementarities, the common challenges of globalization, the regional dynamics in Asia, and the U.S. factor have also dictated mutual need and prudence in handling their relationship. With their international futures interlocked, the two countries have taken care to manage the multiple, crisscross forces if only to ensure their ties ultimately will not break. We do not see ineluctable hostile balancing between them, nor do we see an inevitable amity stemming from economic interdependence. Rather, the outcome depends on their interaction and the broader regional and global forces in which it is embedded. On balance, however, their interdependence goes far beyond economics to include their international status, thus generating cooperative dynamics often overlooked in the literature.

A Friend in Need

The Tiananmen crisis in 1989 created more of an opportunity than a setback for the Sino-Japanese relationship, at least in the short term. Japan's own war guilt and sympathy toward the Chinese government's need to maintain order at home, coupled with its pursuit of self-styled diplomacy and special ties with the PRC, explained the remarkably reserved outrage in Tokyo's response. While Tokyo did join other G7 members at the Paris summit a month later in formally condemning the Tiananmen killings, Japan showed little enthusiasm for imposing sanctions against or isolating the PRC. In fact, at the next G7 meeting in Houston, Texas, Japan announced the resumption of the third yen loan package starting in November 1990, further differentiating itself from other Western powers in its China policy. The PRC appreciation of this much needed help was evidenced by the paramount Chinese Communist Party leader Deng Xiaoping's disparate perspectives on Japan's wartime past before and after the June 4 Tiananmen crackdown. On May 16, 1989, while meeting with the Soviet leader, Mikhail Gorbachev, Deng maintained that "the harms the Japanese inflicted on China are beyond calculation. In terms of death toll alone, tens of millions of Chinese were killed. If we want to settle the historical account, Japan owes China the largest debt." But six months later, Deng told a visiting Japanese business group, "I have a special feeling toward Sino-Japanese friendship. . . . We should have a comprehensive view on history. We should talk about not only the history of Japanese invasion, but also the history of Japanese and numerous Japanese friends struggling for Sino-Japanese friendship."[1]

Also noteworthy was the PRC announcement of its decision to join the Non-proliferation Treaty (NPT), the nuclear weapons

---

[1] Deng Xiaoping, *Deng Xiaoping Wenxuan III* [The Selected Works of Deng Xiaoping, vol. 3] (Beijing: Renmin Chubanshe, 1993), pp. 293, 349.

control regime against which it had long held out, during Prime Minister Takashi Kaifu's visit to Beijing on August 10–13, 1991. The timing, according to the recollection of the then Foreign Minister Qian Qichen, was out of "Chinese understanding of the Japanese concern over nuclear proliferation, as Japan was the only nation victimized by the atomic bombs."[2] Amidst the new euphoria over Sino-Japanese amity, at President Jiang Zemin's invitation Japanese emperor Akihito set foot in China in October 1992, the first ever in the monarchical history. The visit went by without disruption or controversy, much less a firestorm over history. When the Japanese Diet passed the UN peacekeeping operation bill in June 1992, Chinese reaction was that of guarded acquiescence. In the meantime, economic ties with Japan gained momentum, with Japan becoming China's top trading partner. The next year, the value of Japan's China trade stood at only a little less than that with the United States, a pattern that would hold for the following decade.

Against the backdrop of warming bilateral ties, the PRC showed great magnanimity when Japan was leading the way for multilateral institution building in Asia, especially concerning the nascent Asia-Pacific Economic Cooperation (APEC) forum. Japan was instrumental in China's 1991 entry into the APEC, a diplomatic platform that proved vital to facilitate post-Tiananmen China's diplomatic breakthroughs with its Asian neighbors and the mending of political ties with the United States in the early 1990s. Beneath the optimism for cooperation, however, persistent suspicion between the two sides lingered. Japan was wary of the possibility that the PRC was using it to return to the international community. Conversely, the PRC believed that the Japanese were playing the "China card" to strengthen its foothold in Asia in order to counter U.S. and European pressures as the world political economy seemed to be fragmenting into exclusive blocs.

Indeed, the post-Tiananmen *modus vivendi* in Sino-Japanese relations resulted from compatible status needs of the two countries as China sought to end its diplomatic isolation and Japan opted to exercise a greater international role by mediating between the East and

---

[2] Qian Qichen, *Waijiao Shiji* [Ten Episodes in Diplomacy] (Beijing: Shijie Zhishi Chubanshe, 2003), p. 194.

West.[3] The PRC assiduously courted Japan's friendship to break down the Western coalition, which was united in its condemnation of the CCP government. Insofar as Japan was also a suspect by the United States "because of its economic success, political timidity and historical liability," wrote Takashi Inoguchi, it shared a sense of common international destiny with its largest neighbor.[4] While there was some interest on both sides in working together to promote Asian regionalism, the leadership issue in regional affairs was never resolved. The Japanese assumed that its advanced economy and Western membership would secure it an upper hand in dealing with the PRC reeling from blows to its domestic and international transition. But the Chinese were of two minds about Japan's "bridge" role; they appreciated its easing of China's isolation, but they resented the advantage it gave to Japan.[5]

Downward Spiral

As the PRC emerged from its worst diplomatic crisis and relative power began to shift in its favor, the international courses of the two Asian giants started to collide on many levels. A series of events in 1995–96 tipped the shift of contained wariness toward open complaint. Despite repeated calls by Tokyo not to do so, China conducted two nuclear tests in 1995 during a three-month interval. Still another test would take place in June 1996, three months before it signed the comprehensive test ban treaty. The nuclear tests, particularly the second one (August 17, 1995), which happened to be on the fiftieth anniversary of the Japanese surrender in World War II, had the effect of mobilizing anti-China feelings from a wide political spectrum, most notably those on the left who had defended the PRC's legitimate needs for nuclear

---

[3] On Japan, see Yoichi Funabashi, *Asia Pacific Fusion: Japan's Role in APEC* (Washington, DC: Institute for International Economics, 1995); Peter J. Katzenstein and Takashi Shiraishi, eds., *Japan and Asia: Network Power* (Ithaca, NY: Cornell University Press, 1997).

[4] Tadashi Inoguchi, "The Relationship Between Japan and Japan Should Be Viewed from a Worldwide Perspective," *Gaiko Forum*, Nov. 1992, pp. 20–27, in Foreign Broadcast Information Service (hereafter cited as FBIS)-East Asia, Jan. 13, 1993, p. 6.

[5] Yong Deng, *Promoting Asia-Pacific Economic Cooperation: Perspectives from East Asia* (New York: St Martin's Press, 1997), ch. 3, 5, quote on p. 93.

weapons.[6] As a response, Prime Minister Tomiichi Murayama of the Japan Socialist Party (JSP) announced in late August that Japan would reduce its grant aid to China to ¥ 500 million for the 1995 fiscal year (April 1, 1995–March 31, 1996) from the preceding year's ¥ 7.8 billion. Left unaffected were the much more significant yen loans, and a little over a year later the grant started to flow again.[7] This countermeasure represented the first time that Japan had used its official development assistance (ODA) to register displeasure with the Chinese behavior. Murayama's unprecedented move received widespread support in the public as well as in political circles in Japan.

The new Japanese assertiveness had to do with both its changing domestic politics and the shifting international environment. As regards the former, momentous political realignments had occurred, thereby revamping Japan's foreign policy making in general and China policy in particular. "The 1955 system" – with a dominant Liberal Democratic Party (LDP) on the right and the eternal minority party, the Japan Social Party (JSP), on the left – had come to an end after 1993. Rather than the dawning of a two-competitive-party system like the British Westminster model, the LDP made a quick comeback, whereas the JSP fell into oblivion. Ironically, the short-lived first JSP cabinet under Murayama also marked the end of a feisty opposition, with both deep conviction to Japan's pacifist international identity and electoral representation strong enough to defend its ideals.[8] The introduction of the single-member district system in the Japanese Diet in 1994 presumably had an effect on reducing the focus on local issues that had characterized the earlier multimember district system, while

---

[6] See Yoshihide Soeya, "Japan: Normative Constraints Versus Structural Imperatives," in Muthiah Alagappa, ed., *Asian Security Practice: Material and Ideational Influence* (Stanford, CA: Stanford University Press, 1998), p. 205; Mike Mochizuki, "Terms of Engagement: The U.S.-Japan Alliance and the Rise of China," in Ellis S. Krauss and T. J. Pempel, eds., *Beyond Bilateralism: U.S.-Japan Relations in the New Asia-Pacific* (Ithaca, NY: Cornell University Press, 2004), p. 103.

[7] "Chinese Ambassador Terms Aid Cut 'Unwise,'" Kyodo, Aug. 30, 1995, in FBIS: FTS19950830000185; "Tokyo Decides to Resume Grant-in-Aid to Beijing Soon," *Tokyo Nihon Keizai Shimbun*, Nov. 3, 1996, in FBIS: FTS19961103000080.

[8] For reviews of Japanese party politics in the 1990s, see Gerald Curtis, *The Logic of Japanese Politics* (New York: Columbia University Press, 1999); Ronald J. Hrebenar, *Japan's New Party System* (Boulder, CO: Westview Press, 2000).

at the same time spurring politicians to shore up nationalist appeals.[9]
As regards Japan's China policy, the 1990s witnessed the dwindling
influence of the older LDP politicians, whose worldviews were shaped
by war guilt and their own personal stakes in normalizing relations
with the PRC.[10] Also important was the changing Japanese perception
of China. A Japanese governmental survey showed that after 1995 the
share of the Japanese having a "close feeling" toward China fell below
50 percent for the first time since the 1970s.[11]

China, in turn, dismissed the Japanese reactions to its limited nuclear
program as unwarranted and morally unjustified. Disregarding the
fact that Tokyo was quite vocal in criticizing the French testings as
well, Chinese commentators accused Japan of remaining muted on
other powers' nuclear tests. Being "most conspicuous in making irresponsible remarks about China's nuclear testing," they asserted, Japan
proved itself to be hostile to China. For them, its imperialism in Asia
during the Meiji and Showa eras, coupled with its being under the
U.S. nuclear umbrella, put Japan in a dubious position when it come
to criticizing China's nuclear policy.[12] Chinese disregard of Japanese
concern about the nuclear issue stood in sharp contrast to its earlier
empathy with the Japanese position.

Chinese military exercises in the waters adjacent to the island
of Taiwan from June 1995 to March 1996 deeply unnerved the
Japanese, whose misgivings about their giant neighbor had already
been growing. Tokyo responded by strengthening its alliance with the
United States. The result was the revised bilateral defense guidelines
in 1997, which stipulated that the alliance's mission should apply to

---

[9] Yasuhiro Nakasone alluded to this in Tetsushi Kajomoto, "Nakasone Hits Koizumi Populism, Yasukuni Visits," *Japan Times*, Nov. 23,
2005, at http://www.japantimes.co.jp/cgi-bin/getarticle.pl5?nn20051123f1.htm
(accessed Nov. 25, 2005).

[10] On key Japanese political figures with special ties to the PRC, see Quansheng
Zhao, *Japanese Policymaking: The Politics Behind Politics – Informal Mechanisms and the Making of China Policy* (Westport, CT: Praeger, 1993).

[11] Tsuneo Watanabe, "Changing Japanese Views of China: A New Generation
Moves Toward Realism and Nationalism," in Carolyn Pumphrey, ed., *The Rise
of China in Asia: Security Implications* (Carlisle, PA: Strategic Studies Institute,
2002), p. 166.

[12] Guo Zhengping and Zhang Lu, "Where Does the Nuclear Threat Come From?
First of a Series of Articles Refuting the 'China Threat Theory,'" *Jiefangjun
Bao*, June 13, 1996, in FBIS: FTS19960613000008; Ren Xianfong: "Japan:
Big Fuss over Nuclear Tests," *Beijing Review*, Oct. 16, 1995, p. 22, in FBIS:
FTS19951016000056.

"situations in areas surrounding Japan," with the nature and scope of their joint response to be determined on a "situational" basis.[13] Objectively speaking, the attempt to revitalize the U.S.-Japan alliance reflected a complex set of changes in the alliance itself, Japanese politics, regional security dynamics, and international politics, and it was initially prompted by the nuclear crisis on the Korean Peninsula in 1993–94.[14] Even after the conclusion of the new guidelines, the United States and Japan still could not agree on what specific role the situational clause would require of Japan in case of a Taiwan conflict.[15]

Yet for Beijing, the timing of its conclusion suggested a linkage with the Taiwan crisis in 1995–96 and the alliance's anti-China bend. The Japanese government's refusal to explicitly exclude Taiwan in the situational considerations, notwithstanding repeated Chinese pressures, only fueled Beijing's suspicion about Tokyo's motives. The Chinese view clearly fed on a visceral distrust of Japan on the Taiwan issue. The PRC analysts took notice of the fact that the U.S. carrier group *Independence* sailed from Yokosuka, Japan to the vicinity of Taiwan in March 1996.[16] Japan was thus somewhat guilty of interfering in

---

[13] The Guidelines are reprinted in Michael J. Green and Patrick Cronin, eds., *The U.S.-Japan Alliance: Past, Present, and Future* (New York: Council on Foreign Relations Press, 1999), appendix 3, pp. 333–45. For a comprehensive review of Chinese concerns, see Banning Garrett and Bonnie Glaser, "Chinese Apprehensions about Revitalization of the U.S.-Japan Alliance," *Asian Survey*, vol. 37, no. 4 (April 1997), pp. 383–402. For an in-depth assessment of the alliance's security implications, see Thomas J. Christensen, "China, the U.S.-Japan Alliance, and the Security Dilemma in East Asia," *International Security*, vol. 23, no. 4 (Spring 1999), pp. 49–80.

[14] Ni Feng, "Enhanced U.S.-Japan Security Alliance: Cause for Concern," *Beijing Review*, June 16–22, 1997, pp. 7–8, in FBIS: FTS19970616000036. Japanese accounts seem to confirm Chinese suspicion. See, for example, Koji Murata, "Japan's Military Cooperation and Alliances in the Asia-Pacific Region," and Akio Watanabe, "The PRC-Japan Relationship: Heading for a Collision?" in Hung-Mao Tien and Tun-Jen Cheng, eds., *The Security Environment in the Asia-Pacific* (Armonk, NY: M. E. Sharpe, 2000), ch. 4, 5. For a comprehensive account of the emerging dynamics in Sino-Japanese relations since the mid-1990s, see Michael J. Green, *Japan's Reluctant Realism* (New York: Palgrave/Macmillan, 2001), ch. 3. The U.S. objective, according to one key architect of the renewed U.S.-Japan alliance, was to strengthen its engagement policy toward China. See Joseph Nye, Jr., *The Paradox of American Power* (New York: Oxford University Press, 2002), p. 22.

[15] Yoichi Funabashi, *Alliance Adrift* (New York: Council on Foreign Relations Press, 1999), p. 399.

[16] Lu Guozhong, "Japan's Position, Role and Future Trend in the New Situation," *Guoji Wenti Yanjiu*, Jan. 13, 1997, in FBIS: FTS19970506001116.

the Taiwan affair, even though it had had little consultation, much less coordination, with the United States on the U.S. carrier group deployment.[17]

President Jiang Zemin could have used his official visit in November 1998 to set the Sino-Japanese relationship on a forward-looking course. Instead, wrangling over Japan's wartime past hardened the negative Japanese image of China. Prior to Jiang's flight from Moscow to Tokyo, on the heels of his visit to Russia, the PRC had requested a written Japanese apology on its wartime behaviors in the joint statement to be signed by Jiang and Prime Minister Keizo Obuchi. The wording would be similar to the one Obuchi had just issued with the South Korean President, Kim Dae Jung, on October 8. Japan eventually turned down the request, thanks to bureaucratic confusions on both sides, the failure of the last minute behind-the-scene diplomacy, and "apology fatigue" on the part of the Japanese. The Chinese were particularly enraged and humiliated by the Japanese refusal to treat its history with China the same way as it had done with the Republic of Korea.[18] As a result, a joint statement was released without either leader's signature on it. Incensed by the Japanese slight, Jiang took upon himself the crusade to hold the Japanese accountable for the wartime invasions, repeating his history lectures throughout the rest of his tour.[19] Having perhaps misjudged the Japanese national mood vis-à-vis China at this juncture, Jiang's focus on Japan's wartime history backfired, for it did little to provoke critical Japanese self-reflection but a great deal to antagonize the Japanese. The heated public dispute over history fed on the Japanese complaints about the Chinese playing the history card and being ungrateful to the Japanese for its economic assistance.

The Sino-Japanese relationship continued on a downward spiral after the events in 1995–96. Leaders subsequently reciprocated visits

---

[17] For a careful account, see Funabashi, *Alliance Adrift*, pp. 391–401.

[18] Xuanli Liao, *Chinese Foreign Policy Think Tanks and China's Policy Towards Japan* (Hong Kong: Chinese University Press, 2006), pp. 188–93.

[19] See Chang Yi-fan, "Japan Deliberately Sets a Trap, China Makes a Wrong Move: Inside Story of Jiang Zemin's Refusal to Sign 'Joint Declaration.'" Hong Kong Economic Journal, Dec. 1, 1998, in FBIS: FTS19981209000153; Chiang Feng, "A Trip of Striking Blows at Japanese Militarism: Comment on President Jiang's Visit to Japan," Hong Kong Ta Kung Pao, Dec. 1, 1998, in FBIS: FTS19981201000263.

to mark respectively the twenty-fifth and twentieth anniversaries of the diplomatic normalization and the Treaty of Peace and Friendship, but they did little to offer a vision for a joint future. In fact, following Jiang's visit, the Sino-Japanese relationship drifted, with little leadership from either side to chart a common international course.

Interdependent Rivals

After the Sino-Japanese diplomatic normalization in 1972, their bilateral relationship underwent over three decades of substantial growth. By the first years of the new century, their economic ties, people-to-people contacts, and social exchanges were deep and substantial. Yet without a shared political vision to consolidate them, the overall dyadic relationship has seen growing competitive tendencies, even at times jeopardizing long-standing cooperative patterns in supposedly uncontroversial domains.

Economic interdependence has remained the strongest bond between the two countries. As widely reported in Chinese media, for the eleven years between 1992 and 2003 Japan was China's largest trading partner, accounting at times in the 1990s for around 20 percent of China's total trade. The PRC was Japan's second leading trading partner for the decade of 1993–2003. Their respective rankings changed in 2004, when Japan slipped to third place, after the EU and the United States, while China dislodged the United States to become Japan's largest trading partner. Through the period of 1979–2004, Japan invested a total of U.S.$46.1 billion, accounting for 9 percent of the foreign direct investment in China. Japanese businesses in China has created jobs, boosted trade, and generated tax revenues for the Chinese government. Japan is also a major source of paid technological transfers. China's Minister of Commerce Bo Xilai acknowledged amidst the raging anti-Japanese protests in the spring of 2005 that Japanese investments created 9.2 million jobs for his country.[20] Chinese companies have

---

[20] Wang Xusheng: "Can Economic Ties Break Political Impasse?" Beijing Review (Internet), June 3, 2005, in FBIS: CPP20050604000102; Liu Gang, "Experts Say in Interviews: Strengthening Sino-Japanese Exchange, Cooperation, and Nongovernmental Contacts," Xinhua Domestic Service, May 3, 2005, in FBIS: CPP20050503000113; "Trade Policy Towards Japan Unchanged: Commerce Minister," at http://news.xinhuanet.com/english/2005-04/22/content_2866701.htm (accessed June 26, 2006).

also begun to invest in Japan, albeit on a minuscule scale compared to the reverse flow of investment.

For over two decades, Japan's official developmental assistance in the forms of preferential yen loans, grant aid, and technological assistance played a pivotal role in bilateral ties. Starting in 1979, when post-Maoist China was taking its first steps toward economic reforms and opening up to the outside world, the ODA was highly instrumental in the country's economic modernization. By 2002, ¥ 3225.4 billion had been dispensed, with 91 percent in loans, 4 percent in grants, and the remaining 4 percent in technical support.[21] The yen loans represented the bulk of Japanese ODA, with contracted ¥ 320.8 billion by mid-2006.[22] They came with extremely favorable terms, with an annual interest rate as low as less than 1 percent and the maximum repayable period as long as four decades. Specifically tailored to the developmental priorities in the Chinese government's five-year plans, these loans were made in five-year packages. However, with the end of the fourth package in 2000, Japan made several notable changes, including the replacement of multiyear packages with annual assessments and a shift from focusing on building major infrastructure projects to the support of programs directly pertaining to improvement of the environment, the infrastructure in the hinderland, and the welfare of the individual Chinese. As Figure 6.1 shows, set to end yen loans altogether in 2008, when China hosts the Olympic Games, Japan drastically reduced its ODA to the PRC in the early years of the new millennium. Yet that seems to have made no dent in trade, suggesting a strong market force at work in sustaining robust economic ties.

Contacts between the two societies have expanded in line with globalization. According to official Japanese data, there were 70,814 Chinese students in Japan in mid-2003, or 65 percent of the 109,508 total foreign-students population in Japan.[23] Around the same time,

---

[21] Japanese Ministry of Foreign Affairs, *Diplomatic Bluebook 2004*, at http://www.mofa.go.jp/policy/other/bluebook/2004/chap2-a.pdf (accessed Oct. 21, 2005).

[22] *Renmin Ribao* (*People's Daily*, overseas edition, hereafter cited as *RMRB*), April 7, 2007, p. 3.

[23] Japanese Ministry of Education, Culture, Sports, Science and Technology, *Outline of the Student Exchange System in Japan* (2004), at http://www.mext. go.jp/a_menu/koutou/ryugaku/05020201/001.pdf (accessed Sept. 19, 2006), p. 8.

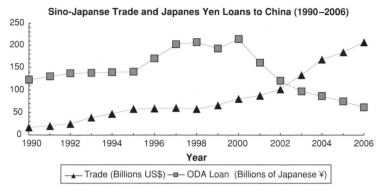

Figure 6.1. Sino-Japanese Trade and Japanese Yen Loans to China (1990–2006) *Sources*: The trade data are from the International Monetary Fund, *Direction of Trade Statistics* (various years), and the Chinese Ministry of Commerce, at http:// zhs.mofcom.gov.cn/tongji.shtml (accessed June 2, 2007). The FY1990–2002 Yen loan data are from the Japanese Ministry of Foreign Affairs, *Diplomatic Bluebook 2004*, at http://www.mofa.go.jp/policy/other/bluebook/2004/ chap2-a.pdf (accessed Oct. 21, 2005), p. 49; the FY2003–04 numbers are from various Japanese media reports; and FY2005–06 data are from http://www.mofa.go.jp/announce/announce/2006/6/0623.html and http://www.mofa.go.jp/announce/announce/2007/3/1172987_822.html (accessed June 3, 2007). Note: The year for ODA refers to the fiscal year (FY), from April 1 of the current year to March 31 of the next year.

Japan had 12,765 students enrolled in Chinese colleges, representing over 16 percent of foreign students in the PRC, second only to the Republic of Korea, which had 35,353. Three years later, Japanese students in China had increased by nearly 6,000.[24] Some estimations indicate that close to half a million Chinese now live in Japan. In 2004, 3.33 million Japanese visited China, and over 1 million Chinese visited Japan. Besides the record numbers in the two-way movement of people, the many sister cities and youth exchange programs, many of which date back to the 1970s and 1980s, continued to play a valuable subgovernmental role in underpinning the nations' bilateral ties.[25]

[24] The Chinese Ministry of Education, "International Students in China," *RMRB*, May 29, 2007, p. 1, at http://www.moe.edu.cn/english/international_3.htm (accessed Nov. 10, 2005).
[25] Liu Gang, "Experts Say in Interviews."

Extensive social interactions in the era of globalization inevitably bring about unconventional, transnational problems that call for cooperative solutions. In that spirit, during the SARS crisis in 2003 the Japanese government was at the forefront in dispatching medical professionals to help China fight the epidemic and was the most generous country in offering financial aid, which totaled ¥ 1.7 billion.[26] Japanese support in the SARS scare earned unqualified Chinese appreciation, but other areas of bilateral cooperation have often generated mixed feelings on both sides. In thirty years, the ODA in China totaled over ¥ 3000 billion, a valuable contribution to the country's development. But not least because the ODA was associated with war reparations, which Maoist China voluntarily forwent during the diplomatic normalization in 1972, its history saw no small share of controversies. The Chinese side invariably emphasized its mutually beneficial nature, arguing that even though the ODA ostensibly had no commercial or political strings attached, in fact it advanced Japanese economic interests in China. The PRC became particularly irate when Japan applied to China its 1992 ODA Charter, which links official aid to human rights compliance, armament policy, and weapons proliferation behaviors of the recipient countries.[27] Insofar as the ODA symbolizes a special relationship defined by Japanese war guilt and Tokyo's willing assistance to China's modernization, its decrease and eventual end in 2008 represented a significant change in bilateral interactions beyond economics.

Large Chinese and Japanese diaspora populations present in the other country enhance mutual understanding, but they also inevitably create frictions. The criminal activities of a small group of Chinese nationals in Japan constituted a sizable share of all crimes perpetrated by foreigners there.[28] The most notorious crime in recent years was the robbery-turned-murder case in which a Japanese family of four in Fukuoka was brutally killed by three Chinese students in June 2003. In the same year, two events involving Japanese citizens in the PRC contributed to anti-Japanese nationalist outcries. Some two hundred

[26] Xinhua, "International Anti-SARS Assistance to China Reached U.S.$38.02 Million," *RMRB*, June 7, 2003, p. 4.

[27] Sun Yafei, "Riben Duiha Yuanzhu de Enyuan Shifei" [The Controversies in Japanese Aid to China], *Renminwang*, June 13, 2003, at http://www.people.com.cn/GB/guoji/14549/1913193.html (accessed June 13, 2003).

[28] Koshin Shisui and Akihiro Yamada, "Japan Needs International Crime Probe Pacts," Asahi Shimbun (Internet), Feb. 2, 2004, in FBIS: PP20040202000025.

Japanese were engaged in prostitution in a Cantonese hotel during September 16–18. That 18 September 1931 was considered the date when imperial Japan expanded its invasion into China helped turn a dishonorable transaction in a formally unlawful but widely practiced business into a minor diplomatic crisis. In a separate occurrence, in late October, one teacher and three students from Japan performed indecent, disrespectful acts at a show held at a Xian'an college that led to anti-Japanese demonstrations in the city.[29] Media reports and Internet instigations centering on these events on both sides amplified the countries' negative nationalist emotions toward each other.

In such a volatile political milieu, the interlocking ties between China and Japan remained fragile. Old problems persisted, and new irritants piled up. The long-standing issue of Japan's attitude toward its fifty years of war (1894–1945) once again became a dominant issue at the beginning of the new century. Much of the Chinese fury over what they perceived to be Japanese denial of its war guilt centered on Prime Minister Kuozumi's visits to the Yasukuni Shrine and the so-called "textbook incidents." Built at the outset of the Meiji era, the Shinto temple is where the 2.46 million Japanese soldiers killed in the wars during the Meiji and Showa eras are commemorated. Included among the war dead since the late 1970s are the fourteen Japanese civilian and military leaders of the Pacific War found guilty, as Class A war criminals, by the Far Eastern tribunal. For the Chinese, a shrine visit by the Japanese leader represents a "gauge for the Japanese government's attitude toward the war of aggression."[30] Because of the emotional symbolism surrounding the shrine, during 1986–2000, except for a secret visit by Prime Minister Miyazawa Kiichi in 1992,[31] only Prime Minister Ryutaro Hashimoto publicly paid homage once (July 29, 1996). In contrast, during his tenure, Prime Minister Junichiro Koizumi visited the shrine on a yearly basis on the following dates:

---

[29] "Yuanxianren Zhuri Jizhe Pingchu 2003 Niandu Zhongri 10 Daxinwen" [Top Ten News Events Selected by Former and Current Correspondents Stationed in Japan], http://www.people.com.cn/GB/guoji/1029/2307193.html (accessed Jan. 23, 2004).

[30] Xia Wenhui, "Zhiyi Canbai Jinguo Shenshe Weishui Zhaohun?" [Insistent Visits to the Yasukuni Shrine: Whose Spirit Does It Want to Call Back?], *RMRB*, June 2, 2001, p. 3.

[31] See Daiki Shibuichi, "The Yasukuni Shrine Dispute and the Politics of Identity in Japan," *Asian Survey*, vol. 45, no. 2 (March/April 2005), citing later Japanese media reports, p. 209.

August 13, 2001, April 21, 2002, January 14, 2003, January 1, 2004, October 17, 2005, and August 15, 2006. To register strong objections, Beijing effectively made his stopping his shrine visits a precondition for any official visit – and, for that matter, for the improvement of Sino-Japanese political relations. So, after his brief visit to China in October 2001, Koizumi was never to return as Japanese Prime Minister.

Similarly, the textbook controversies, which essentially are about how Japan's wartime history is portrayed in several textbooks, returned with a vengeance at the beginning of the new millennium. First erupting in 1982 and then in 1986 over attempts to rewrite history in some textbooks in order to exonerate Japan of its war guilt, the issue would calm down after 1986. Only minor disputes occurred during the 1990s.[32] But another firestorm would break out, due particularly to the establishment of the right-wing Japanese Society for History Textbook Reform in 1997. In 2001 and 2005, the group's textbooks for junior high schools, published by Fusosha, were the center of the furies in China, Korea, and elsewhere in Asia. The revisionist interpretations were attacked for justifying the modern Japanese wars in Asia, whitewashing the Japanese colonial record, and denying any war atrocities. In the end, few schools adopted the Fusosha book. For example, in 2005 fewer than five thousand copies of the book were issued, a 0.4 percent adoption rate that fell far short of the 10 percent its authors had hoped for.[33] But insofar as such reinterpretations of history are associated with official Japanese views, they are considered by the Chinese as evidence of a lack of genuine repentance and a precursor for the revival of Japanese militarism.[34]

Events such as the poison gas incidents and repeated failures by the Chinese citizens said to be victimized by the Japanese to seek justice

---

[32] See the pacifist activist Saburo Ienaga's account "The Glorification of War in Japanese Education," *International Security*, vol. 18, no. 3 (Winter 1993/94), pp. 113–33. The most comprehensive scholarly analysis of the issue in the 1980s is Allen S. Whiting, *China Eyes Japan* (Berkeley: University of California Press, 1989).

[33] *RMRB*, Oct. 7, 2005, p. 4.

[34] Zhang Huanli and Gang Ye, "Japan's Rightists Must Not Tamper with History," Xinhua, April 1, 2004, in FBIS: CPP20010404000078; Tang Tianri, "The Japanese Government Cannot Escape the Blame for the Fact that Textbooks Distorting History Were Assessed as 'Up to Standard,'" Liaowang, no. 15 (April 9, 2001), p. 59, in FBIS: CPP20010419000089.

through legal recourse also served as a constant reminder of the traumatic past. At the end of the Second World War, a massive amount of chemical weapons was left unaccounted for by the retreating Japanese imperial army in Northeast China. Sixty years later, these materials were unexpectedly dug out during China's construction boom, sometimes causing injuries to Chinese citizens. Former Chinese laborers and women allegedly forced to be sex slaves for the Japanese imperial army (known as "comfort women") sought justice and compensation in Japanese courts, but to no avail.

These unsettled historical issues have long haunted the Sino-Japanese relationship. What separated the latest episode from the past was a profound shift in the Japanese official attitude and the Chinese determination to use history to beat back what they perceive to be Japanese attempts to derail China's ongoing rise. In the 1980s, when Japanese officials made ill-conceived remarks offensive to the Chinese, they would profusely apologize and some would even lose their jobs. On the history issue, almost all the controversies ended with the Japanese side backing down. Under strenuous Chinese objections, even the assertive nationalist Prime Minister Yasuhiro Nakasone decided to cease visiting the Yasukuni shrine after 1985.[35] In contrast, under the Koizumi administration, the prime minister repeatedly visited the shrine, and his key cabinet members were markedly less prohibited than their predecessors in criticizing their communist neighbor. Fierce Chinese reactions were often met with equally blunt rebuttals. Polls showed that the majority of the Japanese public wanted Koizumi to stop the shrine visits, but they also lay real blame on the Chinese and Koreans – rather than their politicians – for the deterioration of their bilateral relationship. Not backing down to foreign demands in fact helped shore up Koizumi's image as a refreshingly strong leader among the electorates.[36]

The Chinese have long suspected the Japanese motives on Taiwan, a Japanese colony for half a century (1895–1945). Japanese complaints about China's military threat to Taiwan only reinforce this suspicion.

---

[35] Whiting, *China Eyes Japan*.
[36] Nobuhiro Hiwatari, "Japan in 2004: 'Courageous' Koizumi Carries On," *Asian Survey*, vol. 45, no. 1 (Jan./Feb. 2005), pp. 41–53; ibid, "Japan in 2005: Koizumi's Finest Hour," *Asian Survey*, vol. 46, no. 1 (Jan./Feb. 2006), pp. 22–36.

For Beijing, Taiwan's independence movement was in part egged on by the Japanese, albeit more covertly than by the United States. Chinese commentators were particularly irate at the special ties Taiwanese president Lee Teng-hui and other pro-independence figures have had with Japan. They were extremely wary of Japan-U.S. collusion in extending the theater missile defense to Taiwan or otherwise militarily preventing China's national reunification. Thus, the 2005 joint 2 + 2 statement by the U.S. Department of State and Pentagon chiefs and their Japanese counterparts expressing concern over Taiwan was viewed by the Chinese as aimed against them.[37]

While the PRC has made remarkable strides in settling border disputes on land and at sea, at the same time its territorial dealings with the Koizumi administration in the East China Sea took a negative turn. The Diaoyu Islets, a chain of five uninhabited islets and rocks northeast of Taiwan – which the Japanese call Senkaku – once again became the center of contention. The Chinese have long based their claim to the islands on the historical record of ownership starting in the early fifteenth century, while the Japanese base theirs on effective control of the islands since the late nineteenth century.[38] In 2002, the Japanese government leased three islands from descendants of the Japanese who first discovered the islands. Three years later, the Japanese coast guard took control of these contested islets together with the lighthouse built on them, a measure that would give Tokyo a freer hand to exercise effective management and control.[39]

In conjunction with the Diaoyu Islets disputes, China and Japan were locked in a contest over overlapping claims of the two hundred nautical miles of exclusive economic zones (EEZ) in the East China Sea. Citing different rules in the UN Convention on Law of the Sea (UNCLOS), the Chinese have based their claim on "the natural extension of continental shelf," whereas the Japanese insist on division of the less than four hundred nautical miles–wide territorial waters by the "median line" between the shores of the two countries. The waters adjacent to the

---

[37] The full text of the "Joint Statement of the U.S.-Japan Security Consultative Committee" can be found at http://www.state.gov/r/pa/prs/ps/2005/42490.htm.

[38] Zhong Yan, "China's Claim to Diaoyu Island Chain Indisputable," *Beijing Review*, Nov. 4–10, 1996, pp. 14–19.

[39] "Government Island Tactic Shows Soft Approach," *Daily Yomiuri*, at http://www.yomiuri.co.jp/newse/20030103wo02.htm (accessed Jan. 4, 2003).

islands saw frantic activities during 2004–5 on both sides, involving competitive energy exploration, fishing, and the presence of naval ships and other military assets, all geared toward enforcing unilateral claims over the disputed territorial waters and the natural resources in them and under the seabed. A claimant of the Diaoyu Islands themselves, Taiwan also occasionally joined the foray in protesting the Japanese denial of its fishing rights in the contested waters. The disputes involve not only contested waters, which are not easily amenable to arbitration by international laws, including the UNCLOS (which China ratified in May 1996), but also such resources as natural gas, oil, and fisheries. For example, the Chunxiao gas field off the shores of Zhejiang and Jiangsu provinces, which the PRC began to build in the late 1990s, is technically on the Chinese side by the standard of either the EEZ or the Japanese median line; but as the Japanese fear, it can easily drill natural gas from the Japanese-claimed areas. As the construction was nearing completion in 2004–05 and then began its first stage of gas production in 2006, the two sides held numerous rounds of negotiations, but they failed to reach a settlement on the gas field issue.

Beyond these rather conventional territorial disputes, an unusual incident involving an accusation of sovereignty violation took place in the northeast China city of Shenyang on May 8, 2002, when armed Chinese policemen allegedly forced their way into the Japanese consulate to nab five North Korean refugees. The Japanese claimed that the Chinese had violated the diplomatic immunity afforded to its consulate by international law. The PRC contended that it was legally justified to protect the security of the diplomatic compound and that the entry of its policemen had received prior consent from a Japanese vice-consul. The refugees were soon allowed to leave for a third country.[40] But the incident deteriorated into a diplomatic brawl, for it was not merely about the Chinese treatment of the North Korean refugees, but also added heat to a domestic debate in Japan about its China policy. China's image was hit again in 2006 when the Japanese government

---

[40] On divergent Chinese and Japanese positions and the fate of the refugees, see "FM Spokesman on Consulate Intrusion Accident," Xinhua, May 10, 2002, in FBIS: CPP20020510000197; "Koizumi Urges China Envoy to Settle Consulate Case," Kyodo, May 9, 2002, FBIS: JPP2002050900008; "Five N.K. Defectors to Leave for Manila: Japanese Newspaper," Yonhap, May 15, 2002, in FBIS: KPP20020515000003.

accused the PRC state security agents of entrapping and blackmailing a Japanese diplomat in Shanghai two years earlier, leading to his suicide.

Historical animosities and contemporary disputes fueled mutually hostile nationalism on both sides. In the 1990s, Taiwan, the U.S.-Japanese alliance, and controversies over the Diaoyu Islands spurred much of the anti-Japanese nationalism. Besides these issues, Koizumi's 2001–06 shrine visits, the textbook controversies, a stream of diplomatic incidents, the Japanese bid for a permanent seat in the UN Security Council, and even a soccer match between the two national teams added fuel to the nations' volatile relationship. In spring 2005, such nationalist sentiments culminated in widespread demonstrations in several Chinese cities, including Shanghai and Shengzhen, causing damages to Japanese diplomatic and business properties and injuries to Japanese citizens.[41]

Political volatility even threatened existing cooperation in areas of trade, investment, tourism, and grassroots social ties, where mutual compatibilities had supposedly been strong historically and functionally. Notably, political mistrust had hamstrung energy cooperation, allowing, for example, Russia to play China and Japan against each other in the Siberian oil pipeline deals. Chinese netizens mobilized massive popular opposition to adoption of Japanese technology for the high-speed rail system linking Beijing and Shanghai. Beijing eventually decided against the use of Japanese, German, or French technologies altogether. The public debate over the project showed that the Chinese decision makers were clearly sensitive to popular sentiments. At the height of anti-Japanese demonstrations in early 2005, there were calls for the boycotting of Japanese products. These nationalist acts, although isolated, illustrated the vulnerability of trade and investment to Chinese fury.[42] The threat of a popular backlash against Sino-Japanese economic ties was so real that top Chinese officials, including Foreign Minister Li Zhaoxing and Commerce Minister Bo Xilai, had to publicly urge calm, stressing the inadvisability of such emotional acts.

---

[41] A rundown of these incidents is offered in "China Refuses to Apologize for Anti-Japan Violence," *Japan Times*, April 18, 2005.

[42] Liu Jiangyong, *Zhongguo Yu Riben: Bianhuazhong De "Zhengleng Jingre" Guanxi* [China and Japan: The Relationship of "Political Frigidity and Economic Warmth" in Evolution] (Beijing: Renmin Chuanbanshe, 2007), pp. 131–50.

The cascade of incidents, badly managed on both sides, had eaten away the basis for mutual amity. A joint survey of mutual image of Chinese and Japanese college students conducted in March 2007 by China's *Outlook East Weekly* and Japan's *Yomiuri Shimbun* showed that the shares of the Japanese respondents holding mixed or negative views on China were, respectively, 40 percent and 46 percent, whereas 33.4 percent of the Chinese respondents held a mixed view on Japan and 56.5 percent held a negative view.[43] It appeared that the Sino-Japanese relationship had veered off track. Despite the multifaceted ties between the two countries and the supreme importance they represented to each other, strikingly little consultation and few institutional mechanisms existed to deal with the plethora of bilateral problems. Neither side was willing to do its part in confronting the problems; both opted to shift blame onto the other.

The Politics of Status Competition

With economic cooperation between China and Japan forging ahead amidst stalled political ties, "hot in economics, chilly in politics" has become a standard description of the state of the Sino-Japanese relationship.[44] Taking the seemingly bifurcated development at face value, the extant literature tends to treat the cooperative and competitive domains separately. To the former, the notion of interdependence, as it is commonly defined in liberal international relations theory, is often applied. The emphasis is on material "transactions" and the rational costs-benefits equation in determining the international outcome.[45] While the theory does not preclude conflict between interdependent states, it does seem to have insurmountable difficulties in explaining the intense, multifaceted collision between the two Asian nations,

---

[43] "Zhongri You Duojin, You Duoyuan" [China and Japan: How Close, How Far Away], *RMRB*, April 10, 2007, p. 2.

[44] The most comprehensive study in Chinese is Liu Jiangyong, *China and Japan*.

[45] The classics are Robert O. Keohane and Joseph S. Nye, *Power and Interdependence: World Politics in Transition* (Boston: Little, Brown, 1977); Robert O. Keohane, *After Hegemony: Cooperation and Discord in the World Political Economy* (Princeton, NJ: Princeton University Press, 1984). In this regard, their extensive application of "transactions" from the business world is telling.

particularly during the Koizumi years. Hence, the once popular independence analysis was silenced when the times turned difficult.

As regards the competitive dynamics, nationalism is the most commonly cited domestic cause, but the literature and media seemed two-minded about its usefulness as well as how it is used. Some stress the Chinese government's deliberate manipulation of popular anti-Japanese feelings for diplomatic objectives, be they to pressure Japan on the Diaoyu Islands or to extract economic concessions or to block Japan's bid for UN National Security Council permanent seat or to beat back Japanese resurgent assertivenss abroad. Elsewhere, however, the literature often considers Chinese nationalism as a double-edged sword that the ruling CCP uses to legitimize its rule but that once enflamed could destabilize the government and jeopardize its foreign policy interests. The problem with this argument is two-fold. First, it assumes that nationalism serves none of the government's foreign policy objectives; rather, once out of control it only unnecessarily harms otherwise beneficial Chinese foreign relations, especially economic ties, with the targeted countries. Second, because the emphasis in this argument is on the regime-legitimating function of nationalism, the role of the Chinese government behind the outbursts of popular reactions is subject to greater scrutiny than the bilateral relationship itself.[46] As a result, nationalism becomes a polity-specific stereotypical notion, rather than a variable that explains the interactive dynamics between China and Japan.[47] If this argument held true, one would expect causality between the Chinese leadership's domestic insecurity and Sino-Japanese animosities. But domestically, the most insecure period for the Chinese government in the early 1990s turned out to be the best time for the Sino-Japanese relationship in the post–cold era. Conversely, with continued impressive growth in China's national economy and consolidation of power by the new generation of

---

[46] For a succinct critique of using China's regime as an excuse, see Daqing Yang, "Reconciliation Between Japan and China: Problems and Prospects," in Yoichi Funabashi, ed., *Reconciliation in the Asia-Pacific* (Washington, DC: U.S. Institute of Peace Press, 2003), pp. 84–7.

[47] For a general critique of the static notion of nationalism, see Thomas J. Christensen, Alastair Iain Johnston, and Robert S. Ross, "Conclusions and Future Directions," in Alastair Iain Johnston and Robert S. Ross, eds., *New Directions in the Study of China's Foreign Policy* (Stanford, CA: Stanford University Press, 2006), p. 407.

leadership under Hu Jintao, the relatively calm period on the domestic front in 2004–5 coincided with the worst state of the relationship in the past three decades.[48]

The structural explanation is basically derived from the balancing logic as posited by realism in IR. The problems with applying this proposition to the Sino-Japanese relationship are several. First, the power distribution in Asia is such that there is no inherent logic that Japan and China should view each other as *the* target of strategic planning. As Peter Katzenstein and Nobuo Okawara write, "[Realism] cannot say whether Japan will balance with China against the United States as the preeminent threat or whether it will balance with the United States against China as the rising regional power in East Asia."[49] In fact, by measures of power, geography, and history, a realist could well postulate more potent PRC hostility against India and Russia. Second, as Randall Schweller points out, the balance-of-power proposition assumes the state to be a unitary actor that automatically and properly brings its full national resources to bear in taking counteractive measures against the growing power of the other states – that is, potential enemies.[50] And according to Kenneth Waltz, the state's first and foremost option is self-armament, as "internal balancing [through acquisition of its independent military assets] is more reliable and precise than external balancing [through alliance making]."[51] Again, the evidence in the Sino-Japanese relationship does not bear this out. For one thing, Japan's military expenditures remained at around 1 percent of its gross national product, and its antiviolence strategic culture

---

[48] The Chinese leadership has other, more pressing long-term priorities. For the impact of other concerns on Chinese nationalism, see Suisheng Zhao, *A Nation-State by Construction: Dynamics of Modern Chinese Nationalism* (Stanford, CA: Stanford University Press, 2004); Erica Strecker Downs and Philip C. Saunders, "Legitimacy and the Limits of Nationalism: China and the Diaoyu Islands," *International Security*, vol. 23, no. 3 (Winter 1998/99), pp. 114–46.

[49] Peter Katzenstein and Nobuo Okawara, "Japan, Asia-Pacific Security, and the Case for Analytical Eclecticism," *International Security*, vol. 26, no. 3 (Winter 2001/2), p. 168.

[50] For a critical exposition of the neorealist balance-of-power theory, see Randall L. Schweller, "Unanswered Threats: A Neoclassical Realist Theory of Underbalancing," *International Security*, vol. 29, no. 2 (Fall 2004), pp. 159–201.

[51] Kenneth N. Waltz, *Theory of International Politics* (New York: McGraw-Hill, 1979), p. 168.

and constitutional constraints on foreign adventures remained strong, even if they have been weakened. And even if international structural changes had called for a radical shift in Japanese foreign policy, domestically the country would not be institutionally equipped to wage a robust balancing strategy vis-à-vis the PRC.[52] Granted, things are undoubtedly changing in Japan, with a newly titled ministry of defense, growing strategic awareness, and seemingly inevitable constitutional revisions to the "Peace Clause." Japan may be becoming more like a "normal power," but it is far from being one as predicted by realism. Also important is the extraordinary level of interdependence between the two economies and societies, a phenomenon defying the simple conventional balancing proposition.[53]

Clearly, interdependence, nationalism, and competitive power politics are at play in the Sino-Japanese relationship. But each of their roles needs to be reconsidered in proper perspective. We need to uncover the unifying logic behind the seemingly disjointed domains in economics and politics. To that end, we argue, the totality of the Sino-Japanese relationship can be best understood in terms of the multiple, interrelated dimensions of their respective notion of international status. Fundamentally, China and Japan are critically important to each other's great-power aspirations, but neither has granted the other the recognition it seeks. Bilateral history and Japan's unique position between Asia and the West have made the Sino-Japanese relationship more difficult to manage than any of the other PRC dyadic ties, including, arguably, the tie with the United States. At the same time, the bilateral, regional, and global cooperative dynamics are such that political elites on both sides have held out hope for an entente.

China's Japan experts have attributed the difficulties to the lack of mutual experience in accepting each other as equal great powers in the

---

[52] See also Peter Katzenstein and Nobuo Okawara, "Japan and Asia-Pacific Security," in J. J. Suh, Peter J. Katzenstein, and Allen Carlson, eds., *Rethinking Security in East Asia: Identity, Power, and Efficiency* (Stanford, CA: Stanford University Press, 2004), pp. 97–130; William W. Grimes, "Institutionalized Inertia: Japanese Foreign Policy in the Post–Cold War World," in G. John Ikenberry and Michael Mastanduno, eds., *International Relations Theory and the Asia-Pacific* (New York: Columbia University Press, 2003), pp. 353–85.

[53] For an explication of the realist corollary, see Michael Mastanduno, "Preserving the Unipolar Moment: Realist Theories and U.S. Grand Strategy after the Cold War," *International Security*, vol. 21, no. 4 (Spring 1997), pp. 49–88.

two thousand years of their bilateral history.[54] Indeed, despite glorified stories of cultural exchange in ancient times, bilateral experience was marked by Chinese superiority, neglect, and occasional Japanese defiance in the premodern era. In modern times, it has been marked by Japanese imperialism, military invasions, and clashing nationalist aspirations between them. After they reengaged each other at the full diplomatic level in the early 1970s, the extreme economic asymmetry defined by Japanese advancement was tempered by their common strategic commonality against the Soviet threat and Japanese war guilt. History does suggest it would take the monumental task of a paradigm shift on both sides to come to terms with the reality of each other's new aspirations in world politics.

But it's the unique Japanese role as both a status quo and revisionist power that makes Sino-Japanese accommodation particularly difficult. Postwar Japan had long enjoyed the safety under its alliance with the United States, but not as a fully fledged independent power. The country managed to strike a division of labor with the United States that allowed Japan to capitalize on its economic prowess and unique diplomatic assets to secure it a de facto, if contested, leadership role in Asia.[55] China's rise, along with Asia's reemergence on the world stage, has made Japan more vulnerable than any other power. These challenges to the status quo have shattered the Japanese sense of security, but they have also shaken postwar Japanese assumptions that Asia is where it can "return to" when it sees fit and East Asia needs Japan as a gateway to the West.

Under these circumstances, Japan's history of modern wars took center stage for a contemporary status struggle between the two countries. Unwilling to cede moral ground to the PRC, whose influence was fast growing in Asia and beyond, the maverick Koizumi and other Japanese politicians decided to make a stand on history. Linking the

---

[54] Wu Jinan, "Zhongri Guanxi Zai Zhongguo Guojia Anquan Zhanluezhong De Diwei" [The Role of the Sino-Japanese Relationship in China's National Security Strategy], *Guoji Wenti Luntan*, no. 1 (2003), at http://www.siis.org.cn/gjwtlt/2003/cn200031-2/jnwu.htm; Feng Zhaokui, "Zhongri Guanxi: Cong Lisi Dao Weilai" [Sino-Japanese Relationship: From History to the Future], *Shiji Jingji Yu Zhengzhi*, no. 9 (2005), pp. 35–40.

[55] Katzenstein and Shiraishi, eds., *Japan and Asia: Network Power*; Peter J. Katzenstein, *A World of Regions: Asia and Europe in the American Imperium* (Ithaca, NY: Cornell University Press, 2005).

Japanese position on history to its China policy,[56] the PRC side seized the issue to delegitimize both Japan's China threat theories and its claim for great-power status. As Chapter 4 has shown, for the PRC, responsible for the genesis of the China threat theories dating back to 1990 or even earlier, Japan has consistently been the source of the notion that China's rise is anything but peaceful. Japan's economic woes, combined with a long-standing lack of repentance toward its wartime behavior and rising nationalist efforts to break through the restraints placed on its military and international roles, have explained its persistent interest in fanning the fear of the PRC.[57] For the Chinese, what makes Japan's China threat theories particularly baneful is that they directly justify its alliance with the United States to contain China, its interference in the Taiwan affairs, its revisionist attitude toward its wartime past, and ultimately its abandonment of pacifism to become a traditional great power.[58]

Thus, the spread of China threat theories is seen as being carefully choreographed in tandem with the steps Japan has taken to break free from the constraints on its military power, tighten its security alliance with the United States, and justify joint development with the United States of the Theatre Missile Defense (TMD) system. According to one Chinese commentator, "By disseminating these allegations, Japan hopes to divert the attention of the international community and lull

---

[56] Wu Guangyi, "Jiexi Zhongri Guanxizhong De Lishi Wenti" [Diagnosis of the History Issue in the Sino-Japanese Relationship], *Shijie Jingji Yu Zhengzhi*, no. 2 (2004), pp. 41–6.

[57] Gu Ping, "New Pretext for Joining the TMD system," *Renmin Ribao* (Internet), Aug. 4, 2000, p. 6, in FBIS: CPP 20000804000053; "Japanese 'Dream of Military Power,'" *Liaowang*, no. 37, Sept. 11, 2000, pp. 28–9, in FBIS: CPP20000919000054; Tang Tianri, "Japan Seeks New Pretext to Expanding Military Forces," *Liaowang*, July 16, 2001, in FBIS: CPP20010727000031; Sheng Xin, "What Intentions Does Japan Have in Raising Again the 'China Threat' Theory?" *Jiefangjun Bao* (Internet), July 23, 2001, p. 5, in FBIS: CPP20010723000057.

[58] Ji Yu, "Be More Vigilant Against Japanese Militarism," *Guofang*, Sept. 15, 1996, in FBIS: FTS199660915000350. See also Da Jun, "True Threat Comes from Those Trumpeting 'China Threat,'" *Beijing Review*, Nov. 11–17, 1996, pp. 7–8; Yang Xuejun and Li Hanmei, "Key Factors Affecting Coming Japanese Diplomatic Strategies and Actions," *Zhanlue Yu Guanli*, no. 1, Feb. 1998, pp. 17–23, in FBIS: FTS19980502000166; Ni Feng, "Enhanced U.S.-Japan Security Alliance;" Ni Yanshuo, "Who Is Doing the Threatening?" *Beijing Review*, Jan. 26, 2006, pp. 10–13.

the world into letting down its guard so it may quietly achieve its long-coveted goal of becoming a major political and military power."[59] Spreading fear of a China threat, the reasoning goes, absolves Japan from its responsibility to deal with the war atrocities it committed during the period of 1894–1945. More importantly, it laid the ground for Japan to disregard Article 9 of its constitution and other restrictions placed on its Self-Defense Forces (SDF), including even the development of nuclear weapons. Citing Japanese sources, one Chinese author claimed that Japan "can produce nuclear weapons in seven days. And the nuclear fuel that Japan stores is enough to build 7,500 nuclear warheads."[60] With this technological readiness, all Japan needs to become nuclear-armed is fear mongering of China to break through domestic opposition and international restraint.[61] The Chairman of Japan's Liberal Party, Ichiro Ozawa, remarked in April 2002 that Japan was capable of developing nuclear weapons and should do so to counter Chinese military might were but another signal of Japan's growing domestic opposition to the long-standing "three no's" policy regarding nuclear weapons ("no development, no possession, and no introduction").[62] Having experienced the episode of the Indian linkage of a China threat to its nuclear tests in 1998, the PRC had become particularly vigilant about any nuclear implications of Japan's China threat theories.

For Chinese official and academic experts alike, the notions of a China threat are but a pretext for Japan to remilitarize and to threaten China. With such a frame of mind, Japan's alliance behavior and self-armament are linked to its anti-China scheme. To be sure, the Chinese fear was not altogether unfounded. Under the Koizumi administration, Japan upgraded both its alliance with the United States and its military arsenal, including its missile defense and its war-fighting capabilities, with a doctrinal focus both on China and on expanded Japanese global aspirations.[63] Also reinforcing the Chinese angst were the

---

[59] Da Jun, "True Threat Comes from Those Trumpeting 'China Threat,'" p. 8.

[60] Tang Tianri, "Japan Seeks New Pretext," p. 2.

[61] Garrett and Glaser, "Chinese Apprehensions," pp. 396–7.

[62] Dong Guozheng, "Criticizing Ichiro Ozawa's 'Provocative Remark' on Nuclear Weapons," *Jiefangjun Bao* (Internet), April 14, 2002, p. 4, in FBIS: CPP20020425000126.

[63] This is expertly detailed in Christopher W. Hughes, *Japan's Re-emergence as a "Normal" Military Power*, Adelphi Paper 368-9 (Oxford: Oxford University

concurrent, thinly veiled warnings of China's military threat by Japanese officials and documents – for example, its Defense Guidelines released in December 2004.[64] The events after September 11, 2001 further relaxed the legal and normative prohibitions in the Japanese society, thereby making possible the deployment of its SDF naval ships to the Indian Ocean in support of U.S. military operations against Taliban-controlled Afghanistan and later the stationing of SDF ground troops in Iraq to assist in postwar reconstruction. These unprecedented steps strengthened Japan's position in its alliance with the United States, which in turn allowed it to play a more assertive role in foreign policy.[65]

Growing Japanese confidence abroad, coupled with renewed international calls for UN reforms, spurred Tokyo to launch an all-out diplomatic campaign during 2004–5 to join the permanent members of the UN Security Council, hoping to achieve its long-held goal at the occasion of the organization's sixtieth anniversary. With a plan to first secure an international consensus behind its bid that Beijing would find it hard to reject, Tokyo decided to bypass China. Such slight no doubt hardened Beijing's opposition to Japan's bid. Tokyo naturally felt entitled to the recognition because until most recently it contributed nearly ten times as much as the PRC did to the UN's regular budget. In response, China rejected the notion that the expansion of the powerful UN body should be based on financial contributions, while at the same it enlisted the support of developing countries, particularly members of the African Union, for its position. The PRC made concerted efforts to undermine the Japanese case, including the use of the history issue. Asked about the Japanese bid on his visit to India

Press, 2004); *ibid.*, "Japanese Military Modernization: In Search of a 'Normal' Security Role," in Ashley J. Tellis and Michael Wills, ed., *Strategic Asia 2005–06* (Seattle: National Bureau of Asian Research, 2005), pp. 105–34.

[64] Xinhua Commentary: "Who Is Japan's New Defense Program Outline Intended to Defend Against?" Dec. 11, 2004, in FBIS: CPP20041211000068; Ding Ying, "Who's Threatening Whom?" *Beijing Review*, Jan. 13, 2005, in FBIS: CPP20050113000057.

[65] Richard Tanter, "With Eyes Wide Shut: Japan, Heisei Militarization, the Bush Doctrine," in Mel Gurtov and Peter Van Ness, eds., *Confronting the Bush Doctrine* (London: Routledge, 2005), pp. 153–80; Mike M. Mochizuki, "Japan: Between Alliance and Autonomy," in Ashley J. Tellis and Michael Wills, eds., *Strategic Asia 2004–05* (Seattle: National Bureau of Asian Research, 2004), pp. 103–37.

in April 2005, Chinese Premier Wen Jiabao pointedly replied, "Only countries that respect history, are brave enough to face up to their historical responsibilities, and are able to win people's trust in Asia and the world can play a greater role in international affairs."[66] At the societal level, popular demonstrations targeting Japanese revisionism of its wartime past and the unprecedented massive Internet petition campaigns against Japanese permanent membership organized by Chinese activists also raised questions about Japan's legitimacy for greater global leadership.

The PRC is highly sensitive to the Beijing-Washington-Tokyo trilateral interactions, as the pattern of the three power relationships critically impinges on its international environment. Japan's decision to distance its China policy from that of the United States after the Tiananmen Square crisis led to brief political amity between Beijing and Tokyo in the early 1990s.[67] In 1997–98, the United States seemed to assign greater strategic weight to China while downgrading Japan, particularly during the East Asian financial crisis and the South Asian nuclear crisis.[68] The shifts in the triangular interactions in favor of the PRC proved to have been spurred by international crises and thus were short-lived. In contrast, Chinese analysts have always attributed to the U.S.-Japan alliance dual functions, namely, reining in Japan's international ambitions and serving the U.S. strategic objectives in Asia. Since the late 1990s, the Chinese have seen a diminishing role for the former function, with overall alliance trends turning detrimental to the PRC. They are profoundly worried about the fusion of Japan's remilitarization and the alliance's anti-China bent.[69]

---

[66] "Wen Jiabao Zongli Zai Xindeli Huijian Guoji Meiti Jizhe" [Premier's Wen Jiabao Met with Correspondents from International Media in New Delhi], *RMRB*, April 13, 2005, p. 2. See also Gu Ping [pseudonym], "'Ruchang' Qineng Yixiang Qingyuan" [How Can 'Permanent Membership' Be One's Wishful Thinking?], *RMRB*, April 15, 2005, p. 1.

[67] Michael Oksenberg, "China and Japanese-American Alliance," in Gerald L. Curtis, ed., *The United States, Japan and Asia: Challenges for U.S. Policy* (New York: W. W. Norton, 1994), pp. 98–101.

[68] Mochizuki, "The U.S.-Japan Alliance and the Rise of China," pp. 106–9.

[69] Wang Jisi, "Building a Constructive Relationship," in Morton I. Abramowitz, Yoichi Funabashi, and Wang Jisi, *China-Japan-U.S.: Managing the Trilateral Relationship* (Tokyo: Japan Center for International Exchange, 1998), p. 34. See also Yu Tiejun, "Meiguo De Dongya Junshi Tongmeng" [The U.S. Military Alliance in East Asia], in Yan Xuetong, ed., *Guoji Anquanjuan* [International Security] (Beijing: New World Press, 2007), pp. 61–97; Liu Shilong, "Lengzhan

For the Chinese, the ominous turn in the U.S.-Japan alliance has also manifested itself in the emphasis on shared democratic values and shared responsibility in maintaining regional order. Not only is Japan becoming a more equal ally, but the purpose of the alliance itself has changed to serve as the cornerstone for regional order in Asia.[70] In the early 1990s, Japan's Asia diplomacy focused on improving ties with China and developing nascent regional institutions, such as the APEC and other multilateral initiatives centered on the Association for Southeast Asian Nations (ASEAN). A decade later, the Asian style of multilateralism seemed to do more to facilitate China's growing influence than to serve Japan's interests. The decision of the Koizumi administration to tie its international role first and foremost to its alliance with the United States weakened Japanese interest in Asian regionalism and arguably undercut Japanese influence in the region as well.[71] Suspicious of Tokyo's motives, mainstream Chinese analysts looked at the policy shift as designed to politically hold back China's influence in Asia.[72] Some even drew a parallel between the contemporary alliance and the prevailing "dissociation-from-Asia" idea in the late Tokugawa and subsequent Meiji eras, which invariably viewed China with contempt and Japan as the superior, rightful savior of the uncivilized Asia.[73] They are, of course, not comparing today's China

      Hou Riben De Waijiao Zhanlue" [Japan's Diplomatic Strategy after the Cold War], in Jin Canrong, *Daguo Zhanluejuan* [Strategies of the Great Powers] (Beijing: New World Press, 2007), pp. 384–97.

[70] A concise discussion of Chinese concerns can be found in a major study by the Chinese Academy of Social Sciences. See Zhang Yunling, ed, *Weilai 10–15 Nian Zhongguo Zai Yatai Diqu Bianling de Guoji Huanjing* [China's International Environment in the Asia-Pacific Region in the Next 10–15 Years] (Beijing: Zhongguo Shehui Kexue Chubanshe, 2003), pp. 247–53, quotes on pp. 249, 250. See also Liu Jiangyong, *China and Japan.*

[71] Sarah Suk: "Koizumi's Emphasis on U.S. Ties May Signal Hindering Others," Kyodo World Service, Nov. 16, 2005, in FBIS: JPP20051116969117.

[72] "Rimei Junshi Hezuo Dongtai Jiexi" [Diagnosis of the Trends in Japan-U.S. Military Cooperation], *RMRB*, Nov. 5, 2005, p. 5; Feng Zhaokui, "Meiguo Lejian Zhongri Guanxi Ehua, Liyong Riben Qianzhi Zhongguo" [Happy to See Sino-Japanese Relationship Worsen, the United States Uses Japan to Check China], *International Herald Tribune*, Nov. 29, 2005, at http://news.sina.com.cn/w/2005-11-29/10468436243.shtml (accessed Nov. 29, 2005); Wu Xinbo, "The End of the Silver Lining: A Chinese View of the U.S.-Japanese Alliance," *Washington Quarterly*, vol. 29, no. 1 (Winter 2005/6), pp. 119–30.

[73] Classic studies on this subject in the English literature are Marius B. Jansen, *Japan in the Tokugawa World* (Cambridge, MA: Harvard University Press,

to the Qing China, nor are they suggesting that a violent showdown is inevitable. Rather, in criticizing what the prominent Chinese scholar Liu Jiangyong calls the Japanese mentality of "despising, discriminating against, and even disregarding its Asian neighbors" in its alliance strategy, they are warning the Japanese not to repeat the disastrous choice of the past.[74]

There are multiple reasons for Sino-Japanese tensions, but there are also stabilizing forces at work that have kept a lid on their conflicts. Economic ties are virtually indispensable for both countries. Much of the international identity of post-1945 Japan is defined by its economic and technological prowess. The Chinese leadership's agenda for regaining national greatness entails first and foremost economic modernization. As such, Sino-Japanese political competition has been tempered by the cooperative logic embedded in economic globalization.

Beyond economics, prominent Japanese scholars do not advocate containment, but on the one hand, they hope to have the international constraints and material wherewithal to minimize the dangerous uncertainties in its giant neighbor's foreign trajectory; on the other, they realize that Japan's new international future must retail an active role in Asia where a central Chinese position is already a reality. These engagement ideas represented the consensus in Japan's China policy, circles although the opposition Democratic Party has favored a less U.S.-centered, more Asian-oriented Japanese foreign policy.[75]

1992); Jansen, "Japanese Views of China During the Meiji Period," in Albert Feuerwerker, Rhodes Murphey, and Mary C. Wrights, eds., *Approaches to Modern Chinese History* (Berkeley: University of California Press, 1967), pp. 163–89; Bunso Hashikawa, "Japanese Perspectives on Asia: From Dissociation to Coprosperity," in Akira Iriye, ed., *The Chinese and the Japanese: Essays in Political and Cultural Interactions* (Princeton, NJ: Princeton University Press, 1980), pp. 328–55.

[74] Liu Jiangyong, Fan Yongming, and Lu Yaodong, "Riben Waijiao Quyu Bianyuanhua" [Japanese Diplomacy Tends to Be Marginalized], *RMRB*, Aug. 7, 2006, p. 8. See also Liu Jiangyong, *China and Japan*.

[75] Interview with Akio Watanabe, "Is Japan a UK of the Orient?" *Gaiko Forum*, May 1, 2006, pp. 8–10, in Open Source Center (formerly FBIS), JPP20060419124002; Takashi Shiraishi, "Is It Possible to Create an East Asian Community?" *Chuo Koron*, Jan. 1, 2006, pp. 118–27, in Open Source Center, JPP20060111016002. For comprehensive treatment of the security debate, see Richard J. Samuels, *Securing Japan: Tokyo's Grand Strategy and The Future of East Asia* (Ithaca, NY: Cornell University Press, 2007).

However, these ideas failed to coalesce into a proactive strategy, thereby leaving the Chinese to suspect that Japan has sought to destabilize Asia to thwart China's orderly rise and to help restructure its alliance with the United States to contain China. The United States ultimately does not want to see the Sino-Japanese relationship worsen to the point where the two Asian countries engage in a zero-sum, full-scale balancing. To the extent that the Chinese view the Sino-American relationship through the prism of the Sino-Japanese relationship, excessive rivalry between the Asian powers would jeopardize the U.S. engagement strategy toward the PRC.[76]

Evidently, even during the Koizumi period both sides understood that Sino-Japanese enmity, if uncontrolled, could derail the foreign policy transitions both countries were trying to engineer. While in favor of a hedging strategy toward China, Koizumi repeatedly stated that the PRC rise represented an opportunity rather than a threat. The Chinese, too, sought to stabilize the relationship, as evidenced by the so-called new-thinking debate on Japan during 2003–04. Preceding the formal induction of the new Chinese leadership under President Hu Jintao and Premier Wen Jiabao in 2003, a senior commentator of the *People's Daily*, Ma Licheng, published an essay in the influential bimonthly journal *Strategy and Management* expressing worries about the popular antagonism between China and Japan. He called for "new thinking" in China's Japan policy, which would entail abandoning obsessive, misguided nationalist emotions over Japan's wartime past whilst at the same time duly recognizing contemporary Japan's advanced development as well as its support for China's modernization. Several months later, Shi Yinhong, a professor at the Chinese Renmin University, wrote in the same journal echoing Ma's sentiments. He further proposed that China put the history issue in its proper perspective and proactively support Japan to play a great-power role in order to wean Japan away from the United States.[77] Zhang Tuosheng,

---

[76] The logic is explicated in Christensen, "China, the U.S.-Japan Alliance, and the Security Dilemma." For evidence that the U.S. policy makers are aware of the sensitivity of Japan's role, see "U.S. Finds Strained Japan-China Ties 'Frustrating': Hill," *Kyodo World Service in English*, Nov. 19, 2005, in FBIS: JPP20051119969050.

[77] Ma Licheng, "Duiri Guanxi Xinsiwei: Zhongri Minjianzhiyou" [New Thinking on Sino-Japanese Relations: Worry Trends at Popular Level], *Zhanlue Yu Guanli*, no. 6 (2002), pp. 41–47; Shi Yinhong, "Zhongri Jiejin Yu 'Waijiao

a well-placed strategy analyst in Beijing, agreed. Like Shi, he wrote, China should not ignore Japan for the sake of improving ties with the United States, but rather should grant Japan greater recognition of its independent international role. Worried that the Chinese public image was excessively colored by the history issue and paranoia about Japan's remilitarization, Zhang called for a fairer portrayal of Japan, with due recognition of the Japanese economic assistance to China and the new path postwar Japan had taken.[78]

These new thinkers clearly tied rethinking of history to a fundamental Sino-Japanese realignment, a view that reportedly had its blessing from the incoming Chinese leadership. Yet, to the disappointment of the Chinese, Japanese reactions showed an interest only in the Chinese self-criticisms on the history issue, with little interest in diplomatically reciprocating their goodwill gestures. Thus, these views were soon attacked as selling out China's national interests in intellectual circles and on the Internet in the People's Republic. They were effectively silenced as the Sino-Japanese relationship slipped into a cold spell. However, even during the worst episode since 1972, leaders regularly did meet, albeit not as each other's guest; strategic dialogue over the East China Sea disputes continued, although without a compromise. The PRC quietly repaired the diplomatic facilities damaged in the heat of popular nationalism, and Japan punished the right-wing group member responsible for driving a bus into the Chinese consulate in Osaka in April 2004. Both political leaderships calmed nationalist emotions in their own societies, although their actions played no small part in fueling popular animosities. Ultimately, they failed to agree on the strategic terms with which to engage each other.

It would take a change of leadership in Japan in late September 2006 for the two sides to begin mending their badly tattered political ties.

Geming'" [Sino-Japanese Joining Hands and "Diplomatic Revolution"], *Zhanlue Yu Guanli*, no. 2 (2003), pp. 71–5. For a fairly balanced review of the debate, see Feng Zhaokui, "Duiri Guanxi De Jiannan Qiusuo [The Tortuous Quest in the Sino-Japanese Relationship], *Shijie Jingji Yu Zhengzhi*, no. 5 (2004), pp. 26–31. The full range of Chinese views in the debate is catalogued at http://www.irchina.org/, edited by the School of International Studies of Nankai University in Tianjin, China.

[78] Zhang Tuosheng, "Dui Zhongri Guanxi De Jidian Sikao" [Several Thoughts on Sino-Japanese Relations], *Shijie Jingji Yu Zhengzhi*, no. 9 (2003), pp. 22–6, at http://www.iwep.org.cn/wep/World%20Volume/2003/2003,9/zhangtuosheng. PDF (accessed Feb. 8, 2006).

Within two weeks after assuming office, Shinzo Abe made his first official visits to China and South Korea. Much as China and Japan agreed
to "shelve" the sovereignty dispute over the Diaoyu Islands for the
sake of diplomatic normalization in the early 1970s, the two decided
to leave the issue of future Yasukuni visits unresolved for the moment.
Abe's "Asia first" tour provided some relief to his predecessor's neglect
of Asia. The Chinese were ready to reciprocate. Premier Wen Jiabao
visited Japan in April of the following year. While maintaining a principled PRC stand on history, Wen was more interested in engaging
the Japanese now while looking to the future. Besides the summit with
Abe and a speech at the Diet, Wen's three-day itinerary also included
meeting with Emperor Akihito, playing baseball with Japanese college students, and visiting Japanese farmers. Most importantly, the
two sides reaffirmed their desire to promote bilateral ties based on
shared "strategic" interests between them, in the region, and around
the globe. "Strategic" is a term the PRC has long sought to include
in characterizing their bilateral relationship,[79] and the emphasis on
strategic cooperation in Asia and beyond suggests tentative recognition of each other's rising status. But that's a long way from a genuine
strategic partnership. Compared to the remarkable public attempts by
the two leaders to smooth over bilateral problems, media on both sides,
particularly in Japan, were lukewarm in their coverage, anticipating
uncertainties and lingering difficulties ahead. Yet the Abe-Wen trips
did set warming trends in the relationship, including budding military
exchanges, and a pattern of reciprocal leadership visits, which would
continue with Abe's successor, Prime Minister Yasuo Fukuda's visit to
China at the end of 2007. Again, quite intent on not enflaming the war
guilt issue, both sides showed commitment to build a normal relationship even without settling bilateral irritants, such as the energy dispute
in the East China Sea. Also notable was Fukuda's trip to the hometown
of Confucius to pay homage to the ancient Chinese philisopher, whose
name is synymous with China's historical influence in East Asia and
closely associated with its currect projection of cultural power.

It's more appropriate to view the Sino-Japanese relationship in its
totality in terms of its status dynamics than to compartmentalize
supposedly cooperative economics and irreconcilable politics. The

---

[79] *Sina News*, April 4, 2007, at http://news.sina.com.cn/c/2007-04-04/
024712688170

unresolved issue of each other's role in bilateral, regional, and global politics has intensified balancing logic and nationalist emotions on both sides. Koizumi's personal style also contributed to the latest episode of heightened animosities. The competitive dynamics are real and potent, but their role depends on how the two governments react to their own domestic and international politics. They are not retained by immutable structural force, nor must their rivalry continue unabated because of domestic politics. While the Sino-Japanese relationship could still worsen, the nations' interdependence goes well beyond economics, thus generating cooperative potentials that could transform the bilateral interaction, regional order, and world politics.

7 | *Rediscovering Asia and Africa: The Multilateral Turn*

The idea of Asian regionalism after the Second World War had its genesis with the rising power of Japan in the 1960s. Directly or not, Japan was the architect of the major regional institutions and forums, official and private. The government as well as prominent individuals saw Asian regionalism as a secure footing to facilitate Japan's "return to Asia." Bearing the imprint of the unique Japanese style and interests, these institutional undertakings have made a valuable contribution to the economic development, interdependence, and cooperative dynamics in the region. With the rise of the People's Republic of China, the question inevitably arises as to how it approaches regional integration and multilateral diplomacy in Asia.

The PRC started to seriously consider joining regional institutions in the 1980s. Initially, reformist leaders, such as Premier Zhao Ziyang, wanted to tap into the economic dynamism in East Asia to spur Chinese economic modernization. Later, the ruling Chinese Communist Party elites also began to see institutional involvement as an inescapable part of its regional diplomacy. But they were then worried about the U.S. and Japanese dominance, while at the same time uncertain of the impact of regional integration on Chinese sovereignty and conflicted national identity. The informal, nonintrusive, and gradualist style of the Asian institutional approach assuaged some of these concerns, thereby facilitating tentative PRC engagement. Since the mid-1990s, however, China has demonstrated unprecedented activism and growing leadership in multilateral initiatives in Asia. Such a shift is remarkable, especially in light of the traditional PRC aversion to and suspicion of such institutional entanglements. The change became even more pronounced in light of the unilateral turn in U.S. policy and the bilateral emphasis in Japanese policy after the terrorist attacks on September 11, 2001.[1]

Reflective of its global ambitions in the twenty-first century, the PRC has developed a robust diplomacy in the developing world beyond its neighborhood, most notably in Africa. In these previously far-off places, in lieu of lofty slogans and benign neglect, China is developing substantive ties designed to boost its global status. With its growing reach in Africa, the PRC has extended its multilateral diplomacy to the continent through the Forum on China-Africa Cooperation (FOCAC)–Ministerial Conference, alternatively hosted by China and Africa every three years since its inception in 2000.

This chapter investigates China's multilateral diplomacy in Asia and Africa, with a focus on the former. The new turn in the PRC's foreign policy reveals not only its diplomatic approach to its neighborhood and beyond but also highlight its visions of the regional and global order. The bulk of the chapter is devoted to a close look at China's approaches to the variegated multilateral dynamics across Southeast Asia, Northeast Asia, and Central Asia. For each subregion, I only look at the multilateral process that involves all major players, has a comprehensive agenda, and possesses the greatest capability to transform the Asian regional order at large. Left unaddressed is China's participation in the myriad multilateral platforms that involve a relatively small set of states, that are devoted exclusively to functional issues, and that have limited direct impact beyond the specific issues at hand. I first examine Beijing's multilateral diplomacy toward the Korean peninsula, with a focus on its role in the Six-Party Talks. The multiparty talks deserve special attention, because Northeast Asia is where institutional development is the weakest and the existing regional arrangement poses the greatest challenge to Beijing's foreign policy.[2] I then investigate China's multilateral diplomacy toward Southeast Asia and Central Asia, with the focus, respectively, on regionalism leading to the inaugural East Asian Summit in December 2005 and on the Shanghai Cooperation Organization (SCO). In sketching China's Africa policy, I focus on the

---

[1] On Japan's struggle to balance bilateralism and multilateralism, see Ellis S. Krauss and T. J. Pempel, eds., *Beyond Bilateralism: U.S.-Japan Relations in the New Asia-Pacific* (Stanford, CA: Stanford University Press, 2004).

[2] See Gilbert Rozman, *Northeast Asia's Stunted Regionalism: Bilateral Distrust in the Shadow of Globalization* (Cambridge: Cambridge University Press, 2004).

FOCAC, which has provided the political framework spearheading PRC ties with some fifty countries on the continent. Finally, I draw out insights from the comparative study of China's objectives in Asia and Africa and the limits of its influence in the developing world.

China's Korea Policy and the Six-Party Talks

With the end of the cold war, the beginning of the 1990s witnessed a dramatic wave of Chinese diplomatic normalizations in Asia. The PRC stepped up efforts to establish full relations with the Republic of Korea (ROK), with which it already had a booming economic relationship. To assuage the concern of its traditional ally, the Democratic People's Republic of Korea (DPRK), Beijing deferred formal recognition of the ROK until after both Koreas joined the United Nations. While officially launching a two-Korea policy, the PRC continued to emphasize its "special ties" with the communist North. Propelled by bilateral economic dynamism, however, China's relationship with the ROK soon progressed by leaps and bounds, in contrast to its weakening ties with the North. Even on the security issue, the PRC's commitment to the protection of the DPRK's Kim Jung-il regime weakened, for neither side showed much enthusiasm for reaffirming their 1961 bilateral security treaty. In fact, on several occasions Chinese officials went out of their way to publicly declare that China was by no means unconditionally obligated to militarily assist the DPRK, although the document remained officially in place.[3]

Despite North Korea's many displeasures with the Chinese, it had more reasons to maintain a special bond with them. For one, with lower expectations on both sides, they could continue the trappings of a "lip-and-teeth" friendship through leadership meetings, with a greater emphasis on symbolism than substance. Moreover, China continued to provide North Korea with vital supplies of energy and foodstuffs. And in the diplomatic arena, the PRC remained committed to the security of the Kim regime. In a nutshell, Beijing might not be fully trustworthy, but no other country had comparable power or interest in supporting the North Korean regime.

---

[3] Eric A. McVadon, "Chinese Military Strategy for the Korean Peninsula," in James Lilley and David Shambaugh, eds., *China's Military Faces the Future* (Armonk, NY: M. E. Sharpe, 1999), pp. 279–80.

For the ROK, its economic complementarities with the PRC were demonstrated by the fact that in merely one year after they officially granted each other diplomatic recognition in August 1992, bilateral trade reached $9.1 billion and China jumped to third place on the list of top ROK trading partners.[4] Trade forged ahead afterward, and cultural and social ties thrived, boosting educational exchanges and two-way tourism. In 2006, South Korea traded more with China than with any other country, topping $135 billion. Two-way visits by the two peoples amounted to over 5 million, and 57,504 ROK students were studying in China, accounting for the largest foreign student body there. By the same year, the ROK had invested $35 billion in China, more than in any other country.[5]

Such substantial ties between the PRC and the ROK helped reduce the latter's misgivings toward Beijing. But ultimately, it was Beijing's peninsula policy that enhanced the South Korea's trust. Since the 1990s, China has adopted a conservative "stability" policy, which entails both recognition of the enduring reality of Korea's division and support of measures for inter-Korea rapprochement and reconciliation.[6]

When President Kim Dae Jung launched his ambitious "sunshine policy" toward the DPRK after 1998, the CCP leaders found Kim's vision of a constructively engaged North embracing reforms at home and moderation abroad quite compatible with their own preferences. The Chinese, from President Jiang Zemin to well-placed academics, thus quietly leaned on their North Korean friends to reciprocate Kim's initiative. According to the well-informed Chinese analyst Liu Ming,

---

[4] Victor D. Cha, "The View from Korea," in Alastair Iain Johnston and Robert Ross, eds., *Engaging China: The Management of an Emerging Power* (New York: Routledge, 1999), p. 34; Chung Jae Ho, "South Korea and the Rise of China," *Joint U.S.-Korea Academic Studies*, vol. 15 (2005), p. 3.

[5] Li Dunqiu, "Hanfeng Hanliu Jingfengliu" [Chinese Waves, Korean Trends Competing for Splendor], *Renmin Ribao*, overseas ed. (hereafter cited as *RMRB*), Jan. 5, 2007, p. 1; Xinhua, "Wen Jiabao Jieshou Hanguo Xinwen Meiti Lianhe Caifang" [Wen Jiabao Receives Joint Interviews by Korean News Media], *RMRB*, April 6, 2007, pp. 1, 4; "Qunian Laihua Liuxuesheng Chaoguo 16 Wan," [Foreign Students in China Surpassed 160,000 Last Year], *RMRB*, May 29, 2007, p. 1.

[6] For an overview, see Samuel S. Kim, "The Making of China's Korean Policy in the Era of Reform," in David M. Lampton, ed., *The Making of Chinese Foreign and Security Policy in the Era of Reform* (Stanford, CA: Stanford University Press, 2001), pp. 371–408.

"Many Chinese officials and scholars tried to persuade, even argued with, their North Korean counterparts, urging them to cooperate with [the sunshine policy] in line with Chinese leaders' expectations."[7] In that spirit – while the historical summit meeting between Kim Dae Jung and Kim Jung-il in July 2000 was, as the Korea watcher Scott Snyder aptly characterized it, an *"autonomous* process" between the two Koreas – China played an instrumental role, as evidenced by preceding secret meetings between the two sides held in Chinese cities as well as Kim Jung-il's visit to Beijing prior to the summit.[8]

The United States clearly judges China's intentions on the Korean peninsula in the larger context of overall PRC foreign policy choice and the state of their bilateral relationship. But the touchstone issue is Chinese views on the U.S.-ROK alliance. As Beijing's fear of a forced Korean unification on the South's terms had diminished by the late 1990s, the PRC opposition to the military alliance toned down significantly. So long as China was actively engaged in Korean peninsula affairs, its relationship with the ROK steadily improved, and the Sino-U.S. relationship remained on a relatively stable footing, Beijing was not overly concerned about the U.S.-ROK military alliance.[9]

At the beginning of the new century, to assure the United States of its nonrevisionist regional intentions, Chinese diplomats have publicly stated their recognition of the reality of the U.S. military presence in Asia; and as a matter of principle, they are not opposed to it. Most tellingly, the PRC has not explicitly tied its growing relationship with the ROK to the latter's alliance with the United States. It steered clear of the U.S.-ROK relationship even when anti-Americanism in South Korea reached a new height in 2002–03.[10]

---

[7] Liu Ming, "China's Role on the Korean Peninsula: Its Characteristics and Development," *Joint U.S.-Korea Academic Studies*, vol. 11 (2001), p. 109.

[8] Scott Snyder, "Evaluating the Inter-Korean Peace Process," in Yoichi Funabashi, ed., *Reconciliation in the Asia-Pacific* (Washington, DC: U.S. Institute of Peace Press, 2003), pp. 19–35, quote on p. 24; Liu Ming reconstructed China's intimate involvement in the summit in "China's Role on the Korean Peninsula," *ibid*, pp. 109–11.

[9] For Chinese views on the alliance, see McVadon, "Chinese Military Strategy for the Korean Peninsula," pp. 271–94; Eric McVadon, "China's Goals and Strategies for the Korean Peninsula," in Henry D. Sokolski, ed., *Planning for a Peaceful Korea* (Carlisle, PA: Strategic Studies Institute, 2001), pp. 166–93.

[10] Robert G. Sutter, *China's Rise in Asia: Promises and Perils* (Boulder, CO: Rowman & Littlefield, 2005), p. 163.

Along with growing bilateral confidence in its role in the peninsula's affairs, the PRC had also gained a foothold in major multilateral initiatives. In this regard, its involvement in the Four-Party Talks during 1997–99 – attended by the Koreas, the United States, and China – was particularly important. While the intended goal of the talks – to conclude a peace treaty to end the Korean War (1950–53) in lieu of the armistice – failed to be achieved, the multilateral diplomacy did lay the foundation for the subsequent Six-Party Talks. By all accounts, North Korea initially wanted direct talk with the United States with the exclusion of both China and the ROK. Even after reluctantly agreeing to ROK participation, its mistrust toward China had grown such that it continued to resist, albeit quietly, a full Chinese role. By then, however, South Korea had gained so much confidence in Beijing that it encouraged China's participation in the four-way talks.[11]

During the first nuclear crisis (1993–94), while insisting that the issue be resolved between the DPRK and the United States through diplomatic means, Beijing also exerted influence on Pyongyang (North Korea) in order to make that possible. Though not a member of the Korean Peninsula Energy Development Organization, China's subsequent policy was largely aligned with other regional powers, in the spirit of the 1994 Agreed Framework.[12]

The Agreed Framework, unfortunately, proved to be a failed undertaking. Washington would confront Pyongyang in October 2002 over the latter's purported weapons-grade uranium enrichment program in violation of the framework. By then, Beijing had earned enough diplomatic credit with key individual players and in multilateral forums on peninsular affairs that would enable it to play a high-profile role during the ensuing second nuclear crisis. Also important, the Sino-American relationship had seen great improvement, in part spurred by the events after the terrorist attacks in the United States in September

---

[11] Chae-Jin Lee, "The Evolution of China's Two-Korea Policy," in Bae Ho Hahn and Chae-Jin Lee, eds., *The Korean Peninsula and the Major Powers* (Seoul: Sejong Institute, 1998), pp. 127–8; Liu Ming, "Crafting a Peace Mechanism for the Korean Peninsula," *The Political Economy of Korean Reconciliation and Reform* (Washington, DC: Korean Economic Institute of America, 2001), pp. 26–27, quote on p. 26.

[12] Kim, "Making of China's Korea Policy," pp. 392–4; Lee, "The Evolution of China's Two-Korea Policy," *ibid.*, pp. 136–38; Liu Ming, "China's Role on the Korean Peninsula," pp. 104–5.

2001. With its newfound influence, China proposed and convened the North Korea-U.S.-China trilateral meeting in April 2003 to deal with the nuclear issue.

When the nuclear crisis again erupted, the initial PRC reaction was to call for the United States to hold direct talks with Pyongyang. But the U.S. administration under President George W. Bush made it clear that it would not directly negotiate with the North this time around. Beijing dropped this insistence, as its immediate goal was to kick off a diplomatic process, whatever the format. The only way this could happen was for it to fully participate. To secure Pyongyang's receptivity to the trilateral talks, the PRC employed a combination of blunt warnings and continued reassurances. It even withheld energy supplies to North Korea for three days in mid-March 2003. While Beijing publicly cited technical problems for the interruption, Western and Asian media invariably interpreted it as an extraordinary Chinese step intended to send a stern warning to the Kim regime. In the meantime, Beijing also reassured Pyongyang that it would continue to take to heart the interests of its traditional ally. On April 9, 2003, China, together with Russia, successfully blocked a UN Security Council resolution condemning North Korea's nuclear brinkmanship. Pyongyang eventually forfeited its earlier demand for direct one-on-one negotiation with the United States.

Along with the trilateral talks, Washington also pushed for more robust multilateral pressures on the North. And other regional powers, too, were eager to be involved. China was very agreeable to the idea of membership expansion, hoping that would breathe new life into the diplomatic process. In July 2003, Beijing presented the idea to the DPRK,[13] which initially objected but came around after Russia was included. With the additional participation of the ROK, Japan, and Russia, the Six-Party Talks kicked off in August 2003. In the following four years, Beijing hosted an additional five rounds of talks, in February 2004, June 2004, July–September 2005 (two stages), November 2005–February 2007 (three phases), and March and September 2007 (two stages).

Through this process, the PRC played an active role as the host and as a facilitator. At the early stages, it proposed a lower-level,

---

[13] Liu Ming, "China and the North Korean Crisis: Facing Test and Transition," *Pacific Affairs*, vol. 76, no. 3 (Fall 2003), p. 360.

more frequent consultation mechanism among the countries involved to complement the high-profile, intermittent Six-Party Talks, which proven valuable in facilitating behind-the-scenes dialogues and negotiations. Most notably, at the conclusion of the third round in September 2005, Beijing hammered out a joint statement in which "the six parties unanimously reaffirmed that the goal of the Six-Party Talks is the verifiable denuclearization of the Korean Peninsula in a peaceful manner," but also pledged to address DPRK economic, security, and political concerns.[14]

To maintain forward momentum for these talks, top Chinese diplomats shuttled among the five capitals while keeping in constant communication with their counterparts in the other nations. Sustaining the process required keeping Pyongyang and Washington engaged. To ensure the DPRK's participation, China resorted to both the carrot of assistance and the stick of threat. For example, after the first round of the Six-Party Talks, the head of China's National People's Congress, Wu Bangguo, pledged to North Korea $50 million worth of aid on his visit there in October 2003, which led to the completion of the Da'an Friendship Glass factory two years later. After the North Korean negotiator turned down several drafts of the Chinese-proposed agreement during the first phase of the fourth round, the prominent adviser to the Chinese leadership at the Central Party School of the Communist Party of China, Zhang Liangui, publicly warned Pyongyang of the dire consequences if its recalcitrance aborted the whole process. Following the U.S. initiative, he wrote in the *Beijing Review*, "The [UN] Security Council will probably adopt resolutions condemning North Korea and imposing sanctions on the country, making it possible for the United States to organize a multinational force to enforce sanctions. Then, a war will be unavoidable, as North Korea has reaffirmed that sanctions would lead to war."[15]

Beijing also had to convince the skeptics in Washington about the meaningfulness of the talks. And there were many skeptics, due to the North's erratic behavior and reckless rhetoric as well as broken

---

[14] The Joint State can be found at http://www.state.gov/r/pa/prs/ps/2005/53490.htm.

[15] Zhang Liangui, "Stalemate and Solutions," *Beijing Review*, Aug. 18, 2005, p. 11.

promises on just about all of its past nonproliferation agreements.[16] After all, the "axis of evil," of which the DPRK is a member, is not only defined by its unsavory regimes, but also by its determination to develop weapons of mass destruction. To have faith in the diplomatic process requires some belief that Pyongyang turns to nuclear bombs for deterrence and bargaining and can, therefore, be persuaded to trade its weapons program for a grand deal that would satisfy its security and economic needs. Thus, Beijing through the Six-Party Talks, has to keep Pyongyang publicly committed to a nuclear-free peninsula and ensure, notwithstanding its twists and turns, a multilateral process that explicitly moves forward toward that goal. So far, despite many complaints about and numerous setbacks in the talks, both North Korea and the United States, as well as the other four participants, have remained committed to the process. Given the lack of a better alternative, patience did not run out easily.

As regards the second North Korean nuclear crisis, China's immediate concern was twofold: to prevent a militarized conflict and to contain the weapons proliferation effect. That required first and foremost Pyongyang's openness to giving up its nuclear weapons program, as a North Korea with a permanent nuclear arsenal would likely invite a militarized conflict on China's borders or conceivably trigger proliferation chain reactions in Northeast Asia, leading to a nuclear-armed Japan, South Korea, and even Taiwan. These dangers appeared particularly real in the early stage of the crisis.

Beyond the imperative of crisis management, China's diplomacy never lost sight of its strategic interests. Such linkage is hardly surprising given the pivotal role the Korean peninsula historically played in China's security environment. Thus, in contrast to the Bush administration's fixation on North Korea's nuclear program per se, Beijing all along saw the nuclear crisis as a "political issue," whose resolution required seriously addressing Pyongyang's legitimate demands.[17] Such a solution, in essence, would fundamentally be compatible with the PRC's preferences, which entail a Korean peninsula friendly to its interests and a great-power politics in Northeast Asia significantly less

---

[16] See Victor D. Cha and David C. Kang, *Nuclear North Korea: A Debate on Engagement Strategies* (New York: Columbia University Press, 2003).

[17] Zhang Liangui, "Future Unknown," *Beijing Review*, Sept. 22, 2005, pp. 10–11.

hostile to its rise. With this approach, the Six-Party Talks became a multilateral instrument for Beijing to earn diplomatic capital in and beyond Northeast Asia. Being a key animator of the process, the Chinese leadership could simultaneously earn legitimacy at home and boost the PRC's reputation abroad as a problem-solving, responsible great power. Projecting itself as even-handed between the parties involved, China could take credit for any successes achieved during the talks while blaming others' intransigency for the failures.

Several rounds of talks later, China's relationship with the North seemed to have improved, despite its occasional arm twisting of Pyongyang. Within several months during 2005–06, Hu Jintao and Kim Jung-il exchanged official visits. On Hu's trip in late October 2005, Kim reportedly introduced his son to Hu as his handpicked successor. If true, such an act, rich in symbolic deference to the Chinese leader, would give some real meaning to their "special relationship." In any case, Kim reciprocated Hu's visit with an extended tour of China in January 2006.[18] However, the cooperative momentum was dampened in the summer of the same year after North Korea's missile testing in disregard of Beijing's public pleas to Pyongyang not to do so. Subsequently, with a radical departure from its past diplomatic approach, the PRC went along with the toughly worded UN Security Council resolution condemning the missile firings. South Korean and Japanese media also reported stepped-up Sino-U.S. cooperation in cracking down on illicit DPRK financial activities, as well China's own punitive measures against North Korean counterfeiting of its currency.[19] To register Beijing's displeasure, Zhang Liangui, who had earlier stressed the crisis to be a political one, argued immediately after the missile firings that the North Korean nuclear issue "threatens

---

[18] Wang Ch'ing, "Hu Jintao's Trip to North Korea Affects Successes or Failures of Six-Party Talks," *Hong Kong Zhongguo Tongxun She*, Oct. 29, 2005, in Foreign Broadcast Information Service (hereafter cited as FBIS): CCP20051029061013.

[19] "PRC's Wang Guangya Comments on Security Council Sanctions Against DPRK," Xinhua, Oct. 15, 2006, in Open Source Center (formerly FBIS, hereafter cited as OSC): CPP20061015136002; "China Froze N. Korea Accounts in Macao: S. Korean Lawmaker," Kyodo World Service, July 24, 2006, in OSC: JPP20060724969028; "ROK Official Says DPRK 'Frustrated' by China Freezing DPRK Accounts at BOC," Yonhap, July 24, 2006, in OSC: KPP20060724971039.

the common interests of all human beings," and thus "every responsible country is expected to deal with it seriously."[20] These rebukes were no doubt hard to swallow for Pyongyang, but their relationship had not been all that trustful anyway.

Ultimately, the PRC wanted to persuade Pyongyang to return to the negotiating track without jeopardizing the survival of the DPRK regime. While displeased with the North's provocations in the nuclear crisis, official Chinese analyses were sympathetic to the country's predicament being confronted with a cold war–style division and U.S. hostilities on the peninsula.[21] As Liu Ming, an astute Chinese scholar, wrote in 2000, "No matter how the regional environment changed, North Korea would always be of importance to Chinese security and power diplomacy, and China would not forsake the DPRK's sense of a special relationship."[22] As such, the CCP leadership could tolerate criticisms by individual Chinese scholars of Pyongyang's ill-advised decision to spark the crisis, but only to a degree.[23] These criticisms were useful insofar as they added pressures on North Korea to go along with the negotiated track, but they were not permitted to stray beyond the limits to offend the Pyongyang leadership. In 2004, the Chinese government closed down *Strategy and Management,* the journal popular within a small circle of intellectuals, after it printed an article by a Tianjin-based Chinese analyst that incensed Pyongyang. The article in question accused the DPRK regime of choosing nuclear brinkmanship over feeding its people and advocated siding with the United States to rein in the rogue regime that "practices ultraleftist politics and political persecution in order to maintain dynastic rule."[24] Remarkably, having survived over a decade of publishing some of the most outspoken, unorthodox views on Chinese nationalism, domestic

---

[20] Zhang Liangui, "Talking the Talk," *Beijing Review,* July 13, 2006, p. 16.

[21] For a standard view, see Zhang Tingyan (the first Chinese ambassador to ROK), "Wei Chaoxian Bandao De Heping Yu Wending Ergongtong Nuli" [Let's Struggle Jointly for Peace and Stability on the Korean Peninsula], at http://www.ciis.org.cn/item/2005-06-10/51015.html.

[22] Liu Ming, "China's Role on the Korean Peninsula," p. 100.

[23] Perhaps the best known of such cases is Shi Yinhong, "The DPRK Nuclear Crisis, the Six-Party Talks, and Chinese Diplomacy," *Hong Kong Zhongguo Pinglun,* no. 70 (Oct. 1, 2003), pp. 28–32, in FBIS: CCP20031003000025.

[24] Wang Zhongwen, "Examining the DPRK Issue and Northeast Asian Situation from a New Viewpoint," *Zhanglue Yu Guanli,* no. 4 (July/Aug. 2004), pp. 92–4, in FBIS: CPP20040825000196.

reforms, and foreign policy, the respected journal met its unexpected doom for incurring North Korea's wrath.[25]

In Beijing's judgment, both DPRK security and the PRC's relationship with Pyongyang would benefit from North Korea's economic reforms geared toward moving away from its erstwhile rigid, centrally planned, and autarkic economy in favor of introducing market measures, foreign investment, and greater openness to the outside world.[26] Such reforms would necessitate that the North Koreans learn from the successful Chinese experience, soften the U.S. demand for regime change, and make Pyongyang a less demanding and troublesome ally on issues from aid to refugees and cross-border illicit activities harmful to Chinese interests.

While the PRC has managed to preserve some semblance of a special bond with North Korea, it has strengthened its relationship with South Korea. Most notably, the South Korean public, especially the younger generations, starting in the late 1990s had viewed China overall in a favorable light, consistently more so than Japan and sometimes even better than the United States.[27] But as the historical shadow of the premodern Sino-centric hegemony lingers, the Koreans remain wary in dealing with a China whose power and influence is once again on the rise. Thus, Seoul protested when the Chinese made a formal claim in 2002 that the ancient Korean kingdom Koguryo, which ruled much of the Korean peninsula and parts of northeastern China from 37 B.C. to A.D. 668, was part of an ethnic minority history under the ancient Chinese empire. Two years later, when such an interpretation of Koguryo

[25] Nailen Chou Wiest and Josephine Ma, "Periodical Shut Down after Article on N. Korea," *South China Morning Post* (Hong Kong), Sept. 22, 2004, in FBIS: CPP20040922000074.

[26] For overviews of limited North Korean reforms, see Chistopher D. Hale, "Real Reform in North Korea? The Aftermath of the July 2002 Economic Measures," *Asian Survey*, vol. 45, no. 6 (Nov./Dec. 2005), pp. 823–42; Cha and Kang, *Nuclear North Korea*, pp. 103–14. For Chinese support of North Korean reforms, see Li Dunqiu, "Jicheng Chuantong, Bianxiang Weilai," *RMRB*, Oct. 29, 2005, p. 1.

[27] Chung Jae Ho has tracked Korean public opinion on China as compared to views on the United States. See his "South Korea Between Eagle and Dragon: Perceptual Ambivalence and Strategic Dilemma," *Asian Survey*, vol. 41, no. 5 (2001), pp. 777–96; and "China's Ascendancy and the Korean Peninsula: from Interest Reevaluation to Strategic Realignment?" in David Shambaugh, ed., *Power Shift: China and Asia's New Dynamics* (Berkeley: University of California Press, 2005), pp. 151–69.

history became officially sanctioned on the Chinese foreign ministry's website, it galvanized strenuous Korean opposition. Even North Korea joined the foray by criticizing, albeit more obliquely, Beijing's affront to Korean history. The episode dampened the euphoria about China's relationship with the ROK, but it had little effect on their parallel positions on the nuclear crisis. With greater realism on both sides, their bilateral relationship overall has proceeded well.

Beijing understands that its relationship with the ROK is critical for both its short-term interest and its long-term goal. For Chinese analysts, the ROK insistence on a diplomatic solution to the crisis was the decisive factor preventing the U.S. use of force.[28] Meanwhile, the ROK equally valued the PRC's role in ensuring a peaceful denouement to the nuclear standoff. Because the two countries had a strong, shared interest in the success of the diplomatic process, they pursued de facto parallel policies without high-profile bilateral coordination.

China's diplomacy was driven by its strategic vision, whereas Japan's role in the Six-Party Talks was limited by its overriding concern over the fate of its missing citizens abducted by Northern Korean commandos during the cold war era. The DPRK refused to address the issue, claiming that all thirteen abductees had either died or been repatriated, coinciding with Prime Minister Junichiro Koizumi's two visits to Pyongyang in 2002 and 2004. They further protested that Japan must address the unspeakable Korean sufferings under Japanese colonialism during the years 1910–45. While deadlocked on the abduction issue with North Korea, Japan's relations with the ROK had not seen the materialization of the great promise generated by the breakthrough agreement to set aside history reached on Kim Dae-jung's visit to Tokyo in October 1998. If anything, its relations with the ROK worsened under the Koizumi administration.

As regards the Six-Party Talks themselves, China succeeded in steering the process largely in line with its preferences. The Bush administration initially sought the multilateral format to isolate and pressure the DPRK in order to achieve the goal of denuclearization. As the process moved along, Washington became increasingly receptive to multilateral constraints on itself. Having had to sign the Chinese-drafted Six-Party agreement in September 2005, the United States essentially

---

[28] Yan Xuetong, "Dongya Heping De Jichu" [The Foundation for Peace in East Asia], *Zhijie Jingji Yu Zhengzhi*, no. 3 (2004), pp. 13–14.

adopted the Chinese approach, effectively recognizing many of North Korea's demands and even allowing the statement to acknowledge in principle the DPRK's legitimate desire for the light-water reactor, which the United States had rejected.[29] The spirit of the agreement is closer to China's original preferences than those of the Bush administration.[30]

The heart of China's vision of the East Asian order had to do with its relationship with the United States. That Chinese policy would be guided by such strategic thinking is hardly surprising given that from the PRC perspective while the United States might be temporarily preoccupied with Korea, its long-term concern in Asia would be China.[31] Maintaining that the United States used the Korean threat to justify its hard-line policy toward Pyongyang, to reinvigorate traditional alliances, and to develop missile defense programs, Chinese analysts invariably viewed Washington's policy toward the peninsula as part of the U.S. strategic plan to dominate Asia.[32] Unclear about its role in such a regional order, Beijing was anxious to restrain the U.S. unilateralism while molding the Six-Party Talks according to its strategic preferences in the region.

The most nonthreatening and effective way to do that was to steer the talks away from simply being a U.S. tool for the isolation of North Korea and instead to turn the talks into a more-or-less genuine multilateral mechanism – not simply pressuring the DPRK, but also restraining the United States. In this regard, Beijing achieved notable success. The

[29] Michael Hirsh and Melinda Liu, "North Korea Hold 'Em," *Newsweek*, Oct. 3, 2005, pp. 42–3.

[30] For insightful comparison of the Chinese views and those of the Bush administration, see David Shambaugh, "China and the Korean Peninsula: Playing for the Long Term," *Washington Quarterly*, vol. 26, no. 2 (Spring 2003), pp. 43–56.

[31] See, for example, Wu Guangyi, "Conglaisi De Liuguoxing Kan Meiguo De Yazhou Zhengce" [Rice's Six-Nation Trip and U.S. Asia Policy], *Zhongguo Shehui Kexueyuan Yuanbao*, April 14, 2005, at http://www.iwep.org.cn/shiping/liuguoxing_wgy.pdf.

[32] Yang Chengxu, Zheng Xiangrui, and Song Yiming, eds., *Zhongguo Zhoubian Anquan Huanjing Toushi* [Perspectives on China's Security along Its Boundaries] (Beijing: Zhongguo Qinnian Chubanshe, 2003), pp. 182–5. Avery Goldstein emphasizes China's strategic concerns vis-à-vis the United States in "Across the Yalu: China's Interests and the Korean Peninsula in a Changing World," in Alastair Iain Johnston and Robert R. Ross, eds., *New Directions in the Study of Chinese Foreign Policy* (Stanford, CA: Stanford University Press, 2006), pp. 131–61.

talks effectively enervated the U.S.-Japan-ROK Trilateral Coordination and Oversight Group (TCOG), formally created under American leadership in 1999 to coordinate position with its two allies vis-à-vis the DPRK. After the second nuclear crisis commenced, South Korea found its interests so divergent from those of the United States and Japan that it decided to attach great value to the Six-Party Talks, where it found its positions more closely aligned with China and Russia.[33] Also important, as Table 7.1 shows, if the Six-Party Statement signed in September 2005 were to be implemented, the talks would have to address an agenda expanded beyond exclusively denuclearizing the DPRK to include a joint commitment to "negotiate a permanent peace regime on the Korean Peninsula" and "[promote] security cooperation in Northeast Asia."[34]

China's diplomacy toward the Six-Party Talks cannot be treated as *sui generis*, divorced from its strategic interests. Yet just as international relations in Northeast Asia are rife with profound uncertainties, so, too, have the talks proven to be a tortuous and unwieldy process. The second stage of the fifth round was stalled due to Pyongyang's demand for a light-water reactor for civilian nuclear energy and additional U.S. financial sanctions in retaliation of North Korea's illicit monetary activities, such as money laundering and counterfeiting. Adding yet another twist was North Korea's missile testing in early July 2006, which aggravated its international isolation and sowed discord in its relationship with the PRC.

The regional efforts to create a nuclear-free Korean peninsula suffered yet another major setback when North Korea conducted its nuclear tests in October 2006. In a stunning reversal of its repeated protection of North Korea at the UN Security Council, China went along with the U.S.-drafted resolution for sanctions. Thereafter, with bluntness unimaginable just a few years before, Chinese analysts criticized the DPRK's act as a violation of international laws, as deeply destabilizing to the Northeast Asian region, and as harmful to China's

---

[33] Yukio Kashiyama, "Prelude to Hollowing Out of the Six-Way Talks: Japan, the United States, South Korea in Strains Finally End Cooperation," *Tokyo Sankei Shimbun* (Internet), Dec. 1, 2005, in FBIS: JPP20051201038001; Katsuhisa Furukawa, "Independent vs. Isolated Diplomacy," *Korea Herald* (Internet), Jan. 26, 2004, in FBIS: KPP20040126000024.

[34] See the Joint Statement at http://www.state.gov/r/pa/prs/ps/2005/53490.htm.

Table 7.1. *The 1994 Agreed Framework and 2005 Joint Statement of the Six-Party Talks*

	1994 Agreed Framework	2005 Joint Statement
Parties	U.S. and DPRK	China, DPRK, Japan, ROK, Russia, U.S.
Form of Agreement	*Quid pro quos* between Two Parties	Joint Commitment by Six Parties
Content	**U.S.:** (1) Provision by U.S. (and partners) of heavy fuel and light water reactor; (2) Promise of full diplomatic and economic normalization; and (3) No nuclear threat. **DPRK:** (1) Freezing and dismantling of nuclear weapons program; (2) Compliance with NPT, IAEA, and previous inter-Korean agreements on denuclearization. **U.S. and DPRK:** Joint commitment to a nuclear-free Korean peninsula	(1) Nuclear-free Korean peninsula; (2) Respect of sovereignty, based on which U.S. and Japan will move to normalize relations with the DPRK; (3) Promotion of bilateral and multilateral economic ties; pledges by all five parties to provide energy aid to DPRK; and (4) Promotion of stable, cooperative security on the Korean peninsula and in Northeast Asia.
Implementation	A package-for-package grand bargain	A step-by-step, "commitment for commitment, action for action" reciprocal process

Sources: The 1994 Agreed Framework, at http://www.kedo.org/pdfs/Agreed-Framework.pdf; The Joint Statement, at http://www.state.gov/r/pa/prs/ps/2005/53490.htm.

vital interests.[35] Yet by all accounts, China's implementation of the UN sanctions was superficial, and it continued high-level contacts with North Korea. Chinese commentaries also raised their voices critical of the U.S. inflexibility and hostility toward Pyongyang. The mixed signals were intended again to persuade the DPRK to return to the Six-Party Talks. The Chinese message was clear enough that it could pull the plug on the North Korean regime, thereby making the costs of abandoning the denuclearization process prohibitively high. At the same time, the PRC continued to reassure the DPRK by opposing military options and hostile policies toward the North Korean regime.

Beijing's "tough love" tactics, coupled with corresponding reactions of other parties, persuaded the DPRK to return to the Six-Party Talks in December 2006. In February 2007, the diplomatic forum finally reached a breakthrough in implementing the 2005 Joint Statement, whereby, in addition to reporting its full nuclear program, the DPRK agreed to dismantle the Yongbyon nuclear facility and permit verification by the International Atomic Energy Agency on a fixed timetable. But the implementation was delayed by disputes over how to unfreeze the US$25 million North Korean funds in the Macao-based Banco Belta Asia Bank, which was eventually resolved with a transfer of the funds to a Russian bank in June 2007. In the second half of the year, the Six-Party Talks would continue with the second phase of its sixth round and the DPRKwould fulfill its commitment on the Yongbyon issue but failed to provide a full report of its nuclear program as promised. In the spirit of step-by-step reciprocity, the United States and other parties would take some concrete actions to provide the DPRK with political and security assurances as well as economic aid. Meanwhile, amidst greater intra-Korean reconciliation and U.S.-North Korean direct interactions, Beijing scrambled to secure a central role in the Peninsula affairs. It's clear that the fate of the Six-Party Talks both reflected and was intimately tied to the fluid great-power relations and regional transformation in Northeast Asia.

---

[35] Perhaps the most remarkable indication of China's new position is the principled criticism of North Korea's nuclear testing by a leading international law scholar. See Zeng Lingliang, "Chaoxian Heshiyan De Guojifa Kanliang" [The DPRK Nuclear Testing: Perspective from the International Laws], *World Economics and Politics*, no. 1 (2007), at http://forum.xinhuanet.com/detail.jsp?id=39911414.

The Shanghai Cooperation Organization and East Asian Regionalism

In Central Asia, China has relied on multilateral diplomacy to secure its interests, in a region where historically it had a limited capability to assert any influence. After the collapse of the Soviet Union, the PRC moved quickly to recognize the newly independent central Asian republics and, together with Russia, continued the border demarcation process in the Western Section initiated in the waning years of the Soviet empire. Meanwhile, China, Russia, Kazakhstan, Kyrgyzstan, and Tajikistan jointly started to explore ways to address border security and confidence-building issues. These developments led to the first summit meeting by the leaders of the five countries in 1996 in Shanghai, where they concluded an agreement on measures to enhance military trust along the borders. More importantly, the event gave birth to an annual mechanism known as the Shanghai Five, whereby the leaders would meet again the following year to sign another agreement on specific measures of force reduction along the borders.[36]

With border issues largely settled, the Shanghai Five turned their attention to radical Islamic forces that had plagued regional governments. At their 1998 meeting, held in Almaty, Kazakhstan, the leaders began to institutionalize their collective efforts to combat what would later be called "three evil forces," namely international terrorism, ethnic separatism, and religious extremism. Member states subsequently beefed up cooperative undertakings, including joint military exercises, aimed at fighting various antigovernment "terrorist groups." Meanwhile, realizing that the scourge of economic woes inflicted upon the post-Soviet Central Asian republics had turned the region into a hotbed of radicalism, the countries also looked to the Shanghai Five as an engine for economic development.[37]

---

[36] Deng Hao, "China's Relations with Central Asian Countries: Retrospect and Prospect," Guoji WentiYanjiu, May 13, 2002, pp. 8–12, 7, in OSC: CPP20020712000153.

[37] Xu Tao, "Security Key for SCO – The Shanghai Cooperation Organization May Have the Answers to Global Security Problems," *Beijing Review* (Internet), June 17, 2004, in OSC: CPP20040618000080; "Shanghai Spirit Takes Shape," *China Daily* (Internet), Jan. 16, 2004, in OSC: CPP20040116000009; Wang Xiaoyu and Xu Tao, "Shanghai Hezuo Zhuzhi De Zhonghe Anquan Linian" [The Concept of Comprehensive Security Behind the SCO], in Yan Xuetong, ed., *Guoji Anquanjuan* [International Security], (Beijing: New World Press, 2007), pp. 127–38.

Their collective need for more institutionalized cooperation led to the establishment of the Shanghai Cooperation Organization (SCO) in June 2001. Eager to solidify its warming ties with the West and wary of its neighbors, Uzbekistan did not participate in the Shanghai Five. The PRC had always been in favor of including Tashkent in the multilateral forum, not least because the latter hosts a large Uighur population. Having observed the Shanghai Five summit in 2000, Uzbekistan President Islom Karimov attended the inaugural SCO meeting in Shanghai, marking his country's formal membership in this organization.[38] The SCO quickly underwent institutional growth, adopting a charter in 2002 and creating its secretariat in Beijing and an antiterror center in Tashkent, respectively, in January and June 2004.[39] Former Chinese ambassador to Russia Zhang Deguang was selected as the first SCO general secretary for a three-year term, and thereafter the position would rotate among member states in the alphabetic order of their Russian names.[40] Mongolia became the first SCO observer, and a year later (2005) Iran, Pakistan, and India followed suit. Afghanistan has been regularly involved on issues in which its role heavily bore upon the specific SCO agenda and Turkmen president attended the 2007 SCO summit signaling a strong interest in joining the organization.

By the time the leaders returned to Shanghai to mark the fifth anniversary of the SCO in June 2006, the central mission of the organization had evolved from an antiterror focus to a comprehensive economic, political, and security agenda. Beyond the yearly top-level meeting, regular and functional contacts among various governmental agencies also were in place. At the 2006 meeting, besides formalizing key institutional procedures, the SCO set up the Business Council to complement the Inter-Bank Association, which had been created a year earlier.[41] The economic body and financial network would no doubt help China to utilize the $900 million concessionary importer credit

---

[38] "Backgrounder: Shanghai Cooperation Organization," Xinhua, Jan. 15, 2004, in OSC: CPP20040115000038.

[39] Zhao Huasheng, "Shanghai Hezuo Zuzhi: Pinggu Yu Fazhan Wenti" [The Shanghai Cooperation Organization: Assessment and the Problem of Development], *Xiandai Guoji Guanxi*, no. 5 (2005), at http://www.irchina.org/news/view.asp?id=946 (accessed July 25, 2005).

[40] "SCO Enjoys Bright Future: Secretary-General," Xinhua, Jan. 13, 2004, in OSC: CPP20040113000115.

[41] Sun Zhuangzhi, "Shanghai Fenghui Zaishu Lichengbei" [The Shanghai Summit Erects Yet Another Milestone], *RMRB*, June 16, 2006, p. 1; Yan Wei,

President Hu Jintao first offered in 2004 to promote its exports to the region.[42] Under the SCO umbrella, the PRC completed a major oil pipeline linking Kazakhstan and the Xinjiang Autonomous Region in China and has sought to expand the energy networks that could tap into the oil and gas resources deep into Kazakhstan and elsewhere. At the aegis of the newly created SCO economic and financial institutions, the PRC has financed a number of major infrastructure projects in the cash-strapped Central Asian states.[43]

Militarily, the SCO has enabled the Chinese People's Liberation Army (PLA) and police forces to conduct joint military exercises with its Central Asian counterparts. Under antiterror cover, China and Russia conducted a large-scale joint military exercise, code-named "Peace Mission," in 2005, and in 2007 a full-blown SCO military exercise was held in Russia. More importantly, the organization has facilitated Sino-Russian joint efforts to roll back the U.S. and NATO military presence in the region. The SCO issued a statement in 2005 calling for the early withdrawal of foreign military deployments in member states. Specifically, the issue concerned the military base at the Manas International Airport in Kyrgyzstan and Karshi-Khanabad airbase in Uzbekistan. The coalition forces and U.S. troops had used both facilities in overthrowing the Taliban regime in neighboring Afghanistan in the aftermath of the 2001 terrorist attacks in the United States. Russia and China initially acquiesced to the Western military presence, reckoning that foreign troops would not be tolerated long in this heavily Islamic region.[44] After the active phase of the war was over, suspicions about the intentions of the West started to grow in Russia, China, and

---

"Summit Ascent," *Beijing Review* (Internet), June 30–July 6, 2006, in OSC: CPP20060710715047.

[42] Xinhua, "Hu Jintao Zonglun Shanghe Zhuzhi Jianshe He Fazhan" [Hu Jintao Reviews the Development of the Shanghai Cooperation Organization], *RMRB*, May 31, 2006, p. 1.

[43] Tao Wenzhao, "Shanghai Cooperation Organization Enters Stage of Pragmatic Development," *Hong Kong Ta Kung Bao* (Internet), June 21, 2006, in OSC: CPP20060711715002.

[44] That was clearly the Chinese calculation. See Xu Tao, "On the Shanghai Cooperation Organization under the New Situation," *Xiandai Guoji Guanxi*, June 20, 2002, pp. 6–13, in OSC: CPP20020709000142; Pan Guang, "Shanghai Cooperation Organization under the New Situation and Central Asia's Anti-Terrorism Cooperation," *Hongkong Zhongguo Pinglun*, June 1, 2002, no. 54, pp. 73–7, in OSC:CPP20020604000068.

the hosting countries. In a joint SCO statement, they made public their demand for an end of the Western troop deployments in the region.

Politically, the SCO has served PRC's interests at several levels. Domestically, the organization has proved to be critical in fighting the Uighur separatist elements, which Beijing had labeled terrorists. According to an official Chinese report, Uighur East Turkestan Islamic separatists gained force in the 1990s in Xinjiang and became radicalized, perpetrating during 1990–2001 over two hundred terror attacks in this frontier region that left 162 people dead.[45] A large Uighur population also lives in the near abroad, with one estimate putting the combined number in Kazakhstan and Krygyzstan at 350,000.[46] Cooperation from these Central Asian states is virtually indispensable if Beijing is to root out the problem of Uighur defiance to its central control.

At the regional level, the SCO has cushioned Western pressures on human rights and democracy by lending support to the regional states confronted with popular demand for political change. The role became particularly pronounced when massive popular protests forced a leadership change in Kyrgyzstan and the Uzbek government faced Western condemnation for killing of its own citizens in the city of Andijan in 2005. To help stabilize regional governments, the SCO secretariat began in 2005 to send observers to monitor elections in Kyrgyzstan and other member states for symbolism as well as to better position the organization in proactively coping with such domestic crises.[47] In the end, the Central Asian states held off the wave of "color revolutions," which had brought down a string of autocratic regimes in the former Soviet republics and elsewhere. Regional institutions in Europe and Latin America have contributed to the democratic transitions in their parts of the world, whereas the SCO has lent its institutional support

---

[45] State Information Office of China, "'Dongtu' Kongbu Shili Nantao Zuize" ["East Turkestan" Terrorists Can't Shirk Responsibility for the Crimes], *RMRB*, Jan. 22, 2002, p. 1.

[46] Chien-Peng Chung, "The Shanghai Co-operation Organization: China's Changing Influence in Central Asia," *China Quarterly*, no. 180 (Dec. 2004), p. 995.

[47] Wang Zhen, "Shanghai Cooperation Organization: Maturing While Being Steeled – Exclusive Interview with SCO Secretary General Zhang Deguang," *Shanghai Jiefang Ribao* (Internet), Oct. 5, 2005, in OSC: CPP20051007058001.

to regional governments holding the line amidst demands for uncertain political changes.

In terms of global politics, the SCO has been promoted as the epitome of China's new diplomacy. In celebrating the success of the organization, Chinese commentators invariably attribute to it the so-called Shanghai Spirit of "mutual trust, mutual benefit, equality, consultation, respect of diverse civilizations, and pursuit of joint development."[48] In that spirit, then-Chinese president Jiang Zemin put forward "the new security concept" at the Shanghai Five meeting in 1997, which was supposedly the antidote to the Western cold war mentality.[49] After the 9/11 events, Chinese commentators also emphasized that the Shanghai Spirit constitutes the basis for a "new regionalism" that respects sovereignty *and* embraces globalization, celebrates cultural and political diversity, and promotes win-win economic cooperation.[50]

The Shanghai Five summit proved invaluable as the embryo for the SCO. When the U.S. presence in Central Asia after 9/11 threatened the viability of the freshly formed organization, the PRC and Russia coordinated to lead the SCO toward greater institutional strength and relevance. In important ways, China and Russia have used the SCO as an effective instrument to secure their strategic space in Central Asia free of Western political and military influence. Reflecting on its brief history, Chinese commentators would proudly enumerate the major international crises that the organization had survived, notably from the 9/11 terror attacks to the wars on Afghanistan and Iraq to the "color revolution."[51] When regional leaders gathered in Shanghai to celebrate the SCO's fifth anniversary, the organization had become

---

[48] See, for example, Wang Fang and Sun Li, "Sum up Experience, Deepen Cooperation – Interview with SCO Secretary General Zhang Deguang," *RMRB* (Internet), June 1, 2006, p. 3, in OSC: CPP20060601510003.

[49] Gao Qiang, "Foster New Security Concept Characterized by Mutual Trust, Mutual Benefit, Equality, and Coordination," *Qiushi* (Internet), no. 12 (June 16, 2003), in OSC: CPP20030626000019.

[50] Chung, "The Shanghai Co-operation Organization," pp. 992–93. See also Pang Zhongying, "The Shanghai Cooperation Organization Should Be Built on the Basis of New Regionalism," *Renmin Wang*, June 24, 2002, in OSC: CPP20020625000045.

[51] "SCO Thrives in Face of Common Challenges," *China Daily* (Internet), June 15, 2006, in OSC: CPP20060615053015; Wang Fang and Sun Li, "Sum up Experience."

stronger than ever before. And from Beijing's perspective, the SCO had acquired a comprehensive agenda that was effective in fending off Western pressures on China in Central Asia, as well as in promoting Beijing's economic, security, and political interests in the region and beyond.

In contrast to Northeast Asia and Central Asia, where there was little multilateral experience prior to the 1990s, Pacific Asia had had a long tradition of regional institutional development. The formal and informal institutions have proven extremely valuable for China's diplomatic success in navigating the uncharted waters of its international relations after the cold war. Confronted with the worst foreign policy crisis in its history following the Tiananmen incident, the PRC government looked to the Association for Southeast Asian Nations (ASEAN) to break the international isolation, not least because its member states' championship of "Asian values" dovetailed with China's opposition to Western human rights pressure. In July 1991, ASEAN recognized the PRC as a "consultative partner," in disregard of the U.S. and European call for shunning the CCP leadership. Due in no small part to ASEAN support, China joined the Asia-Pacific Economic Cooperation (APEC) forum in 1991, which subsequently facilitated several informal meetings between Presidents Jiang Zemin and Bill Clinton, which were key in stabilizing the Sino-American relationship. Thus, it was no coincidence that official Chinese media designated 1993 as the year of both China's post-Tiananmen diplomatic breakthrough and "the year of China's ASEAN diplomacy."[52]

The 1997–98 financial crisis dealt a heavy blow to regionalism, for it severely weakened the hard-hit economies and undermined the supposedly distinctive and efficacious Asian brand of political economy and diplomacy. Burdened by aggravated financial woes of its own and suspected of self-interested manipulation of the yen value, Japan's long-standing claim to regional leadership was badly hurt. In contrast, the PRC emerged as a big winner, having held steady with its currency exchange rate and offered several billion U.S. dollars to countries in extreme financial trouble. According to the World Bank, during the two years China managed to pull off a 7.4 percent annual growth rate,

---

[52] "1993: Zhongguo Queli Zai Dangjing Shijie De Youli Weizhi" [1993: China Establishes Advantageous Position in the World], *Liaowang* (Outlook), no. 53 (1993), p. 3.

in contrast to Japan's 2.6 percent rate.[53] Widespread international praise of China's behavior vindicated the notion of responsible power, which its leadership had just embraced, and as such, the Chinese were more ready than ever before to actively participate in regional undertakings.

The financial crisis gave rise to a new sense of shared destiny among the East Asian countries, whose political elites were unhappy about the inadequate responses from the United States and other Western countries as well as the global institutions, such as the International Monetary Fund (IMF). Attempting to take the lead in crafting a regional alternative to IMF, Japan proffered the idea of an Asian Monetary Fund in 1997. Fearing a yen bloc, both the United States and China were opposed to it. Meaningful ideas of regionalism, financial and otherwise, would revolve around the ASEAN, rather than flowing from any other major power. With membership now expanded to ten countries (Brunei, Cambodia, Indonesia, Laos, Malaysia, Myanmar, the Philippines, Singapore, Thailand, and Vietnam), the ASEAN fully represents the whole Southeast Asian region. Meanwhile, the devastating financial crisis made it clear that the smaller economies would benefit greatly from more institutionalized cooperation with the economic powerhouses of Northeast Asia, namely, China, Japan, and South Korea.

At the organization's initiative, the ASEAN Plus Three mechanism was formed in 1997 to facilitate cooperation between the two regions of East Asia. Spearheaded by an annual leadership meeting, the ASEAN Plus Three agreed in 2000 to an array of bilateral currency swap deals under the Chiang Mai Initiative, a multilateral financial arrangement named after its birthplace in Thailand. Significantly less ambitious, more informal than the earlier ill-fated Japanese idea, the initiative nonetheless sought to tackle similar problems of liquidity and balance-of-payments for regional economies, which had been responsible for the 1997–98 financial crisis.[54] The early success of ASEAN Plus Three naturally led regional leaders who had long dreamed of an East Asian

---

[53] Robert D. Blackwill and Paul Dibb, eds., *America's Asian Alliances* (Cambridge, MA: MIT Press, 2000), p. 139.
[54] Chia Siow Yue, "The Rise of China and Emergent East Asian Regionalism," in Kokubun Ryosei and Wang Jisi, eds., *The Rise of China and a Changing East Asian Order* (Tokyo: Japan Center for International Exchange, 2004), pp. 63–4.

community to believe that the time was ripe to push for such an idea. After all, by 2003 intraregional trade in East Asia had reached well over 50 percent of the total trade of the regional economies, a share slightly lower than the European Union but topping the "North America Three" by around 10 percent.[55] China, Japan, and South Korea were clearly the economic leaders, but the ASEAN Plus Three formula appeared to relegate them to the supporting cast. South Korea, in particular, was vocal in proposing the creation of a genuinely East Asian regional forum.[56] After extensive consultations among member states, in 2004 the ASEAN Plus Three decided to hold an annual East Asian summit, whose hosts, like the APEC, would alternate between ASEAN and non-ASEAN members. The PRC immediately expressed interest in being the first Northeast Asian country to host the summit after the inaugural meeting was held in an ASEAN country, but that wish in the end failed to materialize.

Buoyed by its newfound confidence in Southeast Asia, the PRC stepped up cooperation with the ASEAN states. In 2002, ASEAN and China formally kicked off an ambitious plan to build a "Ten Plus One" free-trade zone by 2010. In a major concession, the PRC introduced in 2004 the "Early Harvest" program, which unilaterally opened its markets to over six hundred products from the bordering ASEAN countries.[57] In contrast, Japan and South Korea proved to be much less adroit in making strides with trade with the ASEAN because both – Japan in particular – were tied down by the potent agricultural protectionism in its domestic politics. Beyond the economic area, China signed with ASEAN in 2002 a declaration on the South China Sea issue, pledging along with all other disputants not to take unilateral steps to worsen the situation. Although the statement fell short of the more legally binding code of conduct preferred by the ASEAN states,

---

[55] Takashi Shiraishi, "Is It Possible to Create an East Asian Community?" *Chuo Koron* (in Japanese), Jan. 1, 2006, pp. 118–27, in OSC: JPP20060111016002, p. 4; "Tug of War over the Plan to Create an East Asian Community," *Nihon Keizai Shimbun* (Nikkei Telecom 21 database version; in Japanese), Dec. 8, 2005, in OSC: JPP20051209016003, p. 2.

[56] For the Chinese perspective, see Lu Jianren, "Bright Points and Difficult Problems in East Asian Economic Cooperation," *Shijie Zhishi*, no. 21 (Nov. 1, 2003), pp. 40–41, in OSC: CPP20031118000214.

[57] Li Xia, "Zhongguo-Dongmeng Zimaoqu Jinru Shizhixing Jianshe" [China-ASEAN Free Trade Zone under Substantial Construction], *RMRB*, Sept. 8, 2006, p. 2.

such a multilateral PRC commitment to self-restraint represents a significant departure from its longstanding hardened sovereignty claim and insistence on bilateral dealings on the issue. In the following year, the PRC and ASEAN agreed to form a strategic partnership, in tandem with formal Chinese accession to the Treaty of Amity and Cooperation (TAC), a hallmark of the ASEAN legal and normative prohibition against the violation of sovereignty and the use of violence against the signatory state.

As its trepidation receded, the PRC engagement with ASEAN became a key part of its increasingly sophisticated diplomatic repertoire toward the region. Take, for example, Beijing's handling of the SARS crisis during 2002–3. After being officially sworn in as the new Chinese premier, Wen Jiabao made his first foreign trip to Bangkok, Thailand in late April 2003 to attend an emergency meeting on the epidemic with the ASEAN leaders. There, he admitted Chinese failings in the early stage of the SARS outbreak and pledged full cooperation with the neighboring states to combat this transnational disease. In early June, Beijing sponsored an ASEAN Ten Plus Three meeting devoted exclusively to enhance anti-SARS cooperation. Although this resulted in few concrete measures, these initiatives did help to ameliorate damage to China's reputation caused by Beijing's earlier cover-up and inaction. They also helped to lay some foundation for future regional cooperation in dealing with nontraditional, cross-border threats.

China's Ten Plus One cooperation with the ASEAN strengthened its position in the ASEAN Plus Three mechanism. After the 9/11 events, the United States was preoccupied with fighting global terrorism and Japan seemed to have lost its interest in multilateral institutions in the Asia-Pacific. In comparison, the PRC stepped up its influence in regional initiatives, especially concerning the idea of an East Asian community. China has long supported the idea of an East Asian community, dating back to Malaysian Prime Minister Mahathir bin Mohamad's proposal of an East Asian Economic Caucus in the early 1990s. (Tellingly, Mahathir unveiled his original idea for an "East Asian Economic Grouping" while visiting with Chinese Premier Li Peng in Beijing in December 1990.[58])

---

[58] Linda Low, "The East Asian Economic Grouping," *Pacific Review*, vol. 4, no. 2 (1991), p. 375.

In trying to influence the latest attempts at community building
in East Asia, Beijing eschewed heavy-handedness, remaining instead
deferential to the preeminent role of ASEAN and the interests of its
members.[59] When it did not get its way, the PRC appeared to take
the failure in stride, approaching them with patience and diplomatic
acumen. Leading up to the first East Asian Summit, the PRC opted
to exercise its clout through working with countries, such as Malaysia
and Thailand, whose positions were closely aligned with its own. However, the issue of membership in the East Asian Summit turned out
to be much harder to resolve than many had originally anticipated.
China had hoped that it would consist of ASEAN Ten Plus Three,
all–East Asian members in strictly geographical term. Fearful of being
isolated and dominated by China, Japan wanted the United States to
be present as an observer, if not as a full member.[60] In April 2005,
ASEAN decided that because India, Australia, and New Zealand had
already been involved extensively in regional affairs, they would be
admitted into the summit should they accede to the organization's
TAC. As a result, altogether sixteen countries attended the inaugural
summit held in Kuala Lumpur, Malaysia in December 2005. With such
a diverse membership, the grouping has not been effective in tackling
hard issues impeding regionalism. When the second and third meetings
were convened in early 2007 in the Philippines and later the same year
in Singapore, the summit focused on transnational, relatively noncon-
troversial issues, such as the environment and energy.

The membership expansion was to the liking of the United States,
Japan, and several ASEAN states concerned about China's dominance.
The Chinese were displeased with the diluted East Asian identity,
which meant that the summit meeting would not differ much from the
APEC, whose diverse membership and minimalist approach had done
little to promote East Asian regionalism. Chinese analysts publicly
blamed the outcome on Japan's efforts to invite like-minded democracies.[61] Other than that, they weren't terribly upset – at least not publicly. After all, still ASEAN-centered, future summit meetings would

---

[59] See Alice D. Ba, "China and ASEAN: Re-navigating Relations for a 21st-Century
Asia," *Asian Survey*, vol. 43, no. 4 (2003), pp. 622–47.

[60] "Tug of War over the Plan to Create an East Asian Community."

[61] See, for example, Lu Jianren, "Asia's Long Haul," *Beijing Review*, Dec. 29,
2005, pp. 12–13.

not replace ASEAN Plus Three, supposedly maintaining the latter's somewhat privileged role in Asian regionalism, a desirable compromise for the Chinese. ASEAN, even after it adopted a charter in November 2007, will still be a loosely structured institution but insistent on engaging outside powers on its own terms. Besides, a Chinese imposition of a regional vision on other countries would only give credence to the notion of a Chinese design for an exclusive hegemony in East Asia.

The Forum on China-Africa Cooperation

Starting in the late 1970s, as reformist China scaled down its international ambitions, its Africa diplomacy experienced more than two decades of neglect until the late 1990s. "During the modernization/opening to the West line of the reform decade 1978–1988," as Peter Van Ness writes, "China in fact turned its back on the Third World."[62] The first post-Tiananmen decade saw no major break from earlier times, even though the PRC stepped up its efforts to solicit African support on human rights and Taiwan. Viewed in this light, the renewed Chinese activism in Africa in the early years of the twenty-first century, which culminated in the grandiose November 2006 China-Africa summit in Beijing, is truly astonishing. Attended by forty-eight African countries, the meeting was under the auspices of the Forum on China-Africa Cooperation (FOCAC). As if the PRC had rediscovered Africa, the continent is now being brought back to the center stage of China's diplomacy. But the "third-world" concept as the bedrock of an international united front in Maoist revolutionary diplomacy has lost its relevance. China's African fever reflects not only its ever-extending economic reach, but also its emergence as a new global power.

Starting in the 1950s, the PRC's ties with Africa initially rested on support for the independence struggles on the continent and solidarity with the newly independent countries. Later on, strategic rivalry with the Soviet Union and, to a lesser extent, diplomatic competition with the Republic of China in Taiwan, dictated its policy, sometimes

[62] Peter Van Ness, "China as a Third World State: Foreign Policy and Official National Identity," in Lowell Dittmer and Samuel S. Kim, eds., *China's Quest for National Identity* (Ithaca, NY: Cornell University Press, 1993), p. 206.

overshadowing its concern over the U.S. and Western hegemony.[63] In the first half of the 1970s, Mao Zedong put forth the so-called three-worlds theory, calling for the solidarity of the third world in Asia, Africa, and Latin America in a joint struggle against the first world of the two superpowers: the United States and the Soviet Union.[64] Africa was at the core of China's third-world identity, as underscored by the fact that Mao first spelled out his third-world theory in a meeting with Zambian President Kenneth Kaunda in February 1974. However, starting in the late 1970s, as the reformist China embarked on catch-up modernization through joining the world, the slogans of world revolution began to give way to the mantra of "peace and development."

The early 1980s saw a brief revival of China's identity as a third-world country in its foreign policy rhetoric, when its leadership announced a new line of independence and autonomy. This new official line, however, did less to solidify China's third-world identity than to lessen the stricture on its diplomacy imposed by the earlier fixation on the superpowers. A similar spurt of interest in the third world resurfaced after the Tiananmen crisis, but it quickly died down. As Samuel Kim wrote in the early 1990s, "The third world theory, as a theory of struggle, is obviously incompatible with China's growing enmeshment in the capitalist world system."[65] Fundamentally, reformist China's "reference group" structure in world politics had undergone a drastic change, such that identification with the third world no longer served its international aspirations for power, wealth, and prestige.[66]

---

[63] Philip Snow, "China and Africa: Consensus and Camouflage," in Thomas W. Robinson and David Shambaugh, eds., *Chinese Foreign Policy: Theory and Practice* (Oxford: Oxford University Press, 1994), pp. 283–321.

[64] Zhong Fei, "Mao Zedong Waijiao Zhanluesixiang Weizhongfei Youhaohezuo Guanxi Dianding Jianshi Jichu" [Mao's Diplomatic Strategic Thoughts Lay Solid Foundation for Sino-African Friendship and Cooperation], in Office of Diplomatic History, PRC Ministry of Foreign Affairs, ed., *Mao Zedong Waijiao Sixiang Yanjiu* [Studies on Mao Zedong's Diplomatic Thoughts] (Beijing: Shijie Zhishi Chubanshe, 1994), pp. 281–93.

[65] Samuel S. Kim, "China and the Third World in the Changing World," in Samuel S. Kim, ed., *China and the World: Chinese Foreign Relations in the Post–Cold War Era* (Boulder, CO: Westview Press, 1994), p. 131.

[66] For a seminal treatment of reference groups in Chinese foreign policy, see Lowell Dittmer, *Sino-Soviet Normalization and Its International Implications, 1945–1990* (Seattle: University of Washington Press, 1992); Lowell Dittmer and Samuel S. Kim, "In Search of a Theory of National Identity," in Dittmer and Kim, eds., *China's Quest for National Identity*, pp. 15–16.

As the importance of the third world waned, so did Africa. The PRC shifted its diplomatic focus to neighboring Asian countries starting in the 1990s, but only as a focused regional diplomacy largely divorced from a broader third-world agenda.

China's commercial interests began to expand in Africa sporadically in the 1990s. Perhaps the most notable example of the PRC economic engagement during the decade was its investment in the oil industry in Sudan after Western companies fled the country amidst human rights concerns and domestic instabilities. Chinese capital effectively turned the African country into an oil net exporter and a major supplier of oil to China. However, it was the NATO war on the Federal Republic of Yugoslavia in 1999 that prompted the Chinese leadership to view Africa in a new light. The humanitarian interventionism for which the war was waged threatened to embolden power politics and a disregard of sovereignty by the United States and its allies. For Beijing, African countries represented a natural partner in resisting Western neo-interventionism. So in October 1999, President Jiang Zemin wrote to Secretary General Salim Ahmed Salim of the Organization of African Unity, the predecessor of the African Union (AU), officially proposing the idea of a regular ministerial-level meeting between China and the African states.[67]

After extensive consultations between Beijing and key African capitals as well as among African states, the first FOCAC Ministerial Conference – designed to facilitate consultations and steer ties between China and all African states – was convened during October 10–12, 2000, when Beijing pledged to waive RMB10 billion of debt for the poorest African countries. ("RMB" stands for "Renminbi," the currency of the PRC.) Beyond that, despite the fanfare surrounding the inaugural meeting, FOCAC was mostly a political statement about Sino-African friendship in building a vaguely articulated new international order. Little headway in their unity was made to promote a radical vision of the world, for such rhetoric of a new world order belied a more pragmatic and circumspect Chinese foreign policy agenda.

---

[67] Li Anshan, "Lun 'Zhongguo Jueqi' Yujingzhong De Zhongfei Guanxi" [Sino-African Relations under the "China Rising" Discourse], *Shijie Jingji Yu Zhengzhi*, no. 11, 2006, at http://www.iwep.org.cn/web/200611/lzgjq_lianshan.pdf, p. 10.

The second FOCAC conference was held in December 2003 in Addis Ababa, Ethiopia, where a series of substantial ties were introduced. The PRC promised tariff exemption for certain products from the least-developed countries and granted eight countries Approved Destination Status (ADS), thus simplifying procedures for Chinese citizens to travel to these countries.[68] The China-Africa Business Conference was held on the sidelines of the meeting; and on October 18–20, 2004, FOCAC sponsored a seminar on human rights attended by representatives from China and twenty-seven African countries.[69] When the third FOCAC returned to Beijing in November 2006, a summit was held in conjunction with the ministerial meeting. Chinese president Hu Jintao announced to the forty-three African heads of state and governments his country's three-year action plan to be implemented before the next FOCAC meeting, to be held in Egypt, featuring a promise of U.S.\$10 billion to support African development, bilateral trade, and Chinese investment.[70] Compared to the Western emphasis on humanitarian concerns, the Chinese focus was on government-backed trade and investment expansion. In contrast to the Maoist era, contemporary Chinese leadership has downplayed fraternity and friendship-based aid in favor of projects geared toward sustaining the development of both African states and the rapidly growing PRC economic presence on the continent. At first, the FOCAC appeared destined to wither into oblivion, along with China's third-world identity. But after the second conference, the forum was reinvigorated to spark a renaissance of Sino-African ties. Sino-African trade grew from slightly over U.S.\$10 billion in 2000 to \$18.55 billion in 2003, but it surged to exceed U.S.\$55 billion in 2006, with the leaders having set the goal for bilateral trade to reach \$100 billion in 2010.[71] If successful in achieving that goal, the

---

[68] Xinhua, "Ministerial Meeting of China-Africa Forum Ends with Adoption of Action Plan," Dec. 16, 2003, in OSC: CPP20031216000198.

[69] Xinhua, "First Sino-African Business Conference Opens in Ethiopia," Dec. 14, 2003, in OSC: CPP20031214000015; Xinhua, "Chinese, African Delegates Discuss Human Rights Issues," Oct. 22, 2004, in OSC: CPP20041022000074.

[70] Hu Jintao, "Speech at the Opening Ceremony of the Beijing Summit of China-African Cooperation Forum," *RMRB*, Nov. 5, 2006, p. 3.

[71] "China-African Trade Undergoing Steady Growth," *People's Daily*, Nov. 3, 2006, at http://world.people.com.cn/GB/8212/72927/73385/4994710.html#; "China-African Trade Reaches \$55.5 billion," at http://news.sina.com.cn/c/2007-01-29/153912171205.shtml.

PRC would likely surpass the United States and France to become the number one trading partner of the continent.

Since the second FOCAC, Chinese investment has registered a steady increase to further the country's interests in infrastructure projects, trade, labor export, and natural resources. By the end of 2006, Chinese investment had totaled $11.7 billion throughout the continent,[72] and Africa had supplied roughly one-third of China's oil imports. The historical summit in November 2006 created an even more propitious political and economic environment for Chinese-African business ties. Several days before the Beijing meeting, the China Civil Engineering Construction Corporation inked an $8.3 billion deal to build a 1,315-kilometer railway for Nigeria. In January 2007, the company signed another contract for port repair and restoration worth $128.6 million in the city of Lagos, Nigeria, on whose behalf China also launched several months later a commercial satellite into the space signifying potentials for Sino-African business ties in high tech sectors.[73] The African Development Bank (ADB) held its first Asian meeting in Shanghai in May 2007, further speeding up concrete measures for cooperation in finance and investment. Half a year later, South Africa's Standard Bank agreed to a bid by China's state-owned Industrial and Commercial Bank to invest in it nearly U.S.$5.5 billion, a spectacular deal in both the Chinese and African foreign economic history.[74]

The two sides are also keen to strengthen their cultural and social interactions. With growing number of ADS, more and more middle-class Chinese citizens are traveling to Africa. The PRC government is also intent on funding more students and training more technical and managerial personnel from Africa in China. In December 2005, the first Chinese-sponsored Confucius Institute in Africa, designed to promote local learning of the Chinese language and culture, found its partnership in the University of Nairobi, Kenya. In less than a year, five more such cultural centers sprang up in countries such as South Africa,

---

[72] Xinhua, May 15, 2007, at http://news.xinhuanet.com/english/2007-05/16/content_6105029.htm.

[73] China Civil Engineering Construction Corporation website, at http://www.ccecc.com.cn/2006-11/200611473046.htm; http://www.ccecc.com.cn/2007-1/200712282439.htm.

[74] Xinhua, May 16, 2007, at http://news.xinhuanet.com/english/2007-05/16/content_6106082.htm; *China in Africa Digest* (Oct. 21-31 2007), Nov. 1, 2007, in OSC: AFP: 20071106950055.

Rwanda, Egypt, and Zimbabwe.[75] The PRC also pledged to continue medical assistance, which was traditionally the pride of Chinese assistance to Africa. According to Chinese accounts, during 1963–2005 the PRC dispatched more than fifteen thousand doctors to forty-seven countries, treating some 170 million people on the continent.[76] However, the scale and quality of the medical aid has been eroded as China turns inward to address its own woefully inadequate health care service, and the spirit of the third-world fraternity has dissipated.[77]

African support remains important for the PRC to diplomatically isolate Taiwan. After Liberia severed diplomatic ties with Taiwan in 2003, only four countries on the continent – Burkina Faso, Gambia, São Tomé and Principe, and Swaziland – maintained official ties with the island by the end of 2007. They turned down a Chinese invitation to attend the FOCAC summit as observers, but all of them sent representatives to the ADB meeting in Shanghai.[78] Beyond Taiwan, Africa has proven its diplomatic weight in assisting China's struggle to contest the normative and institutional underpinnings of the world order. The CCP leaders have long appreciated the fact that with twenty-six votes out of the total seventy-six coming from Africa to secure China's reentry into the United Nations in 1971, "it was," in Mao's words, "the African black brothers that carried us into the organization."[79] After the cold war, African support at the UN Human Rights Commission was critical for China's success in defeating the many attempts by Western members to officially censure Beijing's human rights record. African members continue to play a key role in China's efforts to

[75] *Zhongguo Jiaoyubao* [China Education], at http://www.jyb.com.cn/zt/lxzt/2006/c/ (accessed March 12, 2007); Xinhua, "Action Plan Outlines Closer China-Africa Cooperation in Education," at http://news3.xinhuanet.com/english/2006-11/05/content_5292753.htm.

[76] Liu Dongkai and Zhao Wen, "Zhongguo Long Yu Feizhoushi Gongwu" [The Chinese Dragon and African Lion Dancing Together], *RMRB*, Dec. 18, 2006, p. 4.

[77] David H. Shinn, "China, Africa, and the United States: Health Care Cooperation," *Washington Journal of Modern China*, vol. 8, no. 1 (Spring/Summer 2006), pp. 62–3.

[78] *People's Daily*, at http://english.people.com.cn/200610/18/eng20061018_313168.html; China News Service, May 17, 2007, at http://news.sina.com.cn/c/2007-05-17/194713013114.shtml.

[79] Qian Qichen, *Waijiao Shiji* [Ten Episodes in Diplomacy] (Beijing: Shijie Zhishi Chubanshe, 2003), p. 255. Mao's quote from Zhong Fei, "Mao's Diplomatic Strategic Thoughts," p. 290.

reshape the human rights discourse in and outside the newly created UN Human Rights Council.

The PRC has viewed Africa's significance in terms of the continent as a whole, in contrast to its preoccupation through the 1970s–80s with states that might facilitate the Soviet navy threat from the Indian Ocean.[80] China's official policy paper toward Africa released in January 2006 states that it "supports African countries' efforts to grow stronger through unity."[81] Tellingly, President Hu's extended African tour in January–February 2007 took him to a diverse group of countries, including Cameroon, Liberia, Mozambique, Namibia, Seychelles, South Africa, Sudan, and Zambia.[82]

In China's vision of a more democratic (read: less Western-dominated) world, numbers matter. Out of its own interest, the African voting bloc refused to endorse the Group-4 (Brazil, Germany, India, and Japan) proposal that would admit Japan into the UN Security Council as a veto-wielding permanent member in 2004–5. Africa's fifty-two countries have diverse interests. The danger of treating them in terms of a monolith is to exaggerate the continental identity. The PRC has largely avoided this pitfall, insofar as it has pursued ties with individual states in tandem with activism at the FOCAC.

China's Multilateral Diplomacy: Objectives and Realities

China's multilateral diplomacy is derivative of its definition of national interests and its vision of the regional and global order. The Asian financial crisis was the turning point in the evolution of the Chinese view from minimalism to unprecedented activism in multilateral diplomacy. It was around the time that the Chinese embraced such ideas as responsible power, nonconventional threats, the new security concept, and the Shanghai spirit. These ideas underpinned the multilateral turn in China's Asia diplomacy that both dovetails with and reinforces its bilateral ties with individual states and the region as a whole.[83] A

---

[80] Snow, "China and Africa," pp. 292–3.
[81] *People's Daily*, at http://english.people.com.cn/200601/12/eng20060112_234894.html.
[82] He Wenping, "Voyage to Africa," *Beijing Review*, Feb. 8, 2007, pp. 10–11.
[83] Pang Zhongying, "Zhongguo De Yazhou Zhanlue: Linghuo De Duobian Zhuyi" [China's Asia Strategy: Flexible Multilateralism], in Niu Jun, ed., *Zhongguo Waijiao Juan* [China's Foreign Affairs] (Beijing: New World Press, 2007),

similar motive – to set an overarching framework to coordinate its multifaceted engagement in Africa – was also behind the China-Africa forum. Taken together, these variegated forms of multilateral initiative have not only provided the PRC with a political cover to change its international environment, but also added real impetus to extend its reach in Asia and beyond. Through a differentiated multilateral approach, the PRC has sought to achieve three objectives for its rising strategy.

First, multilateral diplomacy serves the Chinese government's agenda of promoting economic development and social stability at home while dealing with transnational threats that directly impinge on its domestic interests in the age of globalization. Most notably, the SCO has played a critical role in the PRC's effort to crack down on Uighur separatism in Xinjiang. In more general terms, by virtue of promoting the sovereignty principle, the multilateral processes lend political support to regional states confronted with subnational and international pressures for domestic liberalization. Through the Six-Party Talks, the PRC was able to defuse the North Korean nuclear crisis enough to fend off a militarized escalation along its border that would have profoundly destabilizing repercussions to its northeast provinces.

On the economic front, the multilateral forums spurred development in the underdeveloped Chinese hinterland of its western and southwestern regions.[84] Under the SCO umbrella, China circumvented Russia's attempt to control the resources of the former Soviet republics. Most notably, the PRC succeeded in diversifying its oil supplies by completing a 1,200 kilometer oil pipeline with Kazakhstan. Whereas the SCO has not been particularly effective in promoting regionwide multilateral cooperation, the ASEAN-centered mechanisms have proven effective in facilitating China's economic integration with Southeast Asia. The FOCAC platform has similarly promoted PRC investment, trade, and energy security in Africa.

---

pp. 132–42; Xiao Huanrong, "Zhongguo De Daguo Zeren Yu Diquzhuyi Zhan-lue" [China's Great Power Responsibility and Strategy of Regionalism], *ibid.*, pp. 143–56.

[84] Zhao Changqing, "ASEAN, the Shanghai Cooperation Organization, and China," *Dangdai Yatai*, no. 11 (Nov. 15, 2003), pp. 11–15, in OSC: CPP20031217000170.

Among Chinese leaders and academic analysts, there clearly is a realization that their country must rely on multilateral settings to cope with nonconventional threats, such as the fragilities in international finance, terrorism, epidemics, and weapons proliferation, which are also transnational in nature.[85] Indeed, as discussed earlier, the Chinese have relied heavily on these instruments to deal with their own Uighur terrorism, SARS, the dangers of financial crisis, and North Korean attempts to acquire nuclear weapons.

Second, multilateral diplomacy undermines China threat theories and facilitates foreign recognition of China as a responsible great power. As we have detailed in Chapter 4, when Deng Xiaoping and other reformist CCP leaders regained political control and restarted the Chinese economic engine in the early 1990s, the fear of an increasingly nationalist China, as reflected in the so-called China threat theories, started to grow. Initially dismissive of these foreign concerns, the CCP leadership quickly realized that a hostile international environment would jeopardize its domestic and international agendas. In response to China threat theories, the PRC has relied heavily on international institutions to reassure the outside world of its unthreatening intentions.

This institutional approach makes sense, if as Lisa Martin argues, "The entire point of institutions is to embody norms and rules, and thus to induce more certainty and predictability in patterns of international interactions."[86] With a severe status deficit after its defeat in World War II, post-1945 Germany successfully capitalized on its newfound institutional role to regain greatness in Europe and beyond. In the words of Jeffrey A. Anderson and John B. Goodman, "Surely, the *magnitude* of Germany's reliance on international institutions to quell unease and to reduce uncertainty about its own intentions was and is unique. Germany conceived its security in part as making other countries less uncertain of itself, and employed different institutions

---

[85] Pang Zhongying, "The Long Road to Long-Term Peace and Stability in East Asia: Creating a New Regionalism," *Shijie Zhishi*, no. 17 (Sept. 1, 2003), p. 62, in OSC: CPP20030908000244.

[86] Lisa L. Martin, "An Institutionalist View: International Institutions and State Strategies," in T. V. Paul and John A. Hall, eds., *International Order and the Future of World Politics* (New York: Cambridge University Press, 1999), p. 91.

to reach overlapping yet distinct audiences."[87] The power of institutions in the case of postwar Germany was perhaps unparalleled, but Germany was not alone in using institutions to achieve great-power status. Similar considerations were behind Japan's interest in regional institutional building after the mid-1960s, although the distinctive dynamics of Asian regionalism significantly limited its leadership role, in comparison to the towering German influence in the robust European regionalism.[88]

Multilateral diplomacy makes China's power less feared but also more welcomed. The PRC has promoted its brand of multilateralism as antithetical to the Western and U.S. approach to international relations. For example, a think tank analyst in Beijing wrote in 2006, "The United States has consistently believed for a long time that its global expansion policy with its basic guidelines of U.S.-style democracy and the free market not only occupies the commanding moral high ground but also has highly effective and wide-ranging attraction in practice." For him, however, the "Shanghai Spirit," as embodied in the SCO, has undermined the U.S. "soft power."[89] Other Chinese scholars similarly believed that East Asian regionalism and the new security concept embraced by China represented an attractive alternative to the unilateralist power politics typified by post-9/11 U.S. foreign policy.

The Chinese concepts, such as harmony and dialogue, might appear self-serving, empty, and high-sounding to the skeptical outside observer. But in the post-9/11 world, the PRC's advocacy of dialogue between civilizations, sovereignty and pluralism, multilateralism, and development did find some resonance across Asia, particularly when its neighbors found Beijing's notions of win-win development and regional stability meaningful. Thus, South Korea found its position

---

[87] Jeffrey A. Anderson and John B. Goodman, "Mars or Minerva? A United Germany in a Post–Cold War Europe," in Robert O. Keohane, Joseph S. Nye, and Stanley Hoffmann, eds., *After the Cold War: International Institutions and State Strategies in Europe, 1989–1991* (Cambridge, MA: Harvard University Press, 1993), p. 59 (italics in original).

[88] The most thorough studies of this topic are Peter J. Katzenstein and Takashi Shiraishi, eds., *Network Power: Japan and Asia* (Ithaca, NY: Cornell University Press, 1997); Peter J. Katzenstein, *A World of Regions: Asia and Europe in the American Imperium* (Ithaca, NY: Cornell University Press, 2005).

[89] Wang Honggang, "Why Is the United States Worried about the Rise of the Shanghai Cooperation Organization?" *Guangzhou Ribao* (Internet), May 30, 2006, in OSC: CPP20060531050001.

more closely aligned with China than with the United States in the early rounds of the Six-Party Talks. While in the early 1990s Beijing stressed its unilateral right to use force in the South China Sea disputes, a decade later it submitted itself to a verbal multilateral restraint with ASEAN to calm the issue. Southeast Asia has overall become more receptive to the PRC's rising power than at any time since 1949.

Third, China's multilateral diplomacy is geared toward both restraining potential hostile powers and gaining initiative in shaping the international environment. For a rising power like China, the logic of multilateralism is virtually embedded in the U.S. hegemony.[90] The Six-Party Talks not only helped prevent war, it also helped prevent a tight U.S.-ROK-Japan united front, while at the same time it secured a joint public commitment to build a unified regional order. The SCO has reinforced unprecedented Sino-Russia cooperation in Central Asia, historically a key battleground between the Chinese and Russians during the Tsarist and Soviet eras.[91] The West's support of the color revolutions and human rights strained relations with Central Asian states, thereby strengthening the latter's reliance on the SCO. This was particularly true with Uzbekistan. The country was not part of the Shanghai Five because of its pro-U.S. policy, and initially avoided getting too involved in SCO even after it joined the group.[92] On the eve of the U.S.-led war on the Taliban regime in Afghanistan, Uzbekistan was eager to provide military bases for the coalition's troops. But several years later, it decided to terminate the Western military presence, while it deepened its ties with the SCO.

As regards potentially hostile powers, from the Chinese perspective the multilateral processes have made it difficult for outside players to wreak havoc on China's peripheral regions, whose stability is essential for the country's development. On the northwestern front, the SCO effectively fended off the NATO expansion to Central Asia, where

[90] Wang Yizhou, *Tanxun Quanqiu Zhuyi Guoji Guanxi* [Exploring Globalist International Relations] (Beijing: Beijing University Press, 2005), pp. 337–9.

[91] Pan Guang, "Shanghai Cooperation Organization under the New Situation and Central Asia's Anti-Terrorism Cooperation," *Hongkong Zhongguo Pinglun*, no. 54, (June 1, 2002), pp. 73–7, in OSC: CPP20020604000068.

[92] Lu Gang, "Shanghai Cooperation Organization Gaining International Influence," *Qiushi* (Internet), no. 18 (Sept. 16, 2005), in OSC: CPP20060302501001; "Why Did Uzbekistan Not Take Part in Joint Military Exercise by the Shanghai Cooperation Organization?" Urumqi Xinjiang Radio in Uyghur, Sept. 15, 2003, in OSC: CPP20031126000226.

it had made some inroads during the latter half of the 1990s. The organization has also provided political cover for building military ties, including joint exercises, between China and other member states. Mechanisms like this could effectively create de facto buffer zones free of the influence of potentially unfriendly powers in China's neighboring regions.

The ASEAN has consistently pursued a policy of engaging China through institutional involvement. The organization's principal mission – to reverse the security dilemma, lessen competition for relative power, and delegitimize the use of violence in regional international relations, coupled with its inclusive and reassuring style and adherence to the sovereignty principle – has proved to be much to Beijing's liking. Especially with the creation in 1994 of the ASEAN Regional Forum, the multilateral security platform that draws in all major powers in the Asia-Pacific, ASEAN has effectively abandoned its long-standing policy of keeping great powers at arms' length in favor of a policy of keeping them engaged and constrained on ASEAN terms.[93] ASEAN autonomy in relating to outside powers and deference to China's interest on Taiwan also eased China's suspicion toward the ASEAN-based multilateral initiatives. Also, from Beijing's perspective, the ASEAN-centered regionalism counteracted the traditional U.S. bilateralism, most notably the U.S.-Japan alliance, as well as the latest U.S. unilateralism and Koizumi's pro-America policy.[94]

---

[93] Amitav Acharya, *Constructing a Security Community in Southeast Asia: ASEAN and the Problem of Regional Order* (New York: Routledge, 2001); Amitav Acharya, "How Ideas Spread: Whose Norms Matter? Norm Localization and Institutional Change in Asian Regionalism, *International Organization*, vol. 58, no. 2 (Spring 2004), pp. 239–75; Alastair Iain Johnston, "The Myth of the ASEAN Way? Explaining the Evolution of the ASEAN Regional Forum," in Robert O. Keohane, Helga Haftendorn, and Celeste Wallander, eds., *Imperfect Unions: Security Institutions over Time and Space* (New York: Oxford University Press, 1999), pp. 287–324; Donald K. Emmerson, "Security, Community, and Democracy in Southeast Asia: Analyzing ASEAN," *Japanese Journal of Political Science*, vol. 6, no. 2 (Aug. 2005), pp. 165–85.

[94] See Liu Jiangyong, *Zhongguo Yu Riben: Bianhuazhong De "Zhengleng Jingre" Guanxi* [China and Japan: The Relationship of "Political Frigidity and Economic Warmth" in Evolution] (Beijing: Renmin Chuanbanshe, 2007); Xia Liping, "Establishing a Security Mechanism on the Korean Peninsula," in *The Political Economy of Korean Reconciliation and Reform* (Washington, DC: Korean Economic Institute of America, 2001), pp. 19–24.

Beijing's incentive to strengthen ties with Africa is not for the sake of maintaining continuity of historical friendship and third-world solidarity, which the Beijing University Professor Li Anshan aptly criticizes his Chinese colleagues of "habitually emphasizing."[95] Nor is it just to advance the PRC's commercial interests.[96] China has capitalized on Sino-African friendship forged in their shared, anti-imperialist struggle. However, that historical friendship has been tapped to serve its more deliberative foreign policy aspirations, particularly after the two sides tempered their earlier protested goal for a radically restructured new international order. As a researcher at the Central Party School of the Chinese Communist Party wrote in 2006, if China is to become a global power, it "should not merely cultivate good-neighborly relations in Asia, but also actively strengthen and expand ties with African countries using its collective weight to simultaneously check attempts by the small number of countries to contain China, on the one hand, and on the other, transform and improve China's position in the international society."[97] Indeed, Africa's positions on human rights, sovereignty, the UN role, and Western dominance align with the PRC interests. Thus, as China rises, Africa's importance and that of the FOCAC will only grow in the Asian power's foreign policy.

While averse to containing the PRC, Asian states along China's periphery have also proven to be skillful in keeping other powers involved in the region, not least because they want to keep China in check as well. During his long tenure as the prime minister of Singapore (1990–2004), Goh Chok Tong was undoubtedly the staunchest defender among Asian leaders of the U.S. role in the region. According to him, the United States was virtually indispensable in ensuring China continued its path of peaceful engagement in Asia.[98] Also tellingly,

---

[95] Li Anshan, "Sino-African Relations under the 'China Rising' Discourse," p. 4.

[96] Western commentary tends to consider China's appetite for natural resources as the primary motive, even though they underscore the broad negative consequences for African development and Western interests. See, for example, the influential report Council on Foreign Relations, *More than Humanitarianism: A Strategic U.S. Approach Toward Africa* (New York: Council on Foreign Relations, 2006), ch. 5.

[97] Luo Jianbo, "Ruhe Tuijin Zhongguo Duifei Duobian Waijiao" [How to Promote China's Multilateral Diplomacy Toward Africa], *Xiandai Guoji Guanxi*, no. 11, 2006, at http://www.irchina.org/news/view.asp?id=1380, p. 2.

[98] "'Full Text' of Singapore Prime Minister Goh Chok Tong's Keynote Address at the U.S.-ASEAN Business Council's Annual Dinner in Washington, DC,"

ASEAN deferred admitting China into its Nuclear Weapons Free Zone when Beijing expressed interest to join it in 2004, presumably out of concern over an unrivaled Chinese presence in the region.[99]

The PRC has also treaded carefully lest its diplomatic activism unduly antagonize the United States. It does not want to be perceived as attempting to establish an exclusive Chinese hegemony in Asia. Leading up to the first East Asian Summit, Chinese ambassador to Japan Wang Yi rejected the notion that his country sought to dominate Asia, arguing instead that "China supports regionalism that is open and respects the objective fact that the United States has a traditional influence on this region and has a realistic stake."[100] Contemplating cooperative scenarios in Northeast Asia, a prominent Shanghai-based analyst held up the APEC "open regionalism" as the standard, urging that "the region's members need to pay attention to the American element and should consider America's interests in this region appropriately in view of its important role in and its close relations with Northeast Asia."[101]

The revitalization of the U.S.-Japan alliance after the mid-1990s and the stabilization of the U.S.-ROK alliance after Roh Moohyun came to power in December 2002 amply demonstrated the resiliency of the U.S. alliance structure in the region. From Beijing's perspective, confronting these alliances is not only futile but also risks being equated with its own revisionist ambitions. Moreover, China does not see its interests as being served if the bilateral alliances are replaced by a new division in Northeast Asia, where it finds itself on the opposite side of the United States. Such concern led prominent Chinese analyst Shi Yinhong to worry that a ROK drawing too close to China in the Six-Party Talks

Straits Times (Internet), June 15, 2001, in OSC: SEP20010615000025; Zuraidah Ibrahim, "Singapore's Goh Urges U.S. to Be More Involved in East Asian Region," *Straits Times*, May 9, 2003, in OSC: SEP 20030509000011.

[99] Elizabeth Economy, "China's Rise in Southeast Asia: Implications for the United States," *Journal of Contemporary China*, vol. 14 (Aug. 2005), p. 417. China's interest is confirmed in Lu Jianren, "Dynamic Cooperation," *Beijing Review*, Oct. 26, 2006, p. 15.

[100] "China Envoy Positive on U.S. Participation in E. Asia Community," Kyodo World Service, May 11, 2005, in OSC: JPP20050511000077.

[101] Ma Ying, "Search for a Peace Community: Regional Cooperation in Northeast Asia," *Journal of East Asian Affairs*, vol. 20, no. 1 (Spring/Summer 2006), p. 36.

might risk creating an undesirable strategic fissure in the region.[102] In essence, the Chinese see the multilateral talks as a low-risk but effective means to soften the U.S.-led alliances and to create a regional order less prone to balancing against China.

Besides the United States, other powers, such as India, Japan, and Russia all compete with China – albeit with varying intensities – for regional influence. The Sino-Japanese rivalry came to a head during 2004–05, leading up to the first East Asian Summit. India only sent its minister of petroleum and natural gas to the 2006 SCO meeting in Shanghai, where heads of all other member and observer states convened to mark the organization's fifth anniversary. In Central Asia, Russia remains wary of China's influence in the region, which Moscow considers as its traditional sphere of influence.

The effectiveness and the fate of the multilateral processes are themselves not at all certain, thanks to their institutional weaknesses and uncertain commitments of the member states. In an interview with Chinese media in 2005, the SCO's General Secretary Zhang Deguang admitted that although both Chinese and Russian are the official languages of the organization, Chinese was rarely used at the secretariat, making translation a cumbersome task for the Beijing-based headquarters.[103] As of the fifth SCO anniversary, member states had yet to smooth over differences over the criteria for new membership. The organization itself seemed to have exerted little influence in enforcing the 2005 statement calling for the foreign troops pullout. While ASEAN settled the standards for membership of the East Asian Summit, the diverse grouping looked too much like the APEC to be taken seriously in forging a genuine East Asian regionalism. The process will continue to be defined by the strong tradition of locally initiated multilateral forums centered on the proud and wary ASEAN. Northeast Asia is the most unsettled region, particularly on the security front. Not surprisingly, the Six-Party Talks have proven to be the most precarious process, as the major powers have struggled to sketch a common vision of the Northeast Asian order.

Along with flourishing Sino-African ties, new problems have also grown. On the economic front, the PRC has been accused of practicing

---

[102] Shi Yinhong makes the point in an interview with the *Beijing Review*, Aug. 18, 2005, p.16.
[103] Wang Zhen, "Shanghai Cooperation Organization."

neocolonialism: plundering natural resources, damaging the environment, exporting Chinese labor, and dumping cheap goods in Africa. The exports of Chinese labor-intensive goods to the continent and the global markets have stymied the development of indigenous manufacturing industries. Fatal industrial accidents and "slavish working conditions" for local workers at Chinese-invested copper and coal mines in Zambia in 2005–6 gave rise to lasting anti-Chinese sentiments in the country.[104] Such business-related conflicts are bound to arise when China's domestic industries fall short of the safety standards and commercial interests drive its engagement on the continent. Several high-profile attacks on Chinese citizens – including the murdering of Chinese businessmen in South Africa and the kidnapping and killing of Chinese workers in Nigeria in the early months of 2007 – also raised the issue of safety for Chinese businesses and personnel on the continent.

Besides doubts over whether the all-round Chinese presence in Africa benefits the sustainable growth of the continent, Beijing's political role has also come under international scrutiny. On major issues of human rights and humanitarian concern, the PRC has generally sided with the African governments involved. Most notoriously, Chinese obstructionism on the Darfur, Sudan crisis at the United Nations prevented Western attempts at a more robust response. Growing international pressures, particularly calls for boycotting the 2008 Beijing Olympics to punish China's support of the Sudanese government, spurred the PRC in 2007 to appoint a special envoy to deal with the crisis and to persuade Khartoum to accept a phased plan leading to deployment of an AU-UN "hybrid peace-keeping force," as proposed by UN Secretary General, Kofi Annan. The PRC also supported Zimbabwe's President Robert Mugabe in disregard of the egregious human rights abuses in his country. Chinese aid and investment has sometimes frustrated conditionality attempts by institutions, such the World Bank and the IMF, to improve governance of the recipient states. China's arms sales in Ethiopia, Sudan, and Zambia also fueled regional conflicts and domestic strife in these countries.

---

[104] Zanis: "Chinese Investors Prevent Minister from Visiting Coal Mine," *Times of Zambia* (Internet), May 26, 2006, in OSC: AFP20060526516006.

Chinese officials and analysts are candid about the problems, except for the human rights and arms transfer issues.[105] They are particularly sensitive to the neocolonialism concerns surrounding PRC economic engagement in Africa and have tried to address these concerns through the FOCAC framework. While publicly rejecting accusations of any wrongdoing on their part, they have been responsive to international criticisms of China's role on issues such as the Darfur conflict. But the PRC suspicion toward Western motives, immediate interests on the continent, aversion to interventionism, and deference to the AU have combined to condition its responsiveness on issues concerning the sovereignty of African states.

China's embrace of multilateral diplomacy in Asia represents one of the most critical shifts in its foreign policy. No doubt both Asia's multilateral trends and China's role are confronted with important uncertainties and limitations. Nor has the region become a sphere of exclusive Chinese sphere of influence. Rather, given its definition of national interest and the dynamics of regional affairs in Asia, support of "open regionalism" is not a choice, but virtually a necessity for Beijing. Thus, a Chinese-dominated East Asian bloc is not even in the offing. The SCO is open to institutional contact with ASEAN, the UN, and the Commonwealth of Independent States; and the Six-Party Talks can only succeed if the major powers can draw the hermit kingdom of the North Korean regime into the tightly interdependent and economic dynamic Northeast Asia region.

However, the country's new power and confidence in realigning Asian international relations does mark a new phase both in the evolution of regional order and in China's quest for great-power status. Chinese flexibility in various multilateral processes, coupled with its bilateral diplomacy and economic ties in Asia, have proven to be an effective means to serve its national interests in the era of globalization, credibly project an image of restraint and responsibility, counter U.S. unilateralism and Japan-U.S. bilateralism, and bring about desirable changes along its periphery. Similarly, through the political framework provided by the FOCAC, the PRC has recast solidarity with African

---

[105] Mei Xinyu, "Doctrine and Issues in Sino-African Economic and Trade Relations," *Zhongguo Jinji Bao* (Internet), Feb. 12, 2007, in OSC: CPP20070221308003; Wang Hongyi, "Sino-African Relations Enter a New Stage," *Guoji Wenti Yanjiu*, Nov. 13, 2006, in OSC: CCP20061212329004.

countries to serve its economic interests and broader foreign policy goals. Notwithstanding the controversies over its role in Africa, the undeniable reality is that in a short period the PRC has firmly established itself as a major player on the continent.

While China has pursued multilateral diplomacy out of instrumental calculations, the new turn in the PRC's foreign policy also reflects a reconstituted national identity that values globalization, responsibility, and win-win international relations.[106] As China's interests become so deeply embedded in these multilateral processes, sometimes it's all but impossible to distinguish behaviors based on instrumental calculations from those driven by normative convictions. Even if China's political elites started out with preset materialist goals in mind, the multilateral processes inevitably have changed what they view as appropriate, credible, and sound policy choices.

---

[106] For a forceful argument, see Su Changhe, "Faxian Zhongguo Xinwaijiao – Duobian Zhidu Yu Zhongguo Waijiao Xinsiwei" [Discovering China's New Diplomacy: Multilateral Institutions and China's New Diplomatic Thinking], *Shjie Jingji Yu Zhengzhi*, no. 4 (2005), at http://www.iwep.org.cn/pdf/2005/faxian.pdf; Su Changhe, "Zoubian Zhidu Yu Zoubian Zhuyi: Dongya Quyu Zili De Zhongguo Tujing" [Institutions and Regionalism on China's Periphery: The Chinese Way of Regional Governance], *Shijie Jingji Yu Zhengzhi*, no. 1 (2006), at http://www.iwep.org.cn/pdf/2006/zbzdyzbzy_suchanghe.pdf; Liu Jianfei, "Be Rooted on the Neighboring Region, and Look onto the World," *Liaowang*, no. 28 (July 11, 2005), p. 48, in OSC: CPP20050719000118. See also Wang Yizhou, *Quanqiu Zhengzhi He Zhongguo Waijiao* [Global Politics and China's Foreign Policy] (Beijing: Shijie Zhishi Chubanshe, 2003).

8 | *Taiwan and China's Rise*

Taiwan is at the center stage of China's foreign relations, and yet mainland China's military threat and coercive diplomacy toward it seem to be removed from its otherwise increasingly sophisticated foreign policy. Exactly how does the Taiwan issue fit into China's quest for great-power status? This chapter addresses the question. It argues that China's concern for reassurance regarding its foreign intentions starkly increases the diplomatic costs of a military option to force unification. Such an assessment of diplomatic costs further dissuades the Chinese Communist Party leadership from a resort to force. Yet as Taiwan has also become a key marker for China's great-power recognition, the gentler turn in Chinese foreign policy ironically has made Taiwan's independence even more intolerable for the People's Republic of China. China's status advancement has made it both imperative and possible for the mainland to pursue a more sophisticated set of preventative measures beyond the blunt instrument of deterrence, designed to maintain a "one China"-oriented status quo across the Taiwan Strait.

International Recognition Versus the Use of Force

When contemplating the use of force, the national leaders of China invariably weigh the costs and benefits of their choice. Regarding a decision by the PRC about Taiwan, what is striking is the juxtaposition of the enormous value the CCP leadership attaches to the issue and the equally enormous costs that a forced solution would entail.[1] When the Chinese leadership makes the fateful decision to go to war, it must carefully calculate the consequences. Although many studies have

---

[1] Yun-han Chu, "The Evolution of Beijing's Policy Toward Taiwan During the Reform Era," in Yong Deng and Fei-ling Wang, eds., *China Rising: Power and Motivation in Chinese Foreign Policy* (Boulder, CO: Rowman & Littlefield, 2005), pp. 245–77.

been devoted to the military balance and possible military outcomes in case of a war across the strait, it's curious that few English-language studies have attempted an inquiry into the diplomatic costs.[2] For different reasons, while vowing to pay any price for national reunification, Chinese officials tend to prevaricate on costs assessment. The late Chinese leader Deng Xiaoping talked about "retrogression" (*Daotui*) in Sino-American relations as a worst-case consequence that China must accept.[3] In early 2004, the PLA's Major General Peng Guanqian merely listed "possible retrogression to relations with certain countries" as one of the costs of war against Taiwan independence without elaborating what that "retrogression" would exactly entail.[4]

At the outset, a few qualifications are in order. The fallout of the war across the Strait will depend upon the circumstances under which it commences. The conflict scenario envisioned here is one that would have been widely considered by the United States and other interested parties as unilaterally initiated by the mainland Chinese to change the status quo. Admittedly, this remains somewhat vague, given the lack of common interpretations of what constitutes the "status quo" and what would represent "provocations." It does, however, clearly apply to the PRC's use of force being driven primarily by either domestic nationalist politics or its *perception* that Taiwan is slipping away or a combination of the two.

In order to gauge the diplomatic consequences of a war on Taiwan, it is necessary to establish what the PRC values most in its foreign relations. From our perspective, in a nutshell, the centrality of the issue notwithstanding, China's status strategy does not hinge upon forcing the return of Taiwan, but rather requires preventing formal

---

[2] An important exception is Andrew Scobell, ed., *The Costs of Conflict: Impact on China of a Future War* (Carlisle, PA: Strategic Studies Institute, U.S. Army War College, 2001), which touches upon certain diplomatic consequences of a Chinese war on Taiwan.

[3] Zhonggong Zhongyang Taiwan Gongzuo Bangongshi He Guowuyuan Taiwan Shiwu Bangongshi [Office of Taiwan Affairs of the Chinese Communist Party Central Committee and Taiwan Affairs Office of the State Council], *Zhongguo Taiwan Wenti* [China's Taiwan Problem] (Beijing: Jiuzhou Tushu Chubanshe, 1998), p. 86.

[4] "Junshi Zhuanjia Tan Fan 'Taidu' Zhanzheng: Liutiao Daijia, Zhanfan Bijiu" [Military Experts on the War Against "Taiwan Independence": Six Prices, War Criminals Bound to Be Punished], *People's Daily* (Internet), at http://www. peope.com.cn/GB/junshi/1076/2223899.html, p. 1.

"loss" of Taiwan through nonviolent means. Historically, power politics geared to territorial disputes were the central cause for war.[5] Territorial defense also characterized Maoist China's rather frequent use of force.[6] Insofar as territorial wars are closely associated with the traditional security paradigm, an unprovoked use of force against Taiwan would undercut the Chinese claims for having chosen an alternative path for great-power status. It would go against the PRC attempt to downplay the militarized nature of international politics. Equally important is the extent to which democratic values are part and parcel of the normative underpinnings of the contemporary great-power system and the world order at large. A military invasion of a democratic Taiwan would amount to an even more egregious act in defiance of the norms of responsible behavior.[7] This suggests high prohibition against the Chinese use of force beyond the CCP leadership's military calculations as to the outcome of a war. But it has also meant that there is no letup in terms of the PRC effort to militarily deter Taiwan independence and to bear down on the island with its full weight through other means.

It is the broad consequences of war that have worried prominent Chinese analysts and influential policy advisers. They are acutely aware of the explosive nature of the Taiwan issue and the danger that a military confrontation across the Strait could derail their nation's great-power rise.[8] Among the most outspoken is Zhang Nianchi, a

[5] John Vasquez, "Reexamining the Steps to War: New Evidence and Theoretical Insights," in Manus I. Midlarsky, ed., *Handbook of War Studies II* (Ann Arbor: University of Michigan Press, 2000), pp. 371–405.

[6] Allen S. Whiting, "China's Use of Force, 1950–96, and Taiwan," *International Security*, vol. 26, no. 2 (Fall 2001), pp. 103–31; Alastair Iain Johnston, "China's Militarized Dispute Behavior, 1949–1992: A First Cut at the Data," *China Quarterly*, no. 153 (March 1998), pp.1–30.

[7] For scholarly illumination of how international relations are shaped by dominant democratic values after the cold war, see, for example, Henry R. Nau, *At Home Abroad: Identity and Power in American Foreign Policy* (Ithaca, NY: Cornell University Press, 2002); Robert Jervis, "Theories of War in an Era of Leading-Power Peace," *American Political Science Review*, vol. 96, no. 1 (March 2002), pp.1–14.

[8] See, for example, "China's International Status and Foreign Strategy after the Cold War: Speech by Pang Zhongying at the Qinghua University on 16 April 2002," *Renmin Wang*, May 5, 2002, in Foreign Broadcast Information Service (hereafter cited as FBIS): CPP20020506000022; Yang Yunzhong, "Some Strategic Reflections on the Main Threats to China's Security in the Early 21st Century," *Dangdai Yatai*, Oct. 15, 2002, pp. 3–12, in FBIS:

key adviser to the Chinese leadership, who has long argued against a myopic hard-line approach to Taiwan lest it jeopardize the overriding goal of China's "national rejuvenation." He urged utmost patience, empathy, and equality in dealing with Taiwan in order to turn the issue from "being an obstruction to being a driving force and a stimulus to the rise of China."[9]

Perhaps, analytically as Iain Johnston argues, given the PRC's positive engagement in the world during the reform era, its intimidation toward Taiwan should be viewed as "a dangerous exception but an exception nonetheless."[10] In the policy world, however, it is all but impossible to separate the Taiwan issue from overall Chinese international orientations. For the United States, Japan, and other Asian countries, how China handles Taiwan is inextricably linked to the broad context of its grand strategy. Even European powers more sympathetic to the PRC position have by no means given it a free hand when military threat is involved. China's ability to separate the coercive side of its Taiwan policy from broader attempt to cultivate acceptance as a responsible power is in itself a form of power that needs to be investigated.[11]

China has always viewed the U.S. position on Taiwan as not only decisive in determining the ebb and flow of Taiwan independence, but also as intertwined with the dynamics of the Sino-American relationship. The PLA missile testing in 1995–96 was to punish Taiwanese President Lee Tenghui's visit to the United States. But according to

CPP20021204000188; Shi Yinhong, "Serious Danger and Strategic Necessity of the Taiwan Issue," *Zhanlue Yu Guanli*, no. 1 (Feb. 1, 2004), pp. 101–6, in FBIS: CPP20040309000257; Brookings Institution China Initiative, "China's Peaceful Rise: Speeches of Zheng Bijian," at http://www.brook.edu/dybdocroot/fp/events/20050616bijianlunch.pdf (accessed July 24, 2005), pp. 28–9; Yang Yi, "Zhanlue Jiyuqi De Zhongguo Guojia Anquan" [China's National Security During the Period of Strategic Opportunity], *Jiaoxue Yu Yanjiu*, no. 4 (2006), at http://www.irchina.org/news/view.asp?id=1201 (accessed July 10, 2006).

9   Zhang Nianchi, "The 16th CPC National Congress and Cross-Strait Relations," *Zhongguo Pinglun* (Hong Kong), no. 60 (Dec. 1, 2002), in FBIS: CPP20021204000033; Zhang Nianchi, "Taiwan Issue and the Future and Destiny of China," *Zhongguo Pinglun*, no. 89 (May 2005), pp. 11–16, in FBIS: CPP20050509000078.

10 Alastair Iain Johnston, "Is China a Status Quo Power?" *International Security*, vol. 27, no. 4 (Spring 2003), pp. 5–56, quote on p. 49.

11 Peter Bachrach and Morton S. Baratz, "Two Faces of Power," *American Political Science Review*, vol. 56, no. 4 (1962), pp. 947–52.

Niu Jun, the underlying goal was to demonstrate resolve vis-à-vis the United States. Against the backdrop of escalating tensions in the Sino-American relationship, Chinese leaders interpreted the U.S. approval of Lee's visit as total disregard of both Chinese concerns and the long-standing mutual understanding on the Taiwan issue.[12]

One lesson that the Clinton administration drew from the missile crisis concerned the need for a more actively engaged and proactive U.S. role in dealing with cross-Strait relations, which had entered into a new state of turbulence because of Chinese nationalism and the fusion of identity struggle and democratic politics in Taiwan.[13] To placate Beijing's concerns, the Clinton administration made an apparent tilt toward mainland China in 1997–98. But in July 1999, President Lee Teng-hui countered with a statement that the cross-Strait relationship should be treated as a "special state-to-state" one, thus setting off another destabilizing round in the Washington-Beijing-Taipei triangle. Such pattern of persistent tensions underscored the inadequacies of the traditional U.S. policy framework in maintaining the balancing act across the Strait.[14] The new realities called for U.S. policy adjustments better suited to serve broad American interests in East Asia and to underpin a more stable cross-Strait relationship.

Upon his inauguration in January 2001, President George W. Bush immediately took measures to strengthen U.S. ties with Taiwan. Most notably, on a morning television show in April, he pledged that the United States would "do whatever it takes to help Taiwan defend itself."[15] His administration subsequently made available the largest high-tech weapons sale to the island in a decade. Taiwan's defense minister Tang Yiau-ming was granted meetings with high-level officials

---

[12] Niu Jun, "Sanci Taiwan Haixia Junshi Douzheng Juece Yanjiu" [Decision-Makings in the Three Military Struggles Across Taiwan Straits], in Niu Jun, ed., *Zhongguo Waijiao Juan* [China's Foreign Affairs] (Beijing: New World Press, 2007), pp. 218–20, 227–30.

[13] Chase Freeman, Jr., "Preventing War in the Taiwan Strait: Restraining Taiwan and Beijing," *Foreign Affairs*, vol. 77, no. 4 (July–Aug. 1998), p. 10; Nancy B. Tucker, "China-Taiwan: U.S. Debates and Policy Choices," *Survival*, vol. 40, no. 4 (Winter 1998/99), p. 15.

[14] For a critique of Clinton's policy of strategic ambiguity biased toward Beijing, see Andrew J. Nathan, "What's Wrong with American Taiwan Policy," *Washington Quarterly*, vol. 23, no. 2 (Spring 2000), pp. 93–106.

[15] Quote from Kelly Wallace, "Bush pledges whatever it takes to defend Taiwan," at http://www.cnn.com/2001/ALLPOLITICS/04/24/bush.taiwan.abc/ (accessed Sept. 30, 2004).

from both the U.S. Defense and State Departments in March 2002. The United States was deeply involved in aiding Taiwan's military modernization, more so than at any time after their official diplomatic ties ended in 1979.

Since the latter half of 2002, however, the need to strategically engage China has led to a more balanced U.S. policy, one that explicitly prevents either the PRC or Taiwan from forcing a resolution. Both before and during his June 1, 2002 visit to attend a conference at the International Institute for Strategic Studies in Singapore, then Deputy Secretary of Defense Paul Wolfowitz stated in unambiguous terms that, in addition to the long-standing opposition to the use of force, "we are opposed to Taiwan independence."[16] Subsequently, when meeting with Presidents Jiang Zemin and Hu Jintao, President Bush reaffirmed the U.S. "one China" stand, although whether the exact wording was "opposing" or "not supporting" Taiwan independence was contested.[17] In any case, since Jiang's visit with Bush in Crawford, Texas in October 2002, the United States has played a more active role than before in reining in independence movement in Taiwan, particularly by holding President Chen Shui-bian accountable for his promises not to change the cross-Strait status quo.

For the United States, its security commitment to Taiwan is heavily defined – albeit somewhat ambiguously, by the Taiwan Relations Act (TRA), a domestic legislation enacted in 1979. Thus, the TRA has been the centerpiece of the U.S. policy evolution regarding cross-Strait relations. The most noteworthy change under the second Bush's administration was the elevation of the TRA to a level on par with the three U.S. communiqués concluded in a decade during the 1970s–80s with the PRC. The juxtaposition of the three communiqués and TRA reflected an unprecedented clarity in the U.S. security

---

[16] *Taipei Times* (Internet), May 31, 2002, in FBIS: CPP20020531000134; *China Post* (Internet), May 31, 2002, in FBIS: CPP20020531000154. His speech at the meeting can be found at htttp://www.defenselink.mil/speeches/2002/s20020601-depsecdef.html.

[17] According to Chinese official media reports on the Bush-Jiang meeting at Crawford, Texas in October 2002, the "opposition" version was used at the private meeting, but Bush stated that Washington "does not support Taiwan independence" at their joint press conference. When meeting with President Hu on June 1, 2003 on the sidelines of the G8 summit, Bush reportedly stated that the United States "is opposed to Taiwan independence." See *Renmin Ribao* (*People's Daily*, overseas edition, hereafter cited as *RMRB*), Oct. 28, 2002, p. 1; June 3, 2003, p. 1.

commitment to Taiwan. Such a policy formula also provided testimony to the strong and increasingly institutionalized U.S. congressional support of Taiwan.[18]

While officially refusing to mention the TRA when publicly characterizing the U.S. one-China policy lest the domestic law be legitimized, Beijing nonetheless understood well that the U.S. policy was deeply embedded in this legislation. In voicing Chinese displeasure at a high-profile forum in Texas in November 2003, the veteran architect of Chinese diplomacy Qian Qichen responded to U.S. Secretary of State Colin Powell's exuberant characterization of the U.S.-China relationship by maintaining that bilateral ties "may and can be even better."[19] According to an influential Chinese commentator, the mainland People's National Congress enacted the antisecession law in March 2005 due in no small part to the PRC's frustration with the U.S. use of the TRA to undercut Beijing's Taiwan policy in the name of maintaining the "status quo."[20] The idea of a counter Chinese legislation to make it legally justified and binding to stop Taiwan independence with any measure necessary, including the use of force, had first come about several years earlier. The emphasis of TRA in the Bush administration's Taiwan policy helped spur Beijing into quick action.

It's clear that China has to deal with the reality that the TRA has become part and parcel of the U.S. deterrence strategy against unilateral PLA attack.[21] Greater emphasis on the TRA may not altogether remove ambiguity regarding the nature of the U.S. military role in a cross-Strait war, but it has greatly removed doubts about the U.S. commitment to secure Taiwan. Amidst the many documents and statements on the U.S. policy, what's not unambiguous is that any forced settlement disagreeable to the democratic choice of Taiwan is

---

[18] Steven M. Goldstein and Randall Schriver, "An Uncertain Relationship: The United States, Taiwan and the Taiwan Relations Act," *China Quarterly*, no. 165 (2001), pp. 147–72.

[19] "China-U.S. Relations Can Be Even Better: Qian," *People's Daily* (Internet), Nov. 6, 2003, at http://english.peopledaily.com.cn/200311/06/eng20031106_127713.shtml.

[20] Xin Qi, "Dalu Duitai Gongzhuo De Zhongda Zhengce Xuanshi" [Important Statement in Mainland China's Taiwan Policy], *RMRB*, March 30, 2005, p. 3.

[21] Robert Ross, "Navigating the Taiwan Strait: Deterrence, Escalation Dominance, and U.S.-China Relations," *International Security*, vol. 27, no. 2 (Fall 2002), pp. 48–85; Thomas Christensen, "The Contemporary Security Dilemma: Deterring a Taiwan Conflict," *Washington Quarterly*, vol. 25, no. 4 (Autumn 2002), pp. 7–21.

ultimately unacceptable.[22] Regardless of the battlefield outcome, the ensuing hostilities held by the United States and its allies against the PRC would be certain, lasting, and costly.[23]

Thanks to its alliance with the United States, colonial legacies in Taiwan, and ambivalent relations with China, Japan assumes a special role in the Taiwan issue. In fact, it is the only major power, other than the United States, and the only Asian country that mainland China is most concerned about on this issue. The 1995–96 cross-Strait crisis marked a turning point in Japanese views regarding Taiwan and the PRC at large. While the effort to revitalize the U.S.-Japan alliance was jump-started in the aftermath of the first Korean nuclear crisis in 1993–94, the process was also clearly influenced by the Chinese military exercises designed to intimidate pro-Taiwan independent elements. The missile firings in waters in close proximity to the island fed into Japanese suspicions of the PRC, at a time when fear and negative perceptions of its neighboring giant had gained momentum.[24] According to Joseph Nye, a key architect of the renewed U.S.-Japan alliance, the 1995–96 crisis offered a rationale for the United States to enlist necessary Japanese support to engage China from a position of strength.[25] The result was the revised defense guidelines released in 1997, pledging joint U.S.-Japanese response to "situations in areas surrounding Japan" on a "situational" basis.[26] Japan's refusal to exclude Taiwan from the

---

[22] For perhaps the best exposition of the U.S. position, see Richard C. Bush, *Untying the Knot: Making Peace in the Taiwan Strait* (Washington, DC: Brookings Institution Press, 2005), pp. 255–65.

[23] David M. Finkelstein, "Chinese Perceptions of the Cost of a Conflict," in Scobell, *The Costs of Conflict*, pp. 9–27.

[24] See Koji Murata, "Japan's Military Cooperation and Alliances in the Asia-Pacific Region," and Akio Watanabe, "The PRC-Japan Relationship: Heading for a Collision?" in Hung-Mao Tien and Tun-Jen Cheng, eds., *The Security Environment in the Asia-Pacific* (Armonk, NY: M. E. Sharpe, 2000), ch. 4, 5; Michael J. Green, *Japan's Reluctant Realism* (New York: Macmillan/Palgrave, 2001), ch. 3; Thomas Berger, "Japan's International Relations: The Political and Security Dimensions," in Samuel S. Kim, ed., *International Relations of Northeast Asia* (Boulder, CO: Rowmand & Littlefield, 2004), pp. 154–6.

[25] Joseph Nye, Jr., *The Paradox of American Power* (New York: Oxford University Press, 2002), p. 22.

[26] For the complete version of the Guidelines, see Michael J. Green and Patrick Cronin, eds., *The U.S.-Japan Alliance: Past, Present, and Future,* (New York: Council on Foreign Relations, 1999), appendix 3, pp. 333–45.

situational considerations, Chinese pressures notwithstanding, only fueled Beijing's suspicion about Tokyo's motives.

Increased Japanese threat perception vis-à-vis China's rising power strengthened support and sympathy in Japan for Taiwan. After becoming Prime Minister in April 2001, Junichiro Koizumi decided to rely on the U.S.-Japan alliance as the cornerstone for Japan's global and regional policy. The war on terror after 9/11 further lessened Japanese domestic restraints on its security role while adding impetus for Japan to face up to the China challenge. As a result, in a joint statement issued by U.S. Secretary of Defense Donald Rumsfeld and Secretary of State Condoleezza Rice and their Japanese counterparts on February 19, 2005, Japan joined the United States in pledging to "[e]ncourage the peaceful resolution of issues concerning the Taiwan Strait through dialogue." Seemingly moderate, this move nonetheless signaled a clearer, more assertive Japanese commitment to a nonviolent outcome of the cross-Strait dispute. With growing suspicion toward Japan, the Chinese naturally viewed the deepening U.S.-Japan alliance as directed against its interests in Taiwan. The subsequent 2+2 statement in 2007 removed explicit reference to Taiwan, but the message of joint U.S.-Japanese interest in the issue remained unmistakable.[27]

Mainland China has long blamed the United States and Japan for abetting the independence movement in Taiwan. The leading think tank analyst Li Jiaquan even attributed the success of the Democratic Progressive Party (DPP) in the 2000 presidential race to the backing of foreign governments with a motive to play the Taiwan card against his country. He pointedly contended, with regard to their interference in Taiwan, "The United States is more open. In contrast, Japan is relatively covert, like what is called 'duck swim, namely motionless above water but active underwater.'"[28] The PRC was particularly irate

---

[27] The full text of the "Joint Statement of the U.S.-Japan Security Consultative Committee" can be found at http://www.state.gov/r/pa/prs/ps/2005/42490.htm (accessed March 8, 2005). For Chinese reactions, see Xiu Chunping, "Meiri Zaixiang 'Taidu' Fachu Cuowu Xinhao" [U.S., Japan Send Wrong Signal to "Taiwan Independence," Yet Again), *RMRB*, March 3, 2005; Weng Xiang, "U.S.-Japan Joint Statement Has Nothing New, But Very Meaningful," *Zhongguo Qingnian Bao* (Internet), Feb. 22, 2005, in FBIS: CPP20050222000062. The 2007 statement is at http://www.state.gov/r/pa/prs/ps/2007//may/84084.htm.

[28] Li Jiaquan, Staff Special Commentator: "Three 'Triangular Relationships' Centering on Taiwan Problem: One Year of Taiwan's Political Situation in

with Lee Teng-hui's ties with Japan, as Lee was held more responsible than anyone else for championing Taiwanese separatism.[29] Pro-Taiwan forces in Japan had long campaigned to secure his visit to Japan while Lee was still in office, but to no avail. After his presidency ended, Lee's first visit quickly materialized in April 2001 for an ostensibly medical reason, and his subsequent nonofficial tours invariably drew Chinese protest vis-à-vis Japan as well as attacks on himself.

Japan insisted that its one-China policy had not changed even after the 2005 U.S.-Japan joint statement that specifically mentioned Taiwan. Indeed, Tokyo expressed reservations over the highly controversial DPP referendum proposals respectively on cross-Strait relations and Taiwan's bid for UN membership in the name of Taiwan leading up to the March 2004 and 2008 presidential elections in the island. What has changed, however, is that Taiwan has become a central factor in Tokyo's relations with China and Japan's overall strategic choice. Putting aside the military role Japan may or may not play in a conflict scenario, an unprovoked PRC military invasion of Taiwan would doubtless fuel the concerns of a China threat, further intensifying the power struggle between the two Asian giants. It would also aggravate Japan's sense of vulnerability, thereby motivating Tokyo to embark on an accelerated path toward "normal power status," with significantly less restraint on the expansion of its military capabilities.

As discussed in the preceding chapter, a hallmark of the PRC regional policy in Asia has been its win-win, economic-centered, and multilateral approach. The aim, as presented by Chinese officials, is not to establish exclusive Chinese dominance in Asia, but to project a pro–status quo, constructive image in the region.[30] Guided by this new strategy, Beijing's regional diplomacy has achieved notable

---

Retrospect and Prospect," *Hong Kong Ta Kung Pao*, Dec. 27, 2000, p. A8, in FBIS: CPP20001227000079.

[29] For the PRC abhorrence to Lee, see Suisheng Zhao, "Taiwan: From Peaceful Offense to Coercive Strategy," in Yong Deng and Fei-ling Wang, eds., *In the Eyes of the Dragon: China Views the World* (Boulder, CO: Rowman & Littlefield, 1999), pp. 221–6.

[30] "Premier Wen Calls for Win-Win Development Path for Asia," *People's Daily* (Internet), at http://fpeng.peopledaily.com.cn/200311/02/print20031102_127404.html; Fu Ying, "China and Asia in a New Era," *China: An International Journal*, vol. 1, no. 2 (Sept. 2003), pp. 304–12.

success, but it has by no means obviated regional concerns over the rapidly growing Chinese power and influence. While most of the neighboring countries do not want to balance against the PRC, they do strive to maintain what former Prime Minister of Singapore Goh Chok Tong called "harmonious balance," whereby an externally restrained China cannot throw its weight around.[31] The PRC would thus forfeit much of its diplomatic gains, should it resort to unilateralism, violence-prone foreign policy, and impatience with the status quo.

No Asian country publicly denounced the PRC missile firings in 1995–96. But as documented by Allen Whiting, the crisis did raise serious questions regarding China's regional role among the strategic analysts and planners throughout the region.[32] While the official positions of regional states on Taiwan have in principle remained unchanged, these governments inevitably would gauge China's strategic choice through its handling of Taiwan. As such, the issue has become more of a regional one, rather than simply China's domestic affair. And China's responses have become more of a signifier of its strategic posture than simply an isolated event. In fact, the PRC has itself conceded that the Taiwan issue impinges on regional security, although it insists peace across the Strait can only be predicated upon the maintenance of "one China." And Beijing has blamed its threat of war on Taipei's provocations. The purpose is to simultaneously minimize the diplomatic cost of its coercive measures and add pressure on Taipei. Chinese leaders are acutely aware that a PRC military attack on Taiwan would cancel out the many important, but by no means secured, gains it has made in its regional diplomacy.

Taiwan Independence: The Unacceptable Costs

The PRC status predicament has been closely tied to its Taiwan conundrum. Its international isolation in the aftermath of the Tiananmen incident and the end of the cold war coincided with the growing assertions of Taiwan's separate identity. The same democratic value

---

[31] Zuraidah Ibrahim, "Singapore's Goh Urges U.S. to Get More Involved in East Asian Region," *Straits Times*, May 9, 2003, in Open Source Center: SEP20030509000011.

[32] See Allen S. Whiting, "ASEAN Eyes China: The Security Dimension," *Asian Survey*, vol. 37, no. 4 (April 1997), pp. 299–322.

that helped relegate China to an inferior status was responsible for providing Taiwan with a new *raison d'être* as an independent entity. Just as Israel has promoted its special bond with the United States based on its liberal democratic identity distinctive from other Arab countries in the Middle East,[33] so, too, did Taiwan capitalize on its democratic achievements to gain international respect and support in its controversy with mainland China.[34] The PRC military threat against Taiwan independence in turn hardened the boundaries separating it from the security community of established great powers.

As the PRC pursues its great-power recognition in earnest, Taiwan is ascribed such substantive and symbolic values by the Chinese elites that their nation's rise is simply unimaginable with a formal loss of Taiwan.[35] As the influential Chinese scholar Wang Jisi observed, "[T]here is the notion among many Chinese that the revival of the Chinese nation would not be meaningful and real if the mainland failed to achieve reunification with Taiwan."[36] Yan Xuetong, director of the Institute of International Studies of Tsinghua University, is more forthright. Having laid out the devastating costs of Taiwan independence, he concludes, "If China lacks the ability to preserve national unity, it cannot rise to be a world power, nor can it achieve

---

[33] On the case of Israel, see Michael Barnett, "Identity and Alliance in the Middle East," in Peter Katzenstein, ed., *The Culture of National Security: Norms and Identity in World Politics* (New York: Columbia University Press, 1996), pp. 400–47. On Taiwan's sovereignty claim based on democracy, see Richard A. Madsen, "The Struggle for Sovereignty Between China and Taiwan," in Stephen D. Krasner, ed., *Problematic Sovereignty: Contested Rules and Political Possibilities* (New York: Columbia University Press, 2001), pp. 141–93; Jacques de Lisle, "The Chinese Puzzle of Taiwan's Status," *Orbis*, Winter 2000, pp. 35–62.

[34] See Ministry of Foreign Affairs of the Republic of China, "Our Position on China's Rise," Dec. 27, 2005, in FBIS: CPP20051227312007.

[35] See Thomas J. Christensen, "Posing Problems Without Catching Up: China's Rise and Challenges for U.S. Security Policy," *International Security* vol. 25, no. 4 (Winter/Spring, 2000/1), pp. 5–40; Suisheng Zhao, ed., *Across the Taiwan Strait: Mainland China, Taiwan, and the 1995–1996 Crisis* (New York: Routledge, 1999).

[36] Jisi Wang, "China's Changing Role in Asia" (Atlantic Council of the United States, 2004), at http://www.acus.org/Publications/occasionalpapers/Asia/WangJisi_Jan_04.pdf, p. 12. See also Zhang Wenmu, "Yatai Diyuan Zhengzhi Yu Taiwan Wenti" [The Geo-Political Landscape in the Asia-Pacific and the Taiwan Issue], *Zhongguo Gaige* [China's Reform], no. 12 (2003), reprinted at http://www.irchina.org/news/view.asp?id=327.

national rejuvenation."[37] Subtly or bluntly stated, these sentiments are widely shared with rather deep conviction by Chinese leaders and analysts alike. Thus, they have explicitly labeled preventing Taiwan's *de jure* independence as China's "core interest" (*Hexin Liyi*). Even moderates, while urging caution in handling the issue, do not see less significance than their more hawkish counterparts in preventing a formal severance of Taiwan from its motherland. Taiwan independence, argues China's liberal international relations scholar Wang Yizhou, would incite separatism and domestic chaos, thereby threatening the viability of the central government. Having experienced the worst victimization during the century after the Opium War, the loss of Taiwan would be a psychological blow that the Chinese nation could not endure.[38]

Outside observers may dismiss these views as nationalist myths propagated by the CCP government. But there is little doubt that the contemporary Chinese elites do believe that the loss of Taiwan would disrupt the social stability, national unity, and international environment essential for China's great-power aspirations. They share the conviction that "a weak China means the loss of Taiwan; a strong China means Taiwan's return."[39] And the immediate task is to prevent Taiwan's independence. This concern explains the quick end to the debate over China's "peaceful rise" from late 2003 to mid-2004. Initially propounded as a strategic choice under the new Hu-Wen leadership, the idea was soon questioned, as the pro-independence movement seemed to gain momentum when Taiwan was gearing up for the presidential

---

[37] Yan Xuetong, "The Pros and Cons of Using Force to Constrain Law-Based Taiwan Independence," *Zhanlue Yu Guanli*, no. 3 (May 2004), pp. 1–5, in FBIS: CPP20040702000233.

[38] Wang Yizhou, *Tanxun Quanqiu Zhuyi Guoji Guanxi* [Exploring Globalist International Relations] (Beijing: Beijing University Press, 2005), pp. 344–5. See also Qingguo Jia, "Beijing and Taipei: Between a Rock and a Hard Place," in Muthiah Alagappa, ed., *Taiwan's Presidential Politics: Democratization and Cross-Strait Relations in the Twentieth-First Century* (Armonk, NY: M. E. Sharpe, 2001), ch. 6.

[39] Huang Jiashu and Zheng Gugu, "Zhonghua Minzu Youshuai Dao Xing De Lishi Zhuanzhe" [The Historical Shift from Decline to Revival of the Chinese Nation], *RMRB*, Aug. 17, 2005, p. 3. For why China's rise cannot tolerate Taiwan independence, see Yan Xuetong, "The Pros and Cons of Using Force to Constrain Law-Based Taiwan Independence;" Ma Hao-liang: "Five Reasons Why 'Taiwan Independence' Can Not Be Allowed," *Hong Kong Ta Kung Pao* (Internet), March 24, 2004, in FBIS: CPP20040324000109.

election. Largely due to its ostensive inability to effectively address the Taiwan problem, "peaceful rise" was no longer officially advocated as a strategic choice by the CCP leadership.

For the Chinese, how other countries approach the Taiwan issue becomes a touchstone of their fundamental attitude toward the PRC. The competitive turns in the Sino-Japanese relationship after the mid-1990s all had to do with what they perceived to be stepped-up Japanese interference in the Taiwan affairs. The Chinese suspicion of American intentions is rooted in a strong belief that the United States plays the "Taiwan card" to constrain China. Through this prism, the U.S. support of Taiwan is viewed as marking its strategic mistrust toward the PRC. Conversely, greater U.S. respect of the PRC's one-China policy is regarded as greater U.S. acceptance of China's rise. As such, the PRC was very optimistic about its international status in 1997–98 due in no small part to President Clinton's "three no's" statement, pledging that the United States would not support the separation of Taiwan from China or Taiwan's representation in international organizations that could confer on it formal sovereignty.[40] By no means a major departure from previous U.S. policy, the statement – which was made against the backdrop of the short-lived U.S.-China "strategic partnership" and cooperation in dealing with the South Asian nuclear proliferation crisis – signaled a substantive recognition of China's interest in Taiwan.[41]

The corollary of such a conception of Taiwan's role is that China's rise may not be predicated upon actual reunification, but it would be unimaginable with the island being forcefully taken away. Securing the one-China–oriented status quo across the Strait thus becomes *sine qua non* and a litmus test of China's great-power recognition. To that end, the PRC has relied heavily on military deterrence and diplomatic isolation, but now it has complemented that with policy adjustments

[40] The verbatim "Three No's" assurance to Beijing is as follows: "We don't support independence for Taiwan or two Chinas or one Taiwan, one China. And we don't believe that Taiwan should be in membership in any organization for which statehood is a requirement." Quote from Robert L. Suettinger, *Beyond Tiananmen: The Politics of U.S.-China Relations, 1989–2000* (Washington, DC: Brookings Institution Press, 2003), p. 348.

[41] Richard C. Bush offers a concise explanation of the statement's continuity with previous U.S. policy in his *At Cross Purposes: U.S.-Taiwan Relations since 1942* (Armonk, NY: M. E. Sharpe, 2004), pp. 231–2.

designed to bring its growing power and influence to bear on cross-Strait developments.

Deterrence under Globalization

The *use* of force may be Beijing's last resort, but the *threat* of war is not. These calculations were revealed by the late Chinese leader Deng Xiaoping, who stated, "We strive for a peaceful solution to the Taiwan issue, but would never rule out the option of force. We cannot make such a promise. What if the Taiwan regime never negotiates with us, what shall we do? Could it be said that we should then give up national reunification? We must remember this. Our next generation must remember this. This is a strategic consideration."[42] The post-Deng generations of Chinese leadership have clearly followed Deng's advice. Through much of the 1990s, Beijing placed its hope on military deterrence, cross-Strait interdependence, and China's own economic growth in dealing with the Taiwan issue. The CCP leadership's belief in the efficacy of the threat of war led to the missile crisis of 1995–96. Its confidence in the economic instrument was made clear by Liu Ji, a close adviser to President Jiang Zemin, who wrote in 1998, "When the economy of mainland China comes close to, equal to, or surpasses the level of Taiwan, there will be no need for negotiation – the issue will be settled naturally."[43]

The PRC's relative complacency was shattered with the successful bid for Taiwanese presidency in 2000 by the pro-independence DPP president, Chen Shui-bian. The support to Taiwan offered by the newly inaugurated Bush, Jr. administration further raised the worst Chinese fear about Taiwan's attempt to formalize its independence over the next few years. The events surrounding the 2004 presidential election in Taiwan underscored the real danger of an imminent clash between China's strategy of peaceful rise and Taiwan independence. Reflecting Beijing's growing sense of urgency, a report by the CCP Propaganda Department in January 2004 warned that the development of both

[42] Office of Taiwan Affairs of the Chinese Communist Party Central Committee and Taiwan Affairs Office of the State Council, *China's Taiwan Problem*, p. 84.
[43] Liu Ji, "Making the Right Choices in Twenty-First Century Sino-American Relations," *Journal of Contemporary China*, vol. 7, no. 17 (March 1998), p. 97.

"positive and negative factors regarding the Taiwan issue are accelerating. The historical process of resolving the Taiwan issue is already approaching a critical period."[44]

Compounding Beijing's anxiety was Chen's winning of his second term of the presidency, albeit by a hair-thin margin and under dubious circumstances surrounding a mysterious shooting incident on the eve of the election. In his inaugural address in March 2004, President Chen acknowledged that the PRC had "chosen peaceful emergence as its keynote for developing international ties."[45] This, however, did nothing to assuage the PRC fear that Chen and his pro-independence supporters might be tempted to take advantage of China's emphasis on peaceful development to promote Taiwan independence. Chen's subsequent, repeated warnings of China's military threats only reinforced Beijing's mistrust.

For the CCP leadership, these developments showed that the instrument of military deterrence proved essential but also inept in maintaining a stable one-China–oriented status quo. According to Thomas Schelling, deterrence is for the initiator "to turn aside and discourage through fear; hence, to prevent from action by fear of consequences."[46] With effective deterrence, one should expect little change in the stalemated conflict, much less change in favor of the target party. With regard to cross-Strait relations, Beijing was frustrated by its inability to prevent the many pro-independence changes initiated by Taiwan. The PRC often felt it had lost the initiative in defining the status quo. China's emphasis on a responsible rise, the age of globalization, and Taiwan's democratization have introduced factors that inherently destabilize deterrence. The likely military interventions of the third parties also undercut the credibility of the PRC deterrence vis-à-vis Taiwan independence.

[44] Zhong Wen, "Chen Shui-bian Yao 2008 Jianguo, Jiejue Taiwan Wenti Bijin Guanjianqi" [With Chen Shui-bian Seeking to Create a Separate State in 2008, Resolution of the Taiwan Issue Is Approaching the Critical Period], *People's Daily* (Internet), at http://www.people.com.cn/GB/shizheng/1025/2309970.html, p. 3.

[45] The full text of Chen Shui-bian's speech is printed at Taipei Public Television Service Foundation, May 20, 2004, in FBIS: CPP20040520000073.

[46] Thomas C. Schelling, *Arms and Influence* (New Haven, CT: Yale University Press, 1966), p. 71.

As we argued earlier, when contemplating the use of force, the grave consequences of China's belligerency are such that the highly security-conscious CCP leadership would be forced to carefully weigh both diplomatic costs as well as the military outcome on the battlefield. In the age of globalization, the all-round costs of a war on China's foreign relations are so credible as to caution the CCP leadership against any rash decision. As Thomas Schelling also argued decades ago, even within a context where the ability for two adversaries to cause equitable, mutual harms does not exist, such "fear of the consequences" can prevent the strong from attacking the weak.[47] This, in turn, inevitably raises doubts about China's deterrence credibility.

High interdependence across the Taiwan Strait, buttressed by myriad commercial and social ties, has made it impossible to sustain an environment of pervasive fear necessary for the credibility of a military threat. During 1979–2006, cross-Strait trade enjoyed spectacular growth, accumulating over U.S.$600 billion, and in 2006 alone bilateral trade topped U.S.$100 billion. After 1987, Taiwanese businesses poured a huge sum of financial resources into mainland China, with actual and contracted investments reaching, respectively, over $44 billion and $100 billion by 2006. During the past two decades or so, personnel exchanges in the form of cross-Strait travels had reached a similarly spectacular level. In 2006, the Taiwanese paid over 4.4 million visits to China, while the mainland residents made over 200,000 trips across the Strait. By the end of 2005, over 600,000 Taiwanese businessmen and -women had investment in mainland China, and about half a million Taiwanese had established residence in Shanghai and its adjacent areas.[48] The level of economic integration between Taiwan and Shanghai is probably higher than that between any two Chinese provinces. Such integrative dynamics inevitably complicate Beijing's scare tactics.

---

[47] Schelling, *Arms and Influence*, p. 36.

[48] The data in this paragraph are from Sun Zhaohui, "Liangan Shixian 'Santong' Haiyou Duoyuan" [How Much Longer Will It Take to Realize the "Three Links" Across the Straits?], *RMRB*, April 6, 2007, p. 3; Li Weina and Hua Xiaohong, "Jingmao Jiaoliu Geiliangan Dailai Jihui" [Cross-Straits Commerce Brings About Opportunities for Both Sides], *RMRB*, April 21, 2006, p. 3; Pan Qing, "Dalu Taishang: Congliye Dao Anjia" [Taiwanese Businessmen in Mainland China: From Establishing Business to Residence], *RMRB*, Dec. 10, 2005, p. 1; Liu Hong, "Bawo Quanju Gaowu Jianling" [Grasp the Overall Situation, Gain Strategic Advantage], *RMRB*, April 26, 2006, p. 3.

Besides, domestic politics on both sides have generated dynamics marring stable deterrence. The competitive political system, pluralistic society, and identity politics in Taiwan often lead to profound internal disagreements over how to interpret and respond to the mainland Chinese military threat. While China's one-party system allows it to speak in one voice, the same system may also undercut the credibility of its threat. With independent institutions, democracies enjoy certain advantages when it comes to credibly signal resolve. Not following through with his or her warnings to the enemy is politically too costly for a popularly elected leader, particularly when the opposition and the public openly back the posturing. Without solid institutions and independent public opinion, explains Kenneth Schultz, "The problems faced by nondemocratic leaders is not that their threats generate no political risks but rather that the political risks generated by their threats are not obvious to outsiders."[49] Indeed, many politicians in Taiwan have dismissed repeated warnings by the mainland Chinese leadership as mere bluffing. Inadequate institutionally based Chinese decision making might also have inclined certain politicians in Taiwan to interpret the mainland's positions as always negotiable and subject to further compromise.

While the PRC has struggled to maintain its deterrence credibility under globalization, it also failed to offer Taiwan an attractive package for reunification. Through the 1980s and 1990s, Beijing insisted on the formula of "One China, Two Systems." But Taiwan has no interest in being treated as less than an equal, much less a subordinate region, regardless of how much more autonomy than post-1997 Hong Kong it was offered. "Communist China has made some adjustment to the size of its cage," Lin Chong-pin, then vice-chairman of the Mainland Affairs Council of Taiwan's Executive Yuan flatly rejected the one country, two systems scheme in 2000, "Why would the Taiwanese people, who have enjoyed full freedom and democracy, want to enter the cage?"[50] Lin's question was not merely rhetorical. Rather, it underscores the futility of dictating the terms of cross-Strait relations

---

[49] Kenneth Schultz, *Democracy and Coercive Diplomacy* (New York: Cambridge University Press, 2001), quote on p. 18.

[50] Quoted in "Chinese Fireworks," *Far Eastern Economic Review*, Feb. 10, 2000, p. 17. Similar official argument is expressed in Lee Teng-hui, "Understanding Taiwan: Bridging the Perception Gap," *Foreign Affairs*, vol. 78, no. 6 (Nov./Dec. 1999), pp. 9–14.

through a declared, preset outcome on Taiwan in mainland China's policy.

Policy Adjustments in the New Century

For the Chinese leaders, forced unification is too costly now, and resistance to Taiwan's return would eventually dissipate when their country fully attains its great-power status. In the interim, however, the PRC needed to gain the initiative in maintaining the one-China–oriented status quo across the Strait. Realizing the ineptitude of its previous approach, the fourth generation of the CCP leadership under President Hu Jintao and Premier Wen Jiabao has adopted a new policy package on Taiwan, designed in the words of the Beijing based think tank analyst Peng Weixue to make "the soft side even softer, the hard side even harder."[51] The two-pronged strategy is to deny and roll back Taiwan's sovereignty claim and support, on the one hand, and on the other hand to more proactively influence the trends in Taiwan in order to undermine the independence momentum.

The PRC has continued its stiff opposition to any step that confers upon Taiwan sovereignty in the international arena. It did not even relent in its campaign to deny Taiwan's representation in the World Health Organization at the height of the SARS crisis in 2003. Originating in late 2002 or earlier in southern China, the epidemic quickly spread to over thirty countries, as well as to Beijing and other Chinese cities, due to belated government action and a lack of transparency. By June 6, 2003, according to the WHO, 8,404 people had been infected, with 779 deaths. Mainland China, Hong Kong, and Taiwan were the hardest hit, with fatalities numbering, respectively, 228, 286, and 81.[52] Against the backdrop of the looming SARS scare, Taipei made yet another bid for observer status at the fifty-sixth World Health Assembly (WHA) in Geneva, the annual WHO conference, during May 19–28, 2003. Even though Taipei had previously made six aborted attempts, the SARS crisis seemed to have strengthened its case

---

[51] Yao Xiaoming and Peng Weixue, "2005 Lianganguanxi: Xinsiwei Kaiqi Xinqianjing" [Cross-Straits Relations in 2005: New Thinking Opens New Prospects], *RMRB*, Dec. 23, 2005, p. 3.

[52] Global SARS Information System, Institute of Remote Sensing Applications, Chinese Academy of Sciences, Beijing, at http://www.digitalearth.net.cn/globesars/ (accessed June 16, 2003).

Table 8.1. *The Three Parties in the Taiwan Issue (2003–)*

United States	Mainland China	Taiwan
One-China Policy	One-China Principle	De facto Independence to *de jure* Independence?
TRA and Three Communiqués	**Toward Taiwan and the U.S.** Coercive Defense of Sovereignty Claim: • Threat of willingness to pay any price to stop Taiwan Independence • Military deterrence • Antisecession law • Diplomatic isolation	**Party Politics** • DPP striving for independence • KMT open to one China – but not now • Shared strong democratic and Taiwanese identity
Opposes Unilateral Change to the Status Quo	**Toward Taiwan** Proactive, Multilevel Engagement to Strengthen Support for One-China–oriented Status Quo	**The Public*** • Large population holds Taiwanese national identity – but slightly larger population holds a national identity inclusive of both Taiwanese-ness and Chinese-ness • Little to no interest in formal unification • Consensus support for the status quo of Taiwan's de facto independence and in favor of beneficial ties with mainland
	Toward the U.S. • Opposition to TRA-based support to Taiwan • Calls for adherence to three communiqués • Reliance on U.S. assistance to rein in Taiwan Independence	

* See Shelley Rigger, *Taiwan's Rising Rationalism: Generations, Politics, and "Taiwanese Nationalism"* (Washington, DC: East-West Center, 2006); Yun-han Chu and Andrew Nathan, "Seizing the Opportunity for Change in the Taiwan Strait," *Washington Quarterly*, vo. 31, no. 1 (Winter 2007–08), pp. 77–91.

enough to produce a different outcome this time around. The spread of the epidemic could be blamed on Beijing's initial mishandling, thus putting the PRC on the defensive. Moreover, as a hardest hit victim, Taiwan had suffered a humanitarian disaster from SARS. Indeed, to mobilize international support, Taiwanese officials compared Taiwan's exclusion from the WHO to "medical apartheid."[53]

Yet, under heavy-handed pressure from Wu Yi, then the vice-premier and newly appointed minister of health, and other Chinese officials, the WHA turned down the motion to consider Taiwan's membership bid on May 19. Emotions over the rejection ran high in Taiwan and were fueled by domestic politics, as political parties started to position themselves for the upcoming presidential election in 2004. Taipei was wounded and enraged by Beijing's bullying tactics. Immediately after the WHO rejection, President Chen Sui-bian threatened to call a national referendum on Taiwan's WHO membership bid. Taipei also turned down Beijing's offer of medical assistance. Officials of the ruling DPP attacked Beijing's callousness and indifference to the well-being of the Taiwanese people. Vice-President Annette Lu lashed out at Beijing's mishandling of the SARS crisis, laying the blame for the spread of the epidemic squarely on the irresponsible mainland government. She called on Beijing to openly apologize to the thirty-three SARS-stricken countries.

The PRC officials were enraged that Taipei would take advantage of their misfortune to promote a separatist agenda by defaming China and politicizing a public health disaster. They maintained that China had not obstructed any international assistance to Taiwan. On the contrary, the mainland compatriots extended great sympathy and support to the Taiwanese people in their fight against SARS in the spirit of "blood is thicker than water." For Beijing, supported by pro-independence forces in Taiwan and abroad, Taipei's bid to join the WHO was nothing but a pretext to legitimize its independence and pave the way for UN membership. The WHO episode underscores the continuity in the PRC's determination to deny Taiwan's search for greater international representation. Such a zero-sum notion of sovereignty over Taiwan had earlier led the PRC to twice exercise its veto power at the UN Security Council, an act it has rarely done in

---

[53] Donald G. McNeil, Jr., "SARS Furor Heightens Taiwan-China Rift," *New York Times*, May 19, 2003.

the international body since 1971. Specifically, Beijing blocked the UN peace missions in Guatemala and Macedonia, respectively, in 1997 and 1999, because of the two countries' diplomatic ties with Taiwan.[54]

To boost the credibility of a military threat, Chinese officials were more forthright than before about the costs of war they were willing to bear. More importantly, through enacting the antisecession law in March 2005, the PRC resorted to an additional legal instrument to effectively demonstrate its resolve to follow through on its repeated warnings. With this law, according to Xu Bodong, "Once a major event leading to 'Taiwan independence' takes place, mainland Chinese leaders will be held accountable if they don't take decisive and effective measures to stop it."[55] Given the fact that few would like to see a war across the Strait, credible military threat remains integral to Beijing's concerted efforts to rein in the independence momentum in Taiwan.

While laying a legal basis against Taiwan independence, the PRC has stepped up preventative measures to earn goodwill and win support for a "one China" in Taiwan. In several major speeches on Taiwan by the Hu-Wen leadership, the PRC noticeably dropped reference to the "one country, two systems" formula, which has been applied to the former British colony Hong Kong. Instead, they only emphasized one China as the inviolable status quo, which was defined by President Hu Jintao as the following: "Although the two sides are yet to be reunified since 1949, the fact that both the mainland and Taiwan belong to one China has never changed."[56] The policy departure, according to Zhang Nianchi, was characterized by what he dubs "process theory" and "joint creation theory," emphasizing positive interaction without a fixed timetable or unilaterally determined formula for unification.[57]

---

[54] Guo Jiading, "Changreng Nishiguo Ruhe Shishi Foujuequan" [How Do Permanent Members of the UN Security Council Exercise Veto Power?" at http://news.xinhuanet.com/world/2005-06/17/content_3098214.htm (accessed July 7, 2005).

[55] Xu Bodong, "Dalu Tiaozheng Duitai Zhengce Celue" [Mainland China Adjusts Its Taiwan Policy Tactics], *RMRB*, June 14, 2005, p. 3.

[56] "Hu Jintao Tichu Xinxinshixia Fazhan Liangan Guanxi Sidian Yijian" [Hu Jintao Puts Forth a Four-Point Proposal in Developing Cross-Strait Relations under New Situation]," *RMRB*, March 5, 2005, p. 1. This definition is expressed in Article 2 of the Anti-Secession Law, at http://news.xinhuanet.com/english/2005-03/14/content_2694317.htm (accessed March 26, 2005).

[57] Zhang Nianchi, "Taiwan Issue and the Future and Destiny of China."

Allowing the one-China idea enough flexibility for interpretation, the CCP leadership succeeded in orchestrating dialogues with Taiwan's Pan-Blue opposition parties. The consecutive visits to the mainland and meetings with Chinese leaders (2005) by the Pan-Blue opposition leaders Lien Chan of Kuomintang (KMT), James Soong of the People First Party (PFP), and Yok Mu-ming of the New Party no doubt represented a landmark event in cross-Strait relations. The visits paved the way for extensive, ongoing exchanges between the CCP and Taiwan's main opposition parties under the idea of one China. Seizing the commemoration of the sixtieth anniversary of the end of World War II to promote a brand of greater-China nationalism, Chinese leaders and analysts showed unprecedented generosity in giving the Nationalists credit for defeating the Japanese in the anti-Japanese war (1937–45). The motive was to emphasize the common bond forged in their nationalist struggle between the CCP, on the one hand, and the KMT and its splinter parties, on the other.[58]

These historical breakthroughs, coupled with the PRC's goodwill gestures – like its offer of two giant pandas as a gift (which was declined by the DPP government) and concessions on a number of functional issues, such as direct cross-Strait flights, mainlander tours to Taiwan, and Taiwan's agricultural exports to the Chinese markets – helped cast a positive light on the mainland among the Taiwanese public. The developments in 2005 reenergized the KMT in terms of both its commitment to the one-China idea and its competition with the ruling DPP in domestic party politics. As regards their effect on cross-Strait relations, these events helped delegitimize independence claims in Taiwan, while at the same time they raised the possibility of positive interactions across the Strait without formally severing Taiwan's ties with China.

In the international arena, the PRC applied its growing influence abroad to elicit support for its Taiwan policy. At the height of the plebiscite controversies in 2003–04, Beijing managed to secure quite explicit statements from President Vladimir Putin of Russia, Chancellor Gerhard Schroeder of Germany, and President Jacques Chirac of France opposing Taiwan's referendums on cross-Strait relations. Most

---

[58] See, for example, Xin Qi, "Hongyang Kangzhan Jingshen, Zhuiqiu Tongyi Fuqiang" [Raising the Spirit of the Anti-Japanese War, Pursuing Wealth and Power under Unification], *RMRB*, July 19, 2005.

notably, the Hu-Wen leadership calibrated China's America policy such that they were able to secure an unprecedented, if still uneasy synergy, with the United States in reining in President Chen's unilateral provocations, including the referendums and attempts at constitutional revisions on the island that would formalize Taiwan's de facto independence.[59] Out of its own "one China" policy, the United States simply did not want to see an escalation of the cross-Strait crisis. Thus when President Chen decided to attach a referendum on the island's bid for UN membership in the name of Taiwan to the 2008 presidential election, the U.S. officials issued pointed criticisms, although they stressed American interest in seeing a "strong" Taiwan, not least in terms of its military capabilities.[60]

To deepen international support for the one-China–oriented status quo across the Taiwan Strait, the PRC has acknowledged Taiwan's importance to regional stability, but at the same time it has equated Taiwan's independence-motivated "provocations" as endangering peace in East Asia.[61] On the one hand, Beijing's recognition of the regional fallout of the Taiwan issue marked a positive change from its long-standing, rigid insistence that Taiwan was purely a Chinese domestic affair. On the other hand, such a notion of peace has enabled Beijing to blame elements of Taiwan independence for the mainland's coercive countermeasures enforced in the name of peace and stability. In this way, Beijing hopes the case for Taiwan independence is undermined while Beijing's notion of a one-China status quo receives greater support.

The mainland Chinese leaders apparently have become heartened by the positive trends in the CCP dialogue with the pan-Blue parties, U.S. opposition to President Chen's attempts to change the status quo, and the overall regional and international dynamics surrounding cross-Strait relationship. Yet there remain heightened angst, as they

[59] Yang Jiemian, *Da Hezuo: Bianhuazhong De Shijie He Zhongguo Guoji Zhan-lue* [Grand Cooperation: The Changing World and China's Global Strategy] (Tianjin: Renmin Chubanshe, 2005), pp. 231, 273.

[60] See the speech by Thomas J. Christensen, Deputy Assistant Secretary of State for East Asian and Pacific Affairs, "A Strong and Moderate Taiwan," Sept. 11, 2007. http://www.state.gov/p/eap/rls/rm/2007/91979.htm (accessed Jan. 14, 2008).

[61] Tang Jiaxuan, "Liangan Tongbao Tuanjie Qilai, Gongtong Wei Zuguo Tongyi Er Nulifendou" [United: Compatriots of the Two Sides of the Strait to Jointly Struggle for the Reunification of Our Motherland), *RMRB*, Jan. 20, 2004, p. 5.

still judge the U.S. policy to be "double-faced," with a continued over-riding goal to constrain China. Prior to the presidential election in 2008, Chinese analysts were also worried over the time-tested DPP electoral tactics of pushing for de-Sinification and *de jure* independence to "uproot" and delegitimize the KMT.[62] But in reality KMT has sunk its roots much deeper in Taiwan than the mainland Chinese commentators thought or would like to admit it has and has proven to have built strong base of society-wide support. Rather than blaming the party politics in Taiwan, mainland China would be better advised to think hard regarding how its own actions may contribute to developments on the island counterproductive to its objectives.

The policy initiatives adopted by the Hu-Wen leadership have effectively laid down the mainland's bottom-line positions for the next ten to fifteen years. The PRC will continue its conscientiously constructed efforts to gain initiative and control over the inherently intractable Taiwan issue. It will not let up its campaign to undercut the momentum for Taiwan independence, while at the same time it will expand cross-Strait ties. Such an all-round, well-coordinated approach may fuel the fear in certain quarters in Taiwan that China's status gains will come at the expense of Taiwan's existential interests. Should the island's domestic politics mobilize such a zero-sum notion to prevail in Taiwan, Beijing's new plan will backfire. Of course, the PRC has not been the paragon of rational decision making when it comes to its Taiwan policy. And Taiwan's struggle for national identity is intimately tied to the unsettled international politics surrounding China's rise. Thus, we will likely see no calm in cross-Strait relations and managing the issue will remain a critical test for China's international relations.

---

[62] Liu Hong, "'Fali Duli' Mengnan Chengzhen" ["De Jure Independence" is an Empty Dream), *RMRB*, March 21, 2007, p. 3; Guo Zhenyuan, interviewed by Xu Lei, "2006: Gengjia Fuza De Meitai Guanxi" [2006: U.S.-Taiwan Relations Get More Complicated], *RMRB*, Dec. 26, 2006, p. 3; Liu Hong, "Yingxiang Taiwan Zhengju Sida Jiaodian" [Four Focal Points Influencing Taiwan's Politics], *RMRB*, Jan. 25, 2007, p. 3; Li Jiaquan, "Minjindang Zhengquan De 'Paogeng' Zhanshu" [The DDP Regime's Uprooting Tactic], *RMRB*, Feb. 13, 207, p. 3

9 | *China's Foreign Relations and the Emerging Great-Power Politics*

After the cold war, Chinese leaders chose a foreign policy course that recognizes the unique set of constraints and opportunities in world politics characterized by an authority structure centered on U.S. hegemony *and* an open, contested great-power politics embedded in globalization. This path of quest for great-power status sets it apart from both the predominant patterns of Chinese foreign policy in the previous eras and traditional great-power politics as posited by mainstream international relations (IR) theories. Focusing on China's foreign policy paradigm in the post–cold war era, this study joins the growing literature taking note of the striking absence of a balance of power in current world politics.[1] It further shows how a reconfigured national identity and interest conception has characterized the PRC's struggle to gain control over cross-Strait relations, extend its influence beyond Asia, and ultimately move from the periphery to the center stage in regional and world politics. In investigating the international politics surrounding China's rise, we also hope to illuminate some emerging dynamics of great-power politics.

China in the World: An Uphill Struggle

In the aftermath of the cold war, Chinese political elites quickly realized their country's foreign policy challenge did not just derive from its material weakness but also from its disadvantaged position in the newly emerging world order. Relegated to a pariah status after

---

[1] See, for example, Ethan Kapstein and Michael Mastanduno, eds., *Unipolar Politics: Realism and State Strategies after the Cold War* (New York: Columbia University Press, 1999); G. John Ikenberry, ed., *America Unrivalled: The Future of the Balance of Power* (Ithaca, NY: Cornell University Press, 2002); T. V. Paul, James J. Wirtz, and Michel Fortmann, eds., *Balance of Power: Theory and Practice in the 21st Century* (Stanford, CA: Stanford University Press, 2004).

the Tiananmen crisis in 1989, the PRC was largely excluded from the restructuring of the world order. The Chinese Communist Party (CCP) leadership soon regained control at home and began to reengage the world. But it found itself confronted with a Western-dominated international hierarchy that promoted democratic value, the idea of a market economy, and great-power responsibility in global management. As China started to experience spectacular growth in its economy, its original outsider status continued to haunt the country's foreign policy, such that it risked being treated as an even more destabilizing "other" to the regional and international status quo.

Meanwhile, notwithstanding their wishful thinking regarding the imminent onset of multipolarity in the early 1990s, Chinese leaders quickly grasped the inescapable reality of the firm hold that the United States had over the world. While dismayed at the disadvantage their country had to endure under such an arrangement, they were at the same time encouraged by the predominant engagement policy the United States and other established powers had adopted. Moreover, just as the dominant interests in Chinese society are closely tied to the globalized world, so is the domestic legitimacy of the CCP party-state inextricably linked to the respect that China receives in international society. An understanding by the Chinese elites of world politics in terms of a fairly durable hierarchy, coupled with the engagement policy by the United States and other great powers, and China's continued embrace of reforms and globalization, spurred a simultaneous Chinese pursuit of both material power and positive recognition in world politics.

The illiberal Chinese polity as manifested in the human rights issue has justified its separate treatment by the established Western powers. To the extent that the rights-respecting great-power community considers human rights as a standard for setting boundaries between the in-group and the out-group, international scrutiny of China's record in this area becomes a political barrier to China's aspirations abroad. In response, Beijing has rejected such political discrimination. It has also tried to remedy its vulnerability through self-paced compliance, whilst at the same time fiercely contesting both the role of the universal standard and its content to minimize its drawbacks. For the sake of social stability and the security of the CCP-state, Chinese leadership has no interest in narrowing the gap between China and the international human rights regime, insofar as it is viewed as the imposition of Western values. Thus, the issue has continued to be an obstacle in achieving China's diplomatic standing. It may not be on the forefront in China's foreign relations, but it is always present as a constitutive principle of world politics. It was invariably invoked whenever at issue were landmark events that would signify status acceptance to the PRC.

Compared to human rights, a more direct and pervasive problem for China's foreign relations are the so-called China threat theories – namely, various forms of foreign attributions to China of a destabilizing and malign character. Realizing that the dynamic of an image formation of threat, if not reversed, could harden its image as a dangerous outsider and invite united anti-China containment, decision makers in Beijing took pains to address the "fear factor" through rhetorical reassurances, such as the notion of "peaceful rise" and "responsible power," and corresponding diplomatic initiatives designed for confidence building regarding its international future. Despite success in the PRC's diplomacy, the alleged China threat has mutated in various ways with China's growing influence abroad. To the extent that the negative reputation threatens to deny the right of a Chinese renaissance, China views its persistence with a heightened sense of vulnerability, nationalism, and power politics. But overall, the PRC has proven adaptable in its rhetorical and policy responses. As the world's fastest growing power has become the focal point of power transition concerns, the PRC has become even more intent on removing the justifications for targeted suspicion and hostile balancing.

In its struggle to realign international relations, the PRC first found a strategic partner in Moscow, when post-Soviet Russia's fast-track domestic transition was derailed and its political elites felt rejected by the West in the early 1990s. For many Russian political and intellectual elites, the NATO expansion, more than anything else, symbolized Western exclusion and mistrust. Strategic partnership with China helped Russia to focus on addressing domestic economic woes and institutional weaknesses, reduce security vulnerabilities in the East, and enhance its overall international leverage. The two outliers in the post–cold war great-power politics needed mutual support to achieve their daunting self-strengthening agendas at home. At present, neither country sees this partnership as a realistic or desirable bloc, alternative to the West. Rather, both see it as essential in strengthening their hands in dealing with the West, securing strategic space, and effecting necessary changes to what they believe to be discriminatory international arrangements. China's strategic partnerships with the EU and India came at the beginning of the twenty-first century. These partnerships are undergirded by various degrees of the member states' discontent with their places under the U.S. hegemony, and more importantly they signal political goodwill between China and the partner states amidst many unresolved bilateral issues. They also differ in origin and intensity. China and Russia have pursued parallel, if not well-coordinated, strategic preferences, whereas Sino-EU and Sino-India strategic partnerships are focused on bilateral ties. Each dyad is characterized by a varying combination of cooperation and competition, limiting its ability to jointly promote change in world politics. Neither China nor any of its partners see its international future as fundamentally lying in these partnerships.

In contrast to the headway China has made with other major powers, its relationship with Japan seemed to be deadlocked in mutual denial of status recognition. In the aftermath of the Tiananmen crisis, Japan was instrumental in facilitating China's reemergence in world politics. However, China's meteoric rise pushed the historically unresolved issue of regional leadership to the fore. In a nutshell, from the Chinese perspective, Japan has attempted to impede China's rise. Tokyo has thus played the role of a barrier to China's regional and global aspirations, most notably by spreading the fear of a China threat and allying itself closely with the United States to contain China. The PRC, in turn, refused to recognize Japan's aspirations to become a more fully developed political and military power. Japan is a step behind the United States in terms of policies designed to constrain the PRC, yet it seems to have borne the brunt of the impact of China's rise. The past *modus vivendi* can no longer hold. But the two countries have yet to find a stable framework that effectively addresses the economic and strategic interdependence that is critically important for both.

The state of the Sino-Japanese relationship underscores the difficulties and uncertainties in both China's great-power diplomacy and its role in Asia. To mold regional affairs to its own liking, the PRC has found multilateral diplomacy to be an efficacious tool. Northeast Asia is the most unsettled and unsettling region. Beijing seized the multilateral initiatives, particularly the Six-Party Talks over the North

Korean nuclear crisis to prevent war and influence events on the Korean peninsula in line with its own vision of the regional order. Given the long tradition of regionalist ideas promoted by the Association for Southeast Asian Nations and the ASEAN receptivity to China's rise, the PRC has opted to work with these regional states in influencing multilateral endeavors. Building on its initial cooperative momentum with Central Asian states stemming from joint efforts to enhance border security in the early 1990s, Beijing (together with Moscow) led the way to create the Shanghai Cooperation Organization (SCO) and has since capitalized on it for China's political, security, and economic interests in the region. Overall, China's multilateral diplomacy is marked by attentiveness to the different dynamics in each subregion and an emphasis on showcasing its win-win, growth-oriented, and nonthreatening foreign policy approach. As its interests and influence extend beyond Asia, the PRC has in the past several years stepped up its diplomatic activities in other parts of the developing world, particularly in Africa. As it rediscovers Africa for economic and political interests, the PRC has heavily relied on the Forum on China-Africa Cooperation (FOCAC) Ministerial Conference to promote its ties with Africa as a collectivity and African states individually. These multilateral processes differ in their missions, collective purposes, and institutional strengths. But they all have served China's interests in complementing bilateral ties, facilitating economic diplomacy, and bringing about desirable changes to the regional and global order.

China's multilateral diplomacy has proven effective in undercutting and isolating Taiwan's claim for sovereignty, an issue that presents a uniquely pressing challenge to China's strategy of peacefully contested rise. The island's quest for independence is fundamentally incompatible with China's notion of its own great-power status. Yet China's status conception, which puts a premium on international legitimacy, exacts prohibitive costs on a military solution to the problem. As such, while the "loss" of Taiwan ironically has become even more intolerable with the recent PRC turn toward an overall cooperative diplomacy, the political consequences, let alone the military ones, associated with a unilateral PRC use of force weighs ever more heavily in its Taiwan policy. Globalization destabilizes mainland China's military deterrence, but it also gives it more policy instruments to fortify a one-China–oriented status quo across the Taiwan Strait. The PRC has most recently integrated the Taiwan issue into its great-power strategy in a more focused and proactive fashion than ever before, hoping to minimizing the risk of explosive developments in the cross-Strait relationship that could imperil its broader international aspirations. In this way, the use of force has become the PRC's last resort, but Taiwan has felt the increasing weight of China's rising power brought to bear by the CCP leadership to box in the island's de jure independence.

From our perspective on China's foreign policy after the cold war, we see a world politics as totally different from that viewed by Kenneth Waltz, who contends, "States are differently placed by their power," and nothing else. If Waltz and other realists were right in attributing such "functional alikeness" to states,[2] the PRC would not be in a position to complain about discrimination, nor would it so vigorously promote a culturally "multicolored" world. Neither would it be so concerned about the impact of human rights issues and a China threat image on its foreign relations. Empirically, the predominant pattern of China's foreign policy simply cannot be adequately explained by the balance-of-power proposition, nor have foreign powers reacted to China's rise in the way posited by various brands of realist theory. The country's uphill battle in world politics is characterized by the Chinese leadership's struggle to simultaneously address its myriad domestic weaknesses, maximize benefits of globalization, and increase its power and positive recognition in the world.

With greater power and confidence, China has become increasingly forceful in pursuing its own course of action abroad. However, considering the PRC's foreign policy in its totality in the past twenty or so years, such a dynamic orientation toward the international status quo is more appropriately viewed in terms of Robert Gilpin's manageable path of seeking "changes *in* an international system," as opposed to the other path of forcing "change *of* an international system" that ends in a hegemonic war.[3] Gilpin did not elaborate on whether the former path can last or, if not, when and how it turns into the latter,

---

[2] The classic realist depiction of the world is Kenneth Waltz, *Theory of International Politics* (New York: McGraw-Hill, 1979). On "functional alikeness" of states, see ch. 5; quote on p. 97.

[3] Robert Gilpin, *War and Change in World Politics* (New York: Cambridge University Press, 1981), quotes on p. 208, with emphasis in original.

violent form. The record of post-Tiananmen Chinese foreign relations has shown that they have by no means always been win-win or harmonious, as its leadership has claimed. Rather, they have been rife with crises, setbacks, competition, and uncertainties. Taken together, however, they have shown how in a largely positive interaction between a rising power and the world it is possible to eschew a violent transition in the age of globalization. The country's international trajectory has been developmentally driven and globally oriented. For political, cultural, and strategic reasons, the PRC has insisted on paving its own path abroad, defining responsibilities on its own terms, and has done everything possible to secure that international environment.

International Status and Chinese Nationalism

Insofar as China's notion of international status heightens sensitivity to how the nation is treated abroad, what then are the implications for Chinese nationalism? Such sensitivity can turn Chinese nationalism into a negative force, setting back its cooperative foreign relations. More powerfully, however, it has limited emotional antiforeignism, while at the same time it has led to China's greater confidence and more active participation in world politics.

Perceived Western insults and bullying have fed on complaints about international unfairness, which have created frustrations directed against foreign provocateurs. Most dramatically, these episodes occurred when China lost its bid to host the 2000 Olympic Games; the U.S. Navy dispatched two carrier groups to the vicinity of Taiwan during the 1995–96 cross-Strait crisis; the NATO bombers accidentally struck the Chinese embassy in Belgrade in May 1999; and a U.S. surveillance plane collided with a Chinese fighter jet near Hainan Island in April 2001. Serving as stinging reminders of past Western humiliations, these events invoked anguished fear among the Chinese of a similar historical fate befalling their country during the century following the Opium War (1839–42).[4]

---

[4] Neta C. Crawford, "The Passions in World Politics: Propositions on Emotion and Emotional Relationships," *International Security*, vol. 24, no. 4 (Spring 2000), pp. 134–5; Peter Hayes Gries, *China's New Nationalism: Pride, Politics, and Diplomacy* (Berkeley: University of California Press, 2004).

As the U.S. engagement with the PRC stabilized after the 9/11 events and China felt more confident abroad, the Chinese public has come to view the United States and Sino-American relations with greater coolheadedness, sophistication, and balance.[5] In the meantime, however, Chinese animosities were turned decidedly against Japan. The main reason for this was the perceived Japanese attempts to neutralize the growing Chinese regional and global influence. The fact that the United States has reacted to China's "peaceful rise" with a policy approach that expresses hope of the PRC evolving into "a responsible stakeholder" in a speech by Deputy Secretary of State Robert Zoellick, whereas Japan has propounded no such positive strategic framework, certainly did not improve Chinese perceptions of Japan.

Despite disagreements over the "standards" of great power in contemporary world politics, what has become increasingly clear is that certain long-held Chinese views of the world are not compatible with its international aspirations.[6] To become a great power, the PRC needs to deepen its participation in the world via economic modernization, but more broadly for affirmative recognition abroad. It must display greater confidence and embrace the idea of international responsibility – however contested that idea is. While denouncing the stigmatization of China on human rights grounds and on the basis of China threat theories by prejudiced foreign parties, ultimately the PRC will have to address the question as to what kind of China it wishes the world to *accept*.

It is true that nationalism continues to be a key source of legitimacy for the ruling CCP. This means that the leadership has an abiding interest in promoting a worldview that suggests a persistent threat to the Chinese nation, whose identity boundaries must be clearly demarcated

---

[5] Zhang Chun, "Lengzhanhou Zhongguoren De Meiguaguan: Liange Meiguo, Shanzhong Taidu, yu Zouxiang Lixin" [The Chinese Views on America after the Cold War: Two Americas, Three Attitudes, and Evolution Toward Rationality], *Kaifang Shidai*, no. 3 (2004), at http://www.irchina.org/news/view.asp?id=530 (accessed Aug. 23, 2004); Wang Jisi, "Reflecting on China," *American Interest*, vol. 1, no. 4 (2006), pp. 74–8.

[6] I discuss some of these in Yong Deng, "Escaping the Periphery: China's National Identity in World Politics," in Weixing Hu, Gerald Chan, and Daojiong Zha, eds., *China's International Relations in the 21st Century* (Lanham, MD: University Press of America, 2000), pp. 41–70.

and vigorously defended.[7] Meanwhile, reforms and opening at home also creates an identity abroad that compels the country to adapt to and comply with mainstream global institutions and commonly accepted standards of "good behavior." With the country so deeply integrated into the globalized world, the Chinese government must rein in antiforeign emotions lest they jeopardize the international ties that are critical for China's domestic and foreign agendas.[8] Great-power recognition and acceptance hints at the CCP leadership's ability to earn international respect. Skillfully managing China's internationalization projects the image of a capable and confident government that is engineering China's economic rise in a globalized world. Thus, while relying on nationalism for legitimacy at home, the CCP has largely brought it under control for the sake of its status quest. In differentiating between domestic and international audiences, elite Chinese nationalism has overall evolved in a way that has facilitated positive "evaluation of the status quo" in world politics, which, according to Jucek Kugler and Douglas Lemke, is the necessary condition for a possible reversal of a violent power transition.[9] The upshot is that Chinese nationalism today entails a quest for international recognition of China as a constructive and cooperative power, rather than a rogue, revolutionary, and threatening power.

Thus, compared to the anti-Western virulence in the first half of the 1990s,[10] Chinese nationalism has since shown greater conviction that how the world views China depends on a successful self-strengthening

---

[7] For further discussion along this line, see Alastair Iain Johnston, "Realism(s) and Chinese Security Policy," in Kapstein and Mastanduno, eds., *Unipolar Politics*, ch. 8.

[8] See Allen S. Whiting, "Chinese Nationalism and Foreign Policy after Deng," *China Quarterly*, no. 142 (June 1995), pp. 295–316; Erica Strecker Downs and Philip C. Saunders, "Legitimacy and the Limits of Nationalism: China and the Diaoyu Islands," *International Security*, vol. 23, no. 3 (Winter 1998/99), pp. 114–46; Yongnian Zheng, *Discovering Chinese Nationalism in China: Modernization, Identity, and International Relations* (New York: Cambridge University Press, 1999); Suisheng Zhao, *A Nation-State by Construction: Dynamics of Modern Chinese Nationalism* (Stanford, CA: Stanford University Press, 2004).

[9] Jucek Kugler and Douglas Lemke, "The Power Transition Research Program: Assessing Theoretical and Empirical Advances," in Manus I. Midlarsky, ed., *Handbook of War Studies II* (Ann Arbor: University of Michigan Press, 2000), p. 158.

[10] Jonathan Unger, ed., *Chinese Nationalism* (Armonk, NY: M. E. Sharpe, 1996).

agenda at home, particularly in securing stable economic development. Even college students, who had just led the demonstrations in front of the U.S. embassy in Beijing against the NATO bombing of the Chinese embassy in Belgrade, expressed overwhelmingly greater concern with their country's domestic self-strengthening reforms than in confronting the United States abroad.[11] More recently, Zheng Bijian, an influential policy adviser, has stressed that China's "national rejuvenation" ultimately depends on its political, economic, and spiritual renewals at home.[12]

There has also been an unprecedented awareness that China's own choices make a huge difference in how it is treated in international society. In the early years of the twenty-first century, the Chinese foreign policy discourse has seen a notable diminution of the self-portrayal of China as the worst victim during the century after the Opium War. Many influential scholars have openly argued that the standard remembrance of the "one hundred years of humiliations" during a bygone era is anachronistic in today's world. Prominent intellectuals and influential IR scholars in China are clearly aware that the irrational nationalist outbursts in the 1990s are now counterproductive to China's rise. The change was even evident during the anti-Japanese protests in 2004–05, when high-ranking officials and mainstream analysts alike warned against excessive emotional response lest it unduly hurt the Sino-Japanese relationship. Compared to nationalist episodes of the past, the political and intellectual elites showed much greater cool-headedness. To be sure, demonstrations of this kind were never pretty, and they showed that Chinese nationalism has retained its explosive force even at the start of the new century.

In wrestling with how best to achieve their nation's international aspirations, Chinese intellectuals and analysts have advocated domestic democratic change, searched in ancient Chinese history for models of benevolent international relations, and proposed a reconfigured

---

[11] Dingxin Zhao, "An Angle on Nationalism in China Today: Attitudes Among Beijing Students after Belgrade 1999," *China Quarterly*, no. 172 (Dec. 2002), pp. 885–905.

[12] "Zhen Bijian Quanshi Zhongguo Jueqi: Shixian Wenming Fuxing He Qiangguomeng" [Zheng Bijian Interprets China's Rise: Reviving Civilization and Great Power Dream], *Study Times*, no. 339 (2006), at http://news.xinhuanet.com/politics/2006-06/14/content_4693905.htm (accessed June 13, 2006).

great-power mentality in order to inspire the nation at home and win respect for China abroad.[13] Debating China's rising strategy, the prominent academic Li Qiang of Peking University wrote in 2004:

> Even thought nationalism helps with social mobilization and providing legitimacy to the political regime, its ideals and standards are after all no more than 'self writ large' (*Dawo*). If a country only bases its national aspirations and policy goals on nationalism, it cannot earn the respect and recognition of other countries. The rise of such a country inevitably spurs power politics and in the end will prove short-lived. The true great power able to rise successfully must possess the ideas and principles that transcend *Dawo*, with goals and standards identified with and respected by other countries.[14]

In the long run, administering "greater China," which includes Hong Kong and even conceivably Taiwan, would appear to require further liberalization of the mainland's polity. In fact, the Kuomintang in Taiwan has pointedly staked out the position that cross-Strait reunification is possible only under a democratic China. Citing the rationale for China's great-power status, calls for embracing universal human rights and democratic value in the mainland proper and beyond become an especially powerful idea insofar as they are couched in nationalist terms. Yet while economic globalization has energized domestic economic and institutional reforms, the CCP leadership has yet to allow an interpretation of international responsibility inclusive of domestic liberalization. It remains uncertain whether the nation's new status in world politics will spur an earnest effort to narrow the political gap separating China and other advanced democracies, just as it has tempered emotional nationalism.

Challenge of Another Kind: China in the Asian Order

The growing Chinese influence in Asia has sparked controversies over how to interpret and respond to it. At one end of the spectrum of

[13] For a typical articulation of these views, see Yu Xintian, "Zhongguo Duiwai Zhanlue De Wenhua Sikao" [Thoughts on the Culture of China's Foreign Strategy], in Niu Jun, ed., *Zhongguo Waijiao Juan* [China's Foreign Affairs] (Beijing: New World Press, 2007), pp. 82–95.

[14] Li Qiang, "Heping Jueqi Yu Zhongguo Fazhan Zhanlue De Xuanze" [Peaceful Rise and the Choice of China's Developmental Strategy], *Zhongguo Shehui Kexue*, no. 5 (2004), p. 2, at http://www.irchina.org/news/view.asp?id=670 (accessed Nov. 24, 2004).

views is the claim that the PRC has created a new, benign, and culturally distinctive regional hegemony, reminiscent of the ancient Chinese-dominated world order.[15] More commonly, however, China's regional policy is looked at in terms of traditional balance-of-power logic suggesting that the United States and/or Japan should respond with a containment policy and regional states must make a dichotomous choice between the United States and China. From our perspective, both approaches misread the regional challenges posed by China's rise.

The premodern Sino-centric East Asian regional order was based on Chinese supremacy in both power and culture. While the nature of this regional arrangement was contested,[16] there is no doubt that prior to the mid-nineteenth century the Chinese dynastic rulers considered the Middle Kingdom as possessing the highest material and normative power. And China was the standard bearer with Confucian principles underpinning *pax sinica*. The Chinese emperor claimed the exclusive right to dispense legitimacy to those local rulers who had manifestly recognized such Chinese authority.[17] An overriding concern of Confucian China's "foreign policy" was to maintain the cultural basis of its superiority over other societies.

True, nearly a decade into the new century, the PRC's regional diplomacy had never experienced this much success as it has in the post–cold war era. But it is misguided to posit a revival of the Chinese regional hegemony, much less to claim that the "Eastern" order is buttressed by some distinctive ancient principles. This interpretation misconstrues the motive behind regional receptivity toward China's rise. As I've argued in this book, rather than itself being the

[15] See, in particular, David C. Kang's work in "Getting Asia Wrong: The Need for New Analytical Frameworks," *International Security*, vol. 27, no. 4 (Summer 2003), pp. 57–85; "Hierarchy, Balancing, and Empirical Puzzles in Asian International Relations," *International Security*, vol. 28, no. 3 (Winter 2003/4), pp. 165–85.

[16] See, for example, Alastair Iain Johnston, *Cultural Realism: Strategic Culture and Grand Strategy in Chinese History* (Princeton, NJ: Princeton University Press, 1995); Takashi Hamashita, "The Intra-regional System in East Asia in Modern Times," in Peter Katzenstein and Takashi Shiraishi, eds., *Network Power: Japan and Asia* (Ithaca, NY: Cornell University Press, 1997), ch. 3.

[17] The two classic treatments of the Sino-centric order are Mark Mancall, *China at the Center: 300 Years of Foreign Relations* (New York: Free Press, 1984); John K. Fairbank, ed., *The Chinese World Order: Traditional Chinese Foreign Relations* (Cambridge, MA: Harvard University Press, 1968).

authoritative source of legitimacy, China in the present era has struggled to gain recognition from the international community. The Chinese political and intellectual elites are indeed referring to history to look for ways to inform and interpret their nation's foreign policy choices in the contemporary era. But the values and lessons they have drawn from the past are meant to suit China's ongoing quest for greatness compatible with global trends. In 2005, with both fanfare and serious reflections, they commemorated the six hundredth anniversary of the start of three decades of naval expeditions led by the Ming Dynasty's Admiral Zheng He that travelled through Southeast Asia to reach as far as East Africa. In marking this defining event in China's tributary history, the lessons they emphasized were that China was peaceful even when it was so strong; China must continue the tradition of technological innovations and embracing economic globalization; and China should confidently engage the world. In the words of one author, "History tells us opening-up, inclusiveness, and determined and dauntless exploration and struggle for the cause of peace could contribute to a powerful and prosperous country. On the contrary, extreme self-preservation and parochial arrogance could only bring death to the fate of a nation."[18]

The foreign polices of most of the smaller regional states are driven first and foremost by their domestic governance and economic agenda vital for regime security and legitimacy at home.[19] Insofar as its interests are compatible with those of ruling elites in neighboring countries, and other states do not see ties with the PRC as limiting to their foreign policy choice China enjoys a diplomatic advantage. As regards its relations with Southeast Asia, the PRC had by the late 1970s ended its public support for the communist insurgencies that had bedeviled the regional states. Moreover, Beijing has taken measures to assuage the concerns over the loyalty of the economically powerful overseas Chinese residing in this region. Ethnic riots and organized crime targeting ethnic Chinese occasionally occurred in Southeast Asia in the 1990s, particularly in Indonesia and the Philippines, testing Beijing's

---

[18] Li Rongxia, "Significance of Zheng He's Voyages," *Beijing Review*, July 14, 2005, p. 25.

[19] For the basic explications of the logic, see Steven R. David, *Choosing Sides: Alignment and Realignment in the Third World* (Baltimore: Johns Hopkins University Press, 1991); Mohammed Ayoob, *The Third World Security Predicament: State Making, Regional Conflict, and the International System* (Boulder, CO: Lynne Rienner, 1995).

diplomatic acumen. Yet China's sensitivity in handling the issue, coupled with effective assimilation efforts by regional states, has succeeded in defusing the historical problem. In Central Asia, the SCO explicitly protects the security of member states in the name of the organization's mission to fight terrorism and radicalism.

Beyond the security issue, China's diplomatic strength has derived from its economic ties in the region extended through rapidly growing trade, investment, and aid. Largely driven by the market force, China has become a new engine for regional economic growth and interdependence that has helped with a reemergence of inchoate regionalism in East Asia. In the meantime, Beijing has vigorously championed the sovereignty principle, instead of imposing its political or cultural conditions on the neighboring countries. In so doing, the PRC effectively aligns its interests with those of neighboring governments whose security is threatened by subnational or transnational forces. Diplomatic finesse is also evident in China's multilateral diplomacy. Its unprecedented activism toward numerous regional institutional initiatives has also reflected an overall favorable Chinese assessment of the general trends in Asian affairs.

China's status strategy is not necessarily predicated upon confronting the United States over regional leadership. To underscore its nonconfrontational orientations in the Asia-Pacific, top Chinese diplomats at the beginning of the new century have openly acknowledged, "The American presence in the region is a product of history and an objective reality."[20] Speaking at a security forum in Singapore in early June 2005, Cui Tiankai, director of the Asian Affairs Bureau at the Chinese Ministry of Foreign Affairs, proclaimed, "China does not pursue exclusive strategic interest in the region, nor does it seek to exclude the strategic existence and strategic interests of the great power(s) concerned in the region."[21] And former Chinese Vice-Premier Qian Qichen was even more explicit when he stated, "China respects the American presence and interests in the Asia-Pacific region. And we welcome the United States playing a positive and constructive role in

[20] Quote from Fu Ying, "China and Asia in a New Era," *China: An International Journal,* vol. 1, no. 2 (Sept. 2003), p. 311.

[21] Xinhua, "Zhongguo Daibiao Chanshu Xinanquanguan, Chengbu Xunqiu Paitaxing Zhanlue Liyi" [Chinese Representative Explains New Security Concept Proclaiming Disinclination to Pursue Exclusive Strategic Interests], June 5, 2005, at http://news.sina.com.cn/c/2005-06-05/00106081722s.shtml (accessed June 11, 2005).

the region."[22] Such public recognition of the U.S. strategic interests in the regional status quo is unprecedented and important, although no one should take these statements at face value. Just as assuring each other of their mutual goodwill is the most difficult part of great-power politics, so is the Chinese attempt to build confidence in its regional intentions an inherently difficult and uncertain process. The reality is that the United States and China remain locked in deeply rooted competitive dynamics.[23] What these statements reveal, however, is a realization that to navigate the evolving Asian international politics, China must assuage the U.S. concern by renouncing its own balancing impulse, while at the same it has to ensure that others do not seek to contain China. In practice, the PRC has relied, among other things, on its multilateral diplomacy to signal its conformist intentions, promote nonexclusive bilateral ties, and bring about orderly changes to Asian international relations. It has actively participated in, and in some cases led, multilateral attempts at crisis management and at building a regional order overtly conducive to peace and prosperity. Through these efforts, China has sought to counter unilateralist U.S. tendencies and U.S.-Japan alliance dynamics its leaders perceive to be deleterious to China's interests.

Meanwhile, the Beijing government has also hoped to solidify regional acceptance of the notion that China pursues a win-win approach in its economic, political, and security engagement in the region. As most of the Asian states are loath to see a balance-of-power politics surrounding China's rise, not least because it would compel them to choose sides in a destructive great-power game, they tended to favorably respond to China's diplomatic approach. For them, to the extent that Beijing eschews an overbearing diplomacy, growing Chinese influence may actually spur a constructive competition among regional and extraregional powers that both benefits minor states and strengthens their diplomatic weight. Notably, China's rise has not eclipsed ASEAN; rather, the organization has seen greater institutionalization and has remained central to Asian regionalism. Beijing's

---

[22] Qian Qichen, "Heping Fazhan Shi Zhongguo de Zhanlue Jueze" [Peace and Development Are China's Strategic Choice], *Renmin Ribao*, Nov. 21, 2005, p. 1.
[23] Yong Deng, "Hegemon on the Offensive: Chinese Perspectives on U.S. Global Strategy," *Political Science Quarterly*, vol. 116, no. 3 (Fall 2001), pp. 343–65.

accession to the ASEAN Treaty of Amity and Cooperation and free trade with the ASEAN Ten has animated Japan, India, and South Korea to follow suit. The United States also has stepped up bilateral free-trade agreements with individual ASEAN states. In the aftermath of the tsunami disaster in late 2004, Beijing's contribution to the relief efforts helped spark a donors' competition, presumably generating more foreign aid than otherwise would be possible.

But there are significant uncertainties in regional institutionalization and China's role in it. The Six-Party Talks proved to be an unwieldy strategic instrument for Beijing. Contested leadership and unresolved identity issues continue to beset the development of an East Asian community. While much of the "community" initiatives have come from Southeast Asia, it's the major power relations in Northeast Asia that have wielded decisive influence over the fate of regionalism. Key questions regarding the U.S. role have remained unresolved. Both China and Japan have shown a serious interest in the idea of regionalism as well as an appreciation that for such an idea to succeed, it must have their common support.[24] Yet with the two Asian giants engaged in status competition in Asia and beyond, each approaches collective Asian endeavors with greater concern over how such undertakings would affect its own regional influence in relation to the other country. Apprehension over being outmaneuvered by its rival in multilateral forums superseded the need for joint leadership in moving regional integration forward. Their competitive notions of regional order have thus stalled many institutional attempts. The Japanese idea for an Asian Monetary Fund to deal with financial crises like the one in 1997–98 met with American and Chinese opposition. Its disputes over history with the PRC and South Korea led to abrupt interruption in 2005 of their trilateral consultation on the sidelines of ASEAN Plus Three, which was first instituted in 1997. Tensions between these major players effectively undercut momentum for regional integration and have derailed attempts to map out a common regional future.

The Sino-Japanese relationship has presented an unusually difficult test of China's foreign policy, at times appearing even more difficult

---

[24] For how Chinese and Japanese views coincided, see Takahara Akio, "Japan's Political Response to the Rise of China," in Kokubun Ryosei and Wang Jisi, eds., *The Rise of China and a Changing East Asian Order* (Tokyo: Japan Center for International Exchange, 2004), pp. 164–6.

than has the Sino-American relationship. Having the responsibility of managing global and regional affairs, the United States faces a greater imperative to elicit Chinese cooperation on a host of issues. However, strategic suspicion between the two Asian powers has inclined the Chinese to interpret U.S. intentions and the U.S.-Japan alliance with deep mistrust. In fact, the worsening Sino-Japanese relationship was in part responsible for the abrupt end to the Chinese official espousal of the "peaceful rise" strategy, reverting instead to the "peaceful development" line by the summer of 2004. The contentious state of the Sino-Japanese relationship has also neutralized the political leadership needed for further institutionalization of the Asian order. As the Junichiro Koizumi administration decided to tie Japan's international future to the alliance with the United States, both Tokyo's interest and position in the value-neutral, sovereignty-based Asian style of diplomacy weakened.[25] Attempts to build financial, economic, security, and political institutions were either aborted or significantly compromised in part due to their mutual denial of regional leadership. It's clear that rivalry with Japan has seriously complicated China's attempt to reconfigure its international relations, particularly in Asia.

The juxtaposition of the first cancellation of the South Korea–Japan–PRC meeting at the ASEAN Plus Three forum and the inaugural East Asian Summit in December 2005 dampened enthusiasm for the idea of an East Asian Community. Indeed, leading up to the historical 2005 summit, ASEAN Plus Three wrangled over whether membership should be strictly limited to the geographical East Asia proper. The result was, like APEC's fomat,[26] a layered arrangement, with the ASEAN being surrounded by ASEAN Plus Three and then the East Asian Summit. The exclusion of the United States raises further questions about the direction and viability of this *modus videndi*. With an ASEAN determined and able to engage an external power – be it the United States, Japan, or China – on its own terms,[27] it is unlikely

---

[25] Christopher W. Hughes and Akiko Fukushima, "U.S.-Japan Security Relations: Toward Bilateralism Plus?" in Ellis S. Krauss and T. J. Pempel, eds., *Beyond Bilateralism: U.S.-Japan Relations in the New Asia-Pacific* (Stanford, CA: Stanford University Press, 2004), pp. 55–86.

[26] Hadi Soesastro, "ASEAN and APEC: Do Concentric Circles Work?" *Pacific Review*, vol. 8, no. 3 (1995), pp. 475–93.

[27] Yuen Foong Khong, "Coping with Strategic Uncertainty: The Role of Institutions and Soft Balancing in Southeast Asia's Post–Cold War Strategy," in

that the curious institutional arrangement can be transcended to form a genuine Asian regionalism any time soon. Stalled growth in such multilateral initiatives in turn limits confirmation of China's regional influence through institutional means.

Besides Sino-Japanese rivalry, China's regional role is also limited by the towering influence of the United States and persistent ambivalence from neighboring countries toward its newfound power.[28] China's growing influence has intensified concerns over its challenge to the regional status quo among established great powers in the Asia-Pacific. Similarly, smaller states in Southeast Asia, particularly Indonesia and Singapore, have become even more wary of Beijing's growing clout. Despite the PRC-ASEAN joint declaration in 2002 pledging responsible behavior on the South China Sea, claimants have continued to dispute territorial claims, energy resources, and fishing rights in the contested areas. During the SARS crisis, some ASEAN countries took drastic preventative measures against Chinese citizens traveling to or studying in the region, some of which Chinese commentators deemed to be excessive and discriminatory. Chinese Premier Wen Jiabao's proposal to establish an anti-SARS regional fund was met with skepticism or indifference by his Southeast Asian colleagues. In the inaugural East Asian summit in December 2005, several ASEAN members insisted on the inclusion of India, Australia, and New Zealand to the original ASEAN Ten Plus Three (the PRC, Japan, and South Korea) to forestall even a semblance of Chinese dominance.

The future of regionalism and China's rise are intertwined. For the PRC, unprecedented institutional entanglement has generated tangible payoffs, but it has also increased the cost of withdrawal and redefined the country's identity and interests in Asia. Beijing's growing influence in regional institutions has become and will remain a new reality in the evolution of Asian international relations. To the extent that China's strategic thinkers see regional multilateral forums as a gateway to the world, their preference is not to form a bloc or a

J. J. Suh, Peter J. Katzenstein, and Allen Carlson, eds., *Rethinking Security in East Asia: Identity, Power, And Efficiency* (Stanford, CA: Stanford University Press, 2004), pp. 172–208.

[28] See Robert Sutter, *China's Rise in Asia: Perils and Promises* (Boulder, CO: Rowman & Littlefield, 2005); David Shambaugh, "China Engages Asia: Reshaping the Regional Order," *International Security*, vol. 29, no. 3 (Winter 2004/5), pp. 64–99.

traditional anti-Western alliance. They see both institutionalization of regional international relations and China's rise as a process whose management requires a great deal of patience and diplomatic acumen. As regards East Asian regionalism and the SCO, Beijing would like to limit institutional membership, but it has insisted on openness both in principle and on future memberships. For these reasons, while China's growing power has intensified the competition for leadership in Asia, it is hopeful that an institutionalized regional order and China's rise can enjoy a compatible pattern of interaction.

Implications for Emerging Great-Power Politics

Various realist theories assume that powerful states, dictated by international anarchy, mechanically succumb to an unmitigated struggle for relative material superiority, leading inexorably to war. IR scholars subscribing to this view fear that China's foreign relations would inescapably repeat the same destructive great-power game of survival.[29] In making these dire claims, they discount evidence of restraint and cooperation in Chinese foreign policy in the past two decades. As documented in this book and in other works as well, it is clear that compared to what mainstream paradigms of great-power politics would predict, balancing has been significantly less salient in the international politics surrounding China's rise. This has been true in China's relations with both aspiring powers and established powers.

The PRC seems determined to avoid forcing great-power recognition through sheer material capacities or war, searching instead for an alternative path to greatness that entails positive affirmation from the international society. Thus, the country has been highly sensitive to the human rights criticisms and China threat theories. Much effort has been expended on minimizing the diplomatic costs of the negative image or replacing it with a positive image that takes the idea of international responsibility seriously. In dealing with other major powers, the PRC has cultivated confidence in its future, with notable success, through its strategic partnerships with Russia, the EU, and India. With

---

[29] Perhaps the best example of these theorists is John J. Mearsheimer. See his *The Tragedy of Great Power Politics* (New York: W. W. Norton, 2001). See also his exchange with Zbigniew Brzezinski, "The Clash of the Titans," *Foreign Policy*, no. 146 (Jan./Feb. 2005), pp. 46–50.

prudence on both sides, the Sino-Russian strategic partnership has not had the kind of military emphasis, mutual security commitment, or anti-Americanism that amounts to an exclusive alliance. True, with time they have proven to be better able to coordinate on international issues where they share compelling interests. But the two aspiring powers have taken pains not to allow their ties to exact irreparable damage to their relationship with the West, which is critical for both their domestic agenda and foreign policy objectives. As regards Taiwan, mainland China's policy has since the mid-1990s shown an acute awareness of the extreme importance of the issue for its broad strategic objectives and the delicacy required for gaining initiative in managing it.

The highly globalized U.S. hegemony has proven to be quite enduring, for it is buttressed by the dominant great-power grouping, although the in-group boundaries are contested from within and without. Hardly acting in unison, established great powers have pursued policies toward China that are sometimes in discord with other members, such as Japan's opening to Beijing after the Tiananmen incident and the more recent EU pursuit of a strategic partnership with the PRC. But overall, their engagements with China have to various degrees entailed steering the rising power toward compliance with the human rights standard, economic liberalization, and foreign policy responsibility.

Lack of a credible vision of a radically restructured world has imposed constraints on the strategic choices of emerging powers like China, Russia, and India. Under the post–cold war international arrangement, they may partner with each other, but they shun alliance making; they compete and hedge against each other, but they also reassure each other. Insofar as the West represents the global mainstream, they all attach supreme importance to relations with it, thereby creating fear of being double-crossed by their partners. Thus, they look over their shoulders lest the others seek unilateral improvements with the West at the expense of their partnerships. The fear of defection also has to do with the fact that in pairs or as a group these countries have weak mutual identification at the social and cultural levels.

In the meantime, China, Russia, and India are also careful to rein in competition while at the same time enhancing cooperation between them. As they each focus on their own relationships with the United States and other established powers, fellow aspiring powers become less of an obstacle than a facilitator in their pursuit of great-power status. Rising together can in fact decrease the pressure and unwanted international attention, which otherwise would be fixated on them individually. To the extent that they share discontent with the U.S./Western unilateralist dominance, their cooperation helps bring about desirable changes in their respective international environment.

There is therefore a great disincentive for any of the aspiring powers to stick its head out to lead an anti-Western coalition. Lack of leadership, in turn, leads to inadequate coordination, thus explaining why their cooperation to effect changes to the existing world order has so far been ad hoc and half-hearted. Certain strategy analysts in China, Russia, and India might find the idea of a tripartite alliance intriguing, but they invariably doubted anyone's sincerity in forming such a separate grouping. Thus, aspiring powers are motivated to work within the existing world order. The United States and its allies enjoy unrivalled leverage to remold great-power politics such that peacefully contested change can be enforced in lieu of violent power transitions.

For the PRC, navigating world politics has not been a smooth ride, nor is the success of its status quest preordained. Along with remarkable improvement in its international environment, China's foreign relations have also been contentious and marked by setbacks, uncertainties, and power politics concerns. At various times, righteous indignation against Western discrimination and suspicion have fueled nationalist rage. Frustrations with a perceived denial by the United States and Japan of its rightful place at the great-power table have turned into mistrust and hostility toward the two countries. Asia remains weakly institutionalized. Japan has seemed to have the greatest difficulties in proactively accommodating the growing Chinese influence. The PRC has failed to assure Japan that China's rise will not come at the expense of its most important neighbor. Taiwan remains intractable and may flare up, despite or because of the mainland's growing clout in denying what's left of Taiwan's sovereignty representation in international institutions, Africa, and elsewhere. As the country ventures into Africa and other parts of the world, the scope of its international responsibility also increases, as do new challenges and questions facing its global role.

Besides the proposition that great powers will fight over power transition, the other IR finding that is generally regarded as empirically scientific is democratic peace. China has not followed the route of liberal peace as paved by unilateral PRC liberalization at home and abroad. The impact of the international human rights regime has manifested itself in a discernible Chinese receptivity to the norm in rhetoric, worldview, and practice. However, the imperative of the CCP party-state security has meant that when domestic concerns clash with external demands, the former often supersedes the latter, thereby perpetuating a political liability in China's foreign relations. The PRC's revisionism on the human rights norm has been geared toward changing its content and role in world politics. In a nutshell, the Chinese government insists that human rights should give equal weight to socioeconomic and civil-political rights, due consideration to relativist arguments, and supreme respect for the collective rights of a nation-state. To further steer the sources of international legitimacy away from domestic politics, the country has emphasized pluralism and sovereignty, while at the same time it has proposed that the great-power standard be based on responsible external behaviors. While the question regarding the broad political repercussions of the rise of an illiberal China remains unsettled, China's revisionism on human rights has so far been focused on securing its immediate economic interests and minimizing the negative impact on its own international standing.

Despite the twists and turns in post–cold war China's foreign relations, the prevailing international and domestic forces behind its status strategy have proven to be potent enough to motivate the PRC to stay on its current course. Its illiberal polity has not prevented the PRC from demonstrating that its rise can represent an opportunity for peaceful change, economic prosperity, and better global governance. In Africa as in Asia, China's presence has spurred economic growth and international attention to the developing countries. Diplomatic success has in turn undermined China's victim mentality, whereby it viewed itself as an innocent party bullied by hostile Western powers. After the 9/11 events, the United States was tied down by the war in Iraq and somewhat constrained by its global campaign against terrorism. Chinese analysts were not rushing to declare that the United States was on the irreversible decline, nor were they rejoicing the onset of a new world order. But there was a growing sense among them that things were going their way, that in what Shi Yihong calls an "asymmetrical race" between the U.S. unilateralism and resort to force and Chinese reliance on multilateralism and economic tools, their country had forged ahead.[30] To the extent that the Chinese government has found its search for national recognition abroad to be suitable for its legitimacy-enhancing agenda at home, growing receptivity to China's rise in Asia and beyond has doubtless vindicated such a foreign trajectory. In this way, its positive orientation abroad is further underpinned by a confident assessment of world politics.

In devising the policy approach to ascending powers like China, it is useful to heed E. H. Carr's warning that rigid "defense of the status quo is not a policy which can be lastingly successful. It will end in war as surely as rigid conservatism will end in revolution."[31] Withholding due status recognition based on zero-sum power politics logic and negative stereotype-driven categorization is a recipe for the repetition of a traditional great-power struggle. Conversely, carefully calibrated engagement undercuts the plausibility of a radically restructured world order. A strong yet flexible hierarchy in world politics compels and encourages compliance with the prevailing institutions and values, insofar as they are viewed as fairly applied and befitting the CCP's domestic agenda. Conversely, to the extent that the PRC complains about Western manipulation of power and standards to justify exclusion and discrimination, it would attempt to bring about change to the world order, especially when the evolution of international arrangements facilitates such change.

Emerging powers respond to constraints and opportunities the world has to offer. Thus, the U.S. engagement toward the PRC should not be just about bilateral interaction. Rather, its success depends on U.S. leadership in shaping a world politics that continues to deny and delegitimize change through radically rewriting the rules of the game. Radical change to the international arrangement, to the prevailing pattern of great-power politics, and to the CCP leadership's own definition of national interests will likely produce a major shift in China's foreign

---

[30] Shi Yinhong, "China's Rise and Prospects of China's Relations with the United States, Japan," Hong Kong *Zhongguo Pinglun*, no. 114 (July 2007), pp. 16–20, in Open Source Center: CPP20070604710001, p. 1.

[31] For Carr's views on peaceful change, see Edward H. Carr, *The Twenty Years' Crisis: 1919–1939*, 2nd edition (first published in 1946) (London: Macmillan, 1961), ch. 13, quote on p. 222.

policy. Viewed in this vein, managing conflicts of interest and dis-agreements in approaching the PRC among the advanced democracies has a decisive bearing on great-power politics beyond transatlantic or transpacific alliances. While the Sino-Russian strategic partnership has received the greatest scrutiny, the Sino-EU strategic partnership also deserves focused attention. Insofar as the Sino-Japanese rivalry could harden the balancing logic in Chinese foreign relations, it behooves the two East Asian giants to accommodate each other's international aspi-rations and the United States to proactively calibrate its engagement of the Japanese regional and global role with farsightedness.

Also important is a realistic appraisal of the strengths and weak-nesses of the U.S. international role. Our study shows that the U.S. leadership role cannot be taken for granted. But the United States occu-pies the central position beyond material supremacy, with unrivaled leverage at its disposal. In responding to China's growing influence in Asia and the world at large, it's important for the United States not to succumb to the simple balance-of-power logic, as such thinking tends to stem from incomplete understanding and an underestimation of U.S. strengths, as well as from misconstrual of the Chinese challenge.

Aspiring powers are ultrasensitive to status recognition in their for-eign relations. Negotiated settlement of conflicting interests is likely to be found so long as disagreements are not cast as foreshadowing inevitable, unmitigated "us-versus-them" struggles. Given that the Tai-wan issue colors so much of how the Chinese elites view the world, the U.S. Taiwan policy should be closely integrated into its broad engage-ment goals with the PRC. Tying Taiwan to the PRC's international treatment also means that the costs for a unilateral Chinese invasion would be prohibitively high for Beijing beyond the battlefield, thereby maximizing the chances of peace across the Strait.

Our study has focused on the dynamic PRC interaction with the out-side world in determining its international course. China will remain a developing, transitional country with lots of growing pains, creating strong imperative for its continued adaptive integration into the world. In the long run, close coordination between China and key interna-tional players in dealing with myriad bilateral and transnational issues may forge social identification to limit enmities. Repeated rounds of win-win conflict resolution and even crisis management could incul-cate the habit of negotiated settlement in the parties involved. A China whose stakes are fully invested in the world order is likely to be a more confident, responsible participant in global governance. While globalization has presented great economic and diplomatic opportunities for China, it has also anchored the country's rise in the world.

Underscoring how China's treatment abroad also depends on its leadership's own choices, our study debunks the myths in some Chinese writings that China is always an innocent victim of the Western powers, that power alone determines status, that China's international treatment can be divorced from domestic changes, and that a single-minded pursuit of preset "national interests" is the solution to China's foreign policy predicament. With the country's diplomatic success, its foreign relations now have in many ways entered a new phase. The competitive dynamics inherent in power transition may intensely drive its relationships with the United States and Japan. Indeed the survey data indicate that when the PRC had achieved unprecedented diplomatic success after 9/11, suspicion of a U.S. attempt to hold back their nation's rightful quest for great-power status actually grew rather than diminished.[32] In linking Taiwan to its status recognition, the CCP elites have made Taiwan's formal independence a more dangerous *casus belli* than in the past. As China grows even stronger, it may be tempted by power politics logic to force its way in world politics. The evidence and arguments presented here suggest that some parameters of joint responsibility are required of both China and the outside world in order to forestall a relapse into an old-fashioned power struggle. The PRC is deeply integrated in the world and finds itself at the most advantageous position than ever before to change it. Yet with the concurrent rise of other nonwestern powers, India, Russia, and countries traditionally known as the third world, the world itself has become increasingly pluralist, less Western-dominated, and even more globalized.

---

[32] Alastair Iain Johnston and Daniela Stockmann, "Chinese Attitudes toward the United States and Americans," Peter Katzenstein and Robert Keohane, eds., *Anti-Amerianism in World Politics* (Ithaca, NY: Cornell University Press, 2007), pp. 157–195.

Index

ABM Treaty. *See* Anti-Ballistic Missile
Treaty
ADB. *See* African Development Bank
Adler, Emanuel, 102
Afghanistan, 95, 162, 192, 218, 219,
221, 237
African Development Bank, 231, 232
Agreed Framework (1994), 205, 215
Akihito (emperor of Japan), 169, 198
Ancient Sino-centric order, 4, 120,
281
Anderson, Jeffrey A., 235
Anti-Ballistic Missile Treaty, 148, 161
APEC. *See* Asia-Pacific Economic
Cooperation
Approved Destination Status, 230
Arunachal Pradesh, 154
ASEAN. *See also* Association for
Southeast Asian Nations
and development of Asian
regionalism, 194, 222–6, 241, 286
and Shanghai Cooperation
Organization, 243
and South China Sea, 237, 287
engagement with China, 238–40,
274, 284–7
institutional features of, 27, 238
ASEAN Plus Three, 223, 225, 227,
286
Asian financial crisis, 285
Chinese behavior in, 222–3
Japanese behavior during, 35, 223
regionalism after, 224
Asia-Pacific Economic Cooperation, 50
and East Asian Summit, 226, 286
Russia's membership in, 149
Sino-Japanese relations in, 169
Association for Southeast Asian
Nations, 19, 27, 194, 222
ten plus one (China), 224

balance-of-power, 6, 19, 56, 65, 142,
155, 167, 187, 270, 275, 280,
284, 293
Barnes, Barry, 104
Barnett, Michael, 102
Beijing Review, 104, 137, 207
Bo Xilai, 184
on anti-Japanese protests, 175
Bolshoi Urruriiski (Black Bear), 134
British School, 13
Brown, Lester, 110
Bush, George W., 32, 124, 206, 249,
250
promotion of democracy by, 94
Buzan, Barry, 73

Carr, E. H., 292
categorization, 22–4
Chen Shui-bian, 109, 250, 259
China
as a big and small power, 10
and "China collapse theories," 110
and liberal peace, 291
as a non-status quo power, 29
as responsible power, 46–8
border disputes with India, 154
concerns about U.S.-Japan alliance,
193
diplomatic "social capital," 61
domestic legitimacy and foreign
policy, 65
domestic sources of foreign policy,
26
energy cooperation with Russia,
160
military exercises with Russia, 137
"one country, two systems," 262,
266
peaceful rise, 3, 12, 59, 119, 257,
259, 272, 277, 286